HEALTH
NAVIGATION
SERIES

NAVIGATING THE U.S. HEALTH CARE SYSTEM

Nancy J. Niles, PhD, MPH, MS, MBA

Associate Professor
Rollins College
Winter Park, Florida

JONES & BARTLETT
LEARNING

World Headquarters
Jones & Bartlett Learning
5 Wall Street
Burlington, MA 01803
978-443-5000
info@jblearning.com
www.jblearning.com

10826-2

Production Credits

VP, Executive Publisher: David D. Cella
Publisher: Michael Brown
Associate Editor: Danielle Bessette
Senior Vendor Manager: Tracey McCrea
Vendor Manager: Juna Abrams
Senior Marketing Manager: Sophie Fleck Teague
Manufacturing and Inventory Control Supervisor: Amy Bacus
Project Management and Composition: Integra Software Services Pvt. Ltd.

Cover Design: Theresa Manley
Rights & Media Specialist: Merideth Tumasz
Media Development Editor: Shannon Sheehan
Cover Image: Monument: © mandritoiu/Shutterstock;
   Nurse: © Robert Kneschke/Shutterstock;
   Cyclists: © monkeybusinessimages/Getty Images
Printing and Binding: LSC Communications
Cover Printing: LSC Communications

Library of Congress Cataloging-in-Publication Data

Names: Niles, Nancy J., author.
Title: Navigating the U.S. health care system / Nancy J. Niles.
Other titles: Health navigation series.
Description: Burlington, MA : Jones & Bartlett Learning, [2018] | Series:
   Health navigation series | Includes bibliographical references and index.
Identifiers: LCCN 2016055917 | ISBN 9781284108163 (pbk. : alk. paper)
Subjects: | MESH: Delivery of Health Care | Insurance, Health | National
   Health Programs | Patient Navigation | Community Health Workers | United States
Classification: LCC RA412.2 | NLM W 84 AA1 | DDC 368.38/200973--dc23 LC record available at
   https://lccn.loc.gov/2016055917

6048

Printed in the United States of America
21 20 19 18 17   10 9 8 7 6 5 4 3 2 1

CONTENTS

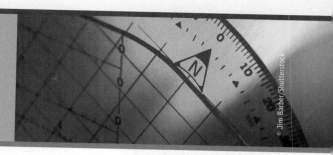

Health Navigator Applied Associate Degree and Academic Certificate Programs

"Health Navigator" is the term used by the Association of Schools and Programs of Public Health (ASPPH) and the League for Innovation in the Community College (League) for applied associate degrees and academic certificate programs that prepare students for employment in existing and emerging fields such as community health worker, patient navigator, and health insurance navigator. These programs also benefit employers and practitioners by offering opportunities for employees to obtain academic credentials that reflect the knowledge, skills, and abilities gained through job experience. As recommended by the Society for Public Health Education (SOPHE), Health Navigator programs should be designed to transfer to bachelor's Health Education degree programs should a graduate wish to do so.

The need for individuals with the skills to help patients obtain and maximally benefit from community services, clinical care, and health insurance is becoming a major issue in the increasingly complex and expensive U.S. health system. Those with Health Navigator training may assist individuals with limited health literacy as well as the elderly with accessing community services and implementing prevention. They may facilitate access to care and follow-up for sick and complicated patients with cancer, HIV, and a range of other complex and chronic health problems. In addition, Health Navigators can assist with identifying and enrolling patients in health insurance plans including those available through the Affordable Care Act exchanges, Medicaid, Medicare, as well as through community health centers.

The recommended Health Navigator applied associate degree program includes 30 semester credit hours of general education as well as 30 semester credit hours of coursework in the following areas:

- **Public Health Core:** 1) Population & Personal Health; 2) Overview of Public Health; and 3) Health Communications
- **Health Navigator Core:** 1) Prevention & Community Health; 2) Accessing and Analyzing Health Information; 3) Healthcare Delivery Systems; 4) Health Insurance
- Experiential learning
- Elective coursework allowing students to tailor their education to specific jobs in the field

This coursework can also form the centerpiece of academic certificate programs designed for nurses and allied health students as a complement to their clinical education. Certificate programs are well-suited for individuals with workforce experience and/or an academic degree who seek to augment their academic portfolio with a Health Navigator credential. Detailed course content outlines are available at www.league.org/ccph/ as part of the *Community Colleges and Public Health* report.

While this need has existed for a long time, until recently it has not been met through paid positions with well-defined roles. This is rapidly changing as a result of the growing commitment to develop specific Health Navigator positions and to integrate these positions into the healthcare and public health systems. Moreover, new funding mechanisms as part of Medicaid, Medicare's 30-day hospital readmission policy, and the Affordable Care Act have dramatically increased demand for employees with Health Navigator credentials. Salaries for Health Navigator graduates range from $30,000 to $55,000 per year. The Department of Labor estimates that by 2022 the demand for Community Health Workers—the only Health Navigator-related job classification it currently tracks— will increase by at least 25 percent.

THE HEALTH NAVIGATION SERIES

FROM JONES & BARTLETT LEARNING

The NEW Jones & Bartlett Learning *Health Navigation* series meets the full range of Health Navigation education competencies of the League for Innovation in the Community College based on the Association of Schools and Programs of Public Health (ASPPH) Community Colleges and Public Health report.

Developed under the editorial direction of Richard K. Riegelman, MD, MPH, PhD, this series of three textbooks and accompanying digital learning materials is designed for Health Navigator associate degree and certificate programs leading to employment as community health workers, patient navigators, and/or health insurance navigators.

Principles of Health Navigation

by Karen Marie Perrin, PhD, MPH, CPH University of South Florida, College of Public Health

This text will provide an overview of the content and knowledge competencies expected as part of health navigation education including health services delivery and health insurance, care of the individual, and accessing and analyzing health information competencies.

Navigating the U.S. Health System

by Nancy Niles, PhD, MPH, MS, MBA, Lander University

This text will comprehensively cover the knowledge competency in healthcare delivery and public health expected as part of health navigation education in the United States.

Navigating Health Insurance

by Alexis Pozen, PhD, and **James Stimpson**, PhD, MA, Both of the CUNY School of Public Health

This text will comprehensively cover the health insurance knowledge competencies needed to understand health insurance and serve as a health insurance navigator.

Each title will serve as a free-standing text designed for a 3 semester hour course. Together the series will cover the required course work recommended for health navigation associate degree and academic certificate programs by the ASPPH Community Colleges and Public Health report.

ABOUT THE AUTHOR

Nancy J. Niles, PhD, MPH, MS, MBA, is in her 12th year of full-time undergraduate teaching. She is in her second year of teaching undergraduate and graduate healthcare management and administration courses at Rollins College in Winter Park, Florida. Prior to Rollins College, she taught 8 years of undergraduate business and healthcare management classes in the AACSB-accredited School of Management at Lander University in Greenwood, South Carolina, having spent 4 years teaching in the Department of Business Administration at Concord University in Athens, West Virginia. She became very interested in health issues as a result of spending two tours with the U.S. Peace Corps in Senegal, West Africa. She focused on community assessment and development, obtaining funding for business- and health-related projects. Her professional experience also includes directing the New York State lead poisoning prevention program and managing a small business development center in Myrtle Beach, South Carolina.

Her graduate education has focused on health policy and management. She received a master of public health from the Tulane School of Public Health in New Orleans, Louisiana, a master of management with a healthcare administration emphasis and a master of business administration from the University of Maryland University College, and a doctorate from the University of Illinois at Urbana, Champaign in health policy.

ACKNOWLEDGMENTS

I would like to thank my husband, Donnie Niles, the love of my life, for his continued love and support. I would also like to thank Mike Brown at Jones & Bartlett Learning, who provided me with this opportunity to contribute to the health navigator series. My thanks to Danielle Bessette, and to Carmel Isaac and Ramanan Sundararajan of Integra Software Services, who have been wonderful. I so appreciate their input into my projects.

The focus of this textbook is on how to navigate the complex U.S. healthcare system from a patient perspective. I have provided an overview of the different components of the healthcare system but in each chapter I have a section that outlines how to navigate that specific component of the healthcare system.

The following is a summary of each chapter.

CHAPTER 1

It is important as a healthcare consumer to understand the history of the U.S. healthcare delivery system, how it operates today, who participates in the system, what legal and ethical issues arise as a result of the system, and what problems continue to plague the healthcare system. We are all consumers of health care. Yet, in many instances, we are ignorant of what we are actually purchasing. If we were going to spend $1,000 on an appliance or a flat-screen television, many of us would research the product to determine if what we are purchasing is the best product for us. This same concept should be applied to purchasing healthcare services.

Increasing healthcare consumer awareness will protect you in both the personal and professional aspects of your life. You may decide to pursue a career in health care either as a provider or as an administrator. You may also decide to manage a business where you will have the responsibility of providing health care to your employees. And last, from a personal standpoint, you should have the knowledge from a consumer point of view so you can make informed decisions about what matters most—your health. The federal government agrees with this philosophy. The Affordable Care Act's health insurance marketplaces provide cost and service data so consumers can determine what is the best healthcare insurance to purchase and what services they will be receiving for that purchase. Recently, the Centers for Medicare and Medicaid Services (CMS) used its claim data to publish the hospital costs of the 100 most common treatments nationwide. The purpose of this effort is to provide data to consumers regarding healthcare costs because the costs vary considerably across the United States. This effort may also encourage pricing competition of healthcare services. The U.S. Department of Health and Human Services is providing funding to states to increase their healthcare pricing transparency. This may change with the new administration's refocus on how to provide health care to individuals in this country.

Each of these areas can have representation for a health navigator. This textbook will cover the health navigator role in all of these areas except insurance. Because the insurance arena is so complicated, an individual textbook will be devoted to this component of the healthcare system.

Health navigators can assist patients with inpatient and outpatient care. Developing a system-wide network of navigators trained to be patient advocate specialists in designated areas can only enhance the philosophy of a patient-centric healthcare system. Healthcare navigators have been shown to be effective at improving chronic disease management, smoking cessation, and adult immunizations.

CHAPTER 2

The U.S. healthcare system is a complicated system that is comprised of both public and private resources. Health care is available to those who have health insurance or who are entitled to health care through a public program. One can think of the healthcare system as several concentric circles that surround the most important stakeholders in the center circle: the healthcare consumers and providers. Immediately surrounding this relationship are health insurance companies and government programs, healthcare facilities, pharmaceutical companies, and laboratories, all of which provide services to consumers to ensure they receive quality health care, as well as support providers to ensure they provide quality health care. The next circle consists of peripheral stakeholders that do not have an immediate impact on the main relationship but are still important to the industry. These consist of the professional associations, the research organizations, and the medical and training facilities. The health navigator has many opportunities to assist a patient with many of the stakeholders that interact with the patient to achieve a desired health outcome. It is the responsibility of the health navigator to receive training in the appropriate areas to successfully assist the patient with their rights and responsibilities.

CHAPTER 3

When many of us think of dealing with government agencies, we think of the typical adage of how government rules and regulations often complicate communication with consumers. Because there are so many government agencies that are responsible for different components of the healthcare system, it can be difficult for healthcare consumer to manage all of these interactions. For example, some elderly patients may be qualified for both Medicare and Medicaid which requires twice the communication needed when receiving care. A health navigator can be very helpful in these types of situations. A health navigator can be a mediator between government agencies and the healthcare consumer. In order to be successful in this role, the navigator should understand government rules and regulations and which agencies are responsible for oversight of these types of rules.

CHAPTER 4

The role of the public health or community navigator can have both a broad and narrow perspective. Public health focuses on providing community health programs that can improve the health of many individuals in a community. A public health navigator can take a leading role in assisting with these types of population based programs. Secondly, the public health navigator can also provide specific health programs to certain targeted demographics that need assistance with improving at risk health behavior. For example, a "womb to tomb" public health navigator model in La Plata county Colorado focused on both children and seniors regarding their health status. This navigator program developed an integrated healthcare and social support services to target those community members that needed assistance with self-care management and disease prevention (Nurse Navigator program, 2016). A nurse can also become a public health navigator as part of his or her role in a public health department. A social worker can also become a health navigator when s/he collaborates with the public health department. From a broader perspective, a state health department could appoint a clinician to oversee public health navigator activities to ensure that more of the population will be reached. It is important to remember that the mission of public health is to increase access to health services as well as to teach individuals health education to ensure they will remain disease free. The public health navigator should be trained in public health as well as have working knowledge of health education. The health navigator could also be used during a public health crisis when communication is needed between victims and health and emergency workers so crisis management training would also be an asset for health navigators. This type of health navigator can be a contributor to improving the community's health.

CHAPTER 5

The role of the health navigator can play a huge role in providing assistance when an individual becomes a patient in a healthcare facility. The focus of the health navigator is to help the patient become empowered. With the ongoing problem of patient deaths resulting from medical errors, it is important that the patient safety is maximized and a health navigator can assist with this goal. Health consumer literacy can play a role in patient safety. Ongoing communication between the providers, patient, and facility also contributes to patient safety. Providing assistance with informed consent for patient care and helping the patient understand the type of care provided is crucial. Assisting with any legal issues such as living wills and advance directives may be needed. A health inpatient service navigator may have to deal with both private and government healthcare insurance when dealing with inpatient services. Overall, having a patient advocate such as a health navigator can be a valuable safeguard for the patient. Health inpatient services navigators should be trained in healthcare insurance which includes both private and public coverage such as Medicare and Medicaid. There should be also training in advance directives and living wills. Having a clinical background can be very helpful so the navigator can provide insight into why certain tests and care are being performed.

CHAPTER 6

The health navigator plays an important role in outpatient service for patients. Because there are so many outpatient services available, it is important for the navigator to ensure that the patient is receiving the appropriate care and testing and that the patient understands why they are having outpatient care. It can be more difficult to deal with outpatients services if the patient must coordinate their care with several agencies. That requires organization of the coordinated care and collaboration with the different providers. Secondly, there are several community organizations that can assist with chronic diseases such as dementia or have a terminal disease. The navigator can work with both the patient and their families to ensure they have contacted the appropriate organizations.

CHAPTER 7

The Health Navigation professions include a large number of job titles. There are three general areas of employment which are often identified as Community Health Workers, Patient Navigators, and Health Insurance Navigators. Employment for a wide range of health navigation professions has grown rapidly in recent years. New funding mechanisms from Medicaid, Medicare, and the Affordable Care Act have dramatically increased interest in developing these types of career positions which need academic Health Navigator training. Community Health Workers are the only Health Navigation employment classification tracked by the U.S. Department of Labor. Community Health workers and health educators are classified together. The Labor Department's Occupational Outlook estimates that the positions for community health workers and health educators will increase 15% by 2024. According to the Department of Labor, insurance companies, employers, and governments are trying to find ways to improve the quality of care and health outcomes, while reducing costs. They hire health educators and community health workers to teach people about how to live healthy lives, obtain screenings, and how to avoid costly diseases and medical procedures. They explain how lifestyle changes can reduce the probability of contracting illnesses such as lung cancer, HIV, heart disease, and skin cancer. Health educators and community health workers also help people understand how to manage their condition and avoid unnecessary trips to the emergency room. Health educators and community health workers help people understand how their actions affect their health. The median annual wage for community health workers was $36,300 in May 2015. A registered nurse who becomes a health navigator may have a salary of $65,000. A social worker who becomes a health navigator may have a salary of $44,000. Health educator positions require more education and therefore their median wage in 2015 was significantly higher at $51,000.

Although the concept of a healthcare navigator has been utilized in different areas of health care, the concept of the navigator was fully introduced to a national audience as part of the Affordable Care Act. The first patient navigation program began in 1990 by Harold Freeman. In 2005, President Bush signed the Patient

Navigator and Chronic Disease Prevention Act which established a research program to examine cost effectiveness of navigation programs. In 2006, the Center for Medicare and Medicaid Services funded six multiyear demonstration programs on navigation programs. In 2000, the Health Resources and Services Administration (HRSA) funded six programs that focused on chronic disease navigation programs and in 2010, added 10 new sites (Huber, Shapiro II, Burke, & Palmer, 2014). Then the ACA established insurance navigators at the state government level to help with the insurance marketplace websites. According to the healthcare.gov website, a navigator is an individual or organization that's trained and able to help consumers, small businesses, and their employees as they look for health coverage options through the Marketplace, including completing eligibility and enrollment forms. These individuals and organizations are required to be unbiased. Their services are free to consumers. The ACA created the Navigator program or In-Person Assister (IPA) as part of their outreach and enrollment assistance to those individuals who were purchasing insurance coverage from the Health marketplace. Any marketplace was required to have a navigator program to assist healthcare consumers. Navigators were required to provide education and to assist with enrollment in insurance programs and contracted directly with the Center for Medicare and Medicaid Services. They were required to complete 30 hours of training. Assuming these navigator positions would be eliminated if the new administration eliminates the marketplaces, hopefully this concept of a navigator would continue to increase information literacy regarding insurance.

Prior to the implementation of the healthcare marketplaces, navigators were used to assist in many areas including mental health, cancer, primary care, uninsured population, clinical ethics consultations, case management, and long-term care. Like the navigators for the healthcare marketplace, their main goal is to assist the healthcare consumer with making educated decisions regarding their health care and the health care of their loved ones. Another term for a healthcare navigator is a patient advocate. As our healthcare system becomes more patient centric and performance based, there will be more navigator roles developed to ensure that patients' comprehension of their healthcare system is clear. The ultimate goal is to ensure that the healthcare system works for the patient so they can achieve the best health outcome.

CHAPTER 8

Being a health navigator for information technology can be very invaluable to a patient. With the increased use of electronic health records, patient portals and telemedicine, many older patients may feel confused. Although the number of elderly individuals who use technology have increased, that population still feels more uncomfortable with information technology. Being an IT Health Navigator could be extremely beneficial to patients. Many patients do not keep copies of their medical records. They are often confused about their medications. Having access to electronic copies of their records and records of their medications could be very beneficial to patients. To be an IT Health Navigator, the navigator would need to be very familiar with electronic health record use as well as be comfortable with technology in general. Microsoft has developed an electronic patient record system that allows individuals to personally keep their medical records electronically. An IT Health Navigator could be very instrumental with this type of electronic record keeping and increase the patient's health technology literacy.

CHAPTER 9

The health navigator can play an instrumental role in helping the patient understand their legal rights as a patient. The patient may or may not understand that the relationship with the provider is a legal relationship and the patient has rights that must be respected. The concept of the Patient Bill of Rights that outlines the patient rights of autonomy in their health care may or may not be adhered to by a provider. The patient navigator can he help the patient be empowered in recognizing their right to refuse treatment, their right to question their provider and to be clearly informed about their patient care. The health navigator should have familiarity with healthcare law to ensure that the patient is treated within his or her legal rights. For example, a provider cannot abandon a patient. There are regulations in place to ensure that cannot occur. The patient may not be aware of that rule. There are 44,000–99,000 medical deaths each year due to medical errors which could have been prevented by improved communication to reduce errors. A health navigator could play a role to ensure that protocols are followed to protect the patient.

CHAPTER 10

The health navigator can play an important patient advocate role when dealing with ethical dilemmas. This is pertinent particularly to the relationship between the patient and clinician. The issue with autonomy and beneficence between the two stakeholders can be difficult. The patient has the absolute right to make a healthcare decision even if the clinician does not agree it may the best decision for the patient. Autonomy focuses on respect for the patient and beneficence focuses on doing the best for the patient's health. The two may conflict if the patient feels differently. The health navigator can be a mediator between the physician and the patient to resolve any issues. Encouraging the patient to develop advance directives so caregivers and their physicians understand and respect their wishes can be very important.

CHAPTER 11

A health navigator can play an integral role in mental health care. Many individuals go undiagnosed because of the patient's fear of being diagnosed with a mental health disorder. They are afraid to tell their family or friends about this type of medical issue. A physician who does not specialize in mental illness may misdiagnose a condition. Health navigators with experience in mental health care can be a valuable liaison with mental healthcare facilities. Navigators may assist with communication with families or the patient's clinicians. They can provide education regarding mental illness. Because mental health care may involve both personal and professional resources, a health navigator could be a coordinator for the individual's care.

CHAPTER 12

The role of the healthcare navigator in long-term care will vary depending on the individual's preference in the type of long-term care services they need, what financial options are available to them, and the state services provided. The long-term care navigator should develop a strategic plan for the individual's long-term care services. The navigator should receive training or have a background in both public and private insurance products. Having experience in long-term care as well as a foundation in basic financial planning would also be an asset. The long-term care navigator should obtain data in the following areas:

1. State options for long-term care
2. Federal options for this individual
3. Insurance options for this individual
4. Personal financial net worth
5. Personal insurance policies

The navigator should collaborate with a personal financial planner to ensure the decision is in the best financial interest of the individual.

CHAPTER 13

The U.S. healthcare system continues to evolve. Technology will continue to have a huge impact on health care. Consumers have more information to make healthcare decisions because of information technology. All of these initiatives are exciting for the healthcare consumer. The implementation of an EHR, which will enable providers to share information about a patient's health history, will provide the consumer with the opportunity to obtain more cost-effective and efficient health care. There are hospitals, physician practices, and other healthcare organizations that utilize EHR systems across the country. Even though implementing the system nationally will be extremely expensive—costs have been estimated in the billions—it will eventually be a cost-saving measure for the United States. The

Affordable Care Act has provided many incentives to improve the quality of and access to the U.S. healthcare system. The Centers for Medicaid and Medicare Innovation has more than 40 demonstration projects that focus on different types of financing models based on the performance of healthcare providers.

All of these changes can improve health outcomes. However, the U.S. healthcare system continues to be complex. The role of patient navigators can vary across the healthcare system. The patient navigator's role can take many forms. Depending on training, a navigator can focus on different parts of the healthcare system or just one component. A navigator can focus on inpatient care; marketplace exchanges; outpatient care including chronic disease management for HIV, cancer, and other chronic diseases; telehealth; mental health; and legal and ethical consultations. Although navigators have been used for decades in cancer care, HIV, and diabetes, the role has been revisited with the implementation of the Affordable Care Act marketplace exchanges and designation of navigators for those exchanges. The Centers for Disease Control and Prevention indicate patient navigation is an effective intervention for HIV care. The National Cancer Institute has funded research to assess the effectiveness of these programs. The Department of Labor, as of this writing, recognizes the community health worker as a navigator for health care. As these navigators prove their success, there are other opportunities for patient navigators to provide advocacy in many areas that are discussed in this chapter. Canada, which provides health care to all of its citizens, has a highly regulated cancer patient navigator system. The system was developed at the request of patients because of the complexity of the system. For example, a cancer patient in Canada may interact with an average of 32 physicians. Having a navigator can assist the patient with this massive communication process. Although the development of navigation programs vary from state to state and may be private or government funded, Canada has a regulated program for cancer. Cancer navigators must have five years of cancer patient experience. The navigator program is expanding its scope to include cultural sensitive navigators for diverse communities. This type of program may be an example that the United States could model particularly as it applies to regulations and standard training. The expansion of the concept of patient navigator will continue to grow as more healthcare facilities hire navigators as a way to improve patient health outcomes. Like Canada, at some juncture, there may need to be regulations to ensure quality training for the patient navigator.

CHAPTER **1**

History of the U.S. Healthcare System

LEARNING OBJECTIVES

The student will be able to:

- Identify five milestones of medicine and medical education and their importance to health care.
- Identify five milestones of the hospital system and their importance to health care.
- Identify five milestones of public health and their importance to health care.
- Identify five milestones of health insurance and its importance to health care.
- Explain the difference between primary, secondary, and tertiary prevention.
- Define and discuss the concept of the health navigator.

DID YOU KNOW THAT?

- When the practice of medicine first began, tradesmen such as barbers practiced medicine. They often used the same razor to cut hair and to perform surgery.
- In 2013, the United States spent 17.4% of the gross domestic product on healthcare spending, which is the highest in the world.
- In 2014, an estimated 36 million people in the United States, approximately 11.5% of the population, had no health insurance, according to the latest report from the National Health Interview Survey's Early Release Program. This is a decrease from the 2010 estimates of 48.6 million uninsured U.S. citizens. As a result of the Affordable Care Act, the number of uninsured is projected to decline to 23 million by 2023.
- The Centers for Medicare and Medicaid Services (CMS) predicts national health expenditures will account for more than 19% of the U.S. gross domestic product.

- The United States is one of only a few developed countries that does not have universal healthcare coverage.
- In 2002, The Joint Commission issued hospital standards requiring them to inform their patients if their results were not consistent with typical care results.

INTRODUCTION

It is important as a healthcare consumer to understand the history of the U.S. healthcare delivery system, how it operates today, who participates in the system, what legal and ethical issues arise as a result of the system, and what problems continue to plague the healthcare system. We are all consumers of health care. Yet, in many instances, we are ignorant of what we are purchasing. If we were going to spend $1,000 on an appliance or a flat-screen television, many of us would research the product to determine if what we are purchasing is the best product for us. This same concept should be applied to purchasing healthcare services.

Increasing healthcare consumer awareness will protect you in both the personal and professional aspects of your life. You may decide to pursue a career in health care either as a provider or as an administrator. Or you may decide to manage a business where you will have the responsibility of providing healthcare insurance to your employees. And lastly, from a personal standpoint, you should have the knowledge from a consumer point of view so you can make informed decisions about what matters most—your health. The federal government agrees with this philosophy. The Affordable Care Act's health insurance marketplaces provide cost and service data so consumers can determine the best healthcare insurance to purchase and the services they will receive for that purchase. Recently, the Centers for Medicare and Medicaid Services (CMS) used its claim data to publish the hospital costs of the 100 most common treatments nationwide. The purpose of this effort is to provide data to consumers regarding healthcare costs because the costs vary considerably across the United States. This effort may also encourage pricing competition of healthcare services. Health and Human Services is providing funding to states to increase their healthcare pricing transparency (Bird, 2013).

As the U.S. population's life expectancy continues to increase—resulting in the **graying of the population**—the United States will be confronted with more chronic health issues because, as people age, chronic health conditions develop. The U.S. healthcare system is one of the most expensive systems in the world. According to 2013 statistics, the United States spent $2.9 trillion, or $9,255 per person, on healthcare expenditures or 17.4% of its gross domestic product. The **gross domestic product (GDP)** is the value of the total finished products or services that are produced in a country within a year. These statistics mean that more than 17% of all of the products made within the borders of the United States within a year are healthcare related. Estimates indicate that healthcare spending will be 19.3% of the gross domestic product (CMS, 2015a).

The Gallup–Healthways Well-Being Index indicates that in 2014, the number of uninsured Americans has dropped to 16%. Among the states, Hawaii had the lowest percentage of uninsured individuals under age 65 in 2014 (2.5%), followed by Massachusetts (3.2%), Delaware (5.4%), and Iowa (6.4%). The District of Columbia also had a low rate of uninsured individuals, at 3.3%. Texas (21.5%), Oklahoma (21.5%), Alaska (21.2%), and Florida (18.8%) had the

highest insurance rates for persons under age 65 in 2014 (Nation at a Glance, 2015). The uninsured rates have dropped most among lower income and black Americans. These drops have been attributed to the insurance mandate of the Affordable Care Act (Levy, 2015).

The Institute of Medicine's (IOM) 1999 report indicated that nearly 100,000 citizens die each year as a result of medical errors. More recent studies indicate this estimate is much higher despite many quality improvement initiatives implemented over the years.

Unlike most developed countries, the United States does not offer a **universal healthcare program**, which means access to all citizens. Many of these systems are typically run by the government, have centralized health policy agencies, are financed through different forms of taxation, and payment of healthcare services are by a single payer—the government (Shi & Singh, 2008). France and the United Kingdom have been discussed as possible models for the United States to follow to improve access to health care, but these programs have problems and may not be the ultimate solution for the United States. However, because the United States does not offer any type of universal healthcare coverage, many citizens who are not eligible for government-sponsored programs are expected to provide the service for themselves through the purchase of health insurance or the purchase of actual services. Many citizens cannot afford these options, resulting in their not receiving routine medical care. The passage of the **Patient Protection and Affordable Care Act of 2010 (PPACA)**, more commonly called the **Affordable Care Act (ACA)**, has attempted to increase access to affordable health care. One of the mandates of the Act was the establishment of electronic health insurance marketplaces, which provide opportunities for consumers to search for affordable health insurance plans. There also is a mandate that individuals who do not have health insurance purchase health insurance if they can afford it or pay a fine. Both of these mandates have decreased the number of uninsured in the United States. At this writing, there is a change in administration so there may be changes to the Affordable Care Act and the marketplace exchanged could be eliminated.

ROLE OF THE HEALTH NAVIGATOR

The health navigation professions include a large number of job titles. There are three general areas of employment, which are often identified as community health workers, patient navigators, and health insurance navigators. Employment for a wide range of health navigation professions has grown rapidly in recent years. New funding mechanisms from Medicaid, Medicare, and the Affordable Care Act have dramatically increased interest in developing these types of career positions that need academic health navigator training. Community health workers are the only health navigation employment classification tracked by the U.S. Department of Labor. The Labor Department's *Occupational Outlook* estimates that the positions for community health workers will increase 21% from 2012 to 2022 (Guide to Public Health and Navigation, 2015).

The U.S. healthcare system is very complex. There are many participants that play a role in providing healthcare services. Because of its complexity, healthcare consumers often are misinformed or uninformed about many aspects of the healthcare system that affect their care. Although the concept of a **health navigator** has been utilized in different areas of health care such as cancer, HIV, and diabetes, the concept of the navigator was fully introduced to a national audience as part of the Affordable Care Act. The first patient navigation program began in 1990 by Harold Freeman. In 2005, President Bush signed the Patient Navigator and Chronic Disease Prevention Act, which established a research program to examine cost effectiveness of navigation programs. In 2006, the Center for Medicare and Medicaid Services funded six multiyear demonstration programs on navigation programs. In 2000, the Health Resources and Services Administration (HRSA) funded six programs that focused on chronic disease navigation programs and in 2010, added 10 new sites. The **Centers for Disease Control and Prevention (CDC)** recognizes that patient navigators can be an effective intervention (Huber, Shapiro II, Burke, & Palmer, 2014). Then the ACA established insurance navigators at the state government level to help with the insurance marketplace websites. According to the healthcare.gov website, a navigator is an individual or organization that is trained and able to help consumers, small businesses, and their employees as they look for health coverage options through the marketplace, including completing eligibility and enrollment forms. These individuals and organizations are required to be unbiased. Their services are free to consumers. The ACA created the navigator program or in-person assister (IPA) as part of the outreach and enrollment assistance to individuals who were purchasing insurance coverage from the health marketplace. Any marketplace was required to have a navigator program to assist healthcare consumers. Navigators were required to provide education and to assist with enrollment in insurance programs and contracted directly with the Center for Medicare and Medicaid Services. They were required to complete 30 hours of training.

Prior to the implementation of the healthcare marketplaces, navigators were used to assist in many areas including mental health, cancer, primary care, uninsured population, clinical ethics consultations, case management, and long-term care. Like the navigators for the healthcare marketplace, their main goal is to assist the healthcare consumer with making educated decisions regarding their health care and the health care of their loved ones. Another term for a health navigator is a patient advocate. As our healthcare system becomes more patient centric and performance based, there will be more navigator roles developed to ensure that patients' comprehension of their healthcare system is clear.

Research indicates that patient navigators that provide assistance to cancer, HIV, and diabetes patients indicate there are improved screening rates for the diseases, improved rates of confirmatory testing which both relate to earlier diagnoses, improved access to care and improved health outcomes, increase in mental health outcomes, and improvement of patient self-management (Broeckhart & Challacombe, 2014).

Regardless of the area of the healthcare system with which a health navigator may assist a patient, the bottom line is increasing patient health literacy. **Health literacy** is the degree to which individuals have the capacity to obtain, process, and understand basic health information and services. The wide range of skills that comprise health literacy and influence a patient's ability to navigate the healthcare system and make appropriate decisions about his or her health include reading, writing, numeracy, communication, and, increasingly, the use of electronic technology.

CONSUMER PERSPECTIVE ON HEALTH CARE

What Is Health?

The World Health Organization (WHO) defines **health** as the state of complete physical, mental, and social well-being and not merely the absence of disease or infirmity (WHO, 1942). IOM defines health as a state of well-being and the capability to function in the face of changing circumstances. It is a positive concept emphasizing social and personal resources as well as physical capabilities (IOM, 1997). According to the Society for Academic Emergency Medicine (SAEM), health is a state of physical and mental well-being that facilitates the achievement of individual and societal goals (SAEM, 1992). All of these definitions focus on the impact an individual's health status has on his or her quality of life.

Several determinants or influences impact the status of an individual's health. Individual lifestyle factors such as exercise, diet, and sexual activity and **constitutional factors** such as age and sex are direct determinants of a person's health. Within the immediate environment of an individual, there are social and community networks, which are external influences on health. In addition to the social and community networks, there also are general macro environmental conditions of socioeconomic, cultural, and environmental factors that impact health, such as education, work environment, living and working conditions, healthcare services, food production, unemployment, water and sanitation, and housing. These **determinants of health** tie

into the activities of the U.S. healthcare delivery system and its impact on the individual's health. These activities often are categorized as primary, secondary, and occasionally tertiary prevention (Determinants of Health, 2013). These concepts are vital to understanding the U.S. healthcare system because different components of the healthcare system focus on different areas of health. This often results in lack of coordination between the different components.

Primary, Secondary, and Tertiary Prevention

According to the *American Heritage Dictionary* (2001), prevention is defined as "slowing down or stopping the course of an event." **Primary prevention** avoids the development of a disease. Promotion activities such as health education are primary prevention. Other examples include smoking cessation programs, immunization programs, and educational programs for pregnancy and employee safety. State health departments often develop targeted, large education campaigns regarding a specific health issue in their area. **Secondary prevention** activities are focused on early disease detection, which prevents progression of the disease. Screening programs, such as high blood pressure testing, are examples of secondary prevention activities. Colonoscopies and mammograms are also examples of secondary prevention activities. Many local health departments implement secondary prevention activities. Tertiary prevention reduces the impact of an already established disease by minimizing disease-related complications. **Tertiary prevention** focuses on rehabilitation and monitoring of diseased individuals. A person with high blood pressure who is taking blood pressure medication is an example of tertiary prevention. A physician who writes a prescription for that blood pressure medication to control high blood pressure is an example of tertiary prevention. Traditional medicine focuses on tertiary prevention, although more primary care providers are encouraging and educating their patients on healthy behaviors (Centers for Disease Control and Pretention [CDC], 2007).

We, as healthcare consumers, would like to receive primary prevention to prevent disease. We would like to participate in secondary prevention activities such as screening for cholesterol or blood pressure because it helps us manage any health problems we may be experiencing and reduces the potential impact of a disease. And, we also would like to visit our physicians for tertiary measures so, if we do have a disease, it can be managed by taking a prescribed drug or some other type of treatment. From our perspective, these three areas of health should be better coordinated for the healthcare consumer so the United States will have a healthier population.

In order to understand the current healthcare delivery system and its issues, it is important to learn the history of the development of the U.S. healthcare system. There are four major sectors

of our healthcare system that will be discussed in this chapter that have impacted our current system of operations: (1) the history of practicing medicine and the development of medical education, (2) the development of the hospital system, (3) the history of public health, and (4) the history of health insurance. In **Tables 1-1** to **1-4**, several important milestones are listed by date and illustrate historic highlights of each system component. The list is by no means exhaustive, but it provides an introduction to how each sector has evolved as part of the U.S. healthcare system.

Milestones of Medicine and Medical Education

The early practice of medicine did not require a major course of study, training, board exams, or licensing, as is required today. During this period,

TABLE 1-1 Milestones of Medicine and Medical Education 1700–2015

- 1700s: Training and apprenticeship under one physician was common until hospitals were founded in the mid-1700s. In 1765, the first medical school was established at the University of Pennsylvania.
- 1800s: Medical training was provided through internships with existing physicians who often were poorly trained themselves. There were only four medical schools in the United States that graduated only a handful of students. There was no formal tuition with no mandatory testing.
- 1847: The AMA was established as a membership organization for physicians to protect the interests of its providers. It did not become powerful until the 1900s when it organized its physician members by county and state medical societies. The AMA wanted to ensure they were protecting their financial well-being. It also began to focus on standardizing medical education.
- 1900s to 1930s: The medical profession was represented by general or family practitioners who operated in solitary practices. A small percentage of physicians were women. Total expenditures for medical care were less than 4% of the gross domestic product.
- 1904: The AMA created the Council on Medical Education to establish standards for medical education.
- 1910: Formal medical education was attributed to Abraham Flexner, who wrote an evaluation of medical schools in the United States and Canada indicating many schools were substandard. The Flexner Report led to standardized admissions testing for students called the Medical College Admission Test (MCAT), which is still used as part of the admissions process today.
- 1930s: The healthcare industry was dominated by male physicians and hospitals. Relationships between patient and physicians were sacred. Payments for physician care were personal.
- 1940s to 1960s: When group health insurance was offered, the relationship between patient and physician changed because of third-party payers (insurance). In the 1950s, federal grants supported medical school operations and teaching hospitals. In the 1960s, the Regional Medical Programs provided research grants and emphasized service innovation and provider networking. As a result of the Medicare and Medicaid Enactment in 1965, the responsibilities of teaching faculty also included clinical responsibilities.
- 1970s to 1990s: During the 1980s, third-party payers reimbursed academic medical centers with no restrictions. In the 1990s with the advent of managed care, reimbursement was restricted.
- 2014: According to the 2014 Association of American Medical Colleges (AAMAC) annual survey, more than 70% of medical schools have or will implement policies and programs to encourage primary care specialties for medical school students.

TABLE 1-2 Milestones of the Hospital and Health care Systems 1820–2015

- 1820s: Almshouses or poorhouses, the precursor of hospitals, were developed to serve the poor primarily. They provided food and shelter to the poor and consequently treated the ill. Pesthouses, operated by local governments, were used to quarantine people who had contagious diseases such as cholera. The first hospitals were built around urban areas in New York City, Philadelphia, and Boston and were used often as a refuge for the poor. Dispensaries or pharmacies were established to provide free care to those who could not afford to pay and to dispense drugs to ambulatory patients.

- 1850s: A hospital system was finally developed but conditions were deplorable because there were unskilled providers. Hospitals were owned primarily by the physicians who practiced in them.

- 1890s: Patients went to hospitals because they had no choice. Providers became more cohesive because they had to rely on each other for referrals and access to hospitals, which gave them more professional power.

- 1920s: The development of medical technological advances increased the quality of medical training and specialization and the economic development of the United States. The establishment of hospitals became the symbol of the institutionalization of health care. In 1929, President Coolidge signed the Narcotic Control Act, which provided funding for hospital construction for drug addicts.

- 1930s to 1940s: Once physician-owned hospitals were now owned by church groups, larger facilities, and government at all levels.

- 1970 to 1980: The first Patient Bill of Rights was introduced to protect healthcare consumer representation in hospital care. In 1974, the National Health Planning and Resources Development Act required states to have CON laws to qualify for federal funding.

- 1980 to 1990: According to the AHA, 87% of hospitals were offering ambulatory surgery. In 1985, the EMTALA was enacted, which required hospitals to provide screening and stabilize treatment regardless of the ability to pay by the consumer.

- 1990 to 2000s: As a result of the Balanced Budget Act cuts of 1997, the federal government authorized an outpatient Medicare reimbursement system.

- 1996: Hospitalists are introduced as clinicians that provide care once a patient is hospitalized.

- 2002: The Joint Commission on the Accreditation of Healthcare Organizations (now The Joint Commission) issued standards to increase consumer awareness by requiring hospitals to inform patients if their results were not consistent with typical results.

- 2007: The Institute for Health Improvement launched the Triple Aim, which focuses on three goals: improving patient satisfaction, reducing health costs, and improving public health.

- 2011: In 1974, a federal law was passed that required all states to have certificate of need (CON) laws to ensure the state approved any capital expenditures associated with hospital/medical facilities' construction and expansion. The Act was repealed in 1987 but as of 2016, 35 states still have some type of CON mechanism.

- 2011: The Affordable Care Act created the Centers for Medicare and Medicaid Services' Innovation Center for the purpose of testing "innovative payment and service delivery models to reduce program expenditures … while preserving or enhancing the quality of care" for individuals who receive Medicare, Medicaid, or Children's Health Insurance Program (CHIP) benefits.

- 2015: The Centers for Medicare and Medicaid Services posted its final rule that reduces Medicare payments to hospitals that have readmission rates of Medicare patients within 30 days.

anyone who had the inclination to set up a physician practice could do so; oftentimes, clergy were also medical providers, as were tradesmen such as barbers. The red and white striped poles outside barber shops represented blood and bandages because the barbers were often also surgeons. They used the same blades to cut hair and to perform surgery (Starr, 1982). Because there were no restrictions, competition was very intense. In most cases, physicians did not possess any technical expertise; they relied mainly on common sense to make diagnoses (Stevens, 1971). During this period, there was no health insurance, so consumers decided when they would visit a physician and paid for their visits out of their own pockets. Often, physicians treated their patients in the patients' homes. During the late 1800s, the medical profession became more cohesive as more technically advanced services were delivered to patients. The establishment of the

TABLE 1-3 Milestones in Public Health 1700–2015

- 1700 to 1800: The United States was experiencing strong industrial growth. Long work hours in unsanitary conditions resulted in massive disease outbreaks. U.S. public health practices targeted reducing epidemics, or large patterns of disease in a population, that affected the population. Some of the first public health departments were established in urban areas as a result of these epidemics.

- 1800 to 1900: Three very important events occurred. In 1842, Britain's Edwin Chadwick produced the General Report on the Sanitary Condition of the Labouring Population of Great Britain, which is considered one of the most important documents of public health. This report stimulated a similar U.S. survey. In 1854, Britain's John Snow performed an analysis that determined contaminated water in London was the cause of the cholera epidemic in London. This discovery established a link between the environment and disease. In 1850, Lemuel Shattuck, based on Chadwick's report and Snow's activities, developed a state public health law that became the foundation for public health activities.

- By 1900 to 1950: In 1920, Charles Winslow defined public health as a focus of preventing disease, prolonging life, and promoting physical health and efficiency through organized community efforts.

- During this period, most states had public health departments that focused on sanitary inspections, disease control, and health education. Throughout the years, public health functions included child immunization programs, health screenings in schools, community health services, substance abuse programs, and sexually transmitted disease control.

- In 1923, a vaccine for diphtheria and whooping cough was developed. In 1928, Alexander Fleming discovered penicillin. In 1946, the National Mental Health Act (NMHA) provided funding for research, prevention, and treatment of mental illness.

- 1950 to 1980: In 1950, cigarette smoke is identified as a cause of lung cancer.

- In 1952, Dr. Jonas Salk developed the polio vaccine.

- The Poison Prevention Packaging Act of 1970 was enacted to prevent children from accidentally ingesting substances. Childproof caps were developed for use on all drugs. In 1980, the eradication of smallpox was announced.

- 1980 to 1990: The first recognized cases of AIDS occurred in the United States in the early 1980s.

- 1988: The Institute of Medicine Report defined public health as organized community efforts to address the public interest in health by applying scientific and technical knowledge and promote health. The first Healthy People Report (1987) was published that recommended a national prevention strategy.

- 1990 to 2000: In 1997, Oregon voters approved a referendum that allowed physicians to assist terminally ill, mentally competent patients to commit suicide. From 1998 to 2006, 292 patients exercised their rights under the law.

- 2000s: The second Healthy People Report was published in 2000. The terrorist attack on the United States on September 11, 2001, impacted and expanded the role of public health. The Public Health Security and Bioterrorism Preparedness and Response Act of 2002 provided grants to hospitals and public health organizations to prepare for bioterrorism as a result of September 11, 2001.

- 2010: The ACA was passed. Its major goal was to improve the nation's public health level. The third Healthy People Report was published.

- 2015: The number of children who have not received vaccines due to parents' beliefs that vaccines are not safe has increased nationally. Due to these beliefs, there have been measles outbreaks throughout the nation even though measles was considered eradicated decades ago.

American Medical Association (AMA) in 1847 as a professional membership organization for physicians was a driving force for the concept of private practice in medicine. The AMA was also responsible for standardizing medical education (AMA, 2013a; Goodman & Musgrave, 1992).

In the early history of medical education, physicians gradually established large numbers of medical schools because they were inexpensive to operate, increased their prestige, and enhanced their income. Medical schools only required four or more physicians, a classroom, some discussion rooms, and legal authority to confer degrees. Physicians received the students' tuitions directly and operated the school from this influx of money. Many physicians would affiliate with

TABLE 1-4 Milestones of the U.S. Health Insurance System 1800–2015

- 1800 to 1900: Insurance was purchased by individuals like one would purchase car insurance. In 1847, the Massachusetts Health Insurance Co. of Boston was the first insurer to issue "sickness insurance." In 1853, a French mutual aid society established a prepaid hospital care plan in San Francisco, California. This plan resembles the modern Health Maintenance Organization (HMO).

- 1900 to 1920: In 1913, the International Ladies Garment Workers began the first union-provided medical services. The National Convention of Insurance Commissioners drafted the first model for regulation of the health insurance industry.

- 1920s: The blueprint for health insurance was established in 1929 when J. F. Kimball began a hospital insurance plan for school teachers at the Baylor University Hospital in Texas. This initiative became the model for Blue Cross plans nationally. The Blue Cross plans were nonprofit and covered only hospital charges so as not to infringe on private physicians' income.

- 1930s: There were discussions regarding the development of a national health insurance program. However, the AMA opposed the move (Raffel & Raffel, 1994). With the Depression and U.S. participation in World War II, the funding required for this type of program was not available. In 1935, President Roosevelt signed the Social Security Act (SSA), which created "old age insurance" to help those of retirement age. In 1936, Vassar College, in New York, was the first college to establish a medical insurance group policy for students.

- 1940s to 1950s: The War Labor Board froze wages, forcing employers to offer health insurance to attract potential employees. In 1947, the Blue Cross Commission was established to create a national doctors network. By 1950, 57% of the population had hospital insurance.

- 1965: President Johnson signed Medicare and Medicaid programs into law.

- 1970s to 1980s: President Nixon signed the HMO Act, which was the predecessor of managed care. In 1982, Medicare proposed paying for hospice or end-of-life care. In 1982, diagnosis-related groups (DRGs) and prospective payment guidelines were developed to control insurance reimbursement costs. In 1985, the Consolidated Omnibus Budget Reconciliation Act (COBRA) required employers to offer partially subsidized health coverage to terminated employees.

- 1990 to 2000: President Clinton's Health Security Act proposed a universal healthcare coverage plan, which was never passed. In 1993, the Family Medical Leave Act (FMLA) was enacted, which allowed employees up to 12 weeks of unpaid leave because of family illness. In 1996, the Health Insurance Portability and Accountability Act (HIPAA) was enacted, making it easier to carry health insurance when changing employment. It also increased the confidentiality of patient information. In 1997, the Balanced Budget Act (BBA) was enacted to control the growth of Medicare spending. It also established the State Children's Health Insurance Program (SCHIP).

- 2000: The SCHIP, now known as the Children's Health Insurance Program (CHIP), was implemented.

- 2000: The Medicare, Medicaid, and SCHIP Benefits Improvement and Protection Act provided some relief from the BBA by providing across-the-board program increases.

- 2003: The Medicare Prescription Drug, Improvement, and Modernization Act was passed, which created Medicare Part D, prescription plans for the elderly.

- 2006: Massachusetts mandated all residents have health insurance by 2009.

- In 2009, President Obama signed the **American Recovery and Reinvestment Act (ARRA)**, which protected health coverage for the unemployed by providing a 65% subsidy for COBRA coverage to make the premiums more affordable.

- 2010: The ACA was signed into law, making it illegal for insurance companies to rescind insurance on their sick beneficiaries. Consumers also can appeal coverage claim denials by the insurance companies. Insurance companies are unable to impose lifetime limits on essential benefits.

- 2013: As of October 1, individuals could purchase qualified health benefits plans from the Health Insurance Marketplaces. If an employer does not offer insurance, effective 2015, consumers can purchase it from the federal Health Insurance Marketplace.

- 2013: The federal government provided states with funding to expand their Medicaid program to increase preventive services.

- In 2015, the CMS also posted its final rule that reduces Medicare payments to hospitals that have Medicare patients readmitted within 30 days. This rule is an attempt to focus hospital initiatives on quality care.

established colleges to confer degrees. Because there were no entry restrictions, as more students entered into medical schools, the existing internship program with physicians was dissolved and the Doctor of Medicine (MD) became the standard (Vault Career Intelligence, 2013). Although there were major issues with the quality of education provided because of the lack of educational requirements, medical school education became the gold standard for practicing medicine (Sultz & Young, 2006). The publication of the **Flexner Report** in 1910, which evaluated medical schools in Canada and the United States, was responsible for forcing medical schools to develop curriculums and admission testing. These standards are still in existence today.

When the Medicare and Medicaid programs were enacted in 1965, Congress recognized that the federal government needed to support medical education, which resulted in ongoing federal funding to teaching hospitals to support medical

resident programs. The responsibilities of teaching now included clinical duties. During the 1970s to 1990s, patient care dollars exceeded research funding as the largest source of medical school support. Academic medical centers would be reimbursed without question by third-party payers. However, with the advent of managed care in the 1990s, reimbursement restrictions were implemented (Rich, Liebow, Srinivasan, Parish, Wollinscroft, Fein, & Blaser, 2002). With the passage of the ACA, which increased the need for primary care providers, more medical schools now focus on primary care curriculum initiatives (AAMAC, 2015).

In 1990, Dr. Harold Freeman established a patient navigation program in the Harlem neighborhood of New York City. The purpose was to increase access to healthcare services such as screening, diagnoses, and treatments for those individuals who were poor and uninsured. The Harold P. Freeman Patient Navigation model (**Figure 1-1**) is considered the gold standard.

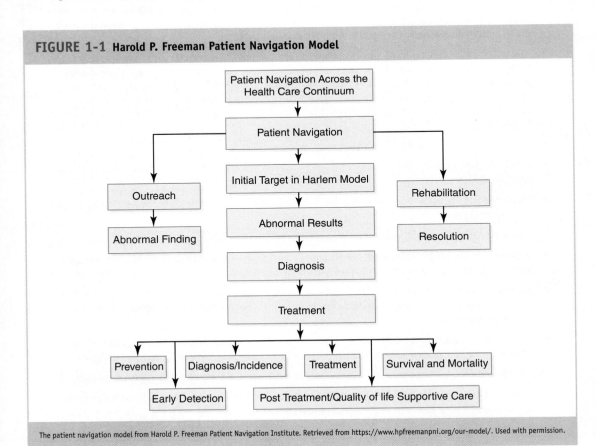

FIGURE 1-1 Harold P. Freeman Patient Navigation Model

The patient navigation model from Harold P. Freeman Patient Navigation Institute. Retrieved from https://www.hpfreemanpni.org/our-model/. Used with permission.

According to its website, the principal function of the navigator is to eliminate any and all barriers to timely screening, diagnosis, treatment, and supportive care for each individual. Navigators act as the support hub for all aspects of patients' movement through the healthcare system. The navigator's role is to promote smooth and timely continuity of care to the point of resolution (Harold Freeman Institute, 2016).

The patient navigator can provide assistance with the following barriers to a healthy outcome:

- Financial barriers (including uninsured and under insured)
- Communication barriers (such as lack of understanding, language/cultural)
- Medical system barriers (fragmented medical system, missed appointments, lost results)
- Psychological barriers (such as fear and distrust)
- Other barriers (such as transportation and need for child care) (Harold Freeman, 2016)

MILESTONES OF THE HOSPITAL SYSTEM

In the early 1800s, almshouses, or poorhouses, were established to serve the indigent. They provided shelter while treating illness. Government-operated pesthouses segregated those who could spread disease. The framework of these institutions set up the conception of the hospital. Initially, wealthy people did not want to go to hospitals because the conditions were deplorable and the providers were not skilled; so hospitals, which were first built in urban areas, were used by the poor. During this period, many of the hospitals were owned by the physicians who practiced in them (Rosen, 1983).

In the early 1900s, with the establishment of a more standardized medical education, hospitals were more accepted across socioeconomic classes and became the symbol of medicine. With the establishment of the AMA, which protected the interests of providers, the reputation of providers became more prestigious. During the 1930s and 1940s, the ownership of the hospitals changed from physician-owned to church-related and government-operated (Starr, 1982).

In 1973, the first Patient Bill of Rights was established to protect healthcare consumers in the hospitals. In 1974, a federal law was passed that required all states to have Certificate of Need (CON) laws to ensure the state approved any capital expenditures associated with hospital/medical facilities' construction and expansion. The Act was repealed in 1987, but as of 2011, 36 states still have some type of CON mechanism (National Conference of State Legislatures [NCSL], 2013). The concept of CON was important because it encouraged state planning to ensure its medical system was based on need. In 1985, the Emergency Medical Treatment and Active Labor Act (EMTALA) was enacted to ensure that consumers were not refused treatment for an emergency. During this period, inpatient hospital use was typical; however, by the 1980s, many hospitals were offering outpatient or ambulatory surgery that continues today. The Balanced Budget Act of 1997 authorized outpatient Medicare reimbursement to support these cost-saving measures (CDC, 2001). Hospitalists, created in 1996, are specialists that focus specifically on the care of patients when they are hospitalized. This new type of provider recognizes the need of providing quality hospital care (American Hospital Association [AHA], 2016; Sultz & Young, 2006). In 2002, The Joint Commission on the Accreditation of Healthcare Organizations (now The Joint Commission) issued standards to increase consumer awareness by requiring hospitals to inform patients if their results were not consistent with typical results (AHA, 2013). In 2007, the Institute for Health Improvement launched the Triple Aim, which focused on the three goals of patient satisfaction, improving public health, and reducing healthcare costs (Zeroing in on Triple Aim, 2015).

In 2011, the Affordable Care Act created the Centers for Medicare and Medicaid Services' Innovation Center for the purpose of developing innovative care and payment models. In 2015, the CMS also posted its final rule that reduces Medicare payments to hospitals that have Medicare patients readmitted within 30 days. This rule is an attempt to focus hospital initiatives on quality care (Rau, 2015).

Hospitals are the foundation of our healthcare system. As our health insurance system evolved, the first type of health insurance was hospital insurance. As society's health needs increased, expansion of different medical facilities increased. There was more of a focus on ambulatory or outpatient services because consumers prefer outpatient services because outpatient services are more cost effective. Although hospitals are still an integral part of our healthcare delivery system, the method of their delivery has changed. More hospitals have recognized the trend of outpatient services and have integrated those types of services in their delivery.

MILESTONES OF PUBLIC HEALTH

The development of public health is important to note because it developed independently of the development of private medical practices. Physicians were worried that government health departments could regulate how they practiced medicine, which could limit their income. Public health specialists also approached health from a collectivistic and preventive care viewpoint—to protect as many citizens as possible from health issues and to provide strategies to prevent health issues from occurring. Private practitioners held an individualistic viewpoint—citizens more often would be paying for physician services from their health insurance or from their own pockets, and physicians would provide guidance on how to cure their diseases, not prevent them. The two contrasting viewpoints still exist today, but there have been efforts to coordinate more of the traditional and public health activities.

During the 1700s into the 1800s, the concept of public health was born. In their reports, Edwin Chadwick, Dr. John Snow, and Lemuel Shattuck demonstrated a relationship between the environment and disease (Chadwick, 1842; Turnock, 1997). As a result of their work, public health law was enacted and, by the 1900s, public health departments were focused on the environment and its relationship to disease outbreaks.

Disease control and health education also were integral components of public health departments. In 1916, The Johns Hopkins University, one of the most prestigious universities in the world, established the first public health school (Duke University Library, 2013). Winslow's definition of public health focuses on the prevention of disease, while the IOM defines public health as the organized community effort to protect the public by applying scientific knowledge (IOM, 1988; Winslow, 1920). These definitions are exemplified by the development of several vaccines for whooping cough, polio, smallpox, diphtheria, and the discovery of penicillin. All of these efforts focus on the protection of the public from disease.

The three most important public health achievements are (1) the recognition by the Surgeon General that tobacco use is a health hazard; (2) the number of vaccines that have been developed that have eradicated some diseases and controlled the number of childhood diseases that exist; and (3) early detection programs for blood pressure and heart attacks and smoking cessation programs, which have dramatically reduced the number of deaths in this country (Novick, Morrow, & Mays, 2008).

Assessment, policy development, and assurance, all core functions of public health, were developed based on the 1988 report, *The Future of Public Health*, which indicated there was an attrition of public health activities in protecting the community (IOM, 1988). There was poor collaboration between public health and private medicine, no strong mission statement and weak leadership, and politicized decision making. **Assessment** was recommended because it focused on the systematic continuous data collection of health issues, which would ensure that public health agencies were vigilant in protecting the public (IOM, 1988; Turnock, 1997). **Policy development** should also include planning at all health levels, not just federally. Federal agencies should support local health planning (IOM, 1988). **Assurance** focuses on evaluating any processes that have been put in place to assure that the programs are being implemented appropriately. These core functions will ensure that public health remains focused on the community, has programs in place that are effective, and has an evaluation process in place to ensure that the programs do work (Turnock, 1997).

The *Healthy People 2000* report, begun in 1987, was created to implement a new national prevention strategy with three goals: increase life expectancy, reduce health disparities, and increase access to preventive services. Also, three categories of health promotion, health prevention, and preventive services were identified and surveillance activities were emphasized. *Healthy People* provided a vision to reduce preventable disabilities and death. Target objectives were set throughout the years to measure progress (CDC, 2013a).

The *Healthy People 2010* report was released in 2000. The report contained a health promotion and disease prevention focus to identify preventable threats to public health and to set goals to reduce the threats. Nearly 500 objectives were developed according to 28 focus areas. Focus areas ranged from access to care, food safety, education, environmental health, to tobacco and substance abuse. An important component of *Healthy People 2010* is the development of an infrastructure to ensure public health services are provided. Infrastructure includes skilled labor, information technology, organizations, and research. In 2010, *Healthy People 2020* was released. It contains 1,200 objectives that focus on 42 topic areas. According to the Centers for Disease Control and Prevention (CDC), a smaller set of *Healthy People 2020* objectives, called Leading Health Indicators (LHIs), have been targeted to communicate high-priority health issues. Healthy People 2020 Progress Review webinars began in early 2013 and are scheduled to run through mid-2017 (CDC, 2015a). The goals for all of these reports are consistent with the definitions of public health in both Winslow's and the IOM's reports.

It is important to mention the impact the terrorist attack on the United States on September 11, 2001, the anthrax attacks, the outbreak of global diseases such as severe acute respiratory syndrome (SARS), and the U.S. natural disaster of Hurricane Katrina had on the scope of public health responsibilities. As a result of these major events, public health has expanded its area of responsibility. The terms "bioterrorism" and "disaster preparedness" have more frequently appeared in public health literature and have become part of strategic planning. The **Public Health Security and Bioterrorism Preparedness and Response Act of 2002** provided grants to hospitals and public health organizations to prepare for bioterrorism as a result of September 11, 2001 (CDC, 2009).

Public health is challenged by its very success because the public now takes public health measures for granted. There are several successful vaccines that targeted almost all childhood diseases, tobacco use has decreased significantly, accident prevention has increased, workplaces are safer because of the Occupational Safety and Health Administration (OSHA), fluoride is added to the public water supply, and there is decreased mortality due to heart attacks (Turnock, 1997). When some major event occurs like anthrax poisoning or a SARS outbreak, people immediately think that public health efforts will automatically control these problems. The public may not realize how much effort, dedication, and research takes place to protect them.

MILESTONES OF THE HEALTH INSURANCE SYSTEM

There are two key concepts in **group insurance**: "risk is transferred from the individual to the group and the group shares the cost of any covered losses incurred by its member" (Buchbinder & Shanks, 2007). Like life insurance or homeowner's insurance, **health insurance** was developed to provide protection should a covered individual experience an event that requires health care. In 1847, a Boston insurance company offered sickness insurance to consumers (Starr, 1982).

During the 1800s, large employers such as coal mining and railroad companies offered medical services to employees by providing company doctors. Fees were taken from their pay to cover the service. In 1913, a union-provided health insurance was provided by the International Ladies Garment Workers where health insurance was negotiated as part of their contract (Duke University Library, 2013). During this period, there were several proposals for a national health insurance program, but the efforts failed. The AMA was concerned that any national health insurance would impact the financial security of its providers. The AMA persuaded the federal government to support private insurance efforts (Raffel & Raffel, 1994).

In 1929, a group hospital insurance plan was offered to teachers at a hospital in Texas. This became the foundation of the nonprofit Blue Cross plans. In order to placate the AMA, Blue Cross initially offered only hospital insurance in order to avoid infringement of physicians' incomes (Blue Cross Blue Shield Association [BCBS], 2007; Starr, 1982). In 1935, the **Social Security Act (SSA)** was created and was considered "old age" insurance. During this period, there was continued discussion of a national health insurance program. But, with the impact of World War II and the Depression, there was no funding for this program. The government felt that the Social Security Act was a sufficient program to protect consumers. These events were a catalyst for the development of a health insurance program that included private participation. Although a universal health coverage program was proposed during President Bill Clinton's administration in the 1990s, it was never passed. In 2006, Massachusetts proposed mandatory health coverage for all citizens, so it may be that universal health coverage would be a state-level initiative (KFF, 2013). In 2009, there was a major public outcry at regional town hall meetings opposing any type of government universal healthcare coverage.

By the 1950s, nearly 60% of the population had hospital insurance (AHA, 2007). Disability insurance was attached to Social Security. In the 1960s, President Johnson signed **Medicare** and **Medicaid** into law, which protects the elderly, disabled, and indigent. President Nixon established the Health Maintenance Organization (HMO), which focused on effective cost measures for health delivery. Also, in the 1980s, diagnostic-related groups (DRGs) and prospective payment guidelines were established to provide guidelines for treatment. These DRGs were attached to appropriate insurance reimbursement categories

for treatment. The **Consolidated Omnibus Budget Reconciliation Act (COBRA)** was passed to provide health insurance protection if an individual changes jobs. In 1993, the **Family Medical Leave Act (FMLA)** was passed to protect an employee if there is a family illness. An employee can receive up to 12 weeks of unpaid leave and maintain his or her health insurance coverage during this period. In 1994, the **Uniformed Services Employment and Reemployment Rights Act (USERRA)** entitled individuals who leave for military service to return to their job. Also, in 1996, the **Health Insurance Portability and Accountability Act (HIPAA)** was passed to provide stricter confidentiality regarding the health information of individuals. In 1997, the Balanced Budget Act (BBA) was passed that required massive program reductions for Medicare and authorized Medicare reimbursement for outpatient services (CMS, 2013b).

Cost, access, and quality continue to be issues for U.S. health care. Employers continue to play an integral role in health insurance coverage. The largest public coverage program is Medicare, which covers 55 million people. In 2014, Medicare benefit payments totaled nearly $600 billion (Facts on Medicare, 2015). The State Children's Health Insurance Program (SCHIP), renamed CHIP, was implemented to ensure that children who are not Medicaid eligible receive health care. The Medicare, Medicaid, and SCHIP Benefits Improvement and Protection Act provided some relief from the BBA of 1997 by restoring some funding to these consumer programs. In 2003, a consumer law, the **Medicare Prescription Drug, Improvement, and Modernization Act**, created a major overhaul of the Medicare system (CMS, 2013b). The Act created Medicare Part D, a prescription plan that became effective in 2006 that provided different prescription programs to the elderly, based on their prescription needs. In 2014, approximately $6 billion Medicare benefit dollars were spent on Medicare Part D (Facts on Medicare, 2015). The Act also renamed the Medicare cost plans to Medicare Advantage, which is a type of managed care program. Medicare contracts with private health insurance programs to provide services.

This program is also called Medicare Part C, and it provides both Medicare Parts A and B benefits. In 2014, approximately $24 billion Medicare benefit dollars were spent on the Medicare Part C plan (Facts on Medicare, 2015). In 2008, the **National Defense Authorization Act** expanded the FMLA to include families of military service members to take a leave of absence if the spouse, parent, or child was called to active military service. In 2009, the **American Recovery and Investment Act** which protected health coverage for the unemployed by providing a 65% subsidy for COBRA coverage to make the premiums more affordable. The 2010 ACA required individuals to purchase health insurance by 2014. Despite these efforts, health insurance coverage continues to be an issue for the United States.

CURRENT SYSTEM OPERATIONS
Government's Participation in Health Care

The U.S. government plays an important role in healthcare delivery. The United States has three governmental levels participating in the healthcare system: federal, state, and local. The federal government provides a range of regulatory and funding mechanisms including **Medicare** and **Medicaid**, established in 1965 as federally funded programs to provide health access to the elderly (65 years or older) and the poor, respectively. Over the years, these programs have expanded to include the disabled. They also have developed programs for military personnel, veterans, and their dependents.

Federal law does ensure access to emergency services regardless of ability to pay as a result of EMTALA (Regenstein, Mead, & Lara, 2007). The federal government determines a national healthcare budget, sets reimbursement rates, and also formulates standards for providers for eligible Medicare and Medicaid patients (Barton, 2003). The state level is responsible for regulatory and funding mechanisms but also provides healthcare programs as dictated by the federal government. The local or county level of government is responsible for implementing programs dictated by both the federal and state level.

The United States has several federal health regulatory agencies including the CDC for public health, the **Food and Drug Administration (FDA)** for pharmaceutical controls, and **Centers for Medicare and Medicaid Services (CMS)** for the indigent, disabled, and the elderly. The Joint Commission is a private organization that focuses on healthcare organizations' oversight, and the **Agency for Healthcare Research and Quality (AHRQ)** is the primary federal source for quality delivery of health services. The **Center for Mental Health Services (CMHS)**, in partnership with state health departments, leads national efforts to assess mental health delivery services. Although the federal government is to be commended because of the many agencies that focus on major healthcare issues, with multiple organizations there is often duplication of effort and miscommunication that results in inefficiencies (KFF, 2013). However, there are several regulations in place that protect patient rights. One of the first pieces of legislation is the **Sherman Antitrust Act of 1890** and ensuing legislation, which ensures fair competition in the marketplace for patients by prohibiting monopolies (Niles, 2013). Regulations such as HIPAA protects patient information; COBRA gives workers and families the right to continue healthcare coverage if they lose their job; the **Newborns' and Mothers' Health Protection Act (NMHPA)** of 1996 prevents health insurance companies from discharging a mother and child too early from the hospital; the **Women's Health and Cancer Rights Act (WHCRA)** of 1998 prevents discrimination of women who have cancer; the **Mental Health Parity Act (MHPA)** of 1996 and its 2008 amendment requires health insurance companies to provide fair coverage for mental health conditions; the **Genetic Information Nondiscrimination Act of 2008** prohibits U.S. insurance companies and employers from discriminating based on genetic test results; the **Lilly Ledbetter Fair Pay Act of 2009** provides protection for unlawful employment practices related to compensation discrimination; and, finally, the Affordable Care Act of 2010 focuses on increasing access to health care, improving the quality of healthcare delivery, and increasing the number of those individuals who have health insurance. All of these regulations are considered **social regulations** because they were enacted to protect the healthcare consumer.

Private Participation in Health Care

The private sector focuses on the financial and delivery aspects of the system. Healthcare costs are paid by a health insurance plan, private, or government, and the enrollee of the plan. Approximately 34% of 2013 healthcare expenditures were paid by private health insurance, offered by a private insurance company such as Blue Cross; private **out-of-pocket payments or expenses**, funds paid by the individual, were 13.7%, and federal, state, and local governments paid 39%. Out-of-pocket payments are considered the individual's **cost share** of his or her healthcare costs. Approximately 57% of private healthcare financing is through **employer health insurance**, a type of **voluntary health insurance** set up by an individual's employer. The delivery of the services provided is through legal entities such as hospitals, clinics, physicians, and other medical providers (National Center for Health Statistics [NCHS], 2014). The different providers are an integral part of the medical care system and need to coordinate their care with the layers of the U.S. government. In order to ensure access to health care, communication is vital between public and private components of healthcare delivery.

ASSESSING YOUR HEALTHCARE SYSTEM USING THE IRON TRIANGLE

Many healthcare systems are evaluated using the **Iron Triangle of Health Care**—a concept that focuses on the balance of three factors: quality, cost, and accessibility to health care (see **Figure 1-2**). This concept was created in 1994 by Dr. William Kissick (Kissick, 1994). If one factor is emphasized, such as cost reduction, it may create an inequality of quality and access because costs are being cut. Because lack of access is a problem in the United States, healthcare systems may focus on increasing access, which could increase costs. In order to assess the success of a healthcare delivery, it is vital that consumers assess their health care

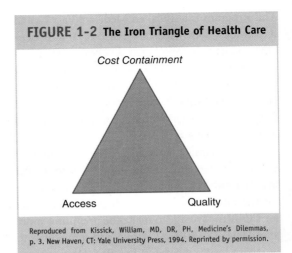

FIGURE 1-2 The Iron Triangle of Health Care

Reproduced from Kissick, William, MD, DR, PH, Medicine's Dilemmas, p. 3. New Haven, CT: Yale University Press, 1994. Reprinted by permission.

by analyzing the balance between cost, access, and quality. Are you receiving quality care from your provider? Do you have easy access to your healthcare system? Is it costly to receive health care? Many experts use the Iron Triangle to analyze large healthcare delivery systems, and, as a healthcare consumer, you also can evaluate your healthcare delivery system using the Iron Triangle. An effective healthcare system should have a balance between the three components.

CONCLUSION

Despite U.S. healthcare expenditures, U.S. disease rates remain higher than many developed countries because the United States has an expensive system that is available to only those who can afford it (Regenstein, Mead, & Lara, 2007). Findings from a recent MetLife annual survey indicate that healthcare costs are worrying employees and their employers. More than 60% of employees are concerned they will not be able to pay out-of-pocket expenses not covered by insurance. Employers are increasing the cost sharing of their employees for healthcare benefits because of the cost increases (Business Wire, 2013). Because the United States does not have universal health coverage, there are more health disparities across the nation. Persons living in poverty are more likely to be in poor health and less likely to use the healthcare system compared to those with incomes above the poverty line.

If the United States offered universal health coverage, the per-capita expenditures would be more evenly distributed and likely more effective. The major problem for the United States is that healthcare insurance is a major determinant of access to health care. Although there has been a decrease in the number of uninsured people in the United States as a result of the individual mandate to purchase health insurance by the Affordable Care Act, there is still limited access to routine health care. In a recent report, the CDC indicates there was a decline in U.S. infant mortality rates between 2005 and 2011 because of declines in certain geographic areas. However, despite this positive result, the United States is still ranked worldwide much lower than other developed countries due to the continued preterm birth rates. This is an important statistic because it is often used to compare the health status of nations worldwide. Although our healthcare expenditures are very high, our infant mortality rates rank higher than many countries. Racial disparities in disease and death rates continue to be a concern (CDC, 2013b). Both private and public participants in the U.S. health delivery system need to increase their collaboration to reduce these disease rates. Leaders need to continue to assess our healthcare system

using the Iron Triangle to ensure there is a balance between access, cost, and quality.

This chapter provides an overview of each broad area of the U.S. healthcare system. In each area, there can be a role for a health navigator. Tables 1-1–1-4 provide an overview of the history of medicine and medical education, hospitals, insurance, and public health. Each of these areas can have representation for a navigator or healthcare consumer advocate. This textbook will cover the navigator role in all of these areas except insurance. Because the insurance arena is so complicated, an individual textbook will be devoted to this component of the healthcare system.

Healthcare navigators can help healthcare providers discuss options with patients. They can assist hospitalized patients with inpatient and outpatient care. Healthcare navigators also can assist people with health insurance choices as well as choices involving healthcare behavior. Developing a system-wide network of navigators trained to be patient advocate specialists in designated areas can only enhance the philosophy of a patient-centric healthcare system. Health navigators have been shown to be effective at improving chronic disease management, smoking cessation, and adult immunizations (Battaglia, McCloskey, Caron, Murrell, Bernstein, Childs, Jong, Walker, & Bernstein, 2012).

© Jim Barber/Shutterstock

Summary

Vocabulary

Affordable Care Act (ACA)
Agency for Healthcare Research and Quality (AHRQ)
Almshouses
American Medical Association (AMA)
American Recovery and Reinvestment Act (ARRA)

Assessment
Assurance
Center for Mental Health Services (CMHS)
Centers for Disease Control and Prevention (CDC)
Centers for Medicare and Medicaid Services (CMS)
Certificate of need (CON)

Consolidated Omnibus Budget Reconciliation
    Act (COBRA)
Constitutional factors
Cost share
Determinants of health
Emergency Medical Treatment and Active Labor
    Act (EMTALA)
Employer health insurance
Epidemics
Family Medical Leave
    Act (FMLA)
Flexner Report
Food and Drug Administration (FDA)
Genetic Information Nondiscrimination Act of
    2008
Graying of the population
Gross domestic product (GDP)
Group insurance
Health
Health navigator
Health insurance
Health Insurance Portability and Accountability
    Act (HIPAA)
Health literacy
Healthy People reports (2000, 2010, 2020)
Hospitalists
Iron Triangle of Health Care
The Joint Commission
Lilly Ledbetter Fair Pay Act of 2009
Medicaid
Medicare

Medicare Prescription Drug, Improvement, and
    Modernization Act
Mental Health Parity Act (MHPA)
National Defense Authorization Act
National Mental Health Act (NMHA)
Newborns' and Mothers' Health Protection Act
    (NMHPA)
Out-of-pocket payments or expenses
Patient Bill of Rights
Patient Protection and Affordable Care Act of
    2010 (PPACA)
Pesthouses
Poison Prevention Packaging Act of 1970
Policy development
Poorhouses
Primary prevention
Public health
Public health functions
Public Health Security and Bioterrorism
    Preparedness and Response Act of 2002
Secondary prevention
Sherman Antitrust Act of 1890
Social regulations
Social Security Act (SSA)
Tertiary prevention
Triple Aim
Uniformed Services Employment and
    Reemployment Rights Act (USERRA)
Universal healthcare program
Voluntary health insurance
Women's Health and Cancer Rights Act (WHCRA)

References

American Heritage Dictionary, 4th ed. (2001). New York, NY: Bantam Dell.

American Hospital Association. (2007). Community accountability and transparency: Helping hospitals better serve their communities. http://www.aha.org/aha/content/2007/pdf/07accountability.pdf.

American Medical Association. (2013a). Our history. https://www.ama-assn.org/ama/pub/about-ama/our-history/ama-history-timeline.page

Barton, P. (2003). *Understanding the U.S. health services system*. Chicago, IL: Health Administration Press.

Battaglia, T., McCloskey, L., Caron, S., Murrell, S., Bernstein, E., Childs, A., Jong, H., Walker, J., & Bernstein, J. (Jan.–March, 2012). Feasibility of chronic disease patient navigation in an urban primary care practice. *J Ambu Care Manag, 35* (1).

Bird, J. (2013). CMS releases hospital price ranges of 100 most common treatments. http://www.fiercehealthfinance.com/story/cms-releases-hospital-price-comparison-data/2013-05-08.

Blue Cross Blue Shield Association. (2016). Blue beginnings. https://www.ama-assn.org/ama/pub/about-ama/our-history/ama history-timeline.page

Broeckhart, L. & Challacombe, L. (2014). Health navigation: A review of the evidence. https://effectiveinterventions.cdc.gov/en/HighImpact Prevention/BiomedicalInterventions/HIVNavigationServices.aspx.

Buchbinder, S., & Shanks, N. (2007). *Introduction to health care management*. Sudbury, MA: Jones and Bartlett Publishers.

Business Wire. (2013). MetLife study finds six out of ten employees are concerned about out-of-pocket medical costs. http://finance.yahoo.com/news/metlife-study-finds-six-ten-130000050.html.

Centers for Disease Control and Prevention. (2001). Trends in hospital emergency department utilization: United States, 1992–1999. *Vital and Health Statistics, 13*(150revised). http://www.cdc.gov/nchs/data/series/sr_13/sr13_150.pdf

Centers for Disease Control and Prevention. (2007). Skin cancer module: Practice exercises. http://www.cdc.gov/cancer/skin/basic_info/prevention.htm

Centers for Disease Control and Prevention. (2009). Selected Federal Legal Authorities Pertinent to Public Health Emergencies. http://www.cdc.gov/phlp/docs/ph-emergencies.pdf.

Centers for Disease Control and Prevention. (2016a). Healthy People 2020: Tobacco use. http://www.cdc.gov/tobacco/basic_information/healthy_people.

Centers for Disease Control and Prevention. (2016b). NCHS Data Brief: Recent Declines in Infant Mortality in the United States, 2005–2011. http://www.cdc.gov/nchs/data/databriefs/db120.htm.

Centers for Medicare and Medicaid Services (2015a). National health expenditure projections. http://www.cms.gov/Research-Statistics-Data-and-Systems/Statistics-Trends-and-Reports/NationalHealthExpendData/nationalHealthAccountsHistorical.html.

Centers for Medicare and Medicaid Services. (2015b). HIPAA: General information. https://www.cms.gov/research-statistics-data-and-systems/statistics-trends-and-reports/nationalhealthexpenddata/nationalhealthaccountshistorical.html.

Chadwick, E. (1842). *The sanitary conditions of the labouring class.* London: W. Clowes,

Classen, D., Resar, R., Griffin, F., Federico, F., Frankel, T., Kimmel, N., James, B. (2011). Global Trigger Tool shows that adverse events in hospitals may be ten times greater than previously measured. *Health Aff., 30*(4): 109.

Determinants of health. (2015). http://healthypeople.gov/2020/implement/assess.aspx.

Duke University Library. (2016). Medicine and Madison Avenue. Timeline. http://library.duke.edu/digitalcollections/mma/timeline.html.

Goodman, J. C., & Musgrave, G. L. (1992). *Patient power: Solving America's health care crisis.* Washington, DC: CATO Institute.

Guide to public health and health navigation in community colleges, part 1. League for Innovation in the community college. https://www.league.org/ccph

Henry J. Kaiser Family Foundation. (2015). Facts on Medicare Spending and Financing. http://kff.org/search/?s=Facts±on±Medicare±spending±and±financing+.

Hersh, L., Salzman, B., & Snyderman, D. (2015). Health literacy in primary care. *Am Fam Physician*, Jul 15;*92*(2):118–124. http://www.aafp.org/afp/2015/0715/p118.html.

Harold Freeman Institute. (2016). http://www.hpfreemanpni.org/our-model/.

United States, 2014. National Center for Health Statistics. http://www.cdc.gov/nchs/data/hus/hus14.pdf

Huber, J., Shapiro, R., II, Burke, H., & Palmer, A. (2014). Enhancing the care navigation model: potential roles for health sciences librarians. *J Med Libr Assoc, 102*(1): 55–61.

Institute of Medicine. (1988). *The future of public health* (1–5). Washington, DC: National Academies Press.

Kissick, W. (1994). *Medicine's dilemmas.* New Haven and New London, CT: Yale University Press.

Kliff, S. (2012). Study: Fewer employers are offering health insurance. http://www.washingtonpost.com/blogs/wonkblog/post/study-fewer-employers-are-offering-health-insurance/2012/04/24/gIQAfGH6eT_print.html.

Levy, J. (2015). U.S. uninsured rate continues to fall. http://www.gallup.com/poll/167798/uninsured-rate-continues-fall.aspx

Ludmerer, K. (2004). The development of American medical education from the turn of the century to the era of managed care. *Clinical, Orthopaedics and Related Research, 422*:256–262.

Nation at a glance: Uninsured Americans. (2015). http://www.cdc.gov/nchs/features/nation_jun2015/nation_at_a_glance_jun2015.htm.

National Center for Health Statistics. (2014). *Health, United States, 2014. With special feature on socioeconomic status and health.* Washington, DC: U.S. Government Printing Office.

National Conference of State Legislatures. (2016). Certificate of need: State health laws and programs. http://www.ncsl.org/issues-research/health/con-certificate-of-need-state-laws.aspx.

Niles, N. (2013). *Basic concepts of health care human resource management* (37–50). Burlington, MA: Jones & Bartlett Learning.

Novick, L., Morrow, C., & Mays, G. (2008). *Public health administration* (2nd ed., 1–68). Sudbury, MA: Jones and Bartlett Publishers.

Raffel, M. W., & Raffel, N. K. (1994). *The U.S. health system: Origins and functions* (4th ed.). Albany, NY: Delmar Publishers.

Rau, J. (2015). 1,700 hospitals with quality bonuses from Medicare, but most will never collect.http://khn.org/news/1700-hospitals-win-quality-bonuses-from-medicare-but-most-will-never-collect/

Regenstein, M., Mead, M., & Lara, A. (2007). The heart of the matter: the relationship between communities, cardiovascular services and racial and ethnic gaps in care. *Manag Care Interface, 20*, 22–28.

Rich, E., Liebow, M., Srinivasan, M., Parish, D., Wollinscroft, J., Fein, O.,& Blaser, R. (2002). Medicare financing of graduate medical education. *J Gen Intern Med., 17*(4): 283–292.

Rosen, G. (1983). *The structure of American medical practice 1875–1941.* Philadelphia, PA: University of Pennsylvania Press.

Starr, P. (1982). *The social transformation of American medicine.* Cambridge, MA: Basic Books.

Stevens, R. (1971). *American medicine and the public interest.* New Haven, CT: Yale University Press.

Sultz, H., & Young, K. (2006). *Health care USA: Understanding its organization and delivery* (5th ed.). Sudbury, MA: Jones and Bartlett Publishers.

Turnock, J. (1997). *Public health and how it works.* Gaithersburg, MD: Aspen Publishers, Inc.

Vault Career Intelligence. (2013). https://career.boisestate.edu/featured/vault-career-intelligence/

Winslow, C. E. A. (1920). *The untilled fields of public health* (30–35). New York, NY: Health Service, New York Chapter of the American Red Cross.

Zeroing in on the Triple Aim (2015). http://www.aha.org/content/15/brief-3aim.pdf

Student Activity 1-1

In Your Own Words

Based on this chapter, please provide a definition of the following vocabulary words in your own words. DO NOT RECITE the text definition.

Epidemics

Gross domestic product (GDP)

Group insurance

Health navigator

Iron Triangle

Pesthouses

Primary prevention

Public health functions

Secondary prevention

Tertiary prevention

Universal healthcare program

Voluntary health insurance

Student Activity 1-2

Complete the following case scenarios based on the information provided in the chapter. Your answer must be IN YOUR OWN WORDS.

Real-Life Applications: Case Scenario One

Your mother knows that you are taking classes for your healthcare management degree. She just returned from a physician checkup and she was confused by the terminology they were using at the office. They recommended surgery and it upset and confused her. You told her about the concept of a navigator as a type of patient advocate for healthcare consumers like her who need assistance.

Activity

Discuss the concept of the health navigator and how this person could assist your mother.

Case Scenario Two

You recently were promoted to assistant to the chief executive officer of the Niles Hospital system. The CEO is interested in building a hospital to expand their healthcare system. She has asked you to investigate the certificate of need (CON) process for this proposal.

Activity

Perform an Internet research on the CON process and provide a report on the necessary steps to achieve this CON.

Case Scenario Three

One of your friends had a serious medical emergency and had to go to the hospital for treatment. She was very upset because upon her arrival, she was asked for her insurance card, which she did not have, and was transferred to another hospital quickly. You had learned there was a law that made this type of treatment by a hospital illegal. However, before giving your friend your opinion, you wanted to find out more about this law and whether it applied to her situation.

Activity

Perform an Internet research on public health regulations and write up a report on whether you think the Emergency Medical Treatment and Active Labor Act (EMTALA) was applicable in this situation. Describe how a health navigator can assist your friend in resolving this issue.

Case Scenario Four

As a public health student, you are interested in different public health initiatives the CDC has put forth over the years and whether they have been successful. You continue to hear the term "Healthy People reports." You are interested in the results of these reports.

Activity

Visit the CDC website and write a report on the Healthy People initiatives and whether or not you think they are successful initiatives.

Student Activity 1-3

Internet Exercises

- Visit each of the websites listed here.
- Name the organization.
- Locate its mission statement or statement of purpose on the website.
- Provide a brief overview of the activities of the organization.
- How does this organization participate in the U.S. healthcare system?

Websites

http://www.ama-assn.org

Organization Name
Mission Statement
Overview of Activities
Importance of Organization to U.S. Health Care

http://www.cdc.gov

Organization Name
Mission Statement
Overview of Activities
Importance of Organization to U.S. Health Care

http://www.health-care-navigators.com

Organization Name
Mission Statement
Overview of Activities
Importance of Organization to U.S. Health Care

http://www.hhs.gov

Organization Name
Mission Statement
Overview of Activities
Importance of Organization to U.S. Health Care

http://www.jointcommission.org

Organization Name
Mission Statement
Overview of Activities
Importance of Organization to U.S. Health Care

http://www.ahrq.gov

Organization Name
Mission Statement
Overview of Activities
Importance of Organization to U.S. Health Care

Student Activity 1-4

Discussion Questions

The following are suggested discussion questions for this chapter:

1. What is the Flexner Report? How did it impact health care in the United States?
2. What are the *Healthy People* report initiatives? Describe three current initiatives to your classmates.
3. Why was health insurance developed? What was Kaiser's role in this?
4. Describe how the Iron Triangle can be used to assess health care. Give specific examples.
5. What is the Patient Bill of Rights? Why was it developed? Have you ever seen the Patient Bill of Rights posted anywhere?
6. Give five examples of public health activities in your personal or work environment.
7. What do you think of the concept of the health navigator. How could this person help you understand the healthcare system?

Student Activity 1-5

Current Events

Perform an Internet search and find a current events topic that relates to this chapter. Provide a summary of the article and the link to the article and explain how the article relates to the chapter.

CHAPTER **2**

Current Operations of the Healthcare System

LEARNING OBJECTIVES

The student will be able to:

- Identify the stakeholders of the U.S. healthcare system and their relationships with each other and the patient.
- Discuss the importance of healthcare statistics.
- Identify at least three current statistics regarding the U.S. healthcare system.
- Discuss complementary and alternative medicine and its role in health care.
- Discuss the role the health navigator can have with healthcare stakeholders.
- Discuss three patient rights and responsibilities.

DID YOU KNOW THAT?

- According to the Bureau of Labor Statistics, the healthcare industry projections for job growth over a 10-year period is 9.8 million jobs by 2024.
- Most healthcare workers have jobs that do not require a four-year college degree but health diagnostic and treatment providers are the most educated workers in the United States.
- Healthcare employment is found predominantly in large states such as California, New York, Texas, and Florida.
- Approximately 40% of U.S. adults use some form of non-traditional medicine.
- The healthcare industry and social assistance industry reported more work-related injuries than any other private industry.
- Life expectancy rates and infant mortality rates are an indication of the health of a population.

INTRODUCTION

The one commonality among the world's healthcare systems is that they all have consumers or users of their systems. Systems were developed to provide a service to their citizens. However, the U.S. healthcare system, unlike other systems in the world, does not provide healthcare access to all of its citizens. It is a very complex system that is comprised of many public and private components. Healthcare expenditures comprise approximately 17.4% of the **gross domestic product (GDP)**, which is the total value of goods produced and services provided in a country during one year. Healthcare costs are very expensive, and most citizens do not have the money to pay for health care themselves. Individuals rely on health insurance to pay a large portion of their healthcare costs. According to a 2014 Centers for Disease Control and Prevention (CDC) survey, there were 35.7 million uninsured people in the United States, which was a decrease from the 2011 reported CDC data of 48.2 million uninsured (CDC, 2016a). The government believes this is the result of the mandate by the Affordable Care for individuals to purchase health insurance coverage.

In the United States there are several **stakeholders** or interested entities that participate in providing healthcare services. Some are trained professionals such as physicians, nurses, dentists, and chiropractors. Others include inpatient and outpatient facilities; the payers such as the insurance companies, the government, and self-pay individuals; and the suppliers of products such as pharmaceutical companies, medical equipment companies, and the research and educational facilities (Sultz & Young, 2006). Each component plays an integral role in the healthcare industry. These different components demonstrate the complexity of the U.S. system. The current operations of the delivery system and utilization statistics will be discussed in this chapter. The role of the health navigator with each of the stakeholders also will be discussed along with how this relationship can help with the care of a patient.

OVERVIEW OF THE CURRENT SYSTEM

Between 2014 and 2024, nearly 10 million jobs are projected to be added in the healthcare industry (Bureau of Labor Statistics [BLS], 2016a). The United States spends the highest proportion of its GDP on healthcare expenditures. The system is a combination of private and public resources. Since World War II, the United States has had a private fee-for-service system that has produced generous incomes for physicians and has been profitable for many participants in the healthcare industry (Jonas, 2003). The healthcare industry operates like traditional business industries. Organizations designated as for-profit, they need to make money in order to operate. The main goal of entities that are designated not-for-profit is based on a particular social goal, but they also have to make money in order to continue their operations.

Several major stakeholders participate or have an interest in the industry. The stakeholders identified as participants in the healthcare industry include consumers, employers, healthcare and non-healthcare employers, healthcare providers, healthcare facilities, government (federal, state, and local), insurance companies, educational and training institutions, professional associations that represent the different stakeholders, pharmaceutical companies, and research institutions.

It is also important to mention the increasing prominence of alternative therapy medicine. Each role will be discussed briefly and the role of the stakeholders with the relationships of the patient and provider.

MAJOR STAKEHOLDERS IN THE HEALTHCARE INDUSTRY
Consumers/Patients

The main group of consumers is patients who need healthcare services from a physician, hospital, or outpatient facility. A **patient** is any individual who is being evaluated by a healthcare professional. Patient rights focus on access to care, patients' informed decision-making and patient confidentiality (Patient rights, 2016). From an organizational perspective, the healthcare consumer is the most important stakeholder for an organization." The healthcare industry operates like a business. If a consumer has the means to pay out-of-pocket, from government sources, or from health insurance, the services will be provided. If an individual does not have the means to pay from any of these sources of funding, a service may not be provided." There is a principle of the U.S. healthcare system, **duty to treat**, which means that any person deserves basic care (Pointer et al., 2007). In some instances, healthcare providers will give care to someone who has no funding source and designate the care provided as a **charitable care or bad debt**, which means the provider either does not expect payment after the person's inability to pay has been determined or efforts to secure the payment have failed (Smith, 2008). Businesses also take the same action. Many of them provide a community service or donate funds to a charitable cause, yet both traditional businesses and healthcare organizations need to charge for their services in order to continue their operations.

There are also other consumer relationships in the healthcare industry. Consumers purchase drugs either from their provider or over the counter from pharmacies. The pharmaceutical companies market their products to physicians who in turn prescribe their products to their patients.

FIGURE 2-1 Major Stakeholders in the Healthcare Industry

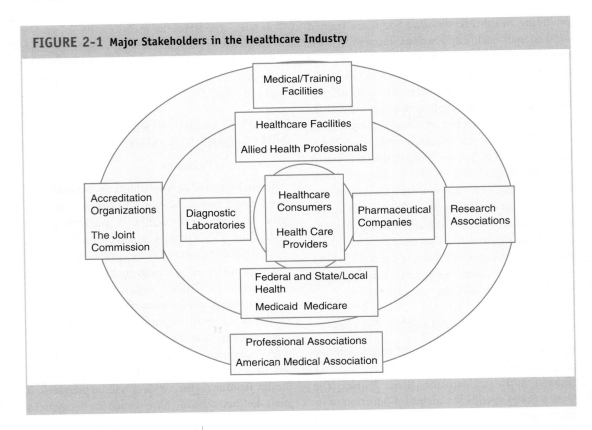

The pharmaceutical companies also market their products to hospitals and outpatient facilities to encourage the use of their drugs in these facilities. Medical equipment companies also sell their products to facilities and individual providers.

Employers

Employers consist of both private and public employers. The healthcare industry is the largest U.S. employer. According to the **Bureau of Labor Statistics (BLS)**, there are several segments of the healthcare industry, including ambulatory healthcare services, hospitals, and nursing and residential care facilities. Ambulatory healthcare services are comprised of physicians, dentists, other health practitioners, outpatient care centers, medical and diagnostic laboratories, home healthcare services, and other ambulatory care. The hospital segment provides inpatient services primarily with outpatient as a secondary source. It includes general and surgical care facilities, psychiatric substance abuse hospitals, and other specialty hospitals. **Residential**

care facilities provide nursing care, mental health treatment, treatment for substance abuse and mental disabilities, community care for the elderly, and other residential care (BLS, 2016b). Healthcare employment opportunities can be more easily found in large states such as California, New York, Texas, and Florida (BLS, 2016c). Employers outside the healthcare industry also are stakeholders because they provide a large percentage of health insurance coverage to individuals nationwide.

Hospitals

There are approximately 11,000 hospitals across the United States. Hospitals provide total medical care that ranges from diagnostic services to surgery and continuous nursing care. They traditionally provide inpatient care, although more hospital systems now also provide outpatient care. Some hospitals specialize in treatments for cancer, children's health, and mental health. It is important to note that hospitals are an integral component of the healthcare system. Many of the uninsured and underinsured present themselves at emergency departments (EDs) across the country and use EDs as their primary care provider. In 2013, more than 136 million individuals presented themselves to the emergency department as their entry into health care. During times of public health crises, hospitals are the backbone of providing care. In 2015, hospitals provided $46.4 billion in uncompensated care, a $7.1 billion increase from 2010 (American Hospital Association, 2016). A health navigator can be instrumental in assisting a patient who needs to be hospitalized to ensure they are proactive in their hospital care. They can also assist the patient when they are discharged from the facility.

Nursing and Residential Care Facilities

These types of facilities provide nursing, rehabilitation, and health-related personal care to those who need ongoing care. There are 76,000 facilities nationwide. Nursing aides provide the majority of care. Residential care facilities provide around-the-clock social and personal care to the elderly, children, and others who cannot take care of themselves. Examples of residential care facilities are drug rehabilitation centers, group homes, and assisted-living facilities (BLS, 2016b). A health navigator can be very helpful to residents of any type of residential care facility to ensure the residents' rights are protected.

Physicians and Other Healthcare Practitioners

In 2014, there were nearly 700,000 U.S. physicians and surgeons. Physicians traditionally practiced solo, but more of them now participate in a group practice to reduce administrative costs. In 2014, there were 151,000 dentists in the United States. Job outlook for both physicians and dentists is very positive due to the aging of the U.S. population. Other healthcare practitioners include chiropractors, optometrists, psychologists, therapists, and alternative medicine practitioners (BLS, 2016c). A health navigator can be helpful to ensure ongoing communication between patients and their providers, and, ultimately, to enable healthy outcomes.

Alternative health or **complementary and alternative medicine (CAM)** practitioners practice unconventional health therapies such as yoga, vitamin therapy, and spiritual healing. Consumers must pay out-of-pocket for these services because health insurance companies generally do not cover them. Chiropractors and acupuncturists, also considered alternative medicine practitioners, are more likely to be covered. Recognizing consumer interest in alternative medicine, in 1998, as part of the National Institutes of Health, the **National Center for Complementary and Alternative Medicine (NCCAM)** was established. Its purpose was to explore these types of practices in the context of rigorous science, train complementary and alternative researchers, and disseminate information. More medical schools now offer some courses in alternative medicine. In the United States, nearly 40% of adults (about 4 in 10) and more than 10% of children (about 1 in 9) use some form of CAM. Adults are most likely to use CAM for musculoskeletal problems such as back, neck, or joint pain (National Center for Health Statistics, 2016). A health navigator can be helpful to a patient who is interested in pursuing nontraditional medicine to ensure the care provided is legitimate. The navigator plays an important role in this area of medicine because this type of treatment often is paid out of pocket by the healthcare consumer.

Home Healthcare Services

Home healthcare services, which offer medical care in the home, are provided primarily to the elderly, chronically ill, and mentally impaired. Mobile medical technology allows more medical problems to be treated in the home. Home health care is one of the fastest-growing components of employment in the industry because of consumer preference and the cost effectiveness of home medical care (BLS, 2016d). The health navigator can assist patients with choosing an appropriate home health agency for their care.

Outpatient Care Centers and Ambulatory Healthcare Services

Outpatient care centers include kidney dialysis centers, mental health and substance abuse clinics, and surgical and emergency centers. Ambulatory healthcare services include transport services, blood and organ banks, and smoking cessation programs (BLS, 2016e). The health navigator can assist the patient to ensure their selection of outpatient centers is appropriate for their needed care.

Laboratories

Medical and diagnostic laboratories provide support services to the medical profession. Workers may take blood, take scans or X-rays, or perform other medical tests. This segment provides the fewest number of jobs in the industry (BLS, 2016f). The health navigator can provide support to the patient to ensure the prescribed tests are appropriate for their diagnosis.

Government

As a result of the Medicare and Medicaid programs, federal and state governments are the largest stakeholders in the U.S. healthcare system. The government at both levels is responsible for financing health care through these programs as well as playing the public provider role through state and local health departments. Veterans' Affairs medical facilities also provide services to those in the armed forces (Sultz & Young, 2006). The health navigator can be extremely helpful to patients when dealing with government programs such as Medicare, Medicaid, and private insurance companies to ensure they understand their insurance coverage.

Insurance Companies

The insurance industry also is a major stakeholder in the healthcare industry. It often is blamed for the problems with the healthcare system because of the millions of people who are underinsured and uninsured. The insurance industry also has been accused of routinely disapproving medical procedures and charging high rates for coverage. There are traditional indemnity plans such as **Blue Cross and Blue Shield**, but managed care, which is also considered an insurance plan, has become more popular for cost control. The Affordable Care Act has placed restrictions on what health insurance companies can do regarding reimbursement restrictions.

Educational and Training Organizations

Educational and training facilities such as medical schools, nursing schools, public health schools, and allied health programs play an important role in the U.S. healthcare industry because they are responsible for the education and training of healthcare employees. These institutions help formulate behaviors of the healthcare workforce. Many health navigators have clinical training or may decide to pursue additional education for their navigator position.

Research Organizations

Government research organizations such as the National Institutes of Health (NIH) and the CDC not only provide regulatory guidance but also perform research activities to improve health care. Private research organizations such as the **Robert Wood Johnson Foundation**, the **Pew Charitable Trusts**, and the **Commonwealth Fund** support research efforts through grants. If a patient has a rare disease, the health navigator may perform research to assist the patient with options for clinical trials.

Professional Associations

Professional associations play an important role in healthcare policy. Associations represent physicians, nurses, hospitals, long-term care facilities, and other health industry stakeholders. Most are represented by a professional organization that offers guidance about their role in the healthcare industry. They also lobby at all government levels in an attempt to influence government regulations in favor of their constituents. The following are examples of professional associations that represent some of the major stakeholder organizations in this industry. Health navigators are encouraged to join a professional association appropriate for their background to ensure they are current with regulations and education and care.

- **American Hospital Association (AHA)** The AHA is the most prominent association for all types of hospitals and healthcare networks. Founded in 1898, the AHA, which is a membership organization, provides education and lobbies for hospital representation in the political process at all governmental levels (AHA, 2016).

- **American Health Care Association (AHCA)** Founded in 1949, the AHCA is a membership organization that represents not-for-profit and for-profit nursing, assisted living, and developmentally disabled and sub-acute providers. Its focus is to monitor and improve standards of nursing home facilities (AHCA, 2016).
- **American Association of Homes and Services for the Aging (AAHSA)** The AAHSA (recently renamed Leading Age), which is a membership organization, represents not-for-profit adult day care services, home healthcare services, community services, senior housing, assisted living facilities, continuous care retirement communities, and nursing homes. It lobbies all government levels regarding legislation that can affect this industry and provides technical assistance for these organizations (LeadingAge, 2016).

Pharmaceutical Companies

A functioning healthcare system needs medicine that is prescribed by a provider or is purchased as an over-the-counter medicine from a pharmacy. The pharmaceutical industry is integral to the success of a healthcare system. Innovative drugs have improved people's quality of life. There has been an internal division within the pharmaceutical industry between the manufacturing of **brand name drugs** and generic or "me too" drugs. **Generic drugs**, which do not have name recognition, are a less costly alternative to a brand name drug. The generic drug manufacturer must provide the same active ingredients as the brand name drugs; however, the generic drug approval process is less costly. Generic drugs have no patent protection and are sold at discounted prices (Zhong, 2012).

Brand name drugs such as Lipitor and Viagra are typically more expensive than generic drugs because they cost a pharma company more than $1 billion over several years to develop. The Food and Drug Administration, which is responsible for approving the drug for human use, has traditionally upheld a very strict and lengthy approval process. However, recently, the FDA has been removing red tape and speeding up the process for drugs that are prescribed for serious diseases. When a patent is awarded, a pharma company typically has 20 years of patent protection to develop a drug. However, because of the length of time it takes to determine the safety and effectiveness of a drug, once the drug is available for the public, the patent may be reduced several years (Mandal, 2014). Once that patent protection has ended, there are more opportunities for generic drug companies to control the market (Herper, 2013).

Like health insurance companies, the pharmaceutical industry often is vilified because of the cost of some prescribed medicines that may preclude some consumers from purchasing without health insurance assistance. The industry's response to why some medicines cost so much is that they take millions of dollars and years of research to develop. The pharmaceutical industry is represented by the **Pharmaceutical Research and Manufacturers of America (PhRMA)** (PhRMA, 2016).

Many medical errors are related to prescription and non-prescription drug errors. A health navigator should have resources available to ensure the patient has received the appropriate drugs for their condition.

PATIENT RIGHTS AND RESPONSIBILITIES AND THE ROLE OF THE HEALTH NAVIGATOR

Each of the stakeholders described plays a direct or indirect role in the relationship between the provider and patient. Because many stakeholders are involved, many lines of communication are required. Patients may have difficulty managing the care needed to achieve a healthy outcome. A patient needs to be proactive in understanding the care required as well as their rights in how care is provided to them. In 1997, President Clinton appointed a commission to provide recommendations for consumer protection and quality in the healthcare industry. These recommendations still apply and include the following: consumer information disclosure, choice of healthcare providers, access to emergency services, participation in treatment decisions, respect and nondiscrimination, health information confidentiality, and complaints and appeals processes (Maldonaldo-Schullo, 2010). The Affordable Care Act provided new guidelines to patients by empowering the patient with opportunities to make informed decisions about their health, which often can be overwhelming. It is the reason why the ACA designated health navigators to assist patients with their healthcare marketplace decisions to assist patients with understanding the information presented to them.

STAKEHOLDERS' ENVIRONMENT

Working Conditions

Healthcare workers have many varied opportunities for workplace settings. Hospitals are a typical work environment, as are physician offices. As outpatient services have become more popular, healthcare professionals can work from their homes. Healthcare professionals can work in outpatient facilities, schools, laboratories, corporations, and other unconventional settings. They are exposed to serious health hazards, including contaminated blood, chemicals, drugs, and X-ray hazards. Depending on the job, there may be ergonomic issues due to heavy lifting of patients and equipment. This industry has one of the highest injury and illness rates. U.S. hospitals recorded nearly 58,000 work-related injuries and illnesses in 2013, amounting to 6.4 work-related injuries and illnesses for every 100 full-time employees. This rate is almost twice as high as the overall rate for private industry (OSHA, 2015). In 2013, healthcare personnel reported seven times the national rate of musculoskeletal disorders compared with all other private sector workers. Nurse assistants and nurses have the highest injury rates of all occupations (Centers for Disease Control, 2015).

Projected Outlook for Employment

The healthcare industry's employment outlook is positive. By 2024, an additional 22 million jobs are projected. Growth will most likely be outside the inpatient hospital centers because cost containment is the major priority for health care. Health care will continue to grow for three major reasons: the aging of the U.S. population, advances in medical technology, and the increased focus on outpatient care.

HEALTHCARE STATISTICS

U.S. Healthcare Utilization Statistics

The National Center for Health Statistics (NCHS), which is part of the CDC, produces an annual report on the health status of the United States. This annual publication, *Health, United States*, 2015, provides an overview of healthcare utilization, resources, and expenditures. This publication examines different aspects of the U.S. healthcare delivery system and assesses the health status of U.S. citizens. The following information was summarized from this publication.

U.S. Demographics and Health Care

Life expectancy rates are an indication of the health of a designated population. This rate indicates the average number of years an individual is expected to live. They are typically calculated by gender. In 2014, life expectancy at birth in the United States was 78.8 years—76 for males and 81.2 years for females. Racial disparities exist in life expectancy at birth rates, although they have narrowed. In 2014, the rate of white male life expectancy at birth was 4.2 years longer than that for black males, and the rate for white females was 3.0 years longer than that for black females. In 2014, Hispanic males (79.2 years) and females (84 years) had longer life expectancy rates than non-Hispanic white or non-Hispanic black males and females (CDC, 2016a).

Healthcare Payers

U.S. statistics (2013) indicate that more than 34% of personal healthcare expenses were paid by private health insurance, 22% were paid by Medicare, and nearly 14% were paid by consumers. The other 30% was paid by other types of programs and insurance. In 2013, the Medicare program had more than 52 million enrollees with expenditures of nearly $585 billion. The Medicare Part D drug program accounted for $68 billion. Children under 21 accounted for nearly 20% of Medicaid expenditures. The aged, blind, and disabled accounted for 61% of Medicaid expenditures.

America's Health Rankings 2014 Edition

The partnership of the United Health Foundation and the American Public Health Association and

Partnership for Prevention, for the past 25 years, has produced the American's Health Rankings, which is an annual assessment of U.S. health by state. Overall, the healthiest states by rank are Hawaii, Vermont, Massachusetts, Connecticut, and Utah. The five unhealthiest states by rank are Arkansas, Louisiana, Kentucky, Oklahoma, and Mississippi. Health status is based on low prevalence of smoking, obesity, poverty, preventable hospitalizations, and small disparity in health status by education, cancer, and cardiovascular deaths. Cardiovascular disease remains the leading killer (NHS, 2014). However, Hawaii has issues with alcohol abuse and low immunization coverage. Although Mississippi has ranked in the bottom of the states for many years, it does have a low prevalence of binge drinking, high immunization coverage for children, and low disparity in health status. Its low ranking is the result of a high prevalence of obesity, low birthweight infants, children in poverty, and limited availability of primary care providers. Despite these rankings, many health issues need to be addressed regardless of the state ranking. Since 2013, there has been a 154% increase in pertussis incidence. Adult obesity increased 7% to nearly 30%, with physical inactivity increasing to nearly 24% of adults who did not exercise in the last 30 days. There was a 3% decrease in adults who smoke, although there has been an increase in using electronic cigarettes. The role of the health navigator could be invaluable in all of the states regardless of their rankings.

CONCLUSION

The U.S. healthcare system is a complicated system comprised of both public and private resources. Health care is available to those who have health insurance or who are entitled to health care through a public program. One can think of the healthcare system as several concentric circles that surround the most important stakeholders in the center circle: the healthcare consumers and providers. Immediately surrounding this relationship are health insurance companies and government programs, healthcare facilities, pharmaceutical companies, and laboratories, all of which provide services to consumers to ensure they receive quality health care, as well as support providers to ensure they provide quality health care. The next circle consists of peripheral stakeholders that do not have an immediate impact on the main relationship but are still important to the industry. These consist of the professional associations, the research organizations, and the medical and training facilities. The health navigator has many opportunities to assist a patient with many of the stakeholders that interact with the patient to achieve a desired health outcome. The health navigator is responsible for receiving training in the appropriate areas to assist the patient with their rights and responsibilities.

© Jim Barber/Shutterstock

Summary

Vocabulary

American Association of Homes and Services for the Aging (AAHSA)
American Health Care Association (AHCA)
American Hospital Association (AHA)

Blue Cross and Blue Shield
Brand name drugs
Bureau of Labor Statistics (BLS)
Charitable care or bad debt

Commonwealth Fund

Complementary and alternative medicine (CAM)

Duty to treat

Generic drugs

Gross domestic product (GDP)

Home healthcare services

Life expectancy rates

National Center for Complementary and Alternative Medicine (NCCAM)

National Center for Health Statistics (NCHS)

Patient

Pew Charitable Trusts

Pharmaceutical Research and Manufacturers of America (PhRMA)

Professional associations

Residential care facilities

Robert Wood Johnson Foundation

Stakeholder

References

American Association of Homes and Services for the Aging (LeadingAge). (2016). http://www.leadingage.org/AAHSA_Becomes_LeadingAge.aspx.

American Hospital Association. (2016). Trendwatch Chartbook 2015. http://www.aha.org/research/reports/tw/chartbook/2015/chart3-8.pdf.

American Hospital Association. (2016). Financial Fact Sheets. http://www.aha.org/content/15/uncompensatedcarefactsheet.pdf0.

American Health Care Association. (2013). https://www.ahcancal.org/about_ahca/Pages/default.

American Hospital Association. (2013). http://www.aha.org.

Bureau of Labor Statistics. (2016a). http://www.bls.gov/news.release/pdf/ecopro.pdf.

Bureau of Labor Statistics. (2016b). Industries at a glance: Nursing and residential care facilities. http://www.bls.gov/iag/tgs/iag623.htm.

Bureau of Labor Statistics. (2016c). Occupational outlook handbook: Healthcare occupations. http://www.bls.gov/ooh/healthcare/.

Bureau of Labor Statistics. (2016d). Occupational outlook handbook: Home health and personal care aides. http://www.bls.gov/ooh/personal-care-and-service/personal-care-aides.htm

Bureau of Labor Statistics. (2016e). Industries at a glance: Ambulatory health care services: NAICS 621. http://www.bls.gov/iag/tgs/iag621.htm.

Bureau of Labor Statistics. (2016f). Occupational outlook handbook: Medical and clinical laboratory technologists and technicians. http://www.bls.gov/ooh/healthcare/medical-and-clinical-laboratory-technologists-and-technicians.htm.

Centers for Disease Control and Prevention. (2016a). Early release of selected estimates based on data from the National Health Interview 2014 Survey (Figure 1.1b). http://www.cdc.gov/nchs/data/nhis/earlyrelease/earlyrelease201506.pdf.

Centers for Disease Control and Prevention. (2015). Occupational traumatic injuries in healthcare facilities. http://www.cdc.gov/mmwr/preview/mmwrhtml/mm6415a2.htm.

Centers for Disease Control and Prevention. (2012b). Chartbook on trends in the health of Americans (Figure 14). http://www.cdc.gov/nchs/hus/contents2012.htm#fig14.

Centers for Disease Control and Prevention. (2012c). Chartbook on trends in the health of Americans (Figure 40). http://www.cdc.gov/nchs/hus/contents2012.htm#fig40.

Centers for Disease Control and Prevention. (2012d). Chartbook on trends in the health of Americans (Figure 19). http://www.cdc.gov/nchs/hus/contents2012.htm#fig19.

Jonas, S. (2003). *An introduction to the U.S. health care system* (17–45). New York, NY: Springer Publishing.

Herper, M. (2013). The cost of creating a new drug now $5 billion, pushing Big Pharma to change. http://www.forbes.com/sites/matthewherper/2013/08/11/the-cost-of-inventing-a-new-drug-98-companies-ranked/.

Maldonaldo-Schullo, D. (2010). Get the best medical care. 1–10.

Mandal, A. (2014). Drug patents and generic pharmaceutical drugs. http://www.news-medical.net/health/Drug-Patents-and-Generics.aspx.

National Center for Health Statistics. (2016). The use of complementary and alternative medicine in the United States. https://nccih.nih.gov/research/statistics/2007/camsurvey_fs1.htm.

Occupational Safety and Health Administration. (2015). https://www.osha.gov/about.html.

Patient rights definition and overview. (2016). http://www.emedicine-health.com/patient_rights/article_em.htm#patient_rights_definition_and_overview.

Pharmaceutical Research and Manufacturers of America. (2013). http://www.phrma.org/.

Pointer, D., Williams, S., Isaacs, S., & Knickman, J. (2007). *Introduction to U.S. health care*. Hoboken, NJ: Wiley Publishing.

Smith, D. (2008). The uninsured in the U.S. health care system. *J Healthc Manag, 53*(2): 79–81.

Sultz, H., & Young, K. (2006). *Health care USA: Understanding its organization and delivery* (5th ed.). Sudbury, MA: Jones and Bartlett Publishers.

Student Activity 2-1

In Your Own Words

Based on this chapter, please provide a definition of the following vocabulary words in your own words. DO NOT RECITE the text definition.

Duty to treat

Infant mortality rate

Life expectancy rates

Charitable care or bad debt

Complementary and alternative medicine

Professional associations

Residential care facilities

Student Activity 2-2

Real-Life Applications: Case Scenario One

You have decided to become a health education teacher for a high school. One of your first class lessons will be on explaining the complexity of the U.S. healthcare system to your students.

Activity

You want to be creative so you have your students role play the stakeholders in the healthcare system. You develop a lesson plan that is outlined below. Your lesson plan outlines the major stakeholders in the system and shows how they interact with each other.

Case Scenario Two

Your grandmother is considering moving to a continuous care retirement community, but she is unsure of how to evaluate them. She asked you for assistance.

Activity

Visit the American Association of Homes and Services for the Aging (AAHSA) website to find out what information is available for continuing care communities. Give that information to your grandmother to help her make a decision.

Case Scenario Three

You eventually would like to work for a pharmaceutical company. You decided to perform research on pharmaceutical companies such as Pfizer and GlaxoSmithKline. You did not realize that there are brand name drugs and generic drugs.

Activity

Perform an Internet search on the difference between generic and brand name drugs. Discuss the difference between the two products.

Case Scenario Four

You are interested in becoming a health navigator for patients who require home health agency services. You are not sure what training you need for this type of service.

Activity

Research home health agency services on the Internet and locally and develop a specific training plan for your health navigator career.

Student Activity 2-3

Internet Exercises

- Visit each of the websites listed here.
- Name the organization.
- Locate its mission statement on the website.
- Provide a brief overview of the activities of the organization.
- How does this organization participate in the U.S. healthcare system?

Websites

http://www.rwjf.org

Organization Name
Mission Statement
Overview of Activities
Importance of Organization to U.S. Health Care

http://www.commonwealthfund.org

Organization Name
Mission Statement
Overview of Activities
Importance of Organization to U.S. Health Care

http://www.phrma.org

Organization Name
Mission Statement
Overview of Activities
Importance of Organization to U.S. Health Care

http://www.oecd.org

Organization Name
Mission Statement
Overview of Activities
Importance of Organization to U.S. Health Care

http://www.bls.gov

Organization Name
Mission Statement
Overview of Activities
Importance of Organization to U.S. Health Care

http://www.ahcancal.org

Organization Name
Mission Statement
Overview of Activities
Importance of Organization to U.S. Health Care

Student Activity 2-4

Discussion Questions

The following are suggested discussion questions for this chapter:

1. Which of the state statistics surprised you about the United States?
2. Identify three stakeholders and their role in the healthcare industry.
3. Do you think the United States should have a universal healthcare system? Defend your answer.
4. Select one of the healthiest states and discuss three of its statistics.
5. Discuss the relationship a health navigator can develop with one of the stakeholders.

Student Activity 2-5

Current Events

Perform an Internet search and find a current events topic that relates to this chapter. Provide a summary of the article and the link to the article and explain how the article relates to the chapter.

CHAPTER 3

Navigating the Government's Role in U.S. Health Care

LEARNING OBJECTIVES

The student will be able to:

- Describe five government organizations and their roles in health care.
- Describe the role of the National Institutes of Health in healthcare research.
- Discuss the U.S. Food and Drug Administration's regulatory responsibility in health care.
- Evaluate the role of the Centers for Medicare and Medicaid Services in health care.
- Define and discuss the Health Insurance Marketplace.
- Discuss the importance of Accountable Care Organizations to the healthcare industry.

DID YOU KNOW THAT?

- Social regulation focuses on actions such as those in the healthcare industry that impact an individual's safety or well-being.
- The U.S. Surgeon General is the chief health educator in the United States.
- The Food and Drug Administration is responsible for accrediting and inspecting mammography facilities.
- The Department of Homeland Security is responsible for ensuring that all government levels have an emergency preparedness plan for catastrophic events.
- The ACA requires most U.S. citizens and legal residents to purchase health insurance if they can afford it or pay a penalty.
- The ACA mandates that every state create a consumer-oriented marketplace where individuals are provided information and can purchase healthcare insurance.

- The ACA established the Medicare and Medicaid Innovation Center, which provides opportunities for innovative healthcare research.
- The Elder Justice Act, passed as part of the Affordable Care Act, targets abuse, neglect, and exploitation of the elderly.

INTRODUCTION

During the Depression and World War II, the United States had no funds to start a universal healthcare program—an issue that had been discussed for years. As a result, a private sector system developed that did not provide healthcare services to all citizens. The government's role of providing healthcare coverage evolved as a regulatory body to ensure that the elderly and poor were able to receive health care. The passage of the **Social Security Act of 1935** and the establishment of the Medicaid and Medicare programs in 1965 mandated the government's increased role in providing healthcare coverage. The **Patient Protection and Affordable Care Act (PPACA)**, more commonly known as the **Affordable Care Act (ACA)**, and its amendment, the **Healthcare and Education Affordability Reconciliation Act of 2010**, was signed into law on March 23, 2010, by President Barack Obama. The goal of the Act is to improve the accessibility and quality of the U.S. healthcare system. It includes nearly 50 healthcare reform initiatives that are being implemented during 2010–2017 and beyond. The passage of this complex landmark legislation has been controversial.

The State Children's Health Insurance Program (SCHIP), now the Children's Health Insurance Program (CHIP), established in 1997 and reauthorized by the Affordable Care Act (ACA) through 2019 with extended funding through 2015, continues to expand the government's role in children's health care (CHIP, 2016). In addition to the reauthorization of the SCHIP program, the ACA has increased government interaction with the healthcare system by developing several government initiatives that focus on increasing the ability of individuals to make informed decisions about their health care.

In these instances, the government increased accessibility to health care as well as provided financing for health care to certain targeted populations. This chapter will focus on the different roles the federal, state, and local governments play in the U.S. healthcare system as well as discuss the basic components of the Affordable Care Act.

ROLE OF THE HEALTH NAVIGATOR

When many of us think of dealing with government agencies, we think of the typical adage of how government rules and regulations often complicate communication with consumers. Because there are so many government agencies responsible for different components of the healthcare system, it can be difficult for healthcare consumers to manage all of these interactions. For example, some elderly patients may be qualified for both Medicare and Medicaid, which requires twice the communication needed when receiving care. A health navigator can be very helpful in these types of situations. A health navigator can be a mediator between government agencies and the healthcare consumer. In order to be successful in this role, the navigator must understand government rules and regulations and which agencies are responsible for oversight of these types of rules.

HISTORY OF THE ROLE OF GOVERNMENT IN HEALTH CARE

Social regulation focuses on organizations' actions, such as those in the healthcare industry,

that impact an individual's safety. Social regulations focus on protecting individuals as employees and consumers (Carroll & Buchholtz, 2015). These types of regulations are common in the U.S. healthcare system. The healthcare industry claims it is the most-regulated industry in the world. It is important to mention that government regulations aside, there are nongovernmental regulations of U.S. health care by accrediting bodies such as The Joint Commission, which began more than 80 years ago and accredits more than 20,000 healthcare organizations (The Joint Commission, 2016). However, regulatory oversight is mainly handled at the federal, state, and local government levels.

U.S. GOVERNMENT AGENCIES

Federal and state governments share the power to regulate health care. State governments have a dominant role of regulating constituents in their jurisdiction. To assure success in this regulatory process, state governments work with local governments to provide direct services to constituents and regulate their geographic region. Their legal authority is derived from legislatures that establish the legal framework for their authority (Jonas, 2003).

Important Federal Government Agencies

Many federal agencies are responsible for regulating health care. The **U.S. Department of Health and Human Services (HHS)** is the most important federal agency. HHS collaborates with state and local governments because many HHS services are provided at those levels. HHS has 11 operating divisions: the **Centers for Disease Control and Prevention (CDC)**, the **Administration for Community Living (ACL)**, the **National Institutes of Health (NIH)**, the **Agency for Toxic Substances and Disease Registry (ATSDR)**, the **Indian Health Service (IHS)**, the **Health Resources and Services Administration (HRSA)**, the **Agency for Healthcare Research and Quality (AHRQ)**, the **Substance Abuse and Mental Health Services Administration (SAMHSA)**, the **U.S. Food and Drug Administration (FDA)**, the **Administration for Children and Families (ACF)**, and the

Centers for Medicare and Medicaid Services (CMS). Each of these agencies will be discussed individually (HHS, 2013).

Centers for Disease Control and Prevention (CDC)

Established in 1946 and headquartered in Atlanta, Georgia, the CDC's mission is to protect health and promote quality of life through the prevention and control of disease, injury, and disability. The CDC has created four health goals that focus on (1) healthy people in healthy places, (2) preparing people for emerging health threats, (3) positive international health, and (4) healthy people at all stages of their life. To achieve these goals, the CDC focuses on six areas: health impact, customer focus, public health research, leadership, globalization, and accountability. The CDC website provides information on disease, healthy living, emergency preparedness, injury prevention, environmental health, workplace safety, data and statistics, and global health. It also provides specific information for travelers, infants and children, pregnancies, and state and tribal associations (CDC, 2016).

Administration for Community Living (ACL)

All Americans—including people with disabilities and older adults—should be able to live at home with the supports they need, participating in communities that value their contributions. To help meet these needs, the HHS created a new organization, the ACL.

Established in 2012, the ACL brings together the efforts and achievements of the Administration on Aging, the Administration on Intellectual and Developmental Disabilities, and the HHS Office on Disability to serve as the federal agency responsible for increasing access to community supports while focusing attention and resources on the unique needs of older Americans and people with disabilities across the lifespan.

The ACL mission is to maximize the independence, well-being, and health of older adults, people with disabilities across the lifespan, and their families and caregivers (ACL, 2016).

Agency for Toxic Substances and Disease Registry (ATSDR)

Established in 1985, headquartered in Atlanta, Georgia, and authorized by the Comprehensive Environmental Response, Compensation, and Liability Act of 1980 (CERCLA; more commonly known as the Superfund law), ATSDR is responsible for finding and cleaning the most dangerous hazardous waste sites in the country. ATSDR's mission is to protect the public against harmful exposures and disease-related exposures to toxic substances. ATSDR is the lead federal public health agency responsible for determining human health effects associated with toxic exposures, preventing continued exposures, and mitigating associated human health risks. ATSDR is administered organizationally with the CDC. The ATSDR has 10 regional offices within the Environmental Protection Agency (EPA) across the country (ATSDR, 2016).

National Institutes of Health (NIH)

Established in 1930 and headquartered in Bethesda, Maryland, this agency is the primary federal agency for research toward preventing and curing disease worldwide. Its mission is the pursuit of knowledge about the nature and behavior of living systems and the application of that knowledge to extend healthy life and reduce the burdens of illness and disability. The agency has 27 institutes and centers that focus on different diseases and conditions including cancer, ophthalmology, heart and lung and blood, genes, aging, alcoholism and drug abuse, infectious diseases, chronic diseases, children's diseases, and mental health. Although the NIH has sponsored external research, it also has a large internal research program (NIH, 2016).

The Health Resources and Services Administration (HRSA)

Created in 1982 and headquartered in Rockville, Maryland, the HRSA is the primary federal agency for improving access to healthcare services for people in every state who are uninsured, isolated, or medically vulnerable. They have six bureaus: primary health care, health professions, healthcare systems, maternal and child, the HIV/AIDS bureau, and the Bureau of Clinician Recruitment and Service. HRSA provides funding to grantees that provide health care to those vulnerable populations. They also oversee organ, bone marrow, and cord blood donation; support programs against bioterrorism; and maintain databases that protect against healthcare malpractice and healthcare waste, fraud, and abuse. Tens of millions of Americans have access to affordable health care and other help through HRSA's 100-plus programs and more than 3,000 grantees (HRSA, 2016).

The Agency for Healthcare Research and Quality (AHRQ)

Created in 1989 and headquartered in Rockville, Maryland, this agency's mission is to improve the quality, safety, efficiency, and effectiveness of health care for all U.S. citizens. AHRQ's cutting-edge research helps people make more informed decisions and improve the quality of healthcare services. AHRQ focuses on the following areas of research: healthcare costs and utilization, information technology, disaster preparedness, medication safety, healthcare consumerism, prevention of illness, and special needs populations (AHRQ, 201). There is a Coalition for Health Services Research (CHSR), an organization of volunteers who advocate for the AHRQ. It is comprised of more than 250 nonprofit organizations that support the AHRQ. Volunteers send letters to Congress encouraging more funds for research (CHSR, 2016).

Indian Health Service (IHS)

Established in 1921 and headquartered in Rockville, Maryland, the mission of IHS is to raise the physical, mental, social, and spiritual health of American Indians and Alaska Natives to the highest level. Its mission also involves assuring that comprehensive, culturally acceptable personal and public health services are available and accessible to American Indian and Alaska Native people. It also is responsible for promoting the communities and cultures of these groups honoring and protecting their inherent sovereign rights. The IHS

provides a comprehensive health service delivery system for approximately 1.9 million American Indians and Alaska Natives who belong to 566 federally recognized tribes (IHS, 2016).

The Substance Abuse and Mental Health Services Administration (SAMHSA)

Established in 1992, SAMHSA is the main federal agency for improving access to quality substance abuse and mental health services in the United States by working with state, community, and private organizations. SAMHSA is the umbrella agency for mental health and substance abuse services, which includes the Center for Mental Health Services (CMHS), the Center for Substance Abuse Prevention (CSAP), and the Center for Substance Abuse Treatment (CSAT). The Center for Behavioral Health Statistics and Quality (CBHSQ) is responsible for data collection, analysis, and dissemination of critical health data to assist policymakers, providers, and the public for use in making informed decisions regarding the prevention and treatment of mental and substance use disorders (SAMHSA, 2016).

U.S. Food and Drug Administration (FDA)

Established in 1906 as a result of the Federal Food, Drug, and Cosmetic Act, the FDA is responsible for ensuring that the following products are safe: food, human and veterinary products, biologic products, medical devices, cosmetics, and electronic products. The FDA also is responsible for ensuring that product information is accurate.

The FDA also advances public health by speeding up innovations to make medicine and food more effective, safer, and more affordable. It also is responsible for ensuring that the public receives accurate information to be able to make informed decisions about using medicine and food products (USFDA, 2016).

The Administration for Children and Families (ACF)

The ACF, which has 10 regional offices, is responsible for federal programs that promote the economic and social well-being of families, children, individuals, and communities. Its mission is to empower people to increase their own economic well-being, support communities that have a positive impact on the quality of life of its residents, partner with other organizations to support Native American tribes, improve needed access to services, and work with those who are special needs populations (ACF, 2016).

Centers for Medicare and Medicaid Services (CMS)

CMS was established when the Medicare and Medicaid programs were signed into law in 1965 by President Lyndon B. Johnson as a result of the Social Security Act. At that time, only half of those 65 years or older had health insurance. Medicaid was established for low-income children, the elderly, the blind, and the disabled and was linked with the Supplemental Security Income program (SSI). In 1972, Medicare was extended to cover people under the age of 65 with permanent disabilities. CMS also has oversight of SCHIP or as more commonly called CHIP – Children's Health Insurance Program, Title XXI of the Social Security Act, which is financed by both federal and state funding, but the program is administered at the state level.

Headquartered in Baltimore, Maryland, the CMS has more than 20 offices that oversee different aspects of its programs. The agency's primary responsibility is to provide policy, funding, and oversight to healthcare programs that serve the elderly and poor. For years, its organizational oversight was a geographically based structure with 10 field offices. In 2007, CMS was reorganized to a consortia structure based on the priorities of Medicare health plans and financial management, Medicare fee for service, Medicaid and children's health, surveys and certification, and quality assurance and improvement. The consortia are responsible for oversight of the 10 regional offices for each priority. In 2010, the Center for Program Integrity was formed as part of the CMS that focuses on best practices for program implementation (CMS, 2013a). As part of the Affordable Care Act, Congress created the Innovation Center for the purpose of testing "innovative payment and service delivery models to reduce program expenditures while preserving or enhancing the quality of care" for those individuals who receive Medicare, Medicaid, or Children's Health Insurance Program (CHIP) benefits (CMS, 2016b).

Occupational Safety and Health Administration (OSHA)

Established on December 29, 1970, and part of the U.S. Department of Labor, the **Occupational Safety and Health Administration (OSHA)** was established to govern workplace environments to ensure that employees have a safe and healthy environment (OSHA, 2016). The **Hazard Communication Standard (HCS)** ensures that all hazardous chemicals are properly labeled and that companies are informed of these risks (Hazard Communication, 2013). The **Medical Waste Tracking Act** requires companies to have medical waste disposal procedures so that there is no risk to employees and the environment (Environmental Protection Agency, 2016). The **Occupational Exposure to Blood-borne Pathogen Standard** developed behavioral standards for employees who deal with blood products, such as wearing gloves and using other equipment, and disposal of blood-collection materials (OSHA Quicktakes, 2016).

Surgeon General/U.S. Public Health Service

The **Surgeon General** is the U.S. chief health educator who provides information on how to improve the health of the U.S. population. The Surgeon General, who is appointed by the President of the United States, and the Office of the Surgeon General oversee the operations of the commissioned **U.S. Public Health Service Corps**, who provide support to the Surgeon General. The U.S. Public Health Service Commissioned Corps consists of 6,500 public health professionals who are stationed within federal agencies and programs. These commissioned employees include various professionals such as dentists, nurses, physicians, mental health specialists, environmental health specialists, veterinarians, and therapists. The Surgeon General serves a four-year term and reports to the Secretary of Health and Human Services. The Surgeon General focuses on certain health priorities for the United States and publishes reports on these issues (Office of the Surgeon General, 2016).

Department of Homeland Security (DHS)

The **Department of Homeland Security (DHS)** was established in 2002 as a result of the 2001 terrorist attack on the United States. It combined 22 different federal departments to form the DHS. The **Federal Emergency Management Agency (FEMA)**, which is responsible for managing catastrophic events, was integrated into DHS in 2003. Together, they are responsible for coordinating efforts at all government levels to ensure **emergency preparedness** for any catastrophic events such as bioterrorism; chemical and radiation emergencies; mass casualties as a result of explosions, natural disasters, and severe weather; and disease outbreaks. They coordinate with the CDC to ensure there are plans in place to quickly resolve these events. DHS has also developed a **National Incident Management System (NIMS)** that provides a systematic, proactive approach to all levels of government and private sector agencies to collaborate and ensure there is a seamless plan to manage any major incidents. The **National Integration Center (NIC)** requires the development of preparedness-related doctrine, policy, and guidance to reflect the collective expertise and experience of the whole community. The NIC has primary responsibility for the maintenance and management of national preparedness doctrine. The NIC develops strategies, doctrine, policies, guidance, and best practices in collaboration with practitioners and subject matter experts from the whole community. The second edition of the **National Response Framework**, updated in 2013, provides context for how the whole community works together and how response efforts relate to other parts of national preparedness (DHS, 2016).

State Health Departments' Role in Health Care

The U.S. constitution gives state governments the primary role in regulating and providing health care for their citizens. Most states have several different agencies that are responsible for specific public health services. There is usually a lead state agency coordinating approximately 20 agencies that target health issues like aging, living, and working environments, as well as alcoholism and substance abuse. Many state agencies are responsible for implementing several different federal acts such as the Clean Water Act; Clean Air Act; Food, Drug, and Cosmetic Act; and Safe Drinking Water Act (Turnock, 2007). **State health departments** monitor communities to identify health problems. Additionally, they diagnose and investigate health problems and provide education about health issues. They also develop policies to support community health. They must enforce laws and regulations to promote health and safety. Most state agencies are responsible for or share responsibility for federal programs related to maternal and infant health services and cancer prevention. They are responsible for providing population-based services for the CDC's health priorities, which include motor vehicle injuries, HIV, obesity, food safety, tobacco use, teen pregnancy, and nutrition. Vital statistics collected include deaths, births, marriages, and health and disease statuses of the population. These statistics are important to collect because they serve as a basis for funding.

Local Health Departments' Role in Health Care

Local health departments are the government organizations that provide the most direct services to the population. There are 2,700 local health departments across the United States. Although their organizational structures may differ across the United States, their basic role is to provide direct public health services to their designated areas. It is difficult to generalize what types of services are offered by local health departments because they do vary according to geographic location, but most are involved in communicable disease control.

AFFORDABLE CARE ACT

The Patient Protection and Affordable Care Act of 2010, or Affordable Care Act, and its amendment have focused on primary care as the foundation for the U.S. healthcare system (Goodson, 2010). The legislation has focused on 10 areas to improve the U.S. healthcare system, including quality, affordable and efficient health care, public health and primary prevention of disease, increasing the healthcare workforce, community health, and increasing revenue provisions to pay for the reform. The goal of the Act is to improve the accessibility and quality of the U.S. healthcare system. The legislation included nearly 50 healthcare reform initiatives that are being implemented over several years. The main bone of contention is the requirement that U.S. citizens and legal residents must purchase health insurance or pay an annual fine for inaction. The second major contentious issue is whether Medicaid expansion requirements were constitutional because the federal government could withhold federal Medicaid funding to states that refuse to expand their Medicaid programs.

Once the bill was signed, several states filed lawsuits. Several of these lawsuits argue that the Act violates the Constitution because of the mandate of individual healthcare insurance coverage as well as infringes on state rights with the expansion of Medicaid (Arts, 2010). On June 28, 2012, the U.S. Supreme Court upheld the constitutionality of the ACA in a 5–4 ruling in the *Florida v. Sebelius* lawsuit regarding individual health insurance mandates and the *National Federation of Independent Businesses v. Sebelius* lawsuits regarding Medicaid expansion (ProCon.org, 2013a). However, the Court found that the federal government could not withhold federal funding to states that refuse the Medicaid expansion because it could be considered coercion. As a result of this decision, the federal government is required to develop state incentives to accept the Medicaid expansion and to restrict the type of funding limitations to states who refuse the Medicaid expansions (Svendiman & Baumrucker, 2012).

The 2012 U.S. Supreme Court Decision that supported the constitutionality of the individual mandates should decrease the number of lawsuits.

Despite these lawsuits, this legislation has provided opportunities to increase consumer empowerment of the healthcare system by establishing the state American Health Benefit Exchanges, providing insurance to those individuals with preexisting conditions, eliminating lifetime and annual caps on health insurance payouts, improving the healthcare workforce, and providing databases so consumers can check the quality of their health care. The 10 titles of this comprehensive legislation also are focused on increasing the role of public health and primary care in the U.S. healthcare system and increasing accessibility to the system by providing affordable healthcare opportunities.

Although this legislation continues to be controversial, a system-wide effort needed to be implemented to curb rising healthcare costs. There are five areas of health care that account for a large percentage of healthcare costs: hospital care, physician and clinician services, prescription drugs, nursing, and home healthcare expenditures (Longest & Darr, 2008). The legislation targets these areas by increasing quality assurance and providing a system of reimbursement tied to quality performance, providing accessibility to consumers regarding the quality of their health care, and increasing access to community health services. Also, the Affordable Care Act has focused on improving the U.S. public health system by increasing the accessibility to primary prevention services such as screenings and wellness visits at no cost. The ACA has mandated, with no cost sharing to the healthcare consumer, 15 preventive services for adults, 22 preventive services for women, 25 preventive services for children, and 23 preventive services for Medicare enrollee (Youdelman, 2013). There are revenue provisions in place to offset some of the costs of this legislation. With continued controversy, it will be difficult to assess quickly how cost effective and effective this health reform will be on improving the health care of U.S. citizens.

CONCLUSION

The government plays an important role in the quality of the U.S. healthcare system. The federal government provides funding for state and local government programs. Federal healthcare regulations are implemented and enforced at the state and local levels. Funding is primarily distributed from the federal government to the state government, which consequently allocates funding to local health departments. Local health departments provide the majority of services for their constituents. More local health departments are working with local organizations such as schools and physicians to increase their ability to provide education and prevention services.

DHS and FEMA now play an integral role in the management and oversight of any catastrophic events such as natural disasters, earthquakes, floods, pandemic diseases, and bioterrorism. DHS and FEMA collaborate closely with the CDC to ensure that both the state and local health departments have a crisis management plan in place for these events. These attacks are often horrific and frightening with a tremendous loss of life, and as a result, the state and local health departments need to be more prepared to deal with catastrophic events. They are required to develop plans and be trained to deal effectively with many of these catastrophic issues. Finally, the Affordable Care Act has increased government involvement in the healthcare industry to increase access to a quality healthcare system.

Summary

© Jim Barber/Shutterstock

Vocabulary

Administration for Children and Families (ACF)

Administration for Community Living (ACL)

Affordable Care Act (ACA)

Agency for Healthcare Research and Quality (AHRQ)

Agency for Toxic Substances and Disease Registry (ATSDR)

Center for Behavioral Health Statistics and Quality (CBHSQ)

Center for Mental Health Services (CMHS)

Center for Substance Abuse Prevention (CSAP)

Center for Substance Abuse Treatment (CSAT)

Centers for Disease Control and Prevention (CDC)

Centers for Medicare and Medicaid Services (CMS)

Department of Homeland Security (DHS)

Emergency preparedness

Federal Emergency Management Agency (FEMA)

Federal Food, Drug, and Cosmetic Act (FDCA)

Hazard Communication Standard (HCS)

Healthcare and Education Affordability Reconciliation Act of 2010

Health Resources and Services Administration (HRSA)

Indian Health Service (IHS)

Local health departments

Medical Waste Tracking Act

National Incident Management System (NIMS)

National Institutes of Health (NIH)

National Integration Center (NIC)

National Response Framework (NRF)

Occupational Exposure to Blood-borne Pathogen Standard

Occupational Safety and Health Administration (OSHA)

Patient Protection and Affordable Care Act (PPACA)

Social regulation
Social Security Act of 1935
State health departments
Substance Abuse and Mental Health Services
Administration (SAMHSA)

Surgeon General
U.S. Department of Health and Human Services
(HHS)
U.S. Food and Drug Administration (FDA)
U.S. Public Health Service Corps

References

Administration for Children and Families (ACF). (2016). What we do. http://www.acf.hhs.gov/about/what-we-do.

Administration for Community Living (ACL). (2016). http://www.acl.gov/About_ACL/Index.aspx.

Agency for Healthcare Research and Quality (AHRQ). (2016). http://www.ahrq.gov/about/mission/glance/index.html.

Agency for Toxic Substances and Disease Registry (ATSDR). (2016). http://www.atsdr.cdc.gov/about/index.html.

Carroll, A., & Buchholtz, A. (2015). *Business and society: Ethics and stakeholder management.* Mason, OH: Cengage.

Centers for Disease Control and Prevention (CDC). (2016). http://www.cdc.gov/about/.

Centers for Medicare and Medicaid Services (CMS). (2016a). About CMS. http://www.cms.gov/About-CMS/About-CMS.html.

Centers for Medicare and Medicaid Services (CMS). (2016b). Innovation Center. http://innovation.cms.gov/.

Children's Health Insurance Program (CHIP). (2016).

Coalition for Health Services Research (CHSR). (2016). http://www.medicaid.gov/medicaid-chip-program-information/by-topics/childrens-health-insurance-program-chip/childrens-health-insurance-program-chip.html.

Council of State and Territorial Epidemiologists (CSTE). (2016). http://www.cste.org/?page=About_CSTE.

Department of Homeland Security (DHS). (2016). https://www.dhs.gov/.

Environmental Protection Agency (EPA). (2016). Medical Waste Tracking Act of 1988. http://www.epa.gov/osw/nonhaz/industrial/medical/tracking.htm.

Health and Human Services (HHS). (2016). About HHS. http://www.hhs.gov/about/.

Health Resources and Services Administration (HRSA). (2016). http://www.hrsa.gov/about/

Indian Health Service (IHS). (2016). https://www.ihs.gov/aboutihs/.

Jonas, S. (2003). *An introduction to the U.S. health care system* (17–45). New York, NY: Springer Publishing.

Mays, G. (2008). Organization of the public health delivery system. In L. Novick & C. Morrow (Eds.), *Public health administration: Principles for population-based management* (69–126). Sudbury, MA: Jones and Bartlett Publishers.

National Institutes of Health (NIH). (2016). http://www.nih.gov/about/mission.htm.

Occupational Safety and Health Administration (OSHA). (2016). http://www.osha.gov/about.html.

OSHA. (2016). Hazard communication. http://www.osha.gov/dsg/hazcom/index.html.

Office of the Surgeon General. (2016). http://www.surgeongeneral.gov/about/index.html.

OSHA Quicktakes. (2016). Bloodborne pathogens. http://www.osha.gov/pls/oshaweb/owadisp.show_document?p_table=standards&p_id=10051.

Substance Abuse and Mental Health Services Administration (SAMHSA). (2016). http://www.samhsa.gov/about-us

The Joint Commission. (2016). About The Joint Commission. http://www.jointcommission.org/about_us/about_the_joint_commission_main.aspx.

Turnock, B. (2007). *Essentials of public health.* Sudbury, MA: Jones and Bartlett Publishers.

U.S. Food and Drug Administration (FDA). (2016). http://www.fda.gov/AboutFDA/default.htm.

Student Activity 3-1

In Your Own Words

Based on this chapter, please provide a description of the following concepts in your own words. DO NOT RECITE the text description.

Administration on Aging

Coalition for Health Services Research (CHSR)

Federal, Food, Drug and Cosmetic Act

Hazard Communication Standard (HCS)

Medical Waste Tracking Act National Incident Management System

National Response Framework (NRF)

Regionalization of public health departments

Social Security Act of 1935

U.S. Public Health Service Corps

U.S. Surgeon General

Student Activity 3-2

Real-Life Applications: Case Scenario One

You will be graduating from college soon with a degree in healthcare management. You are considering different career choices and would like to work for the government. You are thinking of applying to both state and local health departments but are unsure of what types of activities you may be involved with as a healthcare manager.

Activity

Discuss the role that state and local health departments have in health care. Then, using the Internet, look up the state and local health departments in your state and provide an overview of their activities. Finally, decide on where you are going to apply and explain your decision.

Case Scenario Two

You have been assigned as an intern at FEMA for the summer. You are not familiar with this governmental organization but want to be familiar with its mission and activities before you start.

Activity

Perform an Internet search and prepare a report for the class on FEMA and their activities. Be specific about its role in the healthcare system.

Case Scenario Three

You are thinking about continuing your education but are not sure what area of healthcare is of interest to you. Your friend just obtained her master of public health. Before you decide what degree you want to obtain, you think you should make contact with your local public health department.

Activity

Visit your state's health department website and find your local public department. Contact the department to find out what activities it performs for the county. Visit the website or call the department and speak to an employee. Write up a report on your findings.

Case Scenario Four

You have decided you would like to become a federal government worker in the healthcare industry but are unsure of which organization would be of interest to you.

Activity

Select three of the federal government organizations identified in this chapter and provide a summary of their activities.

Student Activity 3-3

Internet Exercises

- Visit each of the websites listed here.
- Name the organization.
- Locate its mission statement on the website.
- Provide a brief overview of the activities of the organization.
- How does this organization participate in the U.S. healthcare system?

Websites

http://www.atsdr.cdc.gov

Organization Name
Mission Statement
Overview of Activities
Importance of Organization to U.S. Health Care

http://www.hrsa.gov

Organization Name
Mission Statement
Overview of Activities
Importance of Organization to U.S. Health Care

http://www.fda.gov

Organization Name
Mission Statement
Overview of Activities
Importance of Organization to U.S. Health Care

http://www.ihs.gov

Organization Name
Mission Statement
Overview of Activities
Importance of Organization to U.S. Health Care

http://www.acl.gov

Organization Name
Mission Statement
Overview of Activities
Importance of Organization to U.S. Health Care

http://www.acf.hhs.gov

Organization Name
Mission Statement
Overview of Activities
Importance of Organization to U.S. Health Care

Student Activity 3-4
Discussion Questions
The following are suggested discussion questions for this chapter.

1. Discuss the role of the FDA in the healthcare industry.
2. Why was the Department of Homeland Security (DHS) established? Why was FEMA integrated into DHS?
3. What is the difference between the role of the state health department and the local health department in providing health services?
4. Go to the ASTHO website. Based on your research, why is it important to state agencies?
5. How can the health navigator assist a patient with government communication with agencies such as Medicare and Medicaid?

Student Activity 3-5
Current Events
Perform an Internet search and find a current events topic that relates to this chapter. Provide a summary of the article and the link to the article and explain how the article relates to the chapter.

CHAPTER 4

Navigating Public Health's Role in Health Care

LEARNING OBJECTIVES

The student will be able to:

- Define and discuss the determinants of health.
- Describe the core public health functions of assessment, policy, and assurance and their role in public health organizations.
- Define and discuss the epidemiology triangle and its importance to public health.
- Discuss the importance of the Prevention and Public Health Fund.
- Evaluate the roles of John Snow, Lemuel Shattuck, and Edwin Chadwick in the development of public health.
- Discuss how the health navigator can assist healthcare consumers with public health issues.
- Analyze the importance of data and surveillance systems in public health policy.

DID YOU KNOW THAT?

- In 1842, Edwin Chadwick reported that the poor had higher rates of disease—a fact that still exists today.
- Established in 1905, the civic organization Rotary International has played a huge role in eradicating polio through international vaccine programs.
- In 1916, the Johns Hopkins University, located in Baltimore, Maryland, established the first school of public health.
- In 1992, a national exercise program for Medicare patients, Silver Sneakers, was created to provide free access to organized exercise at national fitness chains.
- A newer form of surveillance called biosurveillance monitors patterns of unusual disease that may be the result of human intervention.

- Social marketing is an innovative approach to public health practice because it draws from the business discipline of marketing and adds science-based health strategies of promotion and prevention.

INTRODUCTION

There are two important definitions of public health. In 1920, **public health** was defined by Charles Winslow as the science and art of preventing disease, prolonging life, and promoting physical health and efficiency through organized community efforts for the sanitation of the environment, control of community infections, and education of individuals regarding hygiene to ensure a standard of living for health maintenance (Winslow, 1920). Sixty years later, the **Institute of Medicine (IOM)**, in its 1988 *Future of Public Health* report, defined public health as an organized community effort to address public health by applying scientific and technical knowledge to promote health (IOM, 1988). Both definitions point to broad community efforts to promote health activities to protect the population's health status. The Affordable Care Act is also emphasizing the importance of prevention and wellness. The establishment of the Prevention and Public Health Fund has supported several community-based public health programs (APHA, 2016a).

The development of public health is important to note as part of the basics of the U.S. healthcare system because its development was separate from the development of private medical practices. Public health specialists view health from a collectivist and preventive care viewpoint: to protect as many citizens as possible from health issues and to provide strategies to prevent health issues from occurring. The definitions cited in the previous paragraph emphasize this viewpoint. Public health concepts were in stark contrast to traditional medicine, which focused solely on the relationship between a provider and patient. Private practitioners held an individualistic viewpoint, and citizens would pay for their services with the aid of health insurance or from their own pockets. Physicians would provide their patients guidance on how to cure their diseases, not prevent disease. This chapter will discuss the concept of health and healthcare delivery and the role of public health in delivering health care. The concepts of primary, secondary, and tertiary prevention and the role of public health in those delivery activities will be highlighted. Discussion also will focus on the origins of public health, the major role epidemiology plays in public health, the role of public health in disasters, core public health activities, the collaboration of public health and private medicine, and the importance of public health consumers. The chapter begins with a discussion of the role of the health navigator in public health.

THE ROLE OF HEALTH NAVIGATORS

The role of the public health or community navigator can have both a broad and narrow perspective. Public health focuses on providing community health programs that can improve the health of many individuals in a community. A public health navigator can take a leading role in assisting with these types of population-based programs. Secondly, the public health navigator also can provide specific health programs to certain targeted demographics that need assistance with improving at-risk health behavior. For example, a "womb to tomb" public health navigator model in La Plata county, Colorado, focused on the health status of both children and seniors. This navigator program integrated healthcare and social support services to target community members who needed assistance with self-care management and disease prevention (Nurse Navigator Program, 2016). A nurse can also become a public health navigator as part of his or her role in a public health department. A social worker can become a health navigator as well when collaborating with the public health department. From a broader perspective, a state health department could appoint a clinician to oversee public health navigator activities to ensure that more of the population will be reached. It is important to remember that the mission of public health is to increase access to health services as well as to teach individuals health education to ensure they will remain disease free. The public health navigator should be trained in public health as well as have working knowledge of health education. The health navigator also could be used during a public health crisis when communication is needed between victims and health and emergency workers, so crisis management training would also be an asset for health navigators. This type of health navigator can contribute to improving the community's health.

WHAT IS HEALTH?

The World Health Organization (WHO) defines **health** as the state of complete physical, mental, and social well-being and not merely the absence of disease or infirmity (WHO, 1942). IOM defines health as a state of well-being and the capability to function in the face of changing circumstances. It is a positive concept emphasizing social and personal resources as well as physical capabilities (IOM, 1997). According to the Society for Academic Emergency Medicine (SAEM), health is a state of physical and mental well-being that facilitates the achievement of individual and societal goals (SAEM, 1992). All of these definitions focus on the impact an individual's health status has on his or her quality of life.

Health has several determinants or influences that impact the status of an individual's health. The **individual lifestyle factors** such as exercise, diet, and sexual activity as well as **constitutional factors** such as age and sex are direct determinants of a person's health. Within the immediate environment of an individual, there are **social and community networks**, which are external influences on health. In addition to the social and community networks there also are the general **macro-environmental conditions** of socioeconomic, cultural, and environmental conditions that impact health, such as education, work environment, living and working conditions, healthcare services, food production, unemployment, water and sanitation, and housing. These **determinants of health** depicted in **Figure 4-1** tie into the role of public health in the healthcare delivery system because public health focuses on the impact of these determinants on an individual's health. Public health provides health education and other preventive activities to consumers so they will understand the negative impact these determinants may have on their health status. These activities are often categorized

as primary, secondary, and occasionally tertiary prevention (Determinants of Health, 2016).

Primary prevention activities focus on reducing disease development. Smoking cessation programs, immunization programs, educational programs for pregnancy, and employee safety education are all examples of primary prevention programs. **Secondary prevention** activities refer to early detection and treatment of diseases. The goal of secondary prevention is to stop the progression of disease. Blood pressure screenings, colonoscopies, and mammograms are examples of secondary prevention. **Tertiary prevention** activities focus on activities to rehabilitate and monitor individuals during disease progression. Activities also may include patient behavior education to limit disease impact and reduce progression (Shi & Singh, 2008). Although public health professionals may participate in each area of prevention activities, they focus primarily on primary and secondary prevention. See **Table 4-1**.

FIGURE 4-1 Dahlgren and Whitehead Model of Health Determinants, 1991

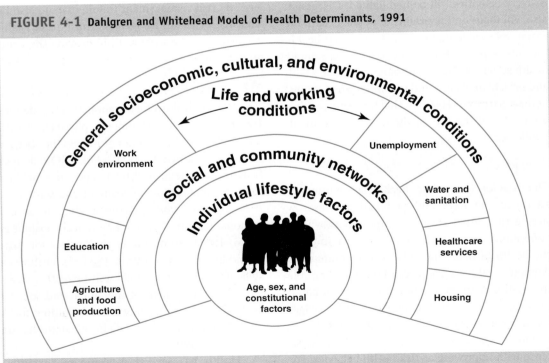

Dahlgren, G., & Whitehead, M. (1991). *Policies and Strategies to Promote Social Equity in Health.* Stockholm, Sweden: Institute for Future Studies. Reprinted by permission.

TABLE 4-1 Primary, Secondary, and Tertiary Prevention

	Primary	Secondary	Tertiary
Aim	Reduce disease development	Prevent disease progression by early detection and intervention	Disease management to reduce progress
Disease Phase	Specific risk factors associated with disease onset Factors associated with protection against disease	Early disease stage	Later disease stages
Target	Total population, selected groups, and healthy individuals	Early disease individuals with established high risk factors	Patients
Examples	–Immunization programs –Education programs for pregnancy –Smoking cessation programs	–Blood pressure screenings –Mammograms –Colonoscopies	–Rehabilitation of stroke patients –Self-management programs for chronic individuals –Patient behavior education

ORIGINS OF PUBLIC HEALTH

The concept of public health was born during the 1700s and 1800s. Edwin Chadwick, Dr. John Snow, and Lemuel Shattuck demonstrated a relationship between the environment and disease that established the foundation of public health.

In 1842, **Edwin Chadwick** published the *Report on the Sanitary Condition of the Labouring Population of Great Britain*. His report highlighted the relationship between unsanitary conditions and disease (Rosen, 1958). As Chief Commissioner of the Poor Law Commission, Chadwick was responsible for relief to the poor in England and Wales. He became the champion of reform for working conditions. His report illustrated that the poor had higher rates of disease than the upper class, a fact that still exists today. His activities became the basis for U.S. public health activities (Rosen, 1958). Chadwick also was responsible for the implementation of the 1848 Public Health Act, which created England's first national board of health. Unfortunately, in 1854, the Parliament did not renew the Act, which consequently dissolved the board of health. Although dissolved, the concept of public health was born because this act, using data, identified several public health issues that were assigned to national and local boards. Public health issues such as water, sewerage,

environment, safety, and food were a focus of the act. By identifying these community issues, people began to focus on improving the community's health status (Ashton & Sram, 1998).

John Snow, a famed British anesthesiologist, is more famous for investigating the cholera epidemics in London in the 1800s. He made the connection between contaminated water and the spread of cholera. Dr. Snow surveyed local London residents and discovered that those who were ill had retrieved water from a specific neighborhood pump on Broad Street. When the pump handle was removed, the disease ceased. This famous Broad Street pump incident became a classic example of an epidemiologic investigation that studies the causes between disease and external sources (Ellis, 2008).

Lemuel Shattuck, who has been called the architect of the public health infrastructure, wrote the landmark report, *Report of the Sanitary Commission of Massachusetts*. It was ignored for many years, but finally in the 1800s, it was central to the development of state and local public health activities (Rosen, 1958).

As a result of their work, public health law was enacted and, by the 1900s, public health departments were focused on the environment and its relationship to disease outbreaks. Disease control and health education also became integral components of public health departments.

WHAT IS PUBLIC HEALTH?

Overview of the Public Health System

According to the Centers for Disease Control and Prevention, public health systems are commonly defined as "all public, private, and voluntary entities that contribute to the delivery of essential public health services within a jurisdiction." **Figure 4-2** provides an overview of the components of public health, which include (CDC, 2016a):

- Public health agencies at state and local levels
- Healthcare providers
- Public safety agencies
- Human service and charity organizations
- Education and youth development organizations
- Recreation and arts-related organizations
- Economic and philanthropic organizations
- Environmental agencies and organizations

In 1945, in conjunction with Haven Emerson and C. E. A Winslow, the **American Public Health Association (APHA)** issued a set of guidelines for the basic functions of the local health department, including (Emerson, 1945):

- Vital statistics: data management of the essential facts on births, deaths, and reportable diseases
- Communicable disease control: management of tuberculosis, venereal disease, and malaria
- Sanitation: management of the environment, including milk, water, and dining
- Laboratory services
- Maternal and child health: management of school-aged children's health
- Health education of the general public

These functions remained the cornerstone of public health until the 1960s when the APHA, reacting to cultural and political changes, revised the definition of the core public health functions.

FIGURE 4-2 Public Health Participants

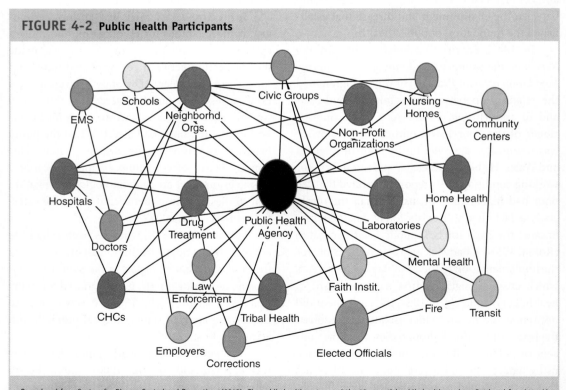

Reproduced from Centers for Disease Control and Prevention. (2013). The public health system and the 10 essential public health services. Retrieved from http://www.cdc.gov/nphpsp/essentialservices.html

The APHA issued the following guidelines for the core public health functions (APHA, 2016b):

- Health surveillance, planning, and program development
- Health promotion of local health activities
- Development and enforcement of sanitation standards
- Health services provisions

The IOM, as a result of an in-depth study of public health, stated that the three **core public health functions** of public health are (IOM, 1988):

- **Assessment**, which includes surveillance, identifying problems, data collection, and analysis
- **Policy development**, which includes developing policies to address public problems
- **Assurance**, which includes evaluating policies that meet program goals

These core public health functions became accepted by public health departments; however, there was some confusion about the terminology. In 1994, the Public Health Steering Committee, as part of the U.S. Public Health Service, issued a list of essential public health services that provided specific information on the implementation of the core public health functions and how they should be implemented (see **Table 4-2**).

THE EPIDEMIOLOGY TRIANGLE

Epidemiology is the study of disease distribution and patterns among populations. Epidemiologists search for the relationship of those patterns of disease to the causes of the disease. They scientifically collect data to determine what has caused the spread of the disease. Epidemiology is the foundation for public health because its focus is to prevent disease from reoccurring. Epidemiologists identify three major risk factor categories for disease. These three factors are called the **epidemiology triangle** (see **Figure 4-3**), which consists of the host, which is the population that has the disease; the agent or organism, which is causing the disease; and the environment, or where the disease is occurring (CDC, 2016b). Public health workers attempt to assess each factor's role in why a disease occurs. Based on this research, public health workers develop prevention strategies to alter the interaction between the host, the disease, and the environment so the disease occurrences will be less severe or will not occur again.

For example, a person (host) can be vaccinated against a disease to prevent the host from carrying the disease (agent). Procedures can be implemented such as sanitary regulations to protect the community condition (environment) from contamination.

TABLE 4-2 10 Essential Public Health Services Describing the Public Health Activities That All Communities Should Undertake

1. Monitor health status to identify and solve community health problems.
2. Diagnose and investigate health problems and health hazards in the community.
3. Inform, educate, and empower people about health issues.
4. Mobilize community partnerships and action to identify and solve health problems.
5. Develop policies and plans that support individual and community health efforts.
6. Enforce laws and regulations that protect health and ensure safety.
7. Link people to needed personal health services and assure the provision of health care when otherwise unavailable.
8. Assure competent public and personal healthcare workforce.
9. Evaluate effectiveness, accessibility, and quality of personal and population-based health services.
10. Research for new insights and innovative solutions to health problems.

Reproduced from Centers for Disease Control and Prevention. (2011). Core Functions of Public Health and How They Relate to the 10 Essential Services. http://www.cdc.gov/nceh/ehs/ephli/core_ess.htm.

FIGURE 4-3 Epidemiological Triangle

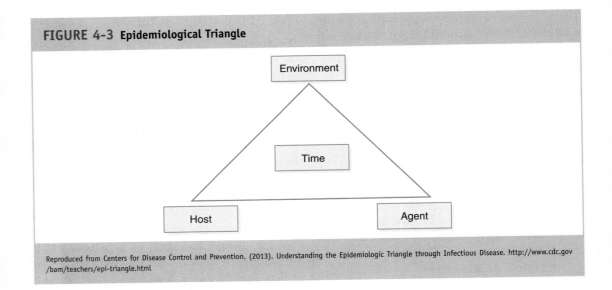

Reproduced from Centers for Disease Control and Prevention. (2013). Understanding the Epidemiologic Triangle through Infectious Disease. http://www.cdc.gov/bam/teachers/epi-triangle.html

EPIDEMIOLOGIC SURVEILLANCE

An important component of epidemiology is surveillance, which is the monitoring of patterns of disease and investigating disease outbreaks to develop public health intervention strategies to combat disease. A new form of surveillance involves biosurveillance, which focuses on early detection of unusual disease patterns that may be due to human intervention. Historically, surveillance activities have been passive and been initiated by public health workers through routine disease reports. However, public health has become more proactive by initiating contact with providers to assess any unusual disease pattern. New surveillance techniques can include pattern recognition software and geographic information systems to determine disease patterns (Turnock, 2007). Depending on the severity of the disease outbreaks, these activities will be investigated by the CDC, a federal public health agency, although public health mostly remains a state responsibility.

ENVIRONMENTAL HEALTH

Because John Snow linked disease with environmental factors, the field of environmental health is an integral component of public health. Environmental health workers often are responsible for investigating environmental hazards in the community and monitoring and enforcing environmental regulations. A subset of environmental health workers is occupational health workers who focus on ensuring employees' environments have safe working conditions. Both state and local health departments have environmental health departments that are responsible for investigating and enforcing local regulations. The Centers for Disease Control and Prevention has identified 10 essential environmental health services that relate to the core functions of public health assessment, policy development, and assurance (CDC, 2016c) (see Table 4-3).

EMERGENCY PREPAREDNESS

Federal Response

Public health emergency preparedness is a term used for planning protocols that are in place to manage a large-scale event such as a natural disaster like a hurricane or massive flooding, chemical or oil spills, or human-caused disasters such as the Boston Marathon bombing in 2013 or the terrorist attack of September 11, 2001. During a public health emergency, such as the California wildfires, Superstorm Sandy in New Jersey, and

> **TABLE 4-3** Essential Health Services and Core Public Health Functions of Environmental Health
>
> **Assessment**
> - Monitor environmental and health status to identify and solve community environmental health problems
> - Diagnose and investigate environmental health problems and health hazards in the community
>
> **Policy Development**
> - Inform, educate, and empower people about environmental health issues
> - Mobilize community partnerships and actions to identify and solve environmental health problems
> - Develop policies and plans that support individual and community environmental health efforts
>
> **Assurance**
> - Enforce laws and regulations that protect environmental health and ensure safety
> - Link people to needed environmental health services and assure the provision of environmental health services when otherwise unavailable
> - Assure a competent environmental health workforce
> - Evaluate effectiveness, accessibility, and quality of personal and population-based environmental health services
> - Research for new insights and innovative solutions to environmental health problems
>
> Reproduced from Centers for Disease Control and Prevention. (2011). Core Functions of Public Health and How They Relate to the 10 Essential Services. http://www.cdc.gov/nceh/ehs/ephli/core_ess.htm.

the tornados in Oklahoma, risk communication protocols are implemented to inform the public regarding the health issue and what should be done during a severe situation. Dissemination of information is handled through multimedia efforts such as the radio, television, and print media.

In the event of a disease outbreak, the federal government may intervene depending on the level of the threat. If the federal government does not intervene, state and local public health departments are responsible for monitoring the disease threat. Unfortunately, severe public health crises can create secondary disease threats. These crises also can have an extreme psychological impact on the public. The public needs to be informed. Since the terrorist attacks in 2001, simulations of public health emergencies have been staged across vulnerable areas of the United States, including large urban areas such as New York City and Las Vegas, to plan for these possible events. Public health funding for state activities such as these are largely from CDC grants and budget allocations (Turnock, 2007).

September 11, 2001, Terrorist Attack Impact on Public Health

As result of the terrorist attacks on the United States in 2001, the Department of Homeland Security (DHS) was created from 23 federal agencies, programs, and offices to coordinate an approach to emergencies and disasters. Several public health functions were transferred to the DHS in 2003 (Turnock, 2007). Within the DHS, the Emergency Preparedness and Response Directorate coordinates emergency medical response in the event of a public health emergency. Some states have created their own Homeland Security offices that coordinate with the federal DHS. The **National Response Framework (NRF)**, created by DHS, presents the guiding principles that enable all response partners to prepare for and provide a unified national response to disasters and emergencies. It establishes a comprehensive, national, all-hazards approach to domestic incident response. The National Response Plan was replaced by the NRF effective March 22, 2008. The NRF defines the principles, roles, and structures that organize how we respond as a nation. It also describes how communities, states, the federal government, the private sector, and nongovernment partners collaborate to coordinate national response. Further, it describes "best practices" for managing incidents and builds on the **National Incident Management System (NIMS)**, which provides a framework for managing incidents. Information on the NRF, including documents, annexes, references, and briefings/trainings, can be accessed from the NRF Resource Center (FEMA, 2016).

STATE AND LOCAL RESPONSE TO DISASTERS

State and Local Health Department Planning in Emergency Preparedness

The state and local health departments play a major role in managing emergencies. The CDC has developed national standards for both state and local health departments to develop capabilities to deal with emergencies as part of their strategic plan. The following are the capabilities as outlined by the CDC (2016d):

- Capability 1: **Community preparedness**: The local health department has to assess the capability of the community and itself to respond quickly to a threat. It also is important to assess the impact of the threat.
- Capability 2: **Community recovery**: The ability to collaborate with community partners (e.g., healthcare organizations, business, education, and emergency management), to plan and advocate for the rebuilding of public health, medical, and mental/behavioral health systems to at least a level of functioning comparable to pre-incident levels, and improved levels where possible.
- Capability 3: **Emergency operations coordination**: The ability to direct and support an event or incident with public health or medical implications by establishing a standardized, scalable system of oversight, organization, and supervision consistent with jurisdictional standards and practices and with the National Incident Management System.

- Capability 4: **Emergency public information and warning system**: The ability to develop, coordinate, and disseminate information, alerts, warnings, and notifications to the public and incident management responders.
- Capability 5: **Fatality management**: The ability to coordinate with other organizations (e.g., law enforcement, health care, emergency management, and medical examiner/coroner) to ensure the proper recovery, handling, identification, transportation, tracking, storage, and disposal of human remains and personal effects; certify cause of death; and facilitate access to mental/behavioral health services to the family members, responders, and survivors of an incident.
- Capability 6: **Information sharing**: The ability to conduct multijurisdictional, multidisciplinary exchange of health-related information and situational awareness data among federal, state, local, territorial, and tribal levels of government, and the private sector. This capability includes the routine sharing of information as well as issuing of public health alerts to federal, state, local, territorial, and tribal levels of government and the private sector in preparation for, and in response to, events or incidents of public health.
- Capability 7: **Mass care**: The ability to coordinate with partner agencies to address the public health, medical, and mental/behavioral health needs of those impacted by an incident at a congregate location. This capability includes the coordination of ongoing surveillance and assessment to ensure that health needs continue to be met as the incident evolves.
- Capability 8: **Medical countermeasure dispensing**: The ability to provide medical countermeasures (including vaccines, antiviral drugs, antibiotics, antitoxins, etc.) in support of treatment or prophylaxis (oral or vaccination) to the identified population in accordance with public health guidelines and/or recommendations.

- Capability 9: **Medical materiel management and distribution**: The ability to acquire, maintain (e.g., cold chain storage or other storage protocol), transport, distribute, and track medical materiel (e.g., pharmaceuticals, gloves, masks, and ventilators) during an incident and to recover and account for unused medical materiel, as necessary, after an incident.
- Capability 10: **Medical surge**: The ability to provide adequate medical evaluation and care during events that exceed the limits of the normal medical infrastructure of an affected community. It encompasses the ability of the healthcare system to survive a hazard impact and maintain or rapidly recover operations that were compromised.
- Capability 11: **Nonpharmaceutical interventions**: The ability to recommend to the appropriate agency (if not public health) and implement, if applicable, strategies for disease, injury, and exposure control. Strategies include the following:

  - Isolation and quarantine
  - Restrictions on movement and travel-advisory/warnings
  - Social distancing
  - External decontamination
  - Hygiene
  - Precautionary protective behaviors

- Capability 12: **Public health laboratory testing**: The ability to conduct rapid and conventional detection, characterization, confirmatory testing, data reporting, investigative support, and laboratory networking to address actual or potential exposure to all hazards. Hazards include chemical, radiological, and biological agents in multiple matrices that may include clinical samples, food, and environmental samples (e.g., water, air, and soil). This capability supports routine surveillance, including pre-event or pre-incident and post-exposure activities.

- Capability 13: **Public health surveillance and epidemiological investigation**: The ability to create, maintain, support, and strengthen routine surveillance and detection systems and epidemiological investigation processes, as well as to expand these systems and processes in response to incidents of public health significance.
- Capability 14: **Responder safety and health**: The ability to protect public health agency staff responding to an incident and the ability to support the health and safety needs of hospital and medical facility personnel, if requested.
- Capability 15: **Volunteer management**: The ability to coordinate the identification, recruitment, registration, credential verification, training, and engagement of volunteers to support the jurisdictional public health agency's response to incidents of public health significance.

Incident Command System and Public Health

Incident Command System (ICS) is used by police, fire, and emergency management agencies. ICS eliminates many communication problems, spans of control, organizational structures, and differences in terminology when multiple agencies respond to an emergency event. The ICS is a coordinator for an emergency event. It is in control of a situation and make decisions about how to manage an emergency. It also coordinates all responders to the event, which increases management effectiveness. Local public health agencies work with first responders such as fire and rescue, emergency medical service, law enforcement, physicians, and hospitals in managing health-related emergencies. Most local public health agencies provide epidemiology and surveillance, food safety, communicable disease control, and health inspections. Many state public health agencies provide laboratory services. Because public health is now considered an integral component to battling terrorism and, consequently, a matter of national security, federal funding has dramatically increased (FEMA, 2013).

BIOTERRORISM

According to the CDC, **bioterrorism** is an attack on a population by deliberately releasing viruses, bacteria, or other germs or agents that will contribute to illness or death in people (CDC, 2016e). These can be spread throughout the environment through the air, water, or in food. These agents can be difficult to detect and may take a period of time to spread. DHS, American Red Cross (ARC), the American Medical Association (AMA), and the Environmental Protection Agency (EPA) have developed educational campaigns regarding the U.S. response to bioterrorism.

More than 20 federal departments and agencies have roles in preparing for a bioterrorist attack. In 2002, the **Public Health Security and Bioterrorism Preparedness and Response Act** provided grants to hospitals and public health organizations to prepare for bioterrorism as a result of September 11, 2001. Funding supports increased public health infrastructures and programs, and increased laboratory testing and programs to detect bioterrorist threats. The **U.S. Food and Drug Administration (FDA)** also has additional responsibilities in the detection of food as a threat to community health (USFDA, 2013). Bioterrorism preparedness involves federal, state, and local health departments as well as input from other organizations. When a disaster occurs such as a bioterrorist attack, responses from both the federal and state level may take 24 hours; therefore, it is vital for local health departments, which are at the front line of public health interventions, to have a plan in place for immediate intervention. In terms of emergency responders, local health departments are the frontline organizations to assess an emergency situation (Turnock, 2007).

PUBLIC HEALTH FUNCTIONS AND ADMINISTRATION

Accreditation of Public Health Departments

The 2003 IOM report discussed previously recommends a national accreditation system for public health agencies because there is no national accrediting body to institute standards. In 2004, the CDC and the Robert Wood Johnson Foundation (RWJF) funded a study, the **Exploring Accreditation Project (EAP)**, to assess accreditation of public health agencies. Based on this information, in 2007, the **Public Health Accreditation Board (PHAB)** was formed as a nonprofit organization dedicated to improving and protecting the health of the public by advancing the quality and performance of tribal, state, local, and territorial public health departments. Since its inception, the PHAB has been working on a set of national accreditation standards for local and state health departments. In 2011, the PHAB awarded five-year accreditation to 11 public health departments.

In 2013, the PHAB awarded five-year accreditation status to three public health departments. Accreditation status also was awarded on May 30 to Polk County Health Department in Balsam Lake, Wisconsin; Summit County Combined General Health District in Stow, Ohio; and Wood County Health Department in Wisconsin Rapids, Wisconsin.

Fast forward 5 years with 141 local and 20 state health departments receiving accreditation. More than 135 health departments are currently preparing to seek national accreditation through the program, which aims to improve and protect the health of the public by advancing the quality and performance of the nation's tribal, state, local, and territorial health departments (PHAB, 2016).

National Association of Local Boards of Health

Established in 1992 as a membership organization, the **National Association of Local Boards of Health (NALBOH)** informs, guides, and is the national voice for boards of health. In today's public health system, the leadership role of boards of health makes them an essential link between public health services and a healthy community. NALBOH provides technical expertise in governance and leadership, board development, health priorities, and public health policy at the local level (NALBOH, 2016).

The Influence of the Institute of Medicine Reports on Public Health Functions

Published in 1988, the IOM published a report, *The Future of Public Health*, which indicated that although the health of the American people has been accomplished through public health measures such as consumer food regulations, water safety standards, and epidemic control of disease, the public has come to take public health measures for granted. The report indicated that there was an attrition of public health activities in protecting the community because of this attitude (IOM, 1988). The report established recommendations for reorganizing public health that emphasized population-based strategies rather than personal healthcare delivery. There was poor collaboration between public health and private medicine, no strong mission statement, weak leadership, and politicized decision making. Three core public health functions were identified: assessment, policy development, and assurance. Assessment was recommended because it focused on systematic continuous data collection of health issues, which would ensure that public health agencies were vigilant in protecting the public. Policy development also was mentioned, but the recommendation was to ensure that any policies be based on valid data to avoid any political decision making. Policy development was recommended to include planning at all health levels, not just at the federal level. Federal agencies should support local health planning. Assurance focused on evaluating any processes that had been put in place to assure that the programs were being implemented appropriately (IOM, 1988). These core functions will ensure that public health remains focused on the community, has programs in place that are effective, and has an evaluation process in place to ensure that the programs do work.

In 2002, the IOM published a second, more in-depth report, *The Future of the Public's Health in the 21st Century*, based on the 1988 report that analyzed public health as a system. The 2002 report discussed several deficiencies first noted in their 1988 report. Deficiencies included:

- Fragmented government public health infrastructures
- Passive community participation in public health activities
- Lack of healthcare delivery coordination
- Lack of participation of businesses in influencing health activities
- Lack of coordination of media with the health arena
- Lack of academic institutions in community-based health activities

Recommendations to rectify these deficiencies included:

- Development of a national commission to establish a framework for state public health law reform
- Development of active partnerships between public health agencies and communities
- Insurance plans should offer preventive services as part of their plans
- Businesses should collaborate with communities to develop health promotion programs
- Media outlets should increase their public service announcements to include health promotion marketing
- Increased funding for researchers who are interested in public health practice research (IOM, 2002)

HEALTHY PEOPLE REPORTS

The *Healthy People* series is a federal public health planning tool produced by the CDC that assesses the most significant health threats and sets objectives to challenge these threats (Novick & Morrow, 2008). The first major report, published in 1979, *Healthy People: The Surgeon General's Report on Health Promotion and Disease Prevention*, discussed five goals of public health: reduce mortality rates among children, adolescents, young adults, and adults and increase independence among older adults.

Objectives were set for 1990 to accomplish these goals (U.S. Department of Health and Human Services [HHS], 1979).

The *Healthy People 2000* report released in 1990, entitled *National Health Promotion and Disease Prevention Objectives*, was created to implement a new national prevention strategy with three major goals: increase life expectancy, reduce health disparities, and increase access to preventive services. Three categories (health promotion, health prevention, and preventive services) and surveillance activities were emphasized. *Healthy People 2000* provided a vision to reduce preventable disabilities and death. Year 2000 target objectives were set throughout the years to measure progress. An evaluation report in 2002 found that only 21% of the objectives were met with an additional 41% indicating progress. Unfortunately, in the critical areas of mental health, there were significant reversals in any progress. There was also minor progress in the areas of chronic diseases and diabetes (CDC, 2016f).

The *Healthy People 2010* report, *Understanding and Improving Health*, based on the previous *Healthy People* reports and their progress, was released in 2000 (HHS, 2000). The report contained a health promotion and disease prevention focus to identify preventable threats to public health and to set goals to reduce the threats. It had two major goals: to increase the quality and years of healthy life and to eliminate health disparities. Nearly 500 objectives were developed according to 28 focus areas. Focus areas ranged from access to care, food safety, education, and environmental health, to tobacco and substance abuse. An important component of the *Healthy People 2010* was the development of an infrastructure to ensure public health services are provided in a systematic approach. Infrastructure includes skilled labor, information technology, organizations, and research (CDC, 2016g). Like *Healthy People 2000*, its major goals were to increase quality and life expectancy and to reduce health disparities. The goals for these reports are consistent with both Winslow's and the IOM's definitions of

public health. In 2010, *Healthy People 2020* was released. It contains 1,200 objectives that focus on 42 topic areas. According to the CDC, a smaller set of Healthy People 2020 objectives, called Leading Health Indicators (LHIs), has been targeted to communicate high-priority health issues (CDC, 2016h).

PUBLIC HEALTH INFRASTRUCTURE

U.S. public health activities are delivered by many organizations, including government agencies at the federal, state, and local levels and nongovernment organizations including healthcare providers, community organizations, educational institutions, charitable organizations, philanthropic organizations, and businesses (Mays, 2008).

GOVERNMENT CONTRIBUTIONS TO PUBLIC HEALTH
Federal Contributions

The federal government has the ability to formulate and implement a national policy agenda for public health (Lee, 1994). It also has the power to allocate funding to both government and nongovernment organizations for public health programs at the state government level. If there is a major health threat in a community, direct federal activity may occur such as investigating a disease outbreak or providing assistance during a major disaster. The majority of their activities focus on policy and regulatory development and funding allocation to public health programs. The major federal agency responsible for public health activities is HHS, which is responsible for the following activities (Pointer, Williams, Isaacs, & Knickman, 2007):

- Data gathering and analysis, and surveillance and control
- Conducting and funding research
- Providing assistance to state and local government programs
- Formulating health policy
- Ensuring food and drug safety

- Ensuring access to health services for the poor and elderly
- Providing direct services to special populations

State Contributions

State public health agencies follow two basic models: a freestanding agency structure that reports directly to the state's governor or an organizational unit with a larger agency structure that includes other healthcare activities. The key feature of state agencies is their relationship with their local public health agencies that are responsible for implementing state policy and regulations. Most states have public health activities distributed across many agencies that include environmental protection, human services, labor, insurance, transportation, housing, and agriculture (Mays, 2008).

Additional activities include (Pointer et al., 2007):

- Licensure of healthcare professionals
- Inspection and licensure of healthcare facilities
- Collection of vital statistics
- Epidemiologic studies
- Crisis management of disease outbreaks
- Disease registry
- Laboratory services
- Implementation and analysis of health policy
- Community health education

Local Contributions

Local government agencies are directly responsible for performing the majority of community public health services. The **National Association of County and City Health Officials (NACCHO)**, which is the national advocacy organization for local health departments, released the operational definition of a local health department, which is defined as "what people in any community can reasonably expect from their local governmental public health presence." It sets forth a series of standards based on the Ten Essential Public Health Services and

serves as the framework for the standards of the Public Health Accreditation Board's (PHAB) national voluntary accreditation program (NACCHO, 2016c).

NONGOVERNMENT PUBLIC HEALTH ACTIVITIES

Community hospitals have been important to public health. The Hill–Burton Act of 1943, which financed hospital construction projects, required them to provide charitable services, which established a tradition of charitable services among community hospitals. Hospitals may operate primary care clinics and sponsor health education programs and health screening fairs. The Joint Commission (TJC) requires hospitals to participate in community health assessment activities (TJC, 2016).

Ambulatory or outpatient care providers such as physician practices also contribute to community public health. Physicians may serve on local public health organizations or provide services to the uninsured for reduced fees. Hospitals, clinics, and nursing homes also may contribute to public health. Health insurers and managed care providers also make important public health contributions. All types of healthcare providers cooperate with state and local health departments by providing immunizations, offering patient education, screening for communicable diseases, and reporting disease information to health departments (Pointer et al., 2007). Health insurers and managed care providers have a large network of clients to encourage health promotion and health education activities. For example, a physical activity program for senior citizens, **Silver Sneakers**, was developed in 1992 and encouraged the elderly to participate in organized exercise at national fitness chains. Data is being collected to assess if those seniors visited their providers less because their health status increased. It is a free program to Medicare or Medicare supplement participants (Healthways Silver Sneakers Fitness Program, 2013). The focus of the 2010 Affordable Care Act is on primary and preventive care as well as increased access and improving the quality of healthcare services.

Nonprofit agencies such as the **American Cancer Society**, **American Heath Association**, and **American Lung Association** have active health promotion and health screening programs at the national, state, and local levels. The **United Way** is a civic organization that is active in identifying health risks and implementing community public health programs to target these risks. Established in 1905, the civic organization **Rotary International** is responsible for efforts to eradicate polio through vaccine programs throughout the world (Rotary International, 2016). Philanthropic organizations such as RWJF have provided funding for public health activities, including community education and intervention programs. The RWJF's goal is to improve the health of all Americans, and it has provided substantial funds for research activities to combat public health issues such as obesity and smoking (RWJF, 2016).

Council of State and Territorial Epidemiologists (CSTE)

Established in 1992 and headquartered in Atlanta, Georgia, the **Council of State and Territorial Epidemiologists (CSTE)** is a professional organization of more than 1,000 public health epidemiologists that work in state and local health departments to provide technical assistance to the **Association of State and Territorial Health Officials (ASTHO)** and to the CDC for research and policy issues. This group provides expertise in the areas of maternal child health, infectious diseases, environmental health, injury epidemiology, occupational health, and public health informatics (CSTE, 2016).

Association of State and Territorial Health Officials (ASTHO)

ASTHO is a not-for-profit organization that provides support for state and territorial health agencies. It provides research, expertise, and guidance for health policy issues. The federal government looks to ASTHO for expertise in developing health policy. ASTHO officials frequently testify in front of Congress regarding major health issues. The group advocates for increased public health funding and campaign against any funding reductions. ASTHO also provides training opportunities for state public health leaders. All states and U.S. territories and the District of Columbia belong to ASTHO (ASTHO, 2016).

National Association for County and City Health Officials (NACCHO)

NACCHO is the advocacy organization for local health departments. Established in 1993 and located in Washington, DC, NACCHO provides support to nearly 3,000 local health department members that include city, county, district, metro, and tribal agencies. The organization is staffed by nearly 100 physicians and public health experts and a 32-member board of directors that lobbies Congress for its public health agenda, promotes public health, and provides support for its membership (NACCHO, 2016a).

NACCHO recently has focused on providing guidance to local health departments on ways to market public health activities and their role in public health. As discussed earlier, in collaboration with the CDC, NACCHO provides support for **Mobilizing for Action through Planning and Partnerships (MAPP)**, which is a community-driven strategic planning process for improving community health. In collaboration with World Ways Social Marketing, NACCHO has developed a logo with the tagline of "Prevent, Promote, Protect," which local health departments can use to help the public understand its role. NACCHO also has developed a communications toolkit with fact sheets regarding public health departments. **Table 4-4** is a fact sheet used to market the importance of public health departments to the community (NACCHO, 2016b).

Public health, nursing, and medical schools are also major contributors to public health activities. Faculty from these schools often provide technical assistance to local public health organizations and often partner with organizations to establish health programs. The schools may also provide specific educational programs that are tailored to community needs. Educational accreditation organizations also encourage educational programs to participate in community health activities. Harvard University's School of Public Health has established several centers to advance research in public health, such as health communication, injury control, AIDS, health promotion, and population and development studies (Harvard School of Public Health, 2016).

PUBLIC HEALTH EDUCATION AND HEALTH PROMOTION

Public health educational strategies are a crucial component to public health interventions. **Health education** focuses on changing health behavior through educational interventions such as multimedia education and classes. **Health promotion**

TABLE 4-4 What Does the Local Public Health Department Do in Your Community?

Your local health department (LHD)—you may know it as your local "health department" or "public health department"—is a leader in improving the health and well-being of your community. This fact sheet describes the roles performed by LHDs in communities throughout the United States.

- Protects you from health threats, the everyday and the exceptional. Your LHD guards multiple fronts to defend you from any health threat, regardless of the source, and works tirelessly to prevent disease outbreaks. Your LHD makes sure the tap water you drink, the restaurant food you eat, and the air you breathe are all safe. It's ready to respond to any health emergency—be it bioterrorism, SARS, West Nile Virus, or an environmental hazard.

"Not content with merely a 'clipboard' role, checking for compliance with regulations, Marquette County (MI) food service health inspectors organize and conduct classes to advise restaurant managers how best to meet current food safety standards. These inspectors are resources as well as enforcers."

- Educates you and your neighbors about health issues. Your LHD gives you information that allows you to make healthy decisions every day, like exercising more, eating right, quitting smoking, or simply washing your hands to keep from spreading illness. They provide this information through public forums in your community, public service announcements in the media, programs in schools, health education in homes and clinics, and detailed websites. During a public health emergency, your LHD provides important alerts and warnings to protect your health.

"Effective health education can be fun and can promote creativity and self-esteem. Marquette County (MI)'s Health Education Division sponsors annual school-based tobacco control billboard contests. Kids' winning designs are displayed on highway billboards throughout the county."

- Provides healthy solutions for everyone. Your LHD offers the preventive care you need to avoid chronic disease and to help maintain your health. It provides flu shots for the elderly and helps mothers obtain prenatal care that gives their babies a healthy start. Your LHD also helps provide children with regular check-ups, immunizations, and good nutrition to help them grow and learn.

- Health professionals and seniors know that foot problems are a major source of disability. Every month, public health nurses hold foot care clinics at every senior center in Marquette County (MI). The nurses examine feet for problems, refer clients for assistance, and provide counseling on how to avoid disease complications and discomfort and "be a friend to your feet."

- Advances community health. Your LHD plays a vital role in developing new policies and standards that address existing and emerging challenges to your community's health while enforcing a range of laws intended to keep you safe. Your LHD is constantly working—through research and rigorous staff training—to maintain its unique expertise and deliver up-to-date, cutting-edge health programs.

"Treatment for HIV/AIDS has evolved rapidly during the last several years. The staff of the Marquette County (MI) health department keeps up to date in preventing the spread of this awful epidemic through periodic, state-run training sessions."

Adapted with permission from the National Association for County and City Officials (NACCHO). http://www.naccho.org/advocacy/marketing/toolkit/upload/Fact_Sheet_1.doc

is a broader intervention term in public health that encompasses not only educational objectives and activities but also organizational, environmental, and economic interventions to support activities conducive to healthy behavior (Pointer et al., 2007).

Public Health Education Campaign

Educational strategies inform the community about positive health behavior, targeting those at risk to change or maintain positive health behavior. Many public health campaigns are performed by the local public health department and in collaboration with community organizations. There are several steps to planning and developing a successful **public health education campaign** (Minnesota Department of Health, 2016).

- The first step in implementing a public health education campaign is to perform a community assessment to determine at-risk populations. Developing an effective educational campaign to target high-risk populations requires community participation.
- The second step is collaborating with the community for their input on health issues and prioritizing target health issues.
- The third step is performing surveillance activities for specific data related to mortality and morbidity rates.
- The fourth step is to develop a pilot study to assess the effectiveness of the proposed campaign.
- The fifth step is to revise the campaign based on the pilot study.
- The sixth step is to implement the chosen campaign for a period of time.
- The seventh step is to perform an evaluation of the impact of the campaign and revise, if needed.

Public Health Education Evaluation

Educational activities can be difficult to measure because of their abstract nature. It is important that specific outcome measures be developed

prior to the campaign. Each measure should address the following parameters: (1) specific target group, (2) change in and type of behavior, (3) time frame for change, and (4) defined geographic area of change (Novick & Morrow, 2008).

Health Promotion Activities

Most health promotion campaigns have more community health objectives than health educational campaigns that focus on specific target populations. Health promotion focuses on a comprehensive coordinated approach to long-term health behavior changes by influencing the community through educational activities (Minnesota Department of Health, 2013). When a focus is at the community level, it is necessary to address **lifestyle behaviors** that include cultural, economic, psychological, and environmental factors. Examples of health promotion include nutritional, genetic, or family counseling that would encompass health education activities. Health promotion also may include other community development activities such as occupational and environmental control and immunization programs (Turnock, 2007).

Social/Public Health Marketing

According to the CDC, health marketing is an innovative approach to public health practice. **Social/public health marketing** draws from the business discipline of marketing theory and adds science-based health strategies of promotion and prevention. It involves creating, communicating, and delivering health information and interventions using customer-oriented and science-based strategies to protect and promote health in diverse populations (CDC, 2016i). Marketing research is used to formulate messages to educate the public on priority health issues.

Social marketing also delivers information through **social media**, which is electronic communication dedicated to community-based input, interaction, content sharing, and collaboration. Websites and applications dedicated to forums, microblogging, social networking, social bookmarking, social curation, and wikis are among the different types of social media (Social Media, 2013). The most well known example is Facebook. Social media can be easily used as part of a health communications program.

Social media also has become a tool for communication among patients, employees, and providers. According to a September 2011 employee survey of IT professionals, administrators, and physicians, 75% use social media for professional purposes within their jobs. The Mayo Clinic and the U.S. Department of Veterans Affairs are exploring ways to use social media for patient engagement, including education (Most Health IT Pros Use Social Media, 2011). Hospitals and academic medical centers are establishing more YouTube channels and Twitter accounts nationwide. Physicians use Twitter to communicate easily and quickly with other physicians. YouTube provides an opportunity for brief videos regarding certain healthcare education.

Because of the continued increase in social media use, the Centers for Disease Control and Prevention Health Communicator's Social Media Toolkit (2011) contains recommendations for social media use in the healthcare industry:

1. Perform market research to determine key educational messages.
2. Review social media sites by user statistics and demographics.
3. Start a social media campaign by using low-risk tools such as podcasts and videos.
4. The educational messages must be based in science.
5. Develop a system of easy viral sharing by patients so everyone can benefit from the message.
6. Social media users should listen to each other. If patients are voicing concerns or questions, they need to be answered.
7. Leverage social networks to expand the message. An average Facebook user has 130 friends with whom he or she can easily share a health message.

In addition to these recommendations, the federal government has established two websites for social media's best practices and governance policies: http://govsocmed.pbworks.com/Web-2-0-Governance-Policies-and-Best-Practices http://socialmediagovernance.com/policies.php (CDC 2016i).

COLLABORATION OF PUBLIC HEALTH AND PRIVATE MEDICINE

Public health and private medicine have traditionally focused on different aspects of U.S. health. Public health focuses on primary prevention, specifically on the prevention of disease. Public health practitioners develop strategies to promote community health. Private medicine has traditionally focused on tertiary care or providing a cure to individuals or patients. These approaches have traditionally been in conflict. In the 1920s, when public health clinics were treating the poor, private medicine felt threatened because these clinics were viewed as competitors (Reiser, 1996).

Prior to these activities, there were some collaborative activities in the early 1800s and early 1900s. Many physicians were involved in public health, and they realized the importance of public health in the role of infectious diseases. However, public health efforts were later resisted by physicians, who resented mandatory tuberculosis reporting as well as immunization programs (Council on Scientific Affairs, 1990). When antibiotics were developed to combat diseases and the financial benefit of reimbursement of tertiary care by health insurance companies was realized, physicians' interest in public health dissipated (Lasker, 1997). They became more hostile because public health was viewed as a direct competitor.

Over the last decade, there has been an increase in the collaboration between public health and private medicine. In 1994, there was a long-term commitment established between the AMA and the APHA that instituted the following initiatives to formalize a partnership: creation of joint research and local and national networks, development of a strategic plan, and development of a shared vision of health care. There has been an increase in collaborative efforts between the AMA and the CDC to develop healthcare programs to combat disease. The AMA is recognizing that obesity is a disease and should be treated as a disease rather than a behavior (AMA, 2016). With the increased prevalence of obesity, diabetes, and other chronic health conditions, this collaboration is crucial to develop strategies to reduce the rates of these diseases in the United States.

CONCLUSION

Public health is challenged by its very success because consumers now take public health measures for granted. There are several successful vaccines that have targeted all childhood diseases, tobacco use has decreased significantly, accident prevention has increased, there are safer workplaces the fluoridation of water was established, and there is a decrease in mortality from heart attacks (Novick & Morrow, 2008). NACCHO and ASTHO are important support organizations for both state and local governments by providing policy expertise, technical advice, and lobbying at the federal level for appropriate funding and regulations. When some major event occurs like a natural disaster, people immediately think that public health will automatically control the problems it causes. They may not realize how much effort, dedication, and research takes place in protecting the public.

As a healthcare consumer, it is important to recognize the role that public health plays in your health care. Public health can provide educational opportunities to help you change a health condition or behavior. You can visit the CDC's website, which provides information about different diseases and health conditions. You can also visit your local health department. Health navigators can play an important role in public health activities by enhancing communication with the community and public health workers, by increasing health education to at-risk individuals, and by assisting public health officials during a health crisis. The health navigator also can provide integrated care with social support workers. Establishing public health navigators at the state level would provide a coordinated opportunity to work with traditional medicine.

The concept of public health has been more publicized since the terrorist attacks of 2001, the anthrax attacks in post offices, the natural disasters of Hurricane Katrina and Superstorm Sandy, the Boston Marathon bombing, and the flooding in the Midwest. Funding has increased for public health activities because of these events. The concept of bioterrorism is now a reality. Because public health is now considered an integral component to battling terrorism, and consequently a matter of national security, federal funding dramatically increased. Lastly, in addition to the Affordable Care Act's goal to improve the accessibility and quality of the U.S. healthcare system, many of its nearly 50 healthcare reform initiatives focus on public health activities. These initiatives are being implemented during 2010–2017 and beyond.

Summary

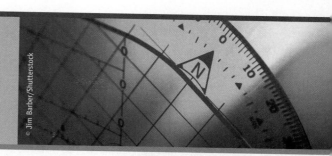
© Jim Barber/Shutterstock

Vocabulary

American Cancer Society
American Public Health Association
American Lung Association
Assessment
Association of State and Territorial Health Officials (ASTHO)
Assurance
Biosurveillance
Bioterrorism
Community preparedness
Community recovery
Constitutional factors
Core public health functions
Determinants of health
Edwin Chadwick
Emergency operations coordination
Emergency public information and warning system
Environmental health
Epidemiology
Epidemiology triangle
Exploring Accreditation Project (EAP)
Fatality management
Health
Health education
Health promotion
Healthy People 2000
Healthy People 2010
Healthy People 2020
Incident Command System (ICS)
Information sharing
Institute of Medicine (IOM)
John Snow
Lemuel Shattuck
Lifestyle behaviors
Macro-environmental conditions

Mass care
Medical countermeasure dispensing
Medical materiel management and distribution
Medical surge
Mobilizing for Action through Planning and Partnerships (MAPP)
National Association of County and City Health Officials (NACCHO)
National Association of Local Boards of Health (NALBOH)
National Incident Management System (NIMS)
National Response Framework (NRF)
Nonpharmaceutical interventions
Policy development
Primary prevention
Public health
Public Health Accreditation Board (PHAB)
Public health/social education campaign
Public health emergency preparedness
Public health laboratory testing
Public Health Security and Bioterrorism Preparedness and Response Act
Public health surveillance and epidemiological investigation
Responder safety and health
Rotary International
Secondary prevention
Silver Sneakers
Social/public health marketing
Social media
Social and community networks
Surveillance
Tertiary prevention
U.S. Food and Drug Administration (FDA)
United Way
Volunteer management

References

American Medical Association (AMA). (2016). http://www.ama-assn.org/ama/pub/advocacy/current-topics-advocacy.shtml.

American Public Health Association (APHA). (2016a). The Prevention and Public Health Fund. http://healthypeople.gov/2020/implement/assess.aspx.

APHA. (2016b). 10 essential public health services. https://www.apha.org/about-apha/centers-and-programs/quality-improvement-initiatives/national-public-health-performance-standards-program/10-essential-public-health-services.

Ashton, J., & Sram, I. (1998). Millennium report to Sir Edwin Chadwick. BMJ, 317:592–596.

Association of State and Territorial Health Officials. (2016). http://www.astho.org/about/.

Centers for Disease Control and Prevention (CDC). (2011). The health communicator's social media toolkit. http://www.cdc.gov/socialmedia/tools/guidelines/pdf/socialmediatoolkit_bm.pdf.

CDC. (2016a). Core functions and capabilities of state public health laboratories. http://www.cdc.gov/mmwr/preview/mmwrhtml/rr5114a1.htm.

CDC. (2016b). Understanding the epidemiologic triangle through infectious disease https://www.cdc.gov/bam/teachers/documents/epi_1_triangle.pdf.

CDC. (2016c). Environmental health services. http://www.cdc.gov/nceh/ehs/ephli/core_ess.htm.

CDC. (2016d). Public health emergency response guide for state, local, and tribal public health directors. https://emergency.cdc.gov/planning/responseguide.asp.

CDC. (2016e). Bioterrorism. http://emergency.cdc.gov/bioterrorism/.

CDC. (2016f). Healthy People 2000. http://www.cdc.gov/nchs/healthy_people/hp2000.htm.

CDC. (2016g). Healthy People 2010. http://www.cdc.gov/nchs/healthy_people/hp2010.htm.

CDC. (2016h). Healthy People 2020. http://www.cdc.gov/nchs/healthy_people/hp2020.htm.

CDC. (2016i). What is health marketing? http://www.cdc.gov/health marketing/whatishm.htm.

Council of State and Territorial Epidemiologists. (2016). About CSTE. http://www.cste.org/?page=About_CSTE.

Council on Scientific Affairs. (1990). The IOM report and public health. JAMA, 264(4): 508–509.

Determinants of health. (2016). http://healthypeople.gov/2020/implement/assess.aspx.

Ellis, H. (2008). John Snow: Early anesthetist and pioneer of public health. British Journal of Hospital Medicine, 69(2): 113.

Emerson, H. (1945). Local health units for the nation (viii). New York, NY: The Commonwealth Fund.

Federal Emergency Management Agency (FEMA). (2016). NRF Resource Center. http://www.fema.gov/nrf.

Harvard School of Public Health. (2016). Research centers. www.hsph.harvard.edu/research/.

Healthways Silver Sneakers Fitness Program. (2016). http://www.silversneakers.com.

Institute of Medicine (IOM). (1988). The future of public health. Washington, DC: National Academies Press.

IOM. (1997). Improving health in the community. Washington, DC: National Academies Press.

IOM. (2002). The future of the public's health in the 21st century. Washington, DC: National Academies Press.

The Joint Commission (TJC). (2016). Hospital Accreditation. http://www.jointcommission.org/AccreditationPrograms/Hospitals/.

Lasker, R. (1997). Medicine & public health: The power of collaboration. New York, NY: Academy of Medicine.

Lee, B. (1994). Health policy and the politics of health care: Nation's health (4th ed.). Boston, MA: Jones and Bartlett Publishers.

Mays, G. (2008). Organization of the public health delivery system. In L. Novick & C. Morrow (Eds.), Public health administration: Principles for population-based management (69–126). Sudbury, MA: Jones and Bartlett Publishers.

Minnesota Department of Health. (2016). Center for health promotion. http://www.health.state.mn.us/divs/hpcd/chp/.

Most health IT pros use social media. (2011). http://www.informationweek.com/healthcare/mobile-wireless/most-health-it-pros-use-social-media/231601331.

National Association of County and City Health Officials (NACCHO). (2016a). About NACCHO. http://www.naccho.org/about/.

NACCHO. (2016b). Mobilizing for action through planning and partnerships. http://naccho.org/topics/infrastructure/mapp/index.cfm?&render.

NACCHO. (2016c). Operational Definition of a Functional Local Health Department. http://www.naccho.org/topics/infrastructure/accreditation/OpDef.cfm.

National Association of Local Boards of Health (NALBOH). (2016). About NALBOH. http://www.nalboh.org/About.htm.

Novick, L., & C. Morrow. (2008). A framework for public health administration and practice. In L. Novick & C. Morrow (Eds.). Public health administration: Principles for population-based management (35–68). Sudbury, MA: Jones and Bartlett Publishers.

Nurse navigator program, bridging public health and primary care with potential to improve chronic disease outcomes. (2016). http://www.publichealthsystems.org/projects/nurse-navigator-program-bridging-public-health-and-primary-care-potential-improve-chronic-0.

Pointer, D., Williams, S., Isaacs, S., & Knickman, J. (2007). Introduction to U.S. health care. Hoboken, NJ: Wiley Publishing.

Public Health Accreditation Board (PHAB). (2016). http://www.phaboard.org/.

Reiser, S. (1996). Medicine and public health. Journal of American Medical Association, 276(17):1429–1430.

Robert Wood Johnson Foundation (RWJF). (2016). http://www.rwjf.org/about/.

Rosen, G. (1958). A history of public health. New York, NY: MD Publications.

Rotary International. (2016). http://www.rotary.org.

Shi, L., & Singh, D. (2008). Essentials of the U.S. health care system. Sudbury, MA: Jones and Bartlett Publishers.

Social Media. (2016). http://whatis.techtarget.com/definition/social-media.

Society for Academic Emergency Medicine (SAEM), Ethics Committee. (1992). An ethical foundation for health care: An emergency medicine perspective. Annals of Emergency Medicine, 21(11): 1381–1387.

Turnock, B. (2007). Essentials of public health. Sudbury, MA: Jones and Bartlett Publishers.

U.S. Department of Health and Human Services (HHS). (1979). Healthy people: The Surgeon General report on health promotion and disease prevention. Publication no. 79-55071. Washington, DC: Public Health Service.

U.S. Department of Health and Human Services (HHS). (2000). Healthy people 1979. https://www.healthypeople.gov/2020/about/History-and-Development-of-Healthy-People

U.S. Food and Drug Administration. (2016). Counterterrorism legislation. http://www.fda.gov/EmergencyPreparedness/Counterterrorism/.

World Health Organization (WHO). (1942). http://www.who.int/about/definition/en/print.html.

World Health Organization (WHO). (2016). Health promotion. http://www.who.int/healthpromotion/en/.

Winslow, C. (1920). The untitled fields of public health. Science, 51(23).

Student Activity 4-1

In Your Own Words

Based on this chapter, please provide a description of the following concepts in your own words. DO NOT RECITE the text description.

Exploring Accreditation Project (EAP)

Determinants of health

Mobilizing for Action through Planning and Partnerships (MAPP)

Healthy People reports

Incident Command System (ICS)

Institute of Medicine (IOM)

Health promotion

National Response Framework (NRF)

Health marketing

Student Activity 4-2

Real-Life Applications: Case Scenario One

Because of all of the media attention on terrorism, your grandparents, who are elderly, are very concerned about terrorist attacks on the United States. They hear the concept of "bioterrorism" and are worried they will be poisoned. They do not understand the role public health departments play in protecting the public from terrorism. As the director of the local health department, you explain that you have a disaster plan prepared in case there is a natural or human-caused disaster in the community.

Activity

(1) Define bioterrorism and how it can impact a community; (2) describe the coordination of the federal, state, and local health departments in a catastrophic event such as bioterrorism; and (3) explain the role that the public health department has in protecting special groups such as the disabled and elderly.

Case Scenario Two

You are business marketing major. You want to provide your expertise to your friend who is a public health nurse. She wants to come up with strategies to reduce cigarette smoking in teens.

Activity

Develop a social media campaign for your friend using three forms of social media.

Case Scenario Three

You have been offered a position with the American Public Health Association. You were not sure if it was a for-profit or nonprofit organization and whether its mission is to make money or help people. You want to be sure that this will be a good fit for you.

Activity

Visit the American Public Health Association website and review its mission statement and level of activities. Develop a list of pros and cons to determine if you should take the job.

Case Scenario Four

As a health navigator, you need to promote primary prevention with your friends who smoke and would like to quit. You are worried they are not taking their health seriously and want to introduce ways to a healthier lifestyle.

Activity

Discuss the concept of primary prevention with your friends. Develop strategies for your friends to focus on a primary prevention plan to stop smoking.

Student Activity 4-3

Internet Exercises

- Visit each of the websites listed here.
- Name the organization.
- Locate its mission statement on the website.
- Provide a brief overview of the activities of the organization.
- How does this organization participate in the U.S. healthcare system?

Websites

http://www.fema.gov/nrf

Organization Name
Mission Statement
Overview of Activities
Importance of Organization to U.S. Health Care

http://www.saem.org

Organization Name
Mission Statement
Overview of Activities
Importance of Organization to U.S. Health Care

http://www.apha.org

Organization Name
Mission Statement
Overview of Activities
Importance of Organization to U.S. Health Care

http://www.hsph.harvard.edu/research

Organization Name
Mission Statement
Overview of Activities
Importance of Organization to U.S. Health Care

http://www.silversneakers.com

Organization Name
Mission Statement
Overview of Activities
Importance of Organization to U.S. Health Care

http://www.naccho.org

Organization Name
Mission Statement
Overview of Activities
Importance of Organization to U.S. Health Care

Student Activity 4-4
Discussion Questions
The following are suggested discussion questions for this chapter.

1. Define public health marketing. Do you think it will help change people's unhealthy behaviors?
2. What is the difference between the role of the state health department and the local health department in providing health services?
3. Go to the ASTHO website. Based on your research, why is it important to state health departments?
4. What is the purpose of the Public Health Accreditation Board? Do you think it has been successful in its goals?
5. Discuss three of the capabilities developed by the CDC as national standards for emergency preparedness.

Student Activity 4-5
Current Events
Perform an Internet search and find a current events topic that relates to this chapter. Provide a summary of the article and the link to the article and explain how the article relates to the chapter.

CHAPTER 5

Navigating Inpatient Services

LEARNING OBJECTIVES

The student will be able to:

- Identify and discuss three milestones of the history of the hospital.
- Define and discuss the different hospitals by their ownership classification.
- Describe the difference between hospitals by who they serve.
- Discuss the roles of the health navigator in the inpatient environment.
- Analyze the utilization trends of inpatient services.

DID YOU KNOW THAT?

- Hospitals are the foundation of our healthcare system.
- Other terms related to "hospital" include hospitality, host, hotel, and hospice.
- Voluntary hospitals are called voluntary because their funding comes from the community voluntarily.
- In 1973, the first Patient Bill of Rights was introduced to represent healthcare consumers in hospitals.
- Public hospitals are the oldest type of hospital and are government owned.
- Religious hospitals were developed as a way to perform spiritual work.
- The Medicare Rural Hospital Flexibility Program was created to allow rural critical access hospitals to receive a cost plus Medicare reimbursement that provides for facility expansion.

INTRODUCTION

Inpatient services are services that involve an overnight stay of a patient. Historically, the U.S. healthcare industry was based on the provision of inpatient services provided by hospitals and outpatient services provided by physicians. As our healthcare system evolved, hospitals became the mainstay of the healthcare system, offering primarily inpatient with limited outpatient services. Over the past two centuries, hospitals have evolved from serving the poor and homeless to providing the latest medical technology to serve the seriously ill and injured (Shi & Singh, 2008). Hospitals have evolved into medical centers that provide the most advanced services. Hospitals can be classified by who owns them, length of stay, and the type of services they provide. Inpatient services typically focus on acute care, which includes secondary and tertiary care levels that most likely require inpatient care. Inpatient care is very expensive and, throughout the years, has been targeted for cost-containment measures. This chapter will discuss the evolution of inpatient healthcare services in the United States and the role the health navigator can play when individuals receive inpatient services.

THE ROLE OF THE HEALTH NAVIGATOR

The role of the health navigator can play a huge role in providing assistance when an individual becomes a patient in a healthcare facility. The focus of the health navigator is to help the patient become empowered. With the ongoing problem of patient deaths resulting from medical errors, it is important to maximize patient safety, and a health navigator can assist with this goal. Health consumer literacy can play a role in patient safety. Ongoing communication between the providers, patient, and facility also contributes to patient safety. Providing assistance with informed consent for patient care and helping the patient understand the type of care provided is crucial. Assisting with any legal issues such as living wills and advance directives also may be needed. A health inpatient service navigator may have to deal with both private and government healthcare insurance when dealing with inpatient services. Overall, having a patient advocate, such as a health navigator, can be a valuable safeguard for the patient. Health navigators who work with inpatient services should be trained in healthcare insurance (both private and public coverage such as Medicare and Medicaid), advance directives, and living wills. Having a clinical background can be very helpful because it will help the navigator to provide insight into why certain tests and care are being performed.

HISTORY OF HOSPITALS

The word "hospital" comes from the Latin word *hospes*, which means a visitor or host who receives a visitor. From this root word, the Latin *hospitalia* evolved, which means an apartment for strangers or guests. The word *hospital* was a word in the Old French language. In England in the 1400s, the word *hospital* came to mean a home for the infirm, poor, or elderly. The modern definition of hospital as "an institution where sick or injured are given medical or surgical care" was developed in the 1500s. The name Hôtel-Dieu, "the hotel of God," was commonly given to hospitals in France during the Middle Ages (American Hospital Association, 2016).

More than 5,000 years ago, Greek temples were the first type of hospital with similar institutions in Egyptian, Hindu, and Roman cultures. Egyptian physicians were the first to use castor oil, opium, and peppermint as medications. Manhattan Island claimed the first U.S. hospital in 1663 for ill soldiers. They were the precursor of the **almshouses** or **poorhouses** that were developed in the 1820s primarily to serve the poor. The first almshouse was in Philadelphia. It was operated by the Quakers and open only to those of their faith. Eventually a public almshouse was established in 1732, which eventually evolved into the Philadelphia General Hospital. The first incorporated hospital in America was the Pennsylvania Hospital in Philadelphia. Philadelphia also is credited with the first quarantine station for immigrants (Pozgar, 2014).

In 1789, the Public Hospital of Baltimore was established for the indigent and, in 1889, it became Johns Hopkins Hospital, which exists today as one of the best hospitals in the world (Sultz & Young, 2006). In the 1850s, a hospital system was finally developed, but the conditions were deplorable because of the staff of unskilled providers.

Hospitals primarily were owned by the physicians who practiced in them (Relman, 2007). The hospitals became more organized because the physicians had to rely on each other for referrals and access to hospitals. This gave the physicians more professional power (Rosen, 1983).

In the early 1900s, with the establishment of standardized medical education, hospitals became accepted across socioeconomic classes and developed to symbolize medicine. With the establishment of the American Medical Association (AMA) that protected the interests of providers, the reputation of providers became more prestigious. In the 1920s, because of the development of medical technological advances, increases in the quality of medical training and specialization, and the economic development of the United States, the establishment of hospitals became the symbol of the institutionalization of health care and the acknowledgment of the medical profession as a powerful presence (Torrens, 1993). During the 1930s and 1940s, the ownership of hospitals changed from physician-owned to church-related and government-operated (Starr, 1982). Religious orders viewed hospitals as an opportunity to perform their spiritual good works, so religion played a major role in the development of hospitals. Several religious orders established hospitals that still exist today.

In 1973, the first Patient Bill of Rights was introduced to represent the healthcare consumer in hospital care (AHA, 2016a). In 1972, the AHA had all hospitals display a "Patient Bill of Rights" in their institutions (Sultz & Young, 2006). In 1974, the National Health Planning and Resources Development Act required states to have **certificate of need (CON)** laws to ensure the state approved any capital expenditures associated with hospital/medical facilities' construction and expansion. The Act was repealed in 1987, but as of January 2016, 36 states still have some type of CON mechanism (National Conference of State Legislatures, 2016). The concept of CON was important because it encouraged state planning to ensure its medical system was based on need.

Hospitals are the foundation of our healthcare system. As our health insurance system evolved, the first type of insurance was hospital insurance. As society's health needs increased, expansion of different medical facilities increased. There was more of a focus on ambulatory or outpatient services because U.S. healthcare consumers preferred outpatient services and, secondly, it was more cost-effective. In 1980, the AHA estimated that 87% of hospitals offered outpatient surgery (Duke University Libraries, 2016). Although hospitals are still an integral part of our healthcare delivery system, the method of their delivery has changed. "Hospitalists," created in 1996, are providers that focus specifically on the care of patients while they are hospitalized (Nabili, 2013). The introduction of this new type of provider recognized the need of providing quality hospital care. More hospitals also have recognized the trend of outpatient services and have integrated those types of services into their delivery. In 2000, as a result of the Balanced Budget Act

cuts of 1997, the federal government authorized an outpatient Medicare reimbursement system, which has supported hospital outpatient services efforts. There are more than 5,700 hospitals in the United States. In 2013, hospitals employed almost 6 million employees, and received more than 600 million outpatient visits and 6,160 million visits to their emergency departments. More outpatient surgeries are now being performed outside the hospital center and in ambulatory surgery centers (American Hospital Association, 2016a).

HOSPITAL TYPES BY OWNERSHIP

There are three major types of hospitals by ownership: (1) public, (2) voluntary or community, and (3) proprietary hospitals. **Public hospitals** are the oldest type of hospital and are owned by the federal, state, or local government. **Federal hospitals** generally do not serve the general public but operate for federal beneficiaries such as military personnel, veterans, and Native Americans. The Veterans Affairs (VA) hospitals are the largest group of federal hospitals. They have high utilization rates by veterans. Taxes support part of their operations. In 2014, there were 211 federal hospitals. County and city hospitals are open to the general population and are supported by taxes. Many of these hospitals are located in urban areas to serve the poor and the elderly. Larger public hospitals may be affiliated with medical schools and are involved in training medical students and other healthcare professionals (Shi & Singh, 2008). Their services are primarily reimbursed by Medicare and Medicaid services and have high utilization rates. In 2014, there were 1,003 state and local hospitals (AHA, 2016b).

Voluntary hospitals are private, not-for-profit, and not government owned. They are considered voluntary because their financial support is the result of community organizational efforts. Their focus is their community. Private, not-for-profit hospitals are the largest group of hospitals. In 2014, there were more than 3,000 not-for-profit hospitals. **Proprietary hospitals**, or investor-owned hospitals, are for-profit institutions and are owned by corporations, individuals, or partnerships. Their primary goal is to generate a profit. They have the lowest utilization rates. In 2014, there were 1,053 proprietary hospitals (AHA, 2016b).

HOSPITAL TYPES BY SPECIALTY

Hospitals may be classified by what type of services they provide and their target population. A general hospital provides many different types of services to meet the general needs of its population. Most hospitals are general hospitals. Specialty hospitals provide services for a specific disease or target population. Some examples are psychiatric, children's, women's, cardiac, cancer, rehabilitation, and orthopedic hospitals.

OTHER HOSPITAL CLASSIFICATIONS

Hospitals can be classified by single- or multiunit operations. Two or more hospitals may be owned by a central corporation. Multiunit hospitals are the result of the merging or acquiring of other hospitals that have financial problems. These chains can be operated as for-profit, not-for-profit, or government owned. These hospitals often formed systems because it was more cost-efficient. In 2014, there were more than 3,000 hospitals or 53% of the hospitals that are part of hospital systems. Hospitals also can be classified by length of stay. A short-stay or **acute care hospital** focuses on patients who stay on an average of less than 30 days. Community hospitals are short term. A **long-term care hospital** focuses on patients who stay on an average of more than 30 days. Rehabilitation and chronic disease hospitals are examples of long-term care hospitals. More than 90% of hospitals are acute or short-term (AHA, 2016b).

Hospitals can be classified by geographic location—rural or urban. Urban hospitals are located in a county with designated urban or city geographic areas. Rural hospitals are located in a county that has no urban areas. In 2014, there were 1,855 rural community hospitals. Urban hospitals tend to pay higher salaries and consequently offer more complex care because of the highly trained providers and staff. In 2014, there were 3,000 urban hospitals. Rural hospitals tend to see more poor and elderly and, consequently, have

financial issues (AHA, 2016b). The **Medicare Rural Hospital Flexibility Program (MRHFP)** was created as part of the Balanced Budget Act of 1997 to address this issue. The MRHFP allows some rural hospitals to be classified as **critical access hospitals** if they have no more than 25 acute care beds and are at least 35 miles away from another hospital, provide emergency care, and are eligible for grants to increase access to consumers. This classification enables them to receive additional Medicare reimbursement called cost plus. **Cost plus reimbursement** brings in additional capital from the federal government, which enables these facilities to expand (Centers for Medicare & Medicaid Services [CMS], 2016).

Teaching hospitals are hospitals that have one or more graduate resident programs approved by the AMA. **Academic medical centers** are hospitals organized around a medical school. There are approximately 400 teaching hospitals that are members of the **Council of Teaching Hospitals and Health Systems** in the United States and Canada. These institutions offer substantial programs and are considered elite teaching and research institutions affiliated with large medical schools (Association of American Medical Colleges, 2016).

Safety-net hospitals are hospitals that provide higher level of charitable care than other hospitals. They receive Hospital Disproportionate Share Payments from the Center for Medicare and Medicaid Services assuming they would be providing more uncompensated care to those populations. However, with the passage of the mandate of the voluntary expansion of Medicaid coverage in the Affordable Care Act, it was assumed there would be less uncompensated care.

As discussed previously, **church-related hospitals** are developed as a way to perform spiritual work. The first church-affiliated hospitals were established by Catholic nuns. These hospitals are community general hospitals. They could be affiliated with a medical school. **Osteopathic hospitals** focus on a holistic approach to care. They emphasize diet and environmental factors that influence health as well as the manipulation of the body. Their focus is preventive care.

Historically, osteopathic hospitals were developed as a result of the antagonism between the different approaches to medicine—traditional or allopathic medicine versus holistic. Current trends indicate that both branches of medicine now serve in each other's hospitals and respect the focus of each others' treatment (Shi & Singh, 2008).

HOSPITAL GOVERNANCE

Hospitals are governed by a **chief executive officer (CEO)**, a board of trustees or board of directors, and the chief of medical staff. The CEO or president is ultimately responsible for the day-to-day operations of the hospital and is a board of trustee's member. CEOs provide leadership to achieve their mission and vision. The **board of trustees** is legally responsible for hospital operations. It approves strategic plans and budgets and has authority for appointing, evaluating, and terminating the CEO. Boards often form different committees such as quality assurance, finance, and planning. In a recent AHA survey, the CEOs indicated the two standing committees were the **finance committee** and the **quality committee**. Economic conditions and legal requirements have forced boards to become more goal oriented and have developed very specific objectives that also focus on quality and safety as well as finances. Hospital governance has evolved as hospital structures have changed. More hospitals belong to a system of hospitals with one board that oversees the system making the individual hospital boards' subsidiary boards (Totten, 2012).

The **chief of medical staff** or **medical director** is in charge of the medical staff/physicians that provide clinical services to the hospital. The physicians may be in private practice and have admitting privileges to the hospital and are accountable to the board of trustees. The medical staff is divided according to specialty or department, such as obstetrics, cardiology, and radiology. There may be a **chief of service** that leads each of these specialties. There also is the **operational staff** that is a parallel line of staff with the medical staff. They are responsible for managing nonmedical staff and performing nonclinical, administrative, and service work (Longest & Darr,

2008; Pointer et al., 2007). It is in the best interest of the institution that both the operational staff and medical staff collaborate to ensure smooth management of the facility.

The medical staff also have committees such as a **credentials committee** that reviews and grants admitting privileges to physicians, a bylaws committee that reviews bylaw changes, a **planning committee** that oversees activities that relate to the mission and vision, **medical records committee** that oversees patient records, a **utilization review committee** that ensures inpatient stays are clinically appropriate, an **infection control committee** that focuses on minimizing infections in the hospital, and a **quality improvement committee** that is responsible for quality improvement programs (Pozgar, 2014). Most hospitals have **ethics committees** that focus on ethical issues involving patient rights and their care.

HOSPITAL LICENSURE, CERTIFICATION, AND ACCREDITATION

State governments oversee the licensure of healthcare facilities including hospitals. States set their own standards. It is important to note that all facilities must be licensed but do not have to be accredited. **State licensure** focuses on building codes, sanitation, equipment, and personnel. Hospitals must be licensed to operate with a certain number of beds.

Certification of hospitals enables them to obtain Medicare and Medicaid reimbursement. This type of certification is mandated by the Department of Health and Human Services (DHHS). All hospitals that receive Medicare and Medicaid reimbursement must adhere to **conditions of participation** that emphasize patient health and safety. **Accreditation** is a private standard developed by accepted organizations as a way to meet certain standards. For example, accreditation of a hospital by The Joint Commission (TJC) means that hospitals have met Medicare and Medicaid standards and do not have to be certified. Medicare and Medicaid also have authorized the American Osteopathic Organization to jointly accredit their types of hospitals with TJC (TJC, 2016 a). It is important to mention that TJC has had tremendous impact on how healthcare organizations are accredited. Since its formation in 1951, TJC has expanded its accreditation beyond hospitals. It accredits ambulatory care, assisted living, behavioral health care, home care, hospitals, laboratory services, long-term care, and office-based surgery centers. Accreditation of managed care organizations such as preferred providers and managed behavioral organizations ended in 2006 (The Joint Commission, 2016b).

International Organization for Standardization

Established in 1947 in Geneva, Switzerland, the **International Organization for Standardization (ISO)** is a worldwide organization that promotes standards from different countries. Although this is not an accrediting organization, organizations that register with the ISO are promoted as having higher standards. ISO 9000 (quality management focus) and ISO 14000 (environmental management focus) are management standards that are applicable to any organization, including healthcare organizations, and many healthcare organizations are registered with the ISO. For example, the ISO has standards for healthcare informatics and medical devices (ISO, 2016).

PATIENT RIGHTS

The **Patient Self-Determination Act of 1990** requires hospitals and other facilities that participate in the Medicare and Medicaid programs to provide patients, upon admission, with information on their rights; it also is referred to as the Patient Bill of Rights. If you enter any hospital, you will see the Patient Bill of Rights posted on its walls. This law requires that the hospital maintain confidentiality of its personal and medical information. Patients also have the right to be provided accurate and easy-to-understand information about their medical condition so they may give **informed consent** for any of their medical care.

The Affordable Care Act (ACA) created an additional Patient Bill of Rights that focuses on implementing consumer-oriented practices from insurance companies, which will help children and adults with preexisting conditions to obtain and keep insurance coverage, to end lifetime reimbursement limits on healthcare insurance reimbursements, and to increase the opportunities for consumers to choose their physicians (Fact Sheet, 2016).

CURRENT STATUS OF HOSPITALS

Many hospitals have experienced financial problems. As a result of the increased competition of outpatient services (which are often more cost-effective, efficient, and consumer friendly) and reduced reimbursement from Medicare and Medicaid, many hospitals have developed strategies to increase their financial stability. Due to pressure to develop cost-containment measures, hospitals are forming huge systems and building large physician workforces. In order to compete with the ACA's mandated state health insurance marketplaces where consumers can purchase health insurance, health insurance companies are developing relationships with hospitals, creating joint marketing plans, and sharing patient data (Matthews, 2011).

Over the years, outpatient services have become the major competitors of hospitals. Advanced technology has enabled more ambulatory surgeries and testing, which has resulted in the development of many specialty centers for radiology and imaging, chemotherapy treatment, kidney dialysis, etc. These services often were performed in a hospital. What is even more interesting is that physicians or physician groups own some of the centers, and they are receiving revenue that used to be hospital revenue. Hospitals have recognized that fact and have embraced outpatient services as part of their patient care. Hospitals have to continue to focus on revenue generation by operating more outpatient service opportunities. They own 25% of urgent care centers in the United States, 21% have ownership interest in ambulatory surgery centers, and 3% have sole ownership of outpatient centers (AHA, 2016a). Because hospitals now compete with outpatient facilities for services, hospitals have begun to develop a digital presence to increase awareness of their brand. A recent 2014 best hospitals study reveals:

- 49% of hospitals lacked a mobile patient website
- 67% failed to offer online rehabilitation and aftercare information
- Only 1 in 5 had online pre-registration to reduce patient wait time
- Nearly 1 in 3 failed to facilitate online bill pay
- At least 18% had onsite errors that hindered the patient experience
- Nearly 1 out of 2 hospitals did not support post-prescription refill requests online (Gamble, 2014).

These data reveal that hospitals have an opportunity to improve their patient care by increasing their technology use.

Cost-Containment Approaches

Hospitals employ different methods to improve quality and control costs.

They use the following models:

- Lean: Based on the Toyota model, this model focuses on increasing efficiency while reducing waste. Staff identify patient care processes that are inefficient and revise them to improve patient care.
- Six Sigma: A Motorola approach that uses statistics to identify and eliminate defects in patient care.
- Plan Do Study Act (PDSA): Developed by the Institute for Healthcare Improvement, a four-step cycle that focuses on improvement of workflow. Providers plan a change in a workflow, and once the change is implemented, they describe what happened with the change, describe the impact of the change, observe and learn from the change, and act upon the change.

Many of the large U.S. hospitals are working with The Joint Commission Center for Transforming Healthcare to implement processes that target safe and quality patient care. For example, the PSDA can be used to reduce medication errors by analyzing the process of providing medications, determining what changes need to be made, and assessing if the changes were successful by the reduction of medication errors (American Hospital Association, 2016b).

Leapfrog Group

The Leapfrog Group was established in 1998 by several large employers that purchase health care to find ways to assess the quality of healthcare services. The founders felt they could take "leaps" forward with their employees by rewarding hospitals that achieve quality and safety performance. In 2001, the Leapfrog Group initiated an annual hospital survey to assess hospital safety performance standards to reduce preventable medical mistakes. The group is endorsed by the National Quality Forum (NQF). The surveys are voluntarily completed by any U.S. hospital and are implemented annually. The survey data is made public so consumers can find out what safety issues are occurring in their local hospitals. The 2015 survey includes data on computerized prescriber order entry, maternity care, and ICU physician staffing.

In June 2012, the Leapfrog Group initiated the Hospital Safety Score, a letter-grade rating of how well hospitals protect patients from accidents, infections, injuries, and errors. These data are collected from the Leapfrog Hospital Survey, CMS, and the American Hospital Association to calculate a letter-grade safety rating (Leapfrog Group, 2016).

Hospital Emergency Services

Hospital emergency medical services are an integral part of the American healthcare system. Emergency departments provide care for patients with emergency healthcare needs. There were 160 million emergency department visits in 2013 (CDC, 2016a). Emergency department use is more likely among the poor, those in fair or poor health, the elderly, infants and young children, and those with Medicaid coverage (CDC, 2016b). Hospitals traditionally provide inpatient services, though nearly all community hospitals provide emergency services that are considered outpatient services. Although emergency departments have the technology to treat emergency situations, many emergency rooms are used for nonemergency issues.

CONCLUSION

Hospitals have been the cornerstone of the U.S. healthcare system. Over the past two centuries, hospitals have evolved from serving the poor and homeless to offering the latest medical technology, which has increased the opportunities for outpatient surgeries. However, as healthcare costs have continued to rise and outpatient services have increased, there have been more mergers and closings and more hospital ownership of outpatient facilities. Despite increasing healthcare costs, the need for hospitals will continue as the graying of the population continues. Hospitals may need to think strategically to determine how they can provide services effectively and efficiently. Part of their strategic plan is to continue to develop a digital presence to increase communication between the patient and facility and to improve their patient services through technology.

Summary

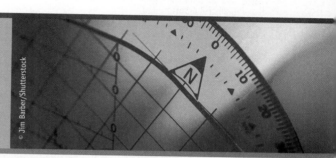
© Jim Barber/Shutterstock

Vocabulary

Academic medical centers
Accreditation
Acute care hospital
Almshouses
Board of trustees
Certificate of need (CON)
Certification
Chief executive officer (CEO)
Chief of medical staff
Chief of service
Church-related hospitals
Conditions of participation
Cost plus reimbursement
Council of Teaching Hospitals and Health Systems
Credentials committee
Critical access hospitals
Federal hospitals
Finance committee
Hospital emergency medical services
Infection control committee
Informed consent
Inpatient services
International Organization for Standardization (ISO)
Long-term care hospital
Medical director
Medical records committee
Medicare Rural Hospital Flexibility Program (MRHFP)
Operational staff
Osteopathic hospitals
Patient Self-Determination Act of 1990
Poorhouses
Proprietary hospitals
Public hospitals
Quality committee
Quality improvement committee
State licensure
Teaching hospitals
Utilization review committee
Voluntary hospitals

References

American Hospital Association (AHA). (2016a). A patient bill of rights http://www.aha.org/about/index.shtml.

American Hospital Association (AHA). (2016b). 2016 Health and hospital trends. http://www.aha.org/research/reports/tw/chartbook/index.shtml.

Ambulatory Surgery Center Association (ASCA). (2016). http://www.ascassociation.org/aboutus/mission.

American Hospital Association. (2016a). Trends affecting hospitals and health systems. http://www.aha.org/research/reports/tw/chartbook/index.shtml.

American Hospital Association (AHA). (2016). Center for hospital and health administration history. http://www.aha.org/research/rc/chhah/index.shtml.

American Hospital Association (AHA). (2016). Community health centers and rural health clinics. http://www.aha.org/advocacy-issues/rural/CHCandRHC.shtml.

Association of American Medical Colleges (AAMC). (2016). Council of Teaching Hospitals and Health Systems (2013). https://www.aamc.org/members/coth/DHHS.

Buchbinder, S., & Shanks, N. (2007). *Introduction to health care management*. Sudbury, MA: Jones and Bartlett Publishers.

Centers for Disease Control and Prevention (CDC). (2016a). National hospital medical care ambulatory survey. http://www.cdc.gov/Nchs/ahcd.htm.

Centers for Disease Control and Prevention (CDC). (2016b). Ambulatory care use and physician visits. http://www.cdc.gov/nchs/fastats/physician-visits.htm.

Centers for Medicare and Medicaid Services (CMS). Home Health Agency (HHA) Center. (2016). http://www.cms.hhs.gov/center/hha.asp.

Department of Health and Human Services (DHHS). (2016). Respite care. http://longtermcare.gov/the-basics/glossary/#Respite_Care.

Duke University Libraries. (2016). Timeline of medicine. http://library.duke.edu/rubenstein/history-of-medicine/.

Fact Sheet: The Affordable Care Act's new patient Bill of Rights. (2016). http://www.healthreform.gov/newsroom/new_patients_bill_of_rights.html.

Gamble M. (2014). Why top hospitals have inadequate websites: 10 things to know. http://www.beckershospitalreview.com/hospital-management-administration/why-top-hospitals-have-inadequate-websites-10-things-to-know.html.

Golia, N. (2016). Three insurers take the plunge into telehealth. http://www.insurancetech.com/three-insurers-take-the-plunge-into-telehealth/d/d-id/13146

Health care law expands community health centers, services more patients. (2012, July 1). http://bphc.hrsa.gov/about/healthcenter factsheet.pdf.

Health Resources and Services Administration. (2016a). Telehealth. http://www.hrsa.gov/ruralhealth/telehealth/.

Health Resources and Services Administration. (2016b). What is a health center? http://bphc.hrsa.gov/about/.

International Organization for Standardization (ISO). (2016). http://www.iso.org.

Jonas, S. (2003). *An introduction to the U.S. health care system*. New York, NY: Springer Publishing.

Leapfrog Group. (2016). Current Leapfrog initiatives. http://www.leapfroggroup.org/about

Longest, B., & Darr, K. (2008). *Managing health services organizations and systems*. Baltimore, MD: Health Professions Press.

Mathews, A. W. (2011, Dec. 12). The future of U.S. healthcare. http://online.wsj.com/article/SB10001424052970204319004577084553869990554.html.

Nabili, S. (2016). What is a hospitalist? http://www.medicinenet.com/script/main/art.asp?articlekey=93946.

National Conference of State Legislatures. (2016). Certificate of need: State health laws and programs. http://www.ncsl.org/default.aspx?tabid=14373.

National Council on Aging. (2016). https://www.ncoa.org/about-ncoa/.

Office of Disability Employment Policy. (2016). Employee Assistance Programs for a new generation of employees. http://www.dol.gov/odep/documents/employeeassistance.pdf.

Pointer, D., Williams, S., Isaacs, S., & Knickman, J. (2007). *Introduction to U.S. health care*. Hoboken, NJ: Wiley Publishing.

Pozgar, G. (2014). *Legal and ethical essentials of health care administration*. Burlington, MA: Jones & Bartlett Learning.

Relman, A. (2007). *A second opinion: Rescuing America's health care*. (15–67). New York, NY: Public Affairs.

Rosen, G. (1983). *The structure of American medical practice 1875–1941*. Philadelphia, PA: University of Pennsylvania Press.

Shi, L., & Singh, D. (2008). *Delivering health care in America*. Sudbury, MA: Jones and Bartlett Publishers.

Starr, P. (1982). *The social transformation of American medicine*. Cambridge, MA: Basic Books.

Substance Abuse and Mental Health Services Administration (SAMHSA). (2016). http://www.samhsa.gov.

Sultz, H., & Young, K. (2006). *Health care USA: Understanding its organization and delivery* (5th ed.). Sudbury, MA: Jones and Bartlett Publishers.

The Joint Commission (TJC). (2016a). Accreditation and certification preparation. https://www.jointcommission.org/accreditation/accreditation_main.aspx.

The Joint Commission (TJC). (2016b). Ambulatory health care. http://www.jointcommission.org/accreditation/ambulatory_healthcare.aspx.

Torrens, P. R. (1993). Historical evolution and overview of health services in the United States. In S. J. Williams & P. R. Torrens (Eds.). *Introduction to health services* (4th ed.). Clifton Park, NY: Delmar Publishers.

Totten, M. (2012). Hospital governance in the US: An evolving landscape. Issue 1, Spring. http://www.greatboards.org/newsletter/2012/greatboards-newsletter-spring-2012.pdf.

Student Activity 5-1

In Your Own Words

Based on this chapter, please provide an explanation of the following concepts in your own words. DO NOT RECITE the text.

Accreditation

Certification

Cost plus reimbursement

Patient Self-Determination Act of 1990

Proprietary hospitals

Public hospitals

Respite care

Voluntary hospitals

Student Activity 5-2

Real-Life Applications: Case Scenario One

You just received your Master of Health Administration degree and decided you would like to pursue a career in hospital management. You cannot decide what type of hospital you would like to apply to and decide to investigate the different types of hospitals that are available.

Activity

(1) Identify three different types of hospitals that are available for your employment. (2) Based on your research, select a hospital type and state why you chose this type of hospital.

Case Scenario Two

One of your friends was just released from the hospital. She was pleased with her care but was not sure about her physician who told her she was a "hospitalist." You had not heard of the term, either.

Activity

Perform an Internet search on the term "hospitalist." Define the term and find out if there are any current statistics on hospitalist use.

Case Scenario Three

Your elderly aunt needs to be hospitalized. She lives alone and has no one to assist her during and after hospital stay. You heard there is a new type of health job called "health navigator" that can assist her while she is in the hospital.

Activity

Perform an Internet search on the subject to understand the role of health navigators. Write up your research and share it with your aunt.

Case Scenario Four

You are a history major and are curious to see how the hospital system has developed in the United States. You can't understand why hospitals are closing.

Activity

Perform an Internet search on the history of hospitals and current trends to find out why hospitals are closing across the United States. Share your information with your classmates.

Student Activity 5-3

Internet Exercises

- Visit each of the websites listed here.
- Name the organization.
- Locate its mission statement on the website.
- Provide a brief overview of the activities of the organization.
- How does this organization participate in the U.S. healthcare system?

Websites

http://www.leapfrog.org

Organization Name
Mission Statement
Overview of Activities
Importance of Organization to U.S. Health Care

http://aha.org

Organization Name
Mission Statement
Overview of Activities
Importance of Organization to U.S. Health Care

http://www.ruralhealthinfo.org

Organization Name
Mission Statement
Overview of Activities
Importance of Organization to U.S. Health Care

https://www.intechnic.com

Organization Name
Mission Statement
Overview of Activities
Importance of Organization to U.S. Health Care

https://www.advisory.com

Organization Name
Mission Statement
Overview of Activities
Importance of Organization to U.S. Health Care

http://www.beckershospitalreview.com

Organization Name
Mission Statement
Overview of Activities
Importance of Organization to U.S. Health Care

Student Activity 5-4

Discussion Questions

The following are suggested discussion questions for this chapter.

1. What was interesting about the history of hospitals?
2. Perform an Internet search and find the 10 top hospitals in the U.S.
3. Have you or anyone you know spent time in a hospital? How was your experience?
4. Perform an internet search and report about how hospitals operate in one other country.
5. How could a health navigator help a patient in a hospital?

Student Activity 5-5

Current Events

Perform an Internet search and find a current events topic that relates to this chapter. Provide a summary of the article and the link to the article and explain how the article relates to the chapter.

CHAPTER **6**

Navigating Ambulatory/Outpatient Services

LEARNING OBJECTIVES

The student will be able to:

- List five types of ambulatory care settings.
- Analyze the utilization trends of ambulatory services.
- Discuss the impact of CON on the increase of ambulatory services.
- Explain the impact of technology on the growth of ambulatory services.

DID YOU KNOW THAT?

- The most common outpatient service is a visit to a physician's office.
- According to the Urgent Care Association, ownership of urgent care centers is split fairly evenly among physicians (35.4%), corporations such as private investors and insurers (30.5%), and hospitals (25.2%).
- Both CVS and Walgreens have outpatient care services in many of their retail operations.
- The most active specialty care to enter the outpatient market is ophthalmology because Medicare reimburses outpatient cataract operations.
- Approximately 75% of urgent care centers are located in suburban areas.

INTRODUCTION

Ambulatory or outpatient services do not require an overnight stay and are less financially taxing on the healthcare system. The terms *outpatient* and

ambulatory often are used interchangeably. Most insurance companies categorize these services as any treatment that does not exceed 24 hours in length regardless of whether there is an overnight stay in an outpatient bed (Barr & Breindel, 2011). As discussed previously, **outpatient services** do not require an overnight stay. Often, the term **ambulatory care** is used interchangeably with outpatient services. The word *ambulatory* literally means a person is able to walk in to receive a service, which may not always be necessarily true. The word *outpatient* is a more general term that encompasses all services other than inpatient services (Jonas, 2003). The term *outpatient services* will be used for the remainder of the chapter.

U.S. healthcare expenditures have increased as part of the gross domestic product, and consequently, more cost-containment measures have evolved. Outpatient services have become more popular because they are less expensive and they are preferred by both consumers and healthcare providers. The increased use of technology in the healthcare setting has provided the opportunity for more outpatient surgical services to be delivered. There are now portable mammography vans and MRI machines that can be used in an outpatient setting. Outpatient care includes medical practices, hospice care, outpatient surgery and testing centers, urgent care, oncology centers, rehabilitation centers, occupational health clinics, endoscopy center, dialysis centers, and hospital-based outpatient facilities. For example, ophthalmology outpatient services increased when Medicare started including cataract operation reimbursement for outpatient service. This chapter will discuss the evolution of outpatient care services in the United States and the role the health navigator can play in coordinating these types of services. A discussion of other health service organizations that provide additional outpatient services also will be discussed.

THE ROLE OF THE HEALTH NAVIGATOR

The health navigator plays an important role in outpatient service for patients. Because there are so many outpatient services available, it is important for the navigator to ensure that the patient is receiving the appropriate care and testing and that the patient understands why they are having outpatient care. Coordinating care among several agencies can make the outpatient care even more difficult for patients to handle. It requires organization of the coordinated care and collaboration with the different providers. Secondly, several community organizations can assist with chronic diseases such as dementia or terminal diseases. The navigator can work with both the patient and their families to ensure they have contacted the appropriate organizations.

OUTPATIENT SERVICES

Physician Offices

The basic form of an outpatient service is a patient seeing his or her physician in the physician's office. Both general practitioners and specialists offer ambulatory care either as solitary practitioners or in group practice. Traditionally, physicians established solitary practices, but as the cost of running a practice became too expensive, more physicians have established group practices (Pointer et al., 2007).

Hospital Emergency Services

Hospital emergency medical services are an integral part of the American healthcare system. Emergency departments provide care for patients with emergency healthcare needs. There were 136 million emergency department visits in 2015. The majority of visits were from individuals 65 years and older followed by 18–44 years of age (CDC, 2016a). Hospitals traditionally provide inpatient services, though nearly all community hospitals provide emergency services that are considered outpatient services. Although emergency departments have the technology to treat emergency situations, many are used for nonemergency issues.

Hospital-Based Outpatient Clinics

Many outpatient clinics are found in teaching hospitals. They use outpatient clinics as an opportunity to teach and perform research. The clinics are categorized as surgical, medical, and other. Larger teaching hospitals may have 100 specialty and subspecialty clinics (Jonas, 2003). They may operate as part of the hospital or as a hospital-owned entity.

Urgent/Emergent Care Centers

Urgent/emergent care centers were first established in the 1970s and are used for consumers who need medical care but their situation is not life threatening. This would take the place of the hospital emergency room visit. The medical issue usually occurs outside traditional physician office hours, so patients seek care at these centers in the evenings and on weekends and holidays. Many of these centers are both walk-in and by-appointment facilities. They do not take the place of a patient's primary care provider. These centers are conveniently located and may be in strip malls or medical buildings so they are accessible for consumers. Many managed care organizations will reimburse member visits because they are less expensive than an emergency room visit (Sultz & Young, 2006). Urgent care centers relieve the hospital emergency departments from seeing patients who do not have life-threatening situations. It is anticipated there will be an increase in urgent care centers in the future.

According to the Urgent Care Association of America (UCAOA), in 2016 there were nearly 7,100 urgent care centers in the United States. The urgent care centers that make up this number have been verified manually by UCAOA and provide full-service urgent care (x-ray, lab, extended hours). There are approximately 2,000 additional urgent care centers that include retail medical clinics. According to an Urgent Care Association of America (UCAOA) survey, approximately 85% of the centers have a physician on site at all times, and 75% of the physicians are board certified in a primary specialty (UCAOA, 2016).

Rite Aid, Walgreen's, and CVS Health (CVS), three national chain pharmacies, have established **drugstore clinics**. CVS, the leader in this innovative type of health care, now has 1,100 Minute Clinics nationwide. CVS has decided to expand treatment options to include conditions typically handled by a physician. The goal is not to replace primary care providers but to increase access to health care. CVS is taking its role in retail health clinics very seriously. In September 2014, CVS stopped selling tobacco products at stores nationwide on grounds it was the ethical thing to do for customers. Walgreens, which has nearly 400 Take Care Clinics nationwide, will follow the CVS policy of stopping tobacco sales. Many of the patients who use drugstore clinics do not have a primary care provider (Modern Healthcare, 2013). According to the **Convenient Care Association (CCA)**, since the first walk-in clinic opened in 2000, retail clinics are now a common feature, with 10.5 million visits occurring annually at more than 1,800 retail clinics. Like urgent care clinics, retail clinics are open late and on weekends, and customers do not need an appointment. This type of access may encourage more individuals to seek health care (Bachrach, Frohlich, Garcimnde, & Nevitt, 2015).

Ambulatory Surgery Centers

Ambulatory surgery centers (ASCs) are for surgeries that do not require an overnight stay. Physicians have taken the lead in developing ASCs. The first ASC was established in 1970 by two physicians. It provided an opportunity for physicians to have more control over their surgical practices as they grew frustrated by hospital policies, wait times for surgical rooms, and delays in new equipment. Advances in technology and newer anesthesia drugs to help patients recover more quickly from grogginess have enabled more

surgeries to be performed on an outpatient basis. ASCs may be general or specialized. General centers may focus on general surgical procedures specialized surgical centers focus on orthopedic surgery, plastic surgery, and gynecologic surgery. Some centers offer a combination of both general and specialized surgeries. Outpatient surgery is a major contributor to growth in ambulatory care. Approximately 8 million surgeries are performed in 4,000 ASCs annually. The most common procedures include ophthalmology; gastroenterology; orthopedic; ear, nose, and throat; gynecology; and plastic surgery. ASCs contribute to healthcare cost containment. Procedures at ASCs cost nearly 50% less than inpatient surgeries. Hospitals have ownership interest in 21% of ASCs and have sole ownership in 3% of ASCs. Patient surveys indicate more than 90% customer satisfaction with their care and service. Most ASCs are accredited by the Joint Commission, the Accreditation for Ambulatory Health Care, or the American Association of Ambulatory Surgery Facilities (ASCA, 2016).

Health Centers

Health centers (HCs), which originated in the 1960s as part of the war on poverty, are organizations that provide culturally competent primary healthcare services to the uninsured or indigent population such as minorities, infants and children living in poverty, patients with HIV, substance abusers, the homeless, and migrant workers. They are outpatient clinics that qualify for specific reimbursement systems under Medicare and Medicaid. Other services that must be provided directly by a health center or by arrangement with another provider include: dental services, mental health and substance abuse services, telehealth services, transportation services necessary for adequate patient care, and hospital and specialty care. Health centers are supported by the Health Resources and Services Administration (HRSA) and share four fundamental characteristics:

1. Location in high service needs community
2. Governed by a community board
3. Provide comprehensive primary care
4. Must achieve performance objectives (HRSA, 2016b)

HCs often are located in urban and rural areas where there is a designated need. They enter a contract with the state or local health department to provide services to these populations. They also provide links with social workers, Medicaid, and Health Insurance Program (HIP) (DHHS, 2016a). HCs may be organized as part of the local health department or other health service and may operate at schools.

Home Health Agencies

Home health agencies and **visiting nurse agencies** provide medical services in a patient's home. The earliest form of home health care was developed by Lillian Wald, who created the Visiting Nurse Service of New York in 1893 to service the poor. In 1909, she persuaded the Metropolitan Life Insurance Company to include home health care in its policies (Longest & Darr, 2008). This care often is provided to the elderly, disabled, or patients who are too weak to come to the hospital or physician's office or have just been released from the hospital. Contemporary home health services include both medical and social services, incorporating skilled nursing care and home health aide care such as dispensing medications, assisting with activities of daily living, and meal planning. Physical, speech, and occupational therapy also can be provided at home. Medical equipment such as oxygen tanks and hospital beds also may be provided (CMS, 2016).

Although the home healthcare industry is popular with patients, there have been continued problems with the quality of home health care being offered, as well as issues with fraudulent Medicare reimbursement for services not needed. Although most states offer licensing for home health agencies, it is important that home health agencies be Medicare certified because they are required to comply with CMS regulations. In 2011, about 3.4 million Medicare beneficiaries received home health services from almost 11,900 home health agencies. Access to home health care is generally adequate: 99% of beneficiaries live in a ZIP code where a Medicare home health agency operates, and 98% live in an area with two or more agencies. There were 12,400

agencies in 2014. In 2011, Medicare implemented two major changes to strengthen program integrity for Medicare home health services. In April 2011, CMS implemented an ACA requirement for a face-to-face encounter with a physician or nurse practitioner when home health care is ordered. They also can receive accreditation from the Community Health Accreditation Program (CHAP) (Medpac, 2016).

Employee Assistance Programs

Employee assistance programs (EAPs) are a type of occupational health program. Established in the 1970s as an intervention for employee drug and alcohol abuse, EAPs offer free and confidential assessment, short-term counseling, referrals, and follow-up services to employees who have personal and/or work-related problems. EAPs address a broad and complex body of issues affecting mental and emotional well-being, stress, grief, family problems, and psychological disorders. EAP counselors also work in a consultative role with managers and supervisors to address employee and organizational challenges and needs. Many EAPs are active in helping organizations prevent and cope with workplace violence, trauma, and other emergency response situations (Employee Assistance Programs, 2016).

OTHER HEALTH SERVICES
Respite Care

Often, family and friends of chronically ill patients become the major caregivers of their friends and family. This continuous care can become stressful for caregivers, especially those who have full-time jobs. As a result of this issue, **respite care programs** or temporary care programs were formally established in the 1970s to provide systematic relief to caregivers who need a mental break or cannot provide full-time care. It also forestalls the ill patient from being placed in a facility. There are many types of respite programs, including in home care services, adult day care, or brief stays in a residential facility. for the patient, and in-home aides. Long-term care insurance may pay for a portion of respite care (DHHS, 2016).

Adult Day Care

Adult day care centers are respite care day programs that provide a medical model of care with medical and therapeutic services. Depending on the needs of the patient, it may a social model that provides meals, recreation, and some basic medical health; or it may be a medical–social model that provides social interaction and intensive medical-related activities. Adult day care centers were developed in the 1960s based on research that indicated a need for a facility that provided a break for informal caregivers as well as provide an opportunity to prolong the patient's life at home. An adult day care center is a professional care setting in which older adults, adults living with dementia, or adults living with disabilities receive individualized therapeutic, social, and health services for some part of the day. The average age of the adult day care center attendee is 72 years old, and two-thirds are female. Nearly half of participants have a form of dementia. Approximately 90% of centers offer cognitive stimulation programs; almost 80% provide memory training programs; and more than 75% offer educational programs. In the United States, the average cost for an adult day care center is about $64 per day, depending on where you live and the services provided (e.g., meals, transportation, nursing supervision). Facilities that provide professional healthcare services charge higher fees. Many facilities offer services on a sliding fee scale, meaning that what you pay is based on your ability to pay. Medicare does not pay for adult day care services, but Medicaid will (DHHS, 2016).

In 1979, the **National Adult Day Services Association (NADSA)** was formed to promote these types of community services. They established national standard criteria for the operation of adult day care centers. Many adult day care centers are regulated by state licensing and may be certified by a particular community agency. They often are affiliated with larger formal healthcare or skilled nursing care facilities, medical centers, or senior organizations. The National Adult Day Services Association (NADSA) identified 5,685 day programs operating in the United States in 2014. Adult day care centers serve as an emerging provider of transitional care and short-term rehabilitation following hospital discharge (NADSA, 2016).

Hospice

Hospice care provides care for patients who have a life-threatening illness and comfort for the patient's family. Medicare, private health insurance, and Medicaid (in 43 states) cover hospice care for qualified patients. Some hospice programs offer healthcare services on a sliding fee scale basis for patients with limited resources. A typical hospice care team includes the following:

- Doctors
- Nurses
- Home health aides
- Clergy or other spiritual counselors (e.g., minister, priest, rabbi)
- Social workers
- Volunteers
- Occupational, physical, and/or speech therapists

The family of the terminally ill patient also is involved in the care giving. Hospice services can be offered both as inpatient and outpatient services. Hospitals may have designated hospice units. Home health agencies also may offer a hospice program. Medicare, Medicaid, Department of Veterans Affairs, and private insurance plans will pay for hospice services. Donations allow hospice care facilities to provide care at no cost to those who cannot afford it (WebMD, 2016). The vast majority of hospices follow Medicare requirements to provide the following, as necessary, to manage the illness for which someone receives hospice care:

- Time and services of the care team, including visits to the patient's location by the hospice physician, nurse, medical social worker, home health aide, and chaplain/spiritual adviser
- Medication for symptom control or pain relief
- Medical equipment such as wheelchairs or walkers and medical supplies such as bandages and catheters

- Physical and occupational therapy
- Speech–language pathology services
- Dietary counseling
- Any other Medicare-covered services needed to manage pain and other symptoms related to the terminal illness, as recommended by the hospice team
- Short-term inpatient care (e.g., when adequate pain and symptom management cannot be achieved in the home setting)
- Short-term respite care (e.g., temporary relief from caregiving to avoid or address "caregiver burnout")
- Grief and loss counseling for patient and loved ones (Hospice Foundation of America, 2016)

Senior Centers

Established by the Older American Act of 1965, senior centers provide a broad array of services for the older population. Services provided include meal and nutrition programs, education, recreational programs, health and wellness programs, transportation services, volunteer opportunities, counseling, and other services.

According to 2016 statistics, there are 11,400 senior centers in the United States, serving approximately 1 million seniors every day; users spend three hours per day, one to three times per week, at the centers; 70% of users are women; and the average age of attendees is 75 years of age (NCOA, 2016). Funding is received from state and local governments, grants, and private donations.

Located in Washington, DC, the National Council on Aging (NCOA) is a not-for-profit advocacy agency for the senior population. As part of the NCOA, the National Institute of Senior Centers (NISC) is a network of senior center professionals that promote senior centers. It is the only national program dedicated to the welfare of senior centers. It sponsors a national voluntary accreditation program for senior centers. Senior centers offer a wide variety of programs and services, including:

- Meal and nutrition programs
- Information and assistance
- Health, fitness, and wellness programs
- Transportation services
- Public benefits counseling
- Employment assistance
- Volunteer and civic engagement opportunities
- Social and recreational activities
- Educational and arts programs
- Intergenerational programs

With the estimated increase in life expectancy, senior centers will continue to expand and offer more services to seniors who have chronic diseases that can be managed on an outpatient basis (NCOA, 2016).

Office of Women's Health

Women have unique health needs that require specialized medical facilities. Recognizing this need, in 1991, HHS established an Office of Women's Health (OWH). Currently 10 regional offices oversee women's health activities nationwide. Women's life expectancy is approximately seven years longer than men's life expectancy, so women represent a larger portion of the elder population. The OWH mission is to promote women's and girls' health by providing gender-specific health activities. The Womenshealth.gov website is recognized as a leader in delivering women's health information. Its content is written and updated according to the most reliable current information in each field of study. The site includes information from the federal government and recommendations from the U.S. Preventive Services Task Force, though it occasionally offers other resources on a case-by-case basis. Before publishing content, all text is reviewed by subject matter experts across the government (DHHS, 2016a).

Meals on Wheels of America

Established in 1954, the Meals on Wheels Association of America (MOWAA) is the oldest and largest national organization composed of and representing 5,000 community-based Senior Nutrition Programs that are members of the association. These programs provide well over 1 million meals to seniors who need them each day. Some programs serve meals at senior centers, some deliver meals directly to the homes of seniors whose mobility is limited, and many provide both services. In 2016, 2.4 million seniors were served meals on wheels meals, including 500,000 veterans. Federal funding for Meals on Wheels is provided by the Senior Nutrition Program that was authorized by the 1972 Older Americans Act. In October of 2011, the U.S. Administration on Aging (AoA) entered into a cooperative agreement with MOWAA to establish a new National Resource Center on Nutrition and Aging. The primary role of the National Resource Center's (NRC) AoA-MOWAA is to cultivate innovative ideas related to nutrition and aging in the United States. Meals on Wheels has partnered with several organizations to perform research on nutrition program barriers to serving seniors (MOWAA, 2016).

Planned Parenthood Federation of America

Planned Parenthood Federation of America (PPFA) is a 90-year-old organization that provides family services to men, women, and teens in local communities regarding sexual health, family planning, and more, both online and at sites across the United States. PPFA also provides important health education to over 1 million individuals. PPFA accepts Medicaid but also offers services based on a sliding fee scale (PPFA, 2016). PPFA is a founding member of the International Planned Parenthood Federation.

American Red Cross

Founded in 1881 and headquartered in Washington, DC, the **American Red Cross (ARC)** provides emergency response to victims of war and natural and human-caused disasters. It also offers services to the indigent and the military, analyzes and distributes blood products, provides education, and organizes international relief programs. Approximately 91 cents of every dollar spent is invested in humanitarian programs. There are more than 700 local chapters with 35,000 employees supported by 500,000 volunteers (ARC, 2016).

Doctors Without Borders

Established in 1971 by physicians and journalists in France, **Doctors Without Borders** is an international medical organization that provides quality medical care in 60 countries to individuals threatened by violence, catastrophe, lack of health care, natural disasters, epidemics, or wars. Nearly 90% of its funding comes from private sources. Staff is derived from the communities where the crises are occurring as well as U.S. aid workers. The organization won the Nobel Peace Prize in 1999. A U.S. component of this organization was established in 1990 and recently raised more than $100 million in funding. In 2015, it sent U.S.-based aid workers on more than 430 assignments overseas (Doctors Without Borders, 2016). It was the first group to respond to the Ebola crisis in West Africa. It has established a training center in Brussels, Belgium. Doctors Without Borders calls itself a movement, and that sensibility infuses the operation. The group created a center, called Crash, devoted to self-criticism of its work. The culture is flinty—aid workers eschew the fancy hotels where government or United Nations workers sometimes stay—and volunteer doctors and top executives alike are paid considerably less than their counterparts at some other aid organizations. Today, Doctors Without Borders is the largest of the relatively few organizations devoted to providing urgent care in medical crises caused by armed conflict or natural disasters. Most of its $1.3 billion in donations in 2015 came from private individuals across the globe, according to financial reports; only 9 percent came from governmental agencies. The charity sent about 6,000 health, logistics, and other experts to 60 countries last year and hired 30,000 local workers (Fink, Nossiter, & Kanter, 2014).

Remote Area Medical Volunteer Corps

Remote Area Medical (RAM) was founded in 1985 to develop a mobile efficient workforce to provide free health care to areas of need worldwide. The first services delivered by Remote Area Medical Volunteer Corps in the United States were in the Appalachian country focusing on using telehealth to increase access to health care. (HRSA, 2016a).

CONCLUSION

The healthcare industry has recognized that outpatient services are a cost-effective method of providing quality health care and has therefore evolved into providing quality outpatient care. This type of service is the preferred method of receiving health care by the consumer (CDC, 2016b). However, as medicine has evolved and more procedures, such as surgeries, can be performed on an outpatient basis, different types of outpatient care have evolved. There are more outpatient surgical centers, imaging centers, urgent/emergent care centers, and other services that were once offered on an inpatient basis. There will continue to be an increase in outpatient services being offered. As a consumer, technology will only increase the quality and efficiency of health care. Telehealth also will become a more widely used model for healthcare delivery because of continued advances in technology.

Summary

© Jim Barber/Shutterstock

Vocabulary

Adult day care centers
Ambulatory care
Ambulatory surgery centers
American Red Cross (ARC)
Convenient Care Association (CCA)
Doctors Without Borders
Drugstore clinics
Employee assistance programs
Health center
Home health agencies
Hospice care
Hospital emergency medical services
Meals on Wheels Association of America (MOWAA)
National Adult Day Services Association (NADSA)
National Institute of Senior Centers (NISC)
Office of Women's Health (OWH)
Outpatient services
Planned Parenthood Federation of America (PPFA)
Remote Area Medical (RAM)
Respite care or temporary care programs
Senior centers
Telehealth
Telemedicine
Urgent/emergent care centers
Visiting nurse agencies

References

Ambulatory Surgery Center Association (ASCA). (2016). http://www.ascassociation.org/home.

American Hospital Association (AHA). Community health centers and rural health clinics. http://www.aha.org/advocacy-issues/rural/CHCandRHC.shtml.

American Red Cross (ARC). (2016). Our history. http://www.redcross.org/about-us/history.

ASCA. (2016b). A positive trend in health care. http://www.ascassociation.org/ASCA/Resources/ViewDocument/?DocumentKey=7d8441a1-82dd-47b9-b626-8563dc31930c.

Bachrach, D., Frohlich, J., Garcimonde, A., & Nevitt, K. (2015). The value proposition of value clinics. http://www.ccaclinics.org/research-a-resources/research.

Eldercare Locator. (2013). Hospice care. http://www.eldercare.gov/ELDERCARE.NET/Public/Resources/Factsheets/Hospice_Care.aspx.

Barr, K. & Breindel, C. (2011). Ambulatory care. *Health care administration: Managing organized delivery systems* (5th ed.). Sudbury, MA: Jones and Bartlett Learning: pp. 433–457.

Buchbinder, S., & Shanks, N. (2007). *Introduction to health care management.* Sudbury, MA: Jones and Bartlett Publishers.

Centers for Disease Control and Prevention (CDC). (2016a). National hospital medical care ambulatory survey. http://www.cdc.gov /Nchs/ahcd.htm.

CDC. (2016b). Ambulatory care use and physician visits. http://www .cdc.gov/nchs/fastats/docvisit.htm.

Centers for Medicare and Medicaid Services (CMS). Home Health Agency (HHA) Center. (2016). http://www.cms.hhs.gov/center/hha.asp.

Department of Health and Human Services (DHHS). (2016). Respite care. http://www.eldercare.gov/ELDERCARE.NET/Public /Resources/Factsheets/Respite_Care.aspx.

DHHS. (2016b). Adult day care. https://www.ncdhhs.gov/assistance /adult-services/adult-day-services.

DHHS. (2016a). Health care law expands community health centers, services more patients. http://bphc.hrsa.gov/about/healthcenter factsheet.pdf.

DHHS. (2016c). Recovery act: Community health centers. http:// www.nhchc.org/wp-content/uploads/2011/09/KaiserCHCsand healthreformAug2010.pdf.

Doctors Without Borders. (2016). History & principles. http://www. doctorswithoutborders.org/aboutus/?ref=nav-footer.

Dolan, P. (2013). Urgent care surge fueled by pressures on health system. http://www.amednews.com/article/20130415/business /130419964/2/.

Fink, S, Nossiter, A., & Kanter, J. (2014). Doctors without borders evolves as it forms the vanguard in Ebola crisis. http://www.nytimes. com/2014/10/11/world/africa/doctors-without-borders-evolves -as-it-forms-the-vanguard-in-ebola-fight-.html?_r=0.

Golia, N. (2013). Three insurers take the plunge into telehealth. http://www.insurancetech.com/three-insurers-take-the -plunge-into-telehealth/d/d-id/1314613?.

Health Resources and Services Administration (HRSA). (2016a). Tele-health. http://www.hrsa.gov/ruralhealth/telehealth/.

HRSA. (2016b). What is a health center? http://bphc.hrsa.gov/about/.

Hospice Foundation of America (HFA). (2016). What is hospice? https:// hospicefoundation.org/End-of-Life-Support-and-Resources /Coping-with-Terminal-Illness/Hospice-Services.

Jonas, S. (2003). *An introduction to the U.S. health care system*. New York, NY: Springer Publishing.

Longest, B., & Darr, K. (2008). *Managing health services organizations and systems*. Baltimore, MD: Health Professions Press.

Mathews, A. W. (2011, Dec. 12). The future of U.S. healthcare. http:// online.wsj.com/article/SB10001424052970204319004577084553869990554.html.

Meals on Wheels Association of America (MOWAA). (2016). Key initiatives, projects and grants. http://www.mowaa.org/page .aspx?pid=296.

Medpac. (2012). Home health care services, Chapter 8. http://www.medpac .gov/docs/default-source/reports/mar12_ch08.pdf?sfvrsn=0.

Modern Healthcare. (2013, April 4). Walgreen clinics expand care into chronic illness. http://www.modernhealthcare.com/article /20130404/INFO/304049978

National Adult Day Services Association (NADSA). (2016). Adult day services: Overview and facts. http://www.nadsa.org/consumers /overview-and-facts/.

National Council on Aging. (2016). https://www.ncoa.org/.

Office of Disability Employment Policy. (2016). Employee Assistance Programs for a new generation of employees. http://www.dol.gov /odep/documents/employeeassistance.pdf.

Planned Parenthood Federation of America (PPFA). (2016). http:// www.plannedparenthood.org/about-us/index.htm.

Pointer, D., Williams, S., Isaacs, S., & Knickman, J. (2007). *Introduction to U.S. health care*. Hoboken, NJ: Wiley Publishing.

Relman, A. (2007). *A second opinion: Rescuing America's health care* (pp. 15–67). New York, NY: Public Affairs.

Remote Area Medical Volunteer Corps (RAM). (2016). https://ramusa. org/about/.

Rodak, S. (2016). 25 things to know about urgent care. http://www.beckers hospitalreview.com/lists/25-things-to-know-about-urgent-care .html.

Rosen, G. (1983). *The structure of American medical practice 1875–1941*. Philadelphia, PA: University of Pennsylvania Press.

Shi, L., & Singh, D. (2008). *Delivering health care in America*. Sudbury, MA: Jones and Bartlett Publishers.

Starr, P. (1982). *The social transformation of American medicine*. Cambridge, MA: Basic Books.

Substance Abuse and Mental Health Services Administration (SAM-HSA). (2013). http://www.samhsa.gov.

Sultz, H., & Young, K. (2006). *Health care USA: Understanding its organization and delivery* (5th ed.). Sudbury, MA: Jones and Bartlett Publishers.

The Joint Commission (TJC). (2016a). Accreditation and certification preparation. https://www.jointcommission.org/accreditation /accreditation_main.aspx.

The Joint Commission. (2016b). Ambulatory health care. http://www. jointcommission.org/accreditation/ambulatory_healthcare .aspx.

Torrens, P. R. (1993). Historical evolution and overview of health services in the United States. In S. J. Williams & P. R. Torrens (Eds.). *Introduction to health services* (4th ed.). Clifton Park, NY: Delmar Publishers.

Urgent Care Association of America (UCAA). (2016). http://www .ucaoa.org/.

Walmart. (2016). Hunger relief & healthy eating. http://walmartstores .com/CommunityGiving/9054.aspx.

WebMD. (2016). Hospice care. http://www.webmd.com/balance/tc /hospice-care-topic-overview?page=2

Student Activity 6-1

In Your Own Words

Based on this chapter, please provide an explanation of the following concepts in your own words. DO NOT RECITE the text.

Emergency departments

Employee assistance programs

Health Centers Ambulatory care

Hospice care

Respite care

Student Activity 6-2

Real-Life Applications: Case Scenario One

You just received your Master of Health Administration degree and decided you would like to establish a home health agency.

Activity

Perform an Internet search on the different types of home health care and discuss your findings with your classmates.

Case Scenario Two

Upon graduating from medical school, you considered going overseas to help those in need but were unsure how to proceed.

Activity

Perform an Internet search on the organization Doctors Without Borders. Discuss your findings with the class.

Case Scenario Three

Your mother is a volunteer at a hospice facility. She often comes home emotionally exhausted. You have never visited a hospice and asked if you could go with her next time. She agrees. Prior to your visit, you want to understand the concept of a hospice.

Activity

Perform an Internet search on the subject to understand their mission and goals. Write up your research and share it with your classmates.

Case Scenario Four

As part of your internship, you will be assigned this semester to an adult day care center. You are only familiar with child day care centers so you decide to do some research before you start your internship.

Activity

Perform an Internet search on adult day care centers in your area and develop and write a report about your findings to share with your classmates. Discuss how a health navigator can assist with this type of service.

Student Activity 6-3

Internet Exercises

- Visit each of the websites listed here.
- Name the organization.
- Locate its mission statement on the website.
- Provide a brief overview of the activities of the organization.
- How does this organization participate in the U.S. healthcare system?

Websites

http://www.doctorswithoutborders.org

Organization Name
Mission Statement
Overview of Activities
Importance of Organization to U.S. Health Care

www.telehealth.com

Organization Name
Mission Statement
Overview of Activities
Importance of Organization to U.S. Health Care

http://www.ramusa.org

Organization Name
Mission Statement
Overview of Activities
Importance of Organization to U.S. Health Care

http://www.swiftmd.com

Organization Name
Mission Statement
Overview of Activities
Importance of Organization to U.S. Health Care

http://www.ncoa.org

Organization Name
Mission Statement
Overview of Activities
Importance of Organization to U.S. Health Care

http://www.ascassociation.org

Organization Name
Mission Statement
Overview of Activities
Importance of Organization to U.S. Health Care

Student Activity 6-4

Discussion Questions

The following are suggested discussion questions for this chapter.

1. Why do you think impatient services are so popular with healthcare consumers? Discuss your experience with outpatient services.
2. What are urgent care centers? Have you or someone you know used these centers?
3. Research an employee assistance program and report on the types of services they provide.
4. Visit the Doctors Without Borders website. Report back to the discussion board on one of their recent activities
5. What is telehealth? Give examples of telehealth. Would you use telehealth to receive care from your healthcare provider?

Student Activity 6-5

Current Events

Perform an Internet search and find a current events topic that relates to this chapter. Provide a summary of the article and the link to the article and explain how the article relates to the chapter.

CHAPTER **7**

Navigating the U.S. Healthcare Workforce

LEARNING OBJECTIVES

The student will be able to:

- Describe five types of physicians and their roles in health care.
- Describe six types of nurse professionals and their roles in health care.
- Describe six types of other health professionals and their roles in health care.
- Discuss the issue of geographic maldistribution of physicians and its impact on access to care.
- Describe the difference between primary, secondary, tertiary, and quaternary care.
- Define allied health professionals and their role in the healthcare industry.
- Discuss the roles and responsibilities of a health navigator.

DID YOU KNOW THAT?

- The healthcare industry is one of the largest employers in the United States with a workforce of 18 million workers.
- Approximately 65% of U.S. physicians are specialists, which includes surgeons, cardiologists, and psychiatrists.
- Quaternary care is an extension of tertiary care and is considered cutting-edge specialty medicine.
- Since the 1990s, physicians who specialize in the care of hospitalized patients have been called "hospitalists."
- Women represent nearly 80% of the healthcare workforce.
- A consumer is eligible to view a physician's credentials in the National Practitioner Data Bank.

INTRODUCTION

The healthcare industry is the fastest-growing industry in the U.S. economy, employing a workforce of 18 million healthcare workers. Considering the aging of the U.S. population and the impact of the Affordable Care Act, it is expected that the healthcare industry will continue to experience strong job growth (Centers for Disease Control and Prevention [CDC], 2013). When we think of healthcare providers, we automatically think of physicians and nurses. However, the healthcare industry is composed of many different health service professionals, including dentists, optometrists, psychologists, chiropractors, podiatrists, nonphysician practitioners (NPPs), administrators, and allied health professionals. It is important to identify allied health professionals because they provide a range of essential healthcare services that complement the services provided by physicians and nurses. This category of health professionals is an integral component of providing quality health.

Health care can occur in varied settings. Physicians have traditionally operated in their own practices, but they also work in hospitals, mental health facilities, managed care organizations, or community health centers. They also may hold government positions or teach at a university. They could be employed by an insurance company. Health professionals, in general, may work at many different organizations, both for profit and nonprofit. In most states, only physicians, dentists, and a few other practitioners may serve patients directly without the authorization of another licensed independent health professional. Those categories authorized include chiropractic, optometry, psychotherapy, and podiatry. Some states authorize midwifery and physical therapy (Jonas, 2003).

Although the healthcare industry is one of the largest employers in the United States, shortages of physicians in certain geographic areas of the country continue. Rural areas continue to suffer physician shortages, which limits consumer access to health care. Incentive programs have been tried to encourage physicians to relocate to rural areas, but shortages still exist. There also continues to be a shortage of registered nurses nationwide. The American Association of Colleges of Nursing (AACN) is publicizing this issue with policy makers (AACN, 2013).

With the passage of the Affordable Care Act, shortages of physicians in certain areas will most likely continue. The Association of American Medical Colleges estimates that by 2015 there will be a shortage of more than 60,000 physicians. The number will double by 2025 because of the aging of the population as well as the impact of the Affordable Care Act, which will increase the number of people with insurance, thus increase the need for primary care doctors because there will be millions of citizens now participating in the healthcare system who will require care. Medicare officials predict that Medicare enrollment will increase by nearly 45% by 2025, which will further place strain on physician shortages (Lowery & Pear, 2012). This chapter will provide a description of the different types of healthcare professionals and their role in providing care in the U.S. system.

RESPONSIBILITIES OF THE HEALTH NAVIGATOR

The health navigation professions include a large number of job titles. There are three general areas of employment that are often identified as community health workers, patient navigators, and health insurance navigators. Employment for a wide range of health navigation professions has grown rapidly in recent years. New funding mechanisms from Medicaid, Medicare, and the Affordable Care Act have dramatically increased interest in developing these types of career positions, which need academic health navigator training. Community health workers, typically hired by healthcare agencies, focus on population-based health such as promoting healthy behavior. They are the only health navigation employment classification tracked by the U.S. Department of Labor. Community health workers and health educators are classified together. The Labor Department's Occupational Outlook estimates that the positions for community health workers and health educators will increase 15% by 2024 (Guide to Public Health and Navigation, 2015). According to the Department of Labor, insurance companies, employers, and governments are trying to find ways to improve the quality of care and health outcomes, while reducing costs. They hire health educators and community health workers to teach people about how to live healthy lives, obtain screenings, and avoid costly diseases and medical procedures. These health educators and community health workers explain how lifestyle changes can reduce the probability of contracting illnesses such as lung cancer, HIV, heart disease, and skin cancer. They help people understand how to manage their condition and avoid unnecessary trips to the emergency room. They also help people understand how their actions affect their health. The median annual wage for community health workers was $36,300 in May 2015. A registered nurse who becomes a health navigator may have a salary of $65,000. A social worker who becomes a health navigator may have a salary of $44,000. Health educator positions require more education, and so the median wage in 2015 for these positions was significantly higher, at $51,000 (BLS, 2016).

Although the concept of a health navigator has been utilized in different areas of health care, the concept of the navigator was fully introduced to a national audience as part of the

Affordable Care Act. The first patient navigation program began in 1990 by Harold Freeman. In 2005, President Bush signed the Patient Navigator and Chronic Disease Prevention Act, which established a research program to examine cost effectiveness of navigation programs. In 2006, the Center for Medicare and Medicaid Services funded six multiyear demonstration programs on navigation programs. In 2000, the Health Resources and Services Administration (HRSA) funded six programs that focused on chronic disease navigation programs and, in 2010, added 10 new sites (Huber, Shapiro II, Burke, & Palmer, 2014). Then the ACA established insurance navigators at the state government level to help with the insurance marketplace websites. According to the healthcare.gov website, a *navigator* is an individual or organization trained and able to help consumers, small businesses, and their employees as they look for health coverage options through the Marketplace, including completing eligibility and enrollment forms. These individuals and organizations are required to be unbiased. Their services are free to consumers. The ACA created the Navigator program or In-Person Assister (IPA) as part of the outreach and enrollment assistance to individuals who were purchasing insurance coverage through the Health marketplace. Any marketplace was required to have a navigator program to assist healthcare consumers. Navigators were required to provide education and to assist with enrollment in insurance programs, and they contracted directly with the Center for Medicare and Medicaid Services. They were required to complete 30 hours of training.

Prior to the implementation of the healthcare marketplaces, navigators were used to assist in many areas including mental health, cancer, primary care, uninsured population, clinical ethics consultations, case management, and long-term care. Like the navigators for the healthcare marketplace, their main goal is to assist the healthcare consumer with making educated decisions regarding their health care and the health care of their loved ones. Another term for a health navigator is a *patient advocate*. As our healthcare system

becomes more patient centric and performance based, more navigator roles will develop to ensure that patients' comprehension of their healthcare system is clear. The ultimate goal is to ensure that the healthcare system works for patients so they can achieve the best health outcomes.

PRIMARY, SECONDARY, TERTIARY AND QUATERNARY CARE

There are three important concepts of care that need to be emphasized: primary, secondary, and tertiary care. **Primary care** is the essential component of the U.S. healthcare system because it is the point of entry into the system—where the patient makes first contact with the system. Primary care focuses on continuous and routine care of an individual. It may be delivered by a physician, nurse practitioner, midwife, or physician's assistant. Categories of primary care practitioners usually include family practitioners, pediatricians, internal medicine providers, obstetricians and gynecologists, psychiatrists, and emergency medicine physicians (Jonas, 2003). The focus of a primary care provider is to ensure patient access to the system by coordinating the delivery of healthcare services. Primary care often is referred to as essential health care and could include health education, counseling, and other preventive services. **Secondary care** focuses on short-term interventions that may require a specialist's intervention. Examples of secondary care include hospitalizations, routine surgery, specialty consultation, and rehabilitation. **Tertiary care** is a complex level of medical care, typically done by surgeons—physicians that perform operations to treat disease, physical problems, and injuries. This type of care is usually based on a referral from a primary care provider. Examples of tertiary care are orthopedic surgeons who operate on broken bones, oncology surgeons who removed cancerous bodies, and cardiac surgeons who operate on the heart. A new term, **quaternary care**, is an extension of tertiary care and refers to highly specialized, cutting-edge tertiary care. This is performed in research facilities and highly specialized facilities. An example of this type of care is proton beam therapy, which is cutting-edge technology used to treat prostate cancer (Torrey, 2011).

PHYSICIAN EDUCATION

Physicians play a major role in providing healthcare services. They have been trained to diagnose and treat patient illnesses. Depending on their training, physicians have participated in primary, secondary, and tertiary care. All states require a license to practice medicine. Physicians must receive their medical education from an accredited school that awards either a **Doctor of Medicine (MD)** or a **Doctor of Osteopathic Medicine (DO)**. Many students prepare for medical school by majoring in a premedical undergraduate program, which often consists of science and mathematics courses. Undergraduate students are required to take the MCAT (the Medical College Admission Test) before applying to medical school.

In order to provide direct patient care, physicians must take a licensing examination in the desired state of practice once they complete a residency. State licensing requirements may vary. This residency or training may take three to eight years. The residency is important because it allows physicians to learn about a certain specialty of interest while providing them with on-the-job training. The length of the residency program can be as short as three years for a family practice and as long as 10 years for a surgery specialty. Most states require physicians to participate in continuing medical education (CME) activities to maintain state licensure.

The major difference between an MD and a DO is the approach to treatment. DOs tend to stress preventive treatments and use a **holistic approach** to treating a patient, which means they focus not only on the disease, but also on the entire person. Most DOs are generalists. MDs use an **allopathic approach**, which means they actively intervene in attacking and eradicating disease and focus their efforts on the disease itself (BLS, 2016a).

In 2014, there were 708,000 jobs for physicians. Growth between 2014 and 2024 is estimated at 14%. Wages of physicians are among the highest of all occupations. According to the Medical Group Management Association, in 2015, physicians practicing primary care received total median annual compensation of $187,200, and physicians practicing in medical specialties received total median annual compensation of $356,885. Due to the difference in wages, there are less primary care physicians in the overall physician population—32.2%. Specialists represent more than 65% of the overall physician population (BLS, 2016b).

GENERALISTS AND SPECIALISTS

Generalists can be primary care physicians, family care practitioners, general internal medicine physicians, or general pediatricians. Their focus is on preventive services such as immunizations and health examinations. They treat less-severe medical problems and often serve as a gatekeeper for a patient, which means they coordinate patient care if the patient needs to see a specialist for more complex medical problems. **Specialists** are required to be certified in their area of specialization. This may require additional years of training, as discussed in the previous paragraph, and require a **board certifying or credentialing examination**. The most common specialties are dermatology, cardiology, pediatrics, pathology, psychiatry, obstetrics, anesthesiology, specialized internal medicine, gynecology, ophthalmology, radiology, and surgery (Shi & Singh, 2008). The board certification often is associated with the quality of the healthcare provider's services because board certification requires more training. A consumer is eligible to view a physician's credentials in the **National Practitioner Data Bank (NPDB)**. The database was created to provide a nationwide system to prohibit incompetent healthcare practitioners from moving state to state without disclosing previous issues.

The database is a depository of negative actions against licenses, or clinical privileges. It also provides information about any medical liability settlements (AMA, 2016). Located on the Centers for Medicare and Medicaid (CMS) website, the **Physician Compare website** helps consumers research physicians who accept Medicare. It provides basic information about their address and contact information, education, languages spoken, gender, hospital affiliation, Medicare acceptance, and specialty (CMS, 2016).

DIFFERENCES BETWEEN PRIMARY AND SPECIALTY CARE

Primary care is the initial contact between the healthcare provider and the patient. If needed, **specialty care** will be a result of a primary care evaluation. The primary care physician will ultimately coordinate the health care of the patient if additional specialty care is required. If a patient has a chronic condition, the primary care provider will coordinate the overall care of the individual (Torrey, 2011). In a managed care environment, which focuses on cost containment, the primary care physician becomes the gatekeeper of the patient's care by referring a patient to a specialist for additional care. Primary care students spend most of their focus in ambulatory settings learning about different diseases, whereas specialty care students spend time in an inpatient setting focusing on special patient conditions.

Patterns of Physician Supply

The concept of **geographic maldistribution** has occurred because physicians prefer to practice in urban and suburban areas where there is a higher probability of increased income. Recruiting physicians to rural areas is difficult because of the working conditions, reduced income, and reduced access to technology, which is more available in urban and suburban areas. Another issue in physician supply is the increasing number of specialists as compared to generalists, which is called **specialty maldistribution**. The supply of specialists has increased more than 100% over the last 20 years, while the supply of generalists has increased only 18%. The Affordable Care Act mandate of expanding health insurance coverage will add an additional 34 million consumers to the healthcare system. President Obama has called for an increase in primary care physicians,

nurse practitioners, and physician assistants to manage this huge increase (Petterson et al., 2012).

TYPES OF HEALTHCARE PROVIDERS

Hospitalists

A **hospitalist** is a physician that provides care to hospitalized patients. This new type of physician, which evolved in the 1990s, usually is a general practitioner and is becoming more popular. Because hospitalists spend so much time in the hospital setting, they can provide more efficient care. They replace a patient's primary care physician while the patient is hospitalized. This was a new model of care that transitioned the patient's primary care provider to the outpatient setting while allowing a hospitalist to take of their patient in the hospital. Hospitalists monitor the patient from admittance to discharge, acting as a primary care provider for inpatient medicine. However, hospitalists normally do not have a relationship with the patient prior to admittance. They coordinate the care within the hospital among the specialty physicians and other healthcare practitioners. Hospitalists comprise 9% of the primary care workforce and 4% of the overall physician workforce, which approximates 35,000 in the United States. Internal medicine physicians comprise 85% of hospitalist jobs (Association of American Medical Colleges [AAMC], 2016).

Nonphysician Practitioners

It is important to mention the general term **nonphysician practitioner (NPP)**, which includes nonphysician clinicians (NPCs) and mid-level practitioners (MLPs). The specific professionals of this category will be discussed in depth in this chapter, but it is important to mention their importance generally in providing health care. They are sometimes called **physician extenders** because they often are used as a substitute for physicians. They are not involved in total care of a patient so they collaborate closely with physicians. Categories of NPPs include physician assistants (PAs), nurse practitioners (NPs), and certified nurse practitioners (CNPs). NPPs have been favorably received by patients because they tend to spend more time with patients (Shi & Singh, 2008).

Physician Assistants

Physician assistants (PAs), a category of NPPs, provide a range of diagnostic and therapeutic services to patients. They take medical histories, conduct patient examinations, analyze tests, make diagnoses, and perform basic medical procedures. They are able to prescribe medicines in all but three states. They must be associated with and supervised by a physician but the supervision does not need to be direct. In many areas where there is a shortage of physicians, PAs act as primary care providers. They collaborate with physicians by telephone and onsite visits. Students take classes and participate in clinical settings. They are required to pass a national certification exam and may take additional education in surgery, pediatrics, emergency medicine, primary care, and occupational medicine. Their median salary is $98,180 (BLS, 2016c).

Nurses

Nurses constitute the largest group of healthcare professionals and provide the majority of care to patients. They are the patient's advocate. There are several different types of nurses that provide patient care and several different levels of nursing care based on education and training.

Although nursing supply and demand is cyclical, during recent years there has been a continued nursing shortage. According to the American Society of Registered Nurses, the recession has minimized the nursing shortage. Nurses who were expecting to retire remained on the job and many former nurses returned to the workforce to recover lost savings (Casselman, 2013). It is expected that the impact of the Affordable Care Act will create another supply shortage. The following is a summary of each type of nurse.

Licensed Practical Nurse/Licensed Vocational Nurse

There are approximately 700,000 **licensed practical nurses (LPNs)** in the United States; these nurses are called **licensed vocational nurses (LVNs)** in California and Texas. They are the largest group of nurses and provide basic nursing care. Expected growth is 14% by 2024. Education for LPNs is offered by community colleges and technical schools. Training takes approximately 12–14 months and includes both education and supervised clinical practice. LPNs have a high school diploma and take a licensing exam. The 2015 median salary is approximately $43,170.

The job responsibilities of LPNs include patient observation, taking vital signs, and keeping records. They also assist patients with **activities of daily living (ADLs)** in aiding with personal hygiene, feeding, and dressing patients. In some states, LPNs administer some medications. They work primarily in hospitals, home health agencies, and nursing homes. Many LPNs work full time and earn their Bachelor of Science in Nursing (BSN) degree to increase their career choices (BLS, 2016d).

Registered Nurse

A **registered nurse (RN)** is a trained nurse who has been licensed by a state board after passing the national nursing examination. An RN can be registered in more than one state. There are different levels of registered nursing based on education.

- **Associate Degree in Nursing (ADN):** Two-year program offered by community colleges.
- Diploma programs: Three-year programs offered by hospitals. There is no degree offered but undergraduate credit may be earned. These programs are very expensive and are being offered less often.
- **Bachelor of Science in Nursing (BSN):** The most rigorous of the nursing programs. Programs offered by colleges and universities normally take four to five years. They perform both classroom activity and clinical practice activity.

Job responsibilities of RNs include recording disease symptoms, implementing care plans, assisting physicians in examinations and the treatment of patients, administering medications and performing medical procedures, supervising other personnel such as LPNs, and educating patients and families about follow-up care. The majority of RNs work in hospitals. Depending on the level of education, the 2015 median annual income was $67,190.

Advanced Practice Nurse

Advanced practice nurse (APN), or midlevel practitioners, are nurses who have experience and education beyond the requirements of an RN. They operate between the RN and MD, which is why they are called midlevel practitioners. They normally obtain a Master of Science in Nursing (MSN) with a specialty in the field of practice. The 2015 median salary was $81,000. Many of the APN certifications allow for a nurse to provide direct care including writing prescriptions (BLS, 2016e). There are four areas of specialization: clinical nurse specialist (CNS), certified registered nurse anesthetist (CRNA), nurse practitioner (NP), and certified nurse–midwife (CNM).

Nurse Practitioners and Certified Nurse–Midwives

As stated earlier, the nonphysician practitioner (NPP) is an integral component of providing quality health care in the United States. Nurse practitioners (NPs) are the largest categories of advanced practice nurses (APNs). The first group of NPs was trained in 1965 at the University of Colorado. In 1974, the American Nursing Association developed the Council of Primary Care Nurse Practitioners, which helped substantiate the role of NPs in patient care. Over the last two decades, several specialty NP boards have been established, such as pediatrics and reproductive health for certification of NPs. On January 1, 2013, the American Academy of Nurse Practitioners (founded in 1985) and the American College of Nurse Practitioners (founded in 1995) merged to form the American Association of Nurse Practitioners (AANP). It is the largest full-service national professional membership organization for NPs.

NPs are required to obtain an RN and a master's or doctoral degree. They may receive a certificate program and complete direct patient care clinical training. NPs emphasize health education

and promotion as well as disease treatment—referred to as "care and cure." NPs spend more time with patients and, as a result, patient surveys indicate satisfaction with NPs' care. NPs may specialize in pediatrics, family, geriatric, or psychiatric care. Most states allow NPs to prescribe medications. They practice in ambulatory, acute, and long-term settings. Their 2015 median salary was $104,740 (AANP, 2016). They are a cost-effective alternative to a physician and will play a role in the expanded health services prescribed by the Affordable Care Act.

Certified nurse–midwives (CNMs) are RNs who have graduated from a nurse–midwifery education program that has been accredited by the American College of Nurse–Midwives' Division of Accreditation. Nurse–midwives have been practicing in the United States for nearly 90 years. They must pass the national certification exam to receive the designation of CNM. Nurse–midwives are primary care providers for women who are pregnant. They must be recertified every eight years. Recent average salaries are reported at $96,970. Certified midwives (CMs) are individuals who do not have a nursing degree but have a related health background. They must take the midwifery education program, which is accredited by the same organization. They also must pass the same national certification exam to be given the designation of CM. The recent average salary is $70,000 (American College of Nurse–Midwives, 2016).

OTHER INDEPENDENT HEALTHCARE PROFESSIONALS

Dentists

Dentists prevent, diagnose, and treat teeth, gum, and mouth diseases. They are required to complete four years of education from an accredited dental school once a bachelor's degree is completed. Dentists are awarded a Doctor of Dental Surgery (DDS) or Doctor of Dental Medicine (DDM) degree. Some states may require a specialty license. The first two years of dental school are focused on dental sciences. The last two years are spent in a clinical environment. Dentists may take an additional two to four years of postgraduate education in orthodontics (teeth straightening), oral surgery, public health dentistry, etc. In 2015, there were more than 150,000 dentists in the United States—more than 90% are in private practice and are primarily general practitioners. Job growth is approximately 18% between 2014 and 2020. The 2015 median salary average was $150,310. There is no industry priority to target this population (BLS, 2016f).

Dentists are often helped by **dental assistants**. Dental assistants work directly with dentists in the preparation and treatment of patients. Some states require assistants to graduate from an accredited program and pass a state exam. Some states have no formal educational requirements. Dental assistants who do not have formal education may learn their duties through on-the-job training. They do not have to be licensed but may become certified. The 2015 median pay was $35,980. Job growth is projected at 18% from 2014 to 2024 (BLS, 2016g).

Dental hygienists clean teeth, examine patients for oral diseases, and provide other preventive dental care. They educate patients on ways to improve and maintain oral health. Dental hygienists typically need an associate's degree in dental hygiene. Every state requires dental hygienists to be licensed, but requirements vary by state. Employment is expected to grow by 38% from 2010 to 2020, much faster than the average for all occupations. Ongoing research linking oral health and general health will continue to spur the demand for the preventive dental services dental hygienists provide. The 2015 median pay was $72,330 (BLS, 2016h).

Pharmacists

Pharmacists are responsible for dispensing medication that has been prescribed by physicians. They also advise both patients and healthcare providers on potential side effects of medications. All Doctor of Pharmacy programs require applicants to have taken postsecondary courses such as chemistry, biology, and anatomy. Applicants need at least two to three years of undergraduate study; for some programs, applicants must have a bachelor's degree. For most programs, applicants also must take the Pharmacy College Admissions Test (PCAT). All states license pharmacists. After they finish the PharmD, prospective pharmacists must pass two exams to get a license: one in pharmacy skills and knowledge and the other in pharmacy law. In May 2015, the median wage of pharmacists was $121,500. Employment of pharmacists is expected to increase by 30% from 2014 to 2024 (BLS, 2016i).

Chiropractors

Chiropractors take a holistic approach to treating their patients, which means they focus on the entire body with emphasis on the spine. They believe the body can heal itself with no medication or surgery. Chiropractors treat patients who have musculoskeletal system health issues (the musculoskeletal system is made up of bones, muscles, ligaments, and tendons). Chiropractors manipulate the body with their hands or with a machine. Becoming a chiropractor requires earning a Doctor of Chiropractic (DC) degree and getting a state license. Doctor of Chiropractic programs take four years to complete and require three years of previous undergraduate college education for admission. Although specific requirements vary by state, all jurisdictions require the completion of an accredited Doctor of Chiropractic program to be licensed in the state. In 2016, the median annual wage of chiropractors was $139,897. Employment of chiropractors is expected to increase by 17% from 2010 to 2020 (BLS, 2016j).

Optometrists

Optometrists, also known as Doctors of Optometry or ODs, are the main providers of vision care. They examine people's eyes to diagnose vision problems. Optometrists may prescribe eyeglasses or contact lenses. Optometrists also test for glaucoma and other eye diseases and diagnose conditions caused by systemic diseases, such as diabetes and high blood pressure, and refer patients to other health practitioners, if necessary. Optometrists often provide preoperative and postoperative care to cataract patients as well as to patients who have had laser vision correction or other eye surgery.

Optometrists need a Doctor of Optometry (OD) degree. In 2011, there were 20 accredited Doctor of Optometry programs in the United States, one of which was in Puerto Rico. All states require optometrists to be licensed. All prospective optometrist must have an OD from an accredited optometry school and must complete all sections of the National Boards in Optometry to be licensed in a state. Some states require an additional exam. Employment of optometrists is expected to grow by 27% from 2014 to 2024. In 2015, the median annual wage of optometrists was $103,900 (BLS, 2016k).

Psychologists

Psychologists study the human mind and human behavior. Some psychologists work independently, doing research or working only with patients. Others work as part of a healthcare team, collaborating with physicians, social workers, and others to treat illness and promote overall wellness. Most clinical, counseling, and research psychologists need a doctoral degree. Psychologists can complete a PhD in psychology or a Doctor of Psychology (PsyD) degree. A PhD in psychology is a research degree that culminates in a comprehensive exam and a dissertation based on original research. In clinical, counseling, school, or health service settings, students usually complete a one-year internship as part of the doctoral program. The PsyD is a clinical degree and often is based on practical work and examinations rather than a dissertation. In most states, practicing psychology or using the title of "psychologist" requires licensure or certification. The American Board of Professional Psychology awards specialty certification in 13 areas of psychology, such as clinical health, couple and family, psychoanalysis, or rehabilitation. Although board certification is not required for most psychologists, it can demonstrate professional expertise in a specialty area. Some hospitals and clinics do require certification. In those cases, candidates must have a doctoral degree in psychology, a state license or certification, and any additional criteria of the specialty field. In May 2015, the median annual wage of psychologists was $72,580. Overall employment of psychologists is expected to grow 30% from 2014 to 2024 (BLS, 2013l).

Podiatrists

Podiatrists provide medical and surgical care for people suffering from foot, ankle, and lower leg problems. They diagnose illnesses, treat injuries, and perform surgery. Podiatrists must have a Doctor of Podiatric Medicine (DPM) degree, which is a four-year degree after earning a bachelor's degree. Admission to DPM programs usually also requires taking the Medical College Admission Test (MCAT). In 2011, there were nine colleges of podiatric medicine in the United States. The 2015 median annual wage of podiatrists was $119,340. Employment of podiatrists is expected to increase 14% from 2014 to 2024 (BLS, 2016m).

ALLIED HEALTH PROFESSIONALS

In the early 1900s, healthcare providers consisted of physicians, nurses, pharmacists, and optometrists. As the healthcare industry evolved with increased use of technology and sophisticated interventions, increased time demands were placed on these healthcare providers. As a result, a broader spectrum of healthcare professionals with skills that complemented these primary healthcare providers evolved. These **allied health professionals** assist physicians and nurses in providing care to their patients. The impact of technology has increased the number of different specialties available. They can be divided into four main categories: laboratory technologists and technicians, therapeutic science practitioners, behavioral scientists, and support services (The Association of Schools of Allied Health Professionals [ASAHP], 2016).

Laboratory or clinical laboratory technologists and technicians have a major role in diagnosing disease, assessing the impact of interventions, and applying highly technical procedures. Examples of this category include radiologic technology and nuclear medicine technology. Therapeutic science practitioners focus on the rehabilitation of patients with diseases and injuries. Examples of this category include physical therapists, radiation therapists, respiratory therapists, dieticians, and dental hygienists.

Behavioral scientists such as social workers and rehabilitation counselors provide social, psychological, and community and patient educational activities (Sultz & Young, 2006). This chapter cannot list all allied health professionals but a list of those allied health careers that have accredited education programs will be discussed.

The **Commission on Accreditation of Allied Health Education Programs (CAAHEP)** accredits 2,000 U.S. programs that offer allied health specialties. This section will provide a brief summary of the different allied healthcare jobs that contribute to providing quality health care. This information was obtained from the CAAHEP website and the Bureau of Labor Statistics (CAAHEP, 2016a).

Anesthesiologist Assistant

Under the direction of an anesthesiologist and as a team member of the anesthesia care component of surgical procedures, this specialty physician assistant helps with implementing an anesthesia care plan. Activities would include performing presurgical and surgical tasks and might also include assistance with administrative and educational activities. The **anesthesiologist assistant (AA)** primarily is employed by medical centers. In 2015, median salaries ranged from $110,000 to $120,000 for 40 hours per week. Acceptance into an AA educational program requires an undergraduate premedical education, which consists of science courses such as biology, chemistry, physics, and mathematics. The AA program length of duration is 24–27 months (CAAHEP, 2016b).

Cardiovascular Technologist

At the request of a physician, **cardiovascular technologists** perform diagnostic examinations for cardiovascular issues. Basically, they assist physicians in treating cardiac (heart) and peripheral vascular (blood vessels) problems. They also may review and or record clinical data, perform procedures, and obtain data for physician review. They may provide services in any medical setting but are primarily in hospitals. They also operate

and maintain testing equipment and may explain test procedures. These allied health professionals generally work a 5-day, 40-hour week that may include weekends. In 2015, their wages averaged $53,050. Employment of cardiovascular technologists and technicians is expected to increase by 26% through the year 2024. A high school diploma or qualifications in a clinically related allied position is required to enter an education program which may last from one to four years depending on the background of the student (CAAHEP, 2016c).

Cytotechnologist

Cytology is the study of the how cells function and their structure. **Cytotechnologists**, a category of clinical laboratory technologists, are specialists who collaborate with pathologists to evaluate cellular material. This material is used by pathologists to diagnose diseases such as cancer and other diseases. Cytotechnologists prepare slides of body cells and examine these cells microscopically for abnormalities that may signal the beginning of a cancerous growth. Most cytotechnologists work in hospitals. In 2015, cytotechnologists averaged $65,000. In order to enter into their educational program, applicants should have a background in the biological sciences. Applicants must have an undergraduate degree in order to quality for national certification (CAAHEP, 2016d).

Diagnostic Medical Sonographer

Under the supervision of a physician, this specialist provides patient services using medical ultrasound, which photographs internal structures. **Sonography** uses sound waves to generate images of the body for the assessment and diagnosis of various medical conditions. Sonography commonly is associated with obstetrics and the use of ultrasound imaging during pregnancy. This specialist gathers data to assist with disease management in a variety of medical facilities including hospitals, clinics, and private practices. They may assist with patient education. In addition to working directly with patients, **diagnostic medical sonographers** keep patient records. They also may prepare work schedules, evaluate equipment purchases, or manage a sonography or imaging department. Diagnostic medical sonographers may specialize in obstetric and gynecologic sonography (the female reproductive system), abdominal sonography (the liver, kidneys, gallbladder, spleen, and pancreas), neurosonography (the brain), breast sonography, vascular sonography, or cardiac sonography.

Sonographers work approximately 40 hours per week but may have weekend and evening hours. In 2015, the median salaries averaged $67,530. Colleges and universities offer formal training in both two- and four-year programs, culminating in an associate or a bachelor's degree. Applicants to a one-year educational program must have relevant clinical experience. Some two-year programs, which are the most prevalent, will accept high school graduates with an education in basic sciences (CAAHEP, 2016e).

Emergency Medical Technician and Paramedic

People who are ill, have had an accident, or have been wounded often depend on the competent care of by an **emergency medical technician (EMT)** or an **emergency medical technician–paramedic (EMT–P)**. All EMT and paramedic patients require immediate medical attention. EMTs and paramedics provide this vital service as they care for and transport the sick or injured to a medical facility for appropriate medical care.

In general, EMTs and EMT-paramedics (EMT–Ps) provide emergency medical assistance needed as a result of an accident or illness that has occurred outside the medical setting. EMTs and paramedics work under guidelines approved by the physician medical director of a healthcare organization to assess and manage medical emergencies. They are trained to provide lifesaving measures. EMTs provide basic life support and EMT-Ps provide advanced life-support measures. They may be employed by an ambulance company, fire department, public emergency medical services company, hospital, or a combination thereof. They may be paid or be volunteers from the community. Both EMTs and EMT–Ps must be proficient in cardiopulmonary resuscitation

(CPR). They learn the basics of different types of medical emergencies. EMs perform more sophisticated procedures. They also receive extensive training in patient assessment. The work is not only physically demanding but can also be stressful, sometimes involving life or death situations. In 2015, their average salaries were approximately $31,700.

Firefighters also may be trained as EMTs. EMT training is offered at community colleges, technical schools, hospitals, and academies. EMTs require 40 hours of training, whereas EMT–Ps require 200–400 hours of training. Applicants for the programs are expected to have a high school diploma or the equivalent. The National Registry of Emergency Medical Technicians (NREMT) certifies emergency medical service providers at five levels: First Responder, EMT–Basic, EMT–Intermediate (which has two levels called 1985 and 1999), and Paramedic. All 50 states require certification for each of the EMT levels (CAAHEP, 2016f).

Exercise Physiologists

Exercise physiologists assess, design, and manage individual exercise programs for both healthy and unhealthy individuals. Clinical exercise physiologists work with a physician when applying programs for patients that have demonstrated a therapeutic benefit for the patient. In 2015, their median wages, depending on geographic area and experience, was $43,000. These allied health professionals may work with fitness trainers, exercise science professionals, or physicians in cardiac rehabilitation in hospital settings. Applicants for their two-year program should have an undergraduate degree in exercise science (CAAHEP, 2016g).

Medical Assistant

Supervised by physicians, **medical assistants** must have the ability to multitask. More than 60% of medical assistants work in medical offices and clinics. They perform both administrative and clinical duties. Medical assistants are employed by physicians more than any other allied health assistant. In 2015, their median salary was $30,000.

Their educational program consists of an associate degree, certificate, or diploma program (CAA-HEP, 2016h).

Medical Illustrator

Medical illustrators are trained artists that portray visually scientific information to teach both the professionals and the public about medical issues. They may work digitally or traditionally to create images of human anatomy and surgical procedures as well as three-dimensional models and animations. Medical illustrators may be self-employed, work for pharmaceutical companies or advertising agencies, or be employed by medical schools. In 2015, median salaries were $62,000. Applicants must have an undergraduate degree with a focus on art and premedical education. The program is two years and results in a master's degree (CAAHEP, 2016i).

Orthotist and Prosthetist

These specialists address neuromuscular/skeletal issues and develop a plan and a device to rectify any issues. The orthotist develops devices called "othoses" that focus on the limbs and spines of individuals to increase function. The prosthetist designs "prostheses" or devices for patients who have limb amputations to replace the limb function. Most of these allied health professionals work in hospitals, clinics, colleges, and medical schools. In 2015, their median salaries were $70,000. Their education may be achieved through a four-year program or a certificate program that varies from six months to two years. Applicants for the four-year program should have a high school diploma. Applicants for the certificate programs must have a four-year degree (CAAHEP, 2016j).

Perfusionist

A perfusionist operates equipment to support or replace a patient's circulatory or respiratory function. Perfusion involves advance life-support techniques. Perfusionists may be responsible for administering blood byproducts or anesthetic products during a surgical procedure. They may be employed by hospitals, surgeons, or group practices. The 2015 median salary range was $65,000. The prerequisites for these educational programs vary depending on the length of the program, which can range from one to four years, depending on the individual's experience (CAAHEP, 2016k).

Personal Fitness Trainer

Personal fitness trainers are familiar with different forms of exercise. They have a variety of clients who they serve one-on-one or in a group. They may work with exercise science professionals or physiologists in corporate, clinical, commercial fitness, country clubs, or wellness centers. In 2015, their median pay was $32,000. Their educational programs consist of a one-year certificate or a two-year associate degree program. Applicants must have a high school diploma or equivalent for program entry (CAAHEP, 2016l).

Polysomnographic Technologist

Polysomnographic technologists perform sleep tests and work with physicians to provide diagnoses of sleep disorders. They monitor brain waves, eye movements, and other physiological activity during sleep; analyze this information; and provide it to the patient's physician. They work in sleep disorder centers that may be affiliated with a hospital or operate independently. In 2015, their median salary was $55,500. Applicants for their education programs should have a high school diploma or equivalent. Their educational program can range from a two-year associate degree to a one-year certificate program (CAAHEP, 2016m).

Recreational Therapist

Recreational therapists provide individualized and group recreational therapy for individuals experiencing limitations in life activities as a result of a disabling condition, illness or disease, aging, and/or developmental factors. Recreational therapists use a variety of educational, behavioral, recreational, and activity-oriented strategies with clients to enhance functional performance and improve positive lifestyle behaviors designed to increase independence, effective community participation, and well-being.

Recreational therapists work in clinical settings, such as hospitals, psychiatric or skilled nursing facilities, substance abuse programs, and rehabilitation centers. Recreational therapists treat and rehabilitate individuals with specific medical, social, and behavioral problems, usually in cooperation with physicians; nurses; psychologists; social workers; and speech, physical, and occupational therapists.

A bachelor's degree with a major in recreational therapy or therapeutic recreation, or a major in recreation with a specialization in recreational therapy or therapeutic recreation, is required for national certification. Specific requirements can be obtained from the National Council for Therapeutic Recreation Certification. Job growth is expected to increase 15% by 2018 due to the aging of the U.S. population. Median pay for 2015 for certified therapists was $51,000 (CAAHEP, 2016n).

Transfusion Medicine Specialist/Specialists in Blood Banking Technology

Transfusion medicine specialists or specialists in blood bank (SBB) technology provide routine and specialized tests for blood donor centers, transfusion centers, laboratories, and research centers. In 2015, the median salary was $55,000. Applicants for their educational programs must be certified in medical technology and have an undergraduate degree from an accredited educational institution. If they are not certified, they must have a degree from an accredited institution with a major in a biological or physical science and have appropriate work experience. This allied health program ranges from one to two years (CAAHEP, 2013o).

Surgical Assistant

A **surgical assistant** is a specialized physician's assistant. The main goal of surgical assistants is to ensure the surgeon has safe and sterile environment in which to perform. They determine the appropriate equipment for the procedure, select radiographs for a surgeon's reference, assist in moving the patient, confirm procedures with the surgeon, and assist with the procedure as directed

by the surgeon. Their educational programs range from 10 to 22 months. In 2015, median annual pay was $75,000. Applicants must have a bachelor of science or higher or an associate degree in an allied health field with three years of recent experience, current CPR/basic life support certification, acceptable health and immunization records, and computer literacy (CAAHEP, 2016p).

Surgeon Technologist

Surgeon technologists are key team members of medical practitioners who provide surgery. They are responsible for preparing the operating room by equipping the room with the appropriate sterile supplies and verifying the equipment is working properly. Prior to surgery, they also interact with the patient to ensure they are comfortable, monitor their vital signs, and review patient charts. During surgery, they are responsible for ensuring all surgery team members maintain a sterile environment and providing instruments to the surgeons. Post surgery, they prepare the room for the next patient. They also may provide follow-up care in the postoperative room. They work in hospitals, outpatient settings, or may be self-employed. In 2015, the median pay was $44,000 per year. Applicants for their educational programs must have a high school diploma or equivalent. The programs range from 12 to 24 months (CAAHEP, 2016q).

NON-CAAHEP ALLIED HEALTH PROFESSIONALS

The following job descriptions are important allied health professionals but are not a CAAHEP program.

Certified Nursing Assistants or Aides

Certified nursing assistants (CNAs) are unlicensed patient attendants who work under the supervision of physicians and nurses. They answer patient call bells that need their service; assist patients with personal hygiene, changing beds, ordering their meals; and assist patients with their ADLs. Most CNAs are employed by nursing care facilities. There are approximately 1.5 million CNAs in the healthcare industry. They are required to receive 75 hours of training and are required to pass a competency examination. Their average pay is $25,000. Although CNAs provide needed services to the patient, they are often overlooked for pay and advancement, creating a high turnover in the field (BLS, 2016f).

Pharmacy Technicians

Pharmacy technicians typically do the following:

- Take from customers or health professionals the information needed to fill a prescription
- Count tablets and measure amounts of other medication for prescriptions
- Compound or mix medications, such as preparing ointments
- Package and label prescriptions
- Accept payment for prescriptions and process insurance claims
- Do routine pharmacy tasks, such as answering phone calls from customers

Many pharmacy technicians learn how to perform their duties through on-the-job training. Others attend postsecondary education programs in pharmacy technology at vocational schools or community colleges, which award certificates. These programs typically last one year or less and cover a variety of subjects, such as arithmetic used in pharmacies, recordkeeping, ways of dispensing medications, and pharmacy law and ethics. Technicians also learn the names, actions, uses, and doses of medications. Many training programs include internships, in which students get hands-on experience in a pharmacy. The median annual wage of pharmacy technicians was $30,410 in 2015, and employment is expected to grow by 9% from 2014 to 2024 (BLS, 2016n).

Psychiatric Technicians and Aides

Psychiatric technicians and aides care for people who have mental illness and developmental disabilities. The two occupations are related, but technicians typically provide therapeutic care, and aides help patients in their daily activities. Psychiatric technicians typically enter the occupation with a postsecondary certificate. Programs

in psychiatric or mental health technology are commonly offered by community colleges and technical schools. Psychiatric technician programs include courses in biology, psychology, and counseling. The programs also may include supervised work experience or cooperative programs, in which students gain academic credit for structured work experience. The median annual wage of psychiatric technicians was $28,710 in 2015. Employment of psychiatric technicians is expected to increase 5% from 2014 to 2024 (BLS, 2016o).

Respiratory Therapist

There are two levels of **respiratory therapists**: the certified respiratory therapist and registered respiratory therapist. The entry-level respiratory therapist performs basic respiratory care procedures under the supervision of a physician or an advance-level therapist. They review patient data, including tests and previous medical history; implement and monitor any respiratory therapy under the supervision of a physician; and may be involved in the home care of a patient. Entry-level therapists are employed in hospitals, nursing care facilities, clinics, sleep labs, and home care organizations. In 2015, the median pay was $57,790. Applicants are required to have a high school degree or equivalent. Their educational program consists of a two-year program leading to an associate's degree. An advanced-level respiratory therapist participates in clinical decision making such as diagnosing lung and breathing disorders, recommending treatment methods, providing patient education, and developing and recommending care plans in collaboration with a physician. Becoming an advanced-level therapist can be achieved through increased education such as a bachelor's or master's degree (BLS, 2016p).

Health Services Administrators

It is important to discuss the importance of **health services administrators** and their role in health care. They can be found at all levels of a healthcare organization. They may manage hospitals, clinics, nursing homes, community health centers, and other types of healthcare facilities. At the top of the organization, they are responsible for strategic planning and the overall success of the organization. They are responsible for financial, clinical, and operational outcomes of an organization. Midlevel administrators also play a leadership role in departments and are responsible for managing their area of responsibility. They may manage departments or individual programs. Administrators at all levels work with top administration to achieve organizational goals. As healthcare costs continue to increase, it is important that health services administrators focus on efficiency and effectiveness at all levels of management (Shi & Singh, 2008).

Health services administration is taught at both the undergraduate and master's levels. The most common undergraduate degree is a degree in healthcare administration, although most generalist manager positions require a master's degree. Undergraduate degrees may be acceptable for entry-level management positions. Salaries vary by administration level. In 2015, the median pay was $94,500. Approximately 40% of hospitals employ health services administrators.

The most common master's degrees are the Master of Health Services Administration (MHA), Master of Business Administration (MBA) with a healthcare emphasis, or a Master of Public Health (MPH). The MHA or MBA degree provides a more business-oriented education that health administrators need for managing healthcare organizations. However, having an MPH degree also provides insight into the importance of public health as an integral component of our healthcare system (BLS, 2016q).

Home Health and Personal Care Aides

Home health and personal care aides help people who are disabled, chronically ill, or cognitively impaired, as well as older adults who may need assistance. They assist with activities such as bathing and dressing, and they provide services such as light housekeeping. In some states, home health aides may be able to give a client medication or check the client's vital signs under the direction of a nurse or other healthcare practitioner. Home health and personal care aides work most often in a client's home or small group homes. There is no formal education required; however, if they work in a certified home health agency or hospice facility, they must receive formal training. The 2015 median pay was $21,920. The projected growth of this occupation between 2014 and 2024 is nearly 38% due to the increased popularity of home health care (BLS, 2016r).

CONCLUSION

Healthcare personnel represent one of the largest labor forces in the United States. As a healthcare consumer and potential employee of the healthcare industry, this chapter provided an overview of the different types of employees in the healthcare industry. Some of them require many years of education; however, some of these positions can be achieved through one- to two-year programs. There are more than 200 occupations and professions among the 13 million healthcare workers (Sultz & Young, 2006). The healthcare industry will continue to progress as U.S. trends in demographics, disease, and public health pattern change, and cost and efficiency issues, insurance issues, technological influences, and economic factors continue to evolve. More occupations and professions will develop as a result of these trends. An example of a new job is the health navigator. The major trend that will affect the healthcare industry is the aging of the U.S. population. The BLS predicts that half of the next decades' fastest-growing jobs will be in the healthcare industry. The Affordable Care Act will have an impact on the continued positive growth for this industry. With the growing popularity of the health navigator, the Department of Labor will eventually develop a navigator category as part of the Occupational Outlook Handbook.

Summary

© Jim Barber/Shutterstock

Vocabulary

Activities of daily living (ADLs)
Advanced practice nurse (APN)
Allied health professionals
Allopathic approach
Anesthesiologist assistant (AA)
Associate degree in nursing (ADN)
Bachelor of Science in Nursing (BSN)
Board certifying or credentialing examination
Cardiovascular technologist
Certified nursing assistants (CNAs)
Certified nurse–midwives (CNMs)
Certified midwives (CMs)
Chiropractors
Commission on Accreditation of Allied Health
    Education Programs (CAAHEP)
Community health workers
Cytotechnologists
Dental assistants
Dental hygienists
Dentists
Diagnostic medical sonographer
Doctor of Medicine (MD)
Doctor of Osteopathic Medicine (DO)
Emergency medical technician (EMT)
Emergency medical technician–paramedic
    (EMT–P)
Exercise physiologists
Generalists
Geographic maldistribution
Health services administrator
Holistic approach
Home health and personal care aides
Hospitalist
Licensed practical nurse (LPN)
Licensed vocational nurse (LVN)

Medical assistant
Medical illustrator
Midlevel practitioners
National Practitioner Data Bank
Nonphysician practitioner (NPP)
Nurse practitioner (NP)
Optometrists
Orthotist
Perfusionists
Personal fitness trainer
Pharmacists
Pharmacy technician
Physician assistant (PA)
Physician Compare website
Physician extender
Podiatrists
Polysomnographic technologist
Primary care
Prosthetist
Psychiatric technicians and aides
Psychologists
Quaternary care
Recreational therapists
Registered nurse (RN)
Respiratory therapist
Secondary care
Sonography
Specialists
Specialty care
Specialty maldistribution
Surgeon technologist
Surgical assistant
Tertiary care
Transfusion medicine specialist

References

American Academy of Nurse Practitioners (AANP). (2016). http://www.aanp.org/AANPCMS2/AboutAANP.

American Association of Colleges of Nursing (AACN). (2016). Nursing shortage. http://www.aacn.nche.edu/media-relations/fact-sheets/nursing-shortage.

American College of Nurse-Midwives (ACNM). (2016). The credentials CNM and CM.(2013). http://www.midwife.org/The-Credential-CNM-and-CM.

American Medical Association (AMA). (2016). National Practitioner Data Bank. http://www.ama-assn.org/ama/pub/physician-resources/legal-topics/business-management-topics/national-practitioner-data-bank.page.

Association of American Medical Colleges (AAMC). (2012). Analysis in brief: Estimating the number and characteristics of hospitalist physicians in the U.S. and their possible workforce implications. https://www.aamc.org/download/300620/data/aibvol12_no3-hospitalist.pdf.

Association of Schools of Allied Health Professionals (ASAHP). (2016). Allied health professionals. http://www.asahp.org/.

Bureau of Labor Statistics (BLS). (2016a). Occupational outlook handbook: Health educators and community health workers. http://www.bls.gov/ooh/community-and-social-service/health-educators.htm.

BLS. (2016b). Occupational outlook handbook: Physicians and surgeons: What physicians and surgeons do. http://www.bls.gov/ooh/healthcare/physicians-and-surgeons.htm#tab-2.

BLS. (2016c). Occupational outlook handbook: Physicians and surgeons: Pay. http://www.bls.gov/ooh/healthcare/physicians-and-surgeons.htm#tab-5.

BLS. (2016d). Occupational outlook handbook: Physician assistants. http://www.bls.gov/ooh/healthcare/physician-assistants.htm.

BLS. (2016e). Occupational outlook handbook: Licensed practical nurses and licensed vocational nurses. http://www.bls.gov/ooh/healthcare/licensed-practical-and-licensed-vocational-nurses.htm.

BLS. (2016e). Occupational outlook handbook: Registered nurses. http://www.bls.gov/ooh/healthcare/registered-nurses.htm.

BLS. (2016f). Occupational outlook handbook: Dentists. http://www.bls.gov/ooh/healthcare/dentists.htm.

BLS (2016g) Occupational outlook handbook: Nursing assistants and orderlies. http://www.bls.gov/ooh/healthcare/nursing-assistants.htm.

BLS. (2016h). Occupational outlook handbook: Dental assistants. http://www.bls.gov/ooh/Healthcare/Dental-assistants.htm.

BLS. (2016i). Occupational outlook handbook: Dental hygienists. http://www.bls.gov/ooh/healthcare/dental-hygienists.htm.

BLS. (2016j). Occupational outlook handbook: Pharmacists. http://www.bls.gov/ooh/Healthcare/Pharmacists.htm.

BLS. (2016k). Occupational outlook handbook: Chiropractors. http://www.bls.gov/ooh/healthcare/chiropractors.htm.

BLS. (2016l). Occupational outlook handbook: Optometrists. http://www.bls.gov/ooh/healthcare/optometrists.htm.

BLS. (2016m). Occupational outlook handbook: Psychologists. http://www.bls.gov/ooh/Life-Physical-and-Social-Science/Psychologists.htm.

BLS. (2016n). Occupational outlook handbook: Podiatrists. http://www.bls.gov/ooh/healthcare/podiatrists.htm.

BLS. (2016o). Occupational outlook handbook: Pharmacy technicians. http://www.bls.gov/ooh/healthcare/pharmacy-technicians.htm.

BLS. (2016p). Occupational outlook handbook: Psychiatric technicians and aides. http://www.bls.gov/ooh/healthcare/psychiatric-technicians-and-aides.htm.

BLS. (2016q). Occupational outlook handbook: Respiratory therapists. http://www.bls.gov/ooh/healthcare/respiratory-therapists.htm.

BLS. (2016r). Occupational outlook handbook: Medical and health services managers. http://www.bls.gov/ooh/Management/Medical-and-health-services-managers.htm.

BLS. (2016s). Occupational outlook handbook: Home healthcare aides. http://www.bls.gov/ooh/healthcare/home-health-aides.htm.

Casselman, B. (2013, April 25). The myth of the Nursing Shortage. http://blogs.wsj.com/economics/2013/04/25/the-myth-of-the-nursing-shortage/

Centers for Disease Control and Prevention (CDC). (2016). Workplace safety & health topics: Healthcare workers. http://www.cdc.gov/niosh/topics/healthcare/.

Centers for Medicare & Medicaid Services (CMS). (2016). About physician compare. http://www.medicare.gov/physiciancompare/staticpages/aboutphysiciancompare/about.html.

Commission on Accreditation of Allied Health Education Programs (CAAHEP). (2016a). About CAAHEP. http://www.caahep.org/Content.aspx?ID=63.

CAAHEP. (2016b). Anesthesiologist assistant. http://www.caahep.org/Content.aspx?ID=20.

CAAHEP. (2016c). Cardiovascular technology. http://www.caahep.org/Content.aspx?ID=21.

CAAHEP. (2016d). Cytotechnology. http://www.caahep.org/Content.aspx?ID=22.

CAAHEP. (2016e). Diagnostic medical sonography. http://www.caahep.org/Content.aspx?ID=23.

CAAHEP. (2016f). Emergency medicine technician–paramedic. http://www.caahep.org/Content.aspx?ID=39.

CAAHEP. (2016g). Exercise physiology. http://www.caahep.org/Content.aspx?ID=40.

CAAHEP. (2016h). Medical assisting. http://www.caahep.org/Content.aspx?ID=43.

CAAHEP. (2016i). Medical illustration. http://www.caahep.org/Content.aspx?ID=44.

CAAHEP. (2016j). Orthotist/prosthetist. http://www.caahep.org/Content.aspx?ID=65.

CAAHEP. (2016k). Perfusion. http://www.caahep.org/Content.aspx?ID=46

CAAHEP. (2016l). Personal fitness training. http://www.caahep.org/Content.aspx?ID=47.

CAAHEP. (2016m). Polysomnographic technology. http://www.caahep.org/Content.aspx?ID=48.

CAAHEP. (2016n). Recreational therapy. http://www.caahep.org/Content.aspx?ID=61.

CAAHEP. (2016o). Specialist in blood bank technology/transfusion medicine. http://www.caahep.org/Content.aspx?ID=51.

CAAHEP. (2016p). Surgical assisting. http://www.caahep.org/Content.aspx?ID=52.

CAAHEP. (2016q). Surgical technology. http://www.caahep.org/Content.aspx?ID=53.

Jonas, S. (2003). *An introduction to the U.S. health care system*. New York, NY: Springer.

Lowery, A., & Pear, R. (2012). Doctor shortage likely to worsen with health law. http://www.nytimes.com/2012/07/29/health/policy/too-few-doctors-in-many-us-communities.html?_r=0&pagewanted=print.

Petterson, S., Liaw, W., Phillips, R., Rabin, D., Meyers, D., & Bazemore, A. (2012). Projecting U.S primary care physician workforce needs: 2010–2015. *Annals of Family Medicine, 10*(6): 503–509.

Pointer, D., Williams, S., Isaacs, S., & Knickman, J. (2007). *Introduction to health care*. New York, NY: Wiley & Sons.

Shi, L., & Singh, D. (2008). *An introduction to health care in America: A systems approach*. Sudbury, MA: Jones and Bartlett Publishers.

Sultz, H., & Young, K. (2006). *Health care USA*. Sudbury, MA: Jones and Bartlett Publishers.

Torrey, T. (2011). Levels of medical care: Primary, secondary, tertiary and quaternary care. http://patients.about.com/od/moreproviders beyonddocs/a/Stages-Of-Care-Primary-Secondary-Tertiary-And-Quaternary-Care.htm.

Student Activity 7-1

In Your Own Words

Based on this chapter, please provide an explanation of the following concepts in your own words. DO NOT RECITE the text.

Allopathic approach

Board certifying or credentialing examination

Certified midwives

Doctor of Medicine

Doctor of Osteopathic Medicine

Emergency medical technician

Psychologist

Respiratory therapist

Transfusion medicine specialist

Student Activity 7-2

Real-Life Applications: Case Scenario One

You have heard that the healthcare industry is a growing industry for employment. You are unsure of the types of careers available to you. You heard there is a new career, a health navigator, which you had not heard of before.

Activity

Perform an Internet search for information on becoming a health navigator. Report back to the class on your findings.

Case Scenario Two

Your friend has decided to research the area of allied health professionals as an opportunity for a career in healthcare and has provided the information here regarding two opportunities in this area. He will provide (1) educational requirements, (2) job responsibilities, and (3) average wages.

Activity

Your friend has decided to visit the CAAHEP website to research two accredited allied health professional jobs that are of interest to him and has added his research below.

Allied Health Professionals

Surgical assistant
Transfusion medical specialist

Case Scenario Three

You just moved to a rural community from an urban community and you want to establish relationships with physicians at your new home. You were surprised to find out how few choices you have. You decide to investigate why this is occurring.

Activity

Look on the Internet to find out information on geographic maldistribution. Write up a report for your family and friends regarding this major issue.

Case Scenario Four

You have just been introduced to the different types of health care typically provided by physicians and other healthcare providers.

Activity

You ask your older sister, who is in medical school, to explain the differences and provide examples of primary, secondary, tertiary, and quaternary care.

Student Activity 7-3

Internet Exercises

- Visit each of the websites here.
- Name the organization.
- Locate its mission statement on the website.
- Provide a brief overview of the activities of the organization.
- How does this organization participate in the U.S. healthcare system?

Websites
http://www.aanp.org

Organization Name
Mission Statement
Overview of Activities
Importance of Organization to U.S. Health Care

http://www.asahp.org

Organization Name
Mission Statement
Overview of Activities
Importance of Organization to U.S. Health Care

http://www.caahep.org

Organization Name
Mission Statement

Overview of Activities
Importance of Organization to U.S. Health Care

http://www.aamc.org

Organization Name
Mission Statement
Overview of Activities
Importance of Organization to U.S. Health Care

http://bhpr.hrsa.gov

Organization Name
Mission Statement
Overview of Activities
Importance of Organization to U.S. Health Care

http://www.aapa.org

Organization Name
Mission Statement
Overview of Activities
Importance of Organization to U.S. Health Care

Student Activity 7-4
Discussion Questions
The following are suggested discussion questions for this chapter.

1. Which of the allied health professional jobs would you like to choose as a career and why?
2. What is a physician extender? Would you as a patient use a physician extender? Defend your decision.
3. What is geographic maldistribution? Do you think it is a problem?
4. What is specialty maldistribution?
5. Discuss the health navigator job and the different areas in health care that the navigator can work. Which one would you choose and why?

Student Activity 7-5
Current Events
Perform an Internet search and find a current events topic that relates to this chapter. Provide a summary of the article and the link to the article and explain how the article relates to the chapter.

CHAPTER **8**

Navigating Information Technology Impact on Health Care

LEARNING OBJECTIVES

The student will be able to:

- Define and discuss health information technology, health information systems, and health/medical informatics.
- Evaluate the importance of the Office of the National Coordinator for Health Information Technology to health care.
- Assess the importance of the National eHealth Collaborative to health information technology policy.
- Discuss the importance of Dr. Octo Barnett to healthcare technology.
- Evaluate the impact of information technology on healthcare stakeholders.
- Discuss the difference between an EMR and an EHR.

DID YOU KNOW THAT?

- Both President Bush and President Obama have supported the initiative for electronic health records.
- E-prescribing is a form of a clinical decision support system
- The average cost to install an EHR software system in a physician's office is $55,000.
- A new product called electronic aspirin is an implant on the side of the head that is normally affected by a headache.
- The Food and Drug Administration (FDA) has approved a medical robot that can make rounds, checking on patients in different rooms.
- The Microsoft HealthVault, Microsoft's version of an electronic patient record, now has a feature that allows a patient to preregister for hospital procedures and admissions.

INTRODUCTION

The term **informatics** refers to the science of computer application to data in different industries. The terms **health informatics** or **medical informatics** refer to the science of computer application that supports clinical and research data in different areas of health care. It is a methodology of how the healthcare industry thinks about patients and how their treatments are defined and evolved. For example, **imaging informatics** applies computer technology to organs and tissue (Coiera, 2003; Open Clinical, 2016). **Health information systems** are systems that store, transmit, collect, and retrieve these data (Anderson, Rice, & Kominski, 2007). The goal of **health information technology (HIT)** is to manage the health data that can be used by patients/consumers, insurance companies, healthcare providers, healthcare administrators, and any stakeholder that has an interest in health care (Goldstein & Blumenthal, 2008).

HIT affects every aspect of the healthcare industry. All of the stakeholders in the healthcare industry use HIT. **Information technology (IT)** has had a tremendous impact on the healthcare industry because it allows faster documentation of every transaction. When an industry focuses on saving lives, it is important that all activities have a written document that describes the activity. Computerization of documentation has increased the management efficiency and accuracy of healthcare data. The focus of HIT is the national implementation of an electronic patient record. Both Presidents Bush and Obama have supported this initiative.

This is the foundation of many IT systems because it will enable different systems to share patient information, which will increase the quality and efficiency of health care. This chapter will discuss the history of IT, different applications of IT health care, the status of electronic health records and barriers for their national implementation, and the role of the health navigator in technology.

ROLE OF THE HEALTH NAVIGATOR

Having a health navigator for information technology can be very invaluable to a patient. With the increased use of electronic health records, patient portals, and telemedicine, many older patients may feel confused. Although the number of elderly individuals who use technology have increased, much of that population still feels uncomfortable with information technology. Many patients do not keep copies of their medical records. They often are confused about their medications. Having access to electronic copies of their records and records of their medications could be very beneficial to patients. An IT health navigator would need to be very familiar with electronic health record use as well as be comfortable with technology in general. Microsoft has developed an electronic patient record system that allows individuals to keep their own medical records electronically. An IT Health Navigator could be instrumental with this type of electronic record keeping and increase the patient's health technology literacy.

HISTORY OF INFORMATION TECHNOLOGY IN THE HEALTHCARE INDUSTRY

The first widespread use of computers in the healthcare industry occurred in the 1960s as a result of the implementation of Medicaid and Medicare. Healthcare providers were inundated with forms to complete for both programs. In order to receive reimbursement from these programs, services needed to be tracked and forms needed to be completed and submitted. Therefore, computers were used to assist with the financial management of these programs (Buchbinder & Shanks, 2007). As a result of computer integration, more healthcare providers recognized the efficiency of computers to manage programs. Hospitals particularly recognized the efficiency of electronic billing. During the 1960s, hospitals developed their own computer systems that housed their financial information. The hospitals were responsible for the maintenance of these systems. These systems, which were large mainframe systems, required a large staff to maintain their operations. All of the hospitals' data was stored on these mainframe computers. Computer programs were developed by the hospitals to extract data reports. These mainframe computers were very expensive. They eventually were replaced in the 1970s with minicomputers, which were more efficient, more cost-effective, and easier to maintain. These minicomputers were connected to a main computer that stored all of the data. They also were used to enter information. Eventually, specific computer systems were developed for laboratories and clinics. It is important to mention Dr. G. Octo Barnett, who is a Professor of Medicine at Harvard Medical School and the senior director at the Laboratory of Computer Science at Massachusetts General Hospital (Appleby, 2008). He developed the first computer program for healthcare applications, called MUMPS, in 1964, which became the basis of very sophisticated programs used today.

During the 1980s and 1990s, the development and widespread use of personal computers (PCs) revolutionized information systems and technology. PCs were not reliant on a main computer for analyses. They were able to generate reports that are more sophisticated. PCs often were linked as a network to share information among different departments in hospitals. The development of the PC also enabled more computerization of physician practices. In the 2000s, the application of IT has increased in the healthcare industry with cutting-edge new applications such as electronic aspirin, needle-free insulin injections, and the national implementation of electronic health information.

The establishment of a **chief information officer (CIO)** in healthcare organizations emphasized how important information systems and technology had become to healthcare organizations. The U.S. healthcare system has been the world leader for developing cutting-edge technology in health care. It has impacted how diagnostic procedures are performed, how data is collected and disseminated, how medicine is delivered, how providers treat their patients, and how surgeries are performed. There are several healthcare stakeholders that are affected by technology. Consumers, providers, employers, researchers, all governmental levels, nonprofit and for-profit healthcare organizations, and insurance payers all have been affected by technology (eJobDescription, 2016). Technological advances have been blamed, in part, for the continued rise of healthcare expenditures, but the results of technological advances cannot be disputed.

ELECTRONIC HEALTH RDS

History

The Institute of Medicine (IOM) has published a series of reports over the past several years that focus on improving the quality of health care in the United States. In 2001, they published the report *Crossing the Quality Chasm: A New Health System for the 21st Century*, which stresses the importance of improving IT infrastructure. IOM emphasized the importance of an **electronic patient or health record (EHR)** which is an electronic record of patients' medical history. The report also discussed the importance of patient safety by establishing data standards for collecting patient information (IOM, 2001).

In 1991 and 1997, the IOM issued reports that focused on the impact of computer-based patients' records as important technology for improving health care (Vreeman, Taggard, Rhine, & Wornell, 2006). There are two concepts in electronic patient records that are used interchangeably but are different—the **electronic medical record (EMR)** and the **electronic health record (EHR)**. The **National Alliance for Health Information Technology (NAHIT)** defines the EMR as the electronic record of health-related information on an individual that is accumulated from one health system and is utilized by the health organization that is providing patient care. The EHR accumulates patient medical information from many health organizations that have been involved in the patient care. Simply, the EMR is an EHR that can be integrated with other systems (MNT, 2016b). The IOM has been urging the healthcare industry to adopt the electronic patient record but initially costs were too high and the health community did not embrace the recommendation. This discussion will focus on the EHR.

As software costs have declined, more healthcare providers have adopted the use of the EHR system. The EHR system can be used in hospitals, healthcare provider offices, and other types of healthcare facilities. It enables healthcare organizations to monitor patient safety and care. In 2003, the Department of Health and Human Services (DHHS) began to promote the use of HIT, including the use of the EHR. The IOM was asked to identify essential elements for the establishment of an EHR. The IOM broadly defined an EHR to include (IOM, 2016):

- The collection of longitudinal data on a person's health
- Immediate electronic access to this information
- Establishment of a system that provides decision support to ensure the quality, safety, and efficiency of patient care

The Health Information Technology for Economic and Clinical Health (HITECH) Act, which was enacted as part of the 2009 American Recovery and Reinvestment Act, was designed to stimulate the adoption of health information technology in the United States. The Office of the National Coordinator (ONC) for Health Information Technology is responsible for implementing the incentives and penalties program. The ONC has developed "meaningful use" guidelines for physicians and others that will help them receive incentive payments and avoid penalties in the future (DHHS, 2016).

Incentives to Use Electronic Health Records: Meaningful Use

In accordance with the HITECH Act, the Centers for Medicaid and Medicare established incentives to encourage **meaningful use** of EHRs to increase patient care, quality, and safety. Meaningful use, as defined by the CMS, has established core measures that healthcare providers must meet to determine whether they are using the EHR system adequately. For example, providers must have entered one medication using the CPOE for at least 30% of their patients (Centers for Medicare and Medicaid Services [CMS], 2016c). In order to qualify for the incentive program, their EHR system must store data in a structured format that adheres to the standards developed by the Centers for Medicare and Medicaid. The EHR system also must be certified specifically for the incentive program. Both healthcare professionals and hospitals are eligible for the program. They can participate in the Medicare, Medicare Advantage, or Medicaid program but can only receive incentives from one of the programs, and they must choose the program from which they will receive the incentive.

The initial incentive program started in 2011 and concluded in 2016. There will be additional incentive programs extended passed 2016. Eligible healthcare professionals can participate for up to five continuous years and receive up to $44,000 for those years. Providers must demonstrate meaningful use on an annual basis. The last year for provider enrollment is 2014; however, to receive maximum participation, providers must have enrolled by 2012. Effective 2015, providers who do not demonstrate meaningful use will be subject to a fine up to 5% of their incentive amount. Medicaid professionals also can be involved in the meaningful use EHR system. Nearly all states are administering the program. Medicaid incentives are higher than the Medicare program—up to $63,750 over six years. Specified criteria for meaningful use for hospitals was

established to review their EHR systems. As of September 2016, more than 509,484 received payment for participating in the Medicare and Medicaid EHR Incentive Programs (CMS, 2016d).

Through the EHR Incentive Programs' requirements for 2015 through 2017 (Modified Stage 2) and Stage 3, CMS will focus on advanced use of certified EHR technology to support health information exchange and interoperability, advanced quality measurement, and maximizing clinical effectiveness and efficiencies.

Changes to Meaningful Use Requirements

- All providers are required to attest to a single set of objectives and measures, beginning in 2015.
- For all eligible professionals in 2015 through 2017 (Modified Stage 2), there are 10 objectives. For all eligible hospitals and CAHs, there are 9 objectives.
- Beginning on a voluntary basis in 2017 and required beginning in 2018, all providers will attest to Stage 3 objectives and measures (CMS, 2016e).

Benefits of Electronic Health Records

- Several studies have been performed to assess the impact of the EHR on healthcare delivery. Administrators of several healthcare delivery systems reported many benefits to the implementation of an EHR. Many administrators cited the capability of more comprehensive reporting that integrated both clinical and administrative data. An EHR also provides an opportunity to analyze and review patient outcomes because of the standardization of the clinical assessments. Also noted was the development of electronic automated reports that improve the discharge of a patient. The reports also provide an opportunity for the administrator to assess the workload of a department. The EHR was also found to improve operational efficiency and had excellent capabilities to process and store data. Administrators further reported that the computerized documentation takes

30% less time than the previous handwritten notes (Shields et al., 2007).

- Several studies indicated an improvement in interdepartmental communication. The EHR provided aggregate data in the patient records to other departments and the information about the patient was legible. The actual design and implementation of an EHR system contributed to the development of a more interdisciplinary approach to patient care (Ventres & Shah, 2007; Whitman & David, 2007). The implementation of an EHR system led to improved data accuracy because it reduced the need to replicate data. The EHR system also provided a platform for routine data quality assessments, which was important to maintain the accuracy of the EHR data. The EHR system provides an opportunity for future research. The data captured in the database can be used to analyze outcomes and develop baseline data for future research.

BARRIERS TO ELECTRONIC HEALTH RECORD IMPLEMENTATION

From the perspective of a user such as a physician's office, a major issue with EHR implementation is the cost of implementing the system. Software purchases, hardware, network upgrades, training, and computer personnel must be considered in the purchase of the system. The average cost of installation for a practice is $55,000 (Daigrepont & McGrath, 2011).

According to Valerius (2007), migrating from a hard copy system to an electronic system requires several components, including a physician order communication/results retrieval, electronic document/control management, point-of-care charting, electronic physician order entry and prescribing, clinical decision support system, provider patient portals, personal health records, and population health. When an organization implements an electronic system, there are changes in the workflow because much of the process was previously manual. Training is required for both healthcare professionals and staff to utilize the system fully.

When purchasing a system for patient electronic records, some users found that there were equipment or software inadequacies that created a much slower system for processing data. If the system failed, it created frustration for healthcare professionals and administrators. Both of these problems emphasized the need for adequate training for both the providers and staff. Much of the initial training required overtime for the staff. Most of the training lasted approximately four months. Continued training also was required for maintenance of the system (Valerius, 2007).

The critical success factors medical practices need to consider for successful HIT implementation include (Daigrepont & McGrath, 2011):

- Uniform adoption of technology by all participants
- Reliable HIT infrastructure
- A system that is appropriate for the practice
- A plan that details the milestones of the implementation of the system
- Ongoing training of all employees to ensure optimal use of the EHR

One focus of EHR implementation is the development of standards for the type of data collected so it can be exchanged between two systems. However, the American Academy of Pediatrics has indicated that that EHRs lack specific functions for pediatric patients such as child abuse reporting and newborn screening. The AAP has developed additional standards that EHR vendors could integrate into their products (Robeznieks, 2013).

Computerized information systems that are seen in finance, manufacturing, and retail have not achieved the same penetration in health care. EHRs have captured the attention of politicians, insurance companies, and practitioners as a way to improve patient safety because patient information will be more complete and standardized, which will enhance the decision-making process of a practitioner (Murer, 2007). Major barriers to EHR implementation have been discussed, including training and financial impact of an organization as the system becomes integrated with daily operations. However, there also are legal issues associated with the implementation of an EHR.

There may be medical malpractice concerns when a physician initially adopts an EHR due to errors when transferring patient data from a paper system to an electronic system. Another legal issue is the electronic definition of a legal patient record. A traditional patient record is a folder containing a paper trail of patient visits, prescriptions, and tests. During a trial, what constitutes an electronic patient record? A report is generated by the EHR software that does not look like the actual screen data of the patient. As with patient paper files, there are certainly issues with medical errors related to entering the patient information into the system. For example, a family physician using an EHR system nearly prescribed the incorrect medication because of an incorrect click of the mouse. Lastly, the other issue is the protection of the data. Depending on who has access to the patient data in the healthcare facility, there may be breaches of confidentiality (Gamble, 2012).

In October 2008, Microsoft announced its **HealthVault** website (HealthVault, 2016) that enables patients to develop **electronic patient records** free of charge. These electronic health records are the patient component of the electronic health record. It is up to the individual as to how much medical information the person wants to store online with this website. The website also has links to several health websites that can assist with issues such as exercise programs, heart problems, drug reactions, and sharing medical information with providers. In November 2008, the Cleveland Clinic agreed to pilot data exchanges between HealthVault and the Cleveland Clinic's personal health record system. The Clinic enrolled 250 patients in the areas of diabetes, hypertension, and heart disease to test the system. The patients tested their health status at home using blood pressure monitors, weight scales, heart rate monitors, and glucometers. The patients tested themselves and uploaded the reports to the clinic using HealthVault. They also were able to access health education material on HealthVault regarding their diseases. This is the first pilot study in the country to assess this tool. The 2010 results of the pilot study indicated that there was a 26–71% increase in time intervals between doctor appointments. Heart patients made more appointments with their physicians as well (iMedicalApps, 2013). In 2010, Microsoft released a new version of HealthVault, HealthVault Community Connect, which allows patients to preregister for hospital procedures and admissions via the hospital's web portal. Patients can create a HealthVault personal e-health record account. When patients are discharged from the hospital, copies of their hospital care are uploaded to the patient's HealthVault account for the patient's accessibility. Microsoft HealthVault can now communicate with many healthcare websites, mobile applications, and personal health devices, which enable patients to more quickly upload their health data (HealthVault, 2016).

PRIMARY CARE INFORMATION PROJECT IN NEW YORK CITY MODEL

In 2008, the New York City Department of Health and Mental Hygiene (DOHMH), as part of a $27 million mayoral initiative to improve the quality and efficiency of health care in New York City, developed the **Primary Care Information Project (PCIP)** to support the adoption and use of prevention-oriented EHRs primarily among providers who care for the city's underserved and vulnerable populations. PCIP is a bureau in the Division of Prevention and Primary Care at the New York City Department of Health and Mental Hygiene. PCIP's mission is to advance population health through supporting and promoting high quality primary care and prevention. PCIP assists medical practices to use EHRs and other forms of health information technology to increase the delivery of evidence-based preventive care services, such as blood pressure control and cancer screenings, and to track chronic disease risk factors and disease management (PCIP, 2016).

CLINICAL DECISION SUPPORT SYSTEMS

Artificial intelligence (AI) is a field of computerized methods and technologies created to imitate human decision making. One application of AI is an **expert system (ES)**, which imitates experts' knowledge in decision making (Coiera, 2003). An **electronic clinical decision support system (CDSS)** is designed to integrate medical information, patient information, and a decision-making tool to generate information to assist with cases. CDSS systems are a type of knowledge-based system. The key functions of a CDSS are (1) administrative, (2) case management, (3) cost control, and (4) decision support. Administrative protocols consist of clinical coding and documentation for procedure approval and patient referrals if necessary. Case management control focuses on the management of patients to ensure they are receiving timely interventions. Cost control is a focus because the system monitors orders for tests and medication, which reduces unnecessary interventions (Perreault & Metzger, 1999).

Expert systems can be used to alert and remind healthcare providers of a patient's condition change, or to have a laboratory test or an intervention performed. An ES can also assist with a diagnosis using the system's database. The system can expose any weaknesses in a treatment plan or check for drug interactions and allergies. A system can also interpret imaging tests routinely to flag any abnormalities. It is important to note that the more complex duties of a system require the integration of an EHR system so the system can interface with the patient data (Coiera, 2003).

Research over the past several years has indicated that CDSSs have many potential benefits that can be classified into three categories: (1) improved patient safety, (2) improved quality of care, and (3) improved efficiency in healthcare delivery. Although the barriers to implementation were identified previously, the benefits for many institutions have outweighed those barriers so they have found ways to utilize these CDSSs. More CDSSs are being developed to provide information for various types of diseases (Open Clinical, 2016).

COMPUTERIZED PHYSICIAN ORDER ENTRY

Computerized physician order entry (CPOE) systems are CDSSs that enable a patient's provider to enter a prescription order or order for a lab or diagnostic test in a computer system. The order

entry has four components: (1) information can be entered from a handheld device, laptop, or desktop computer; (2) it enables the provider to order a test, prescription, or procedure; (3) it is connected to a decision support system that alerts providers to any problems with their orders; and (4) it can be integrated into the overall computer system of the organization. The CPOE first appeared in 1971 when NASA Space Center and Lockheed Corporation developed a system for a hospital in California. It improves quality assurance in patient care, thus reducing medical errors, (Ash, Gorman, Seshardri, & Hersch, 2004). Similar to the EHR, barriers to implementing a CPOE system are the initial financial investment, the customization requirement with the current organization's computer system, medical and administrative training to use this system, and staff's fear of change. These barriers can be addressed before successful implementation of a CPOE.

E-prescribing, a form of CPOE, consists of medication history, benefits information, and processing new and existing prescriptions. With an e-prescribing system, the user-clinician signs into a system with a password to verify identify. The user clinician provides a patient identification code so the user clinician can review the patient's medication list, prescribe a new drug, and designate which pharmacy will fill the prescription (HRSA, 2016)

More than 90% of pharmacies can accept electronic prescriptions (Surescripts, 2016). Medication ordering and the administration of these medications can be incorrectly given to a patient because of similar sounding names, similar dosages, and similar labeling. E-prescribing can be performed on a desk computer, laptop, or handheld device that will record physicians' prescription orders, which eliminates having an individual read a handwritten prescription. CPOE also includes a decision support system that includes possible drug interactions and dosage information that assist with the physician making the best decision possible for a patient.

Section 132 of the Medicare Improvements for Patients and Providers Act of 2008 (MIPPA) authorized incentives to encourage physicians to e-prescribe. In January 2009, Medicare and some private healthcare plans began paying a bonus to physicians who e-prescribe medications for their Medicare patients. Since 2012, Medicare has also penalized physicians who do not e-prescribe by reducing their reimbursement rates by 1% for 2012, 1.5% for 2013, and 2% for 2014 and all subsequent years (CMS, 2016b). IT companies are providing free software to physicians to encourage them to electronically prescribe. This system can be used alone, but it is best used with the EHR system because it integrates the information from the patient's EHR into its decision making.

PATIENT PORTALS

A **patient portal** is a secure online website that gives patients convenient 24-hour access to personal health information from anywhere with an Internet connection. Using a secure username and password, patients can view health information including their recent physician visits, medications, and lab results. They can also communicate with their physician electronically. Patient portals can enhance patient-provider communication and enable patients to check test results, refill prescriptions, review their medical record, and view education materials. In addition, patient portals can simplify administrative tasks such as streamlining registration, scheduling appointments, and providing patient reminders. They also allow providers to generate electronic statements and facilitate online payments (HIT, 2016).

BLUE RIBBON PROJECT

In 2010, the Markle Foundation Work Group on Consumer Engagement convened to discuss how to increase healthcare consumer's engagement in their health care. Their recommendation was to increase patient access to their health data. The Department of Veterans Affairs was one of the first government agencies to develop a Blue Button function on their patient portal; in August 2010, MyHealthVet allowed veterans to download their data by clicking on the Blue Button. This enabled patients to review their health information to ensure its accuracy. This initiative has grown nationally with both government and nongovernment health agencies using the Blue Button on their websites to promote electronic access for patients (HIT, 2016).

PHARMACY BENEFIT MANAGERS

Technology-based tools provide exceptional value to the prescription benefits of a health insurance program. E-prescribing will become more commonplace with the mandates of Medicare. In order to manage this technology effectively and efficiently, a **pharmacy benefit manager (PBM)** uses technology-based tools to assess and evaluate the management of the prescription component so it can be customized to address the needs of the organization. PBMs are companies that administer drug benefits for employers and health insurance carriers. They contract with managed care organizations, self-insured employers, Medicaid and Medicare managed care plans, federal health insurance programs, and local government organizations. Approximately 95% of all patients with drug coverage received benefits through a PBM. They manage approximately 70% of more than 3 billion prescriptions in the United States each year. The PBM integrates medical and pharmacy data of the population to determine which interventions are the most cost-effective and clinically appropriate (Federal Trade Commission, 2016).

DRUG–DRUG INTERACTIONS

Drug–drug interaction (DDI) alerts are used by software programs to warn pharmacists and clinicians about potential drug interactions. These alerts can notify the provider that two drugs may interact or there may be management strategies provided regarding the DDIs. DDI software programs can be very beneficial to providers but must be updated continually to ensure they contain current information regarding drug interactions (Murphy et al., 2009).

TELEHEALTH

Telehealth is the broad term that encompasses the use of IT to deliver education, research, and clinical care. An important activity of telehealth is the use of email between providers and their patients. **E-health** refers to the use of the Internet by both individuals and healthcare professionals to access education, research, and products and services. There are several websites such as WebMD and Healthline that provide consumers with general healthcare information. Sometimes telemedicine is best understood in terms of the services provided and the mechanisms used to provide those services.

Telemedicine refers to the use of IT to enable healthcare providers to communicate with rural care providers regarding patient care or to communicate directly with patients regarding treatment. The ultimate goal of telemedicine is to improve the patient's health status. The basic form of telemedicine is a telephone consultation. There are growing IT applications for telemedicine, including smart phones, video conferencing, and email (American Telemedicine Association, 2016). Telemedicine is most frequently used in pathology and radiology because images can be transmitted to a distant location where a specialist will read the results. Telemedicine is becoming more common because it increases healthcare access to remote locations such as rural areas. It is also a cost-effective mode of treatment. Telemedicine includes:

1. Synchronous consulting between primary care providers and specialists electronically
2. Monitoring patients remotely, which includes sending patient data to a remote location electronically
3. Providing electronic health consumer information
4. Providing medical education to healthcare professionals

The information can be sent electronically via networks and websites (American Telemedicine Association, 2016).

AVERA eCARE

Beginning in 1993, Avera offered eConsult services to rural, frontier, and critical access hospitals that were part of the Avera Health system (Avera e-care, 2016). Avera eConsult completes more than 900 virtual visits each month with patients

in 100+ clinics and hospitals. Since eConsult services launched in 1993, it has provided support to approximately 35 medical specialties. Ten years later, eCARE expanded to provide eICU care, the first 24-hour, on-demand service that allows staff at partner facilities to connect virtually via a video and audio call for immediate assistance from board-certified providers. In addition, Avera eCARE delivers 24/7 access to medical specialists for underserved populations and communities.

Since it began in 2008, Avera ePharmacy services has provided remote pharmacy coverage for more than 744,000 patients. For the 60+ facilities currently in its network, 630,000 medication orders in the last year have been reviewed for adverse drug events.

Avera eCare established eEmergency in 2009, which provides electronic immediate access of emergency-certified physicians and nurses to rural providers to help them with diagnosis of patients with critical conditions. It is an example of tele-emergency services. Rural clinicians and administrators agreed that eEmergency services have demonstrated significant impact on the quality of clinical services provided in rural areas.

Avera eCare recently established eCorrectionalHealth, which provides medical consults to South Dakota prisons. In 2015, it completed 500 video consults and 150 service-related calls. It also instituted eLongTermCare, which serves 30 long-term care facilities. In all of these instances, this type of electronic medical service provides cost savings to medical facilities because it requires no onsite visits (Avera eCare, 2016).

CHIEF INFORMATION OFFICER

As more healthcare services are delivered electronically, many healthcare organizations have designated a chief information officer (CIO) to manage the organization's information systems. Some organizations may also refer to this position as a **chief technology officer (CTO)**, or they may have both. Normally, the CIO is a vice president of the organization and the CTO reports to that position. The CIO also integrates HIT into the organization's strategic plan. The CIO must have knowledge of current information technologies as they apply to the healthcare industry and how new technology can apply to the organization. The CIO is also responsible for motivating employees whenever there is any technological change (Oz, 2006). C. Martin Harris, CIO of the Cleveland Clinic, feels that the challenge of the CIO (who he believes is a change agent) is to move from the implementing of the EHR to continuing to provide quality care to the patient by developing an integrated system model regardless of the size or location of the organization. As more health care is being delivered by technology, the CIO will be responsible for developing a model that is patient-oriented rather than operations-oriented (Harris, 2008).

COUNCIL FOR AFFORDABLE QUALITY HEALTH CARE

The Council for Affordable Quality Health Care (CAQH), a nonprofit organization, consists of alliances of health plans and trade associations that discuss efficiency initiatives to streamline healthcare administration by working with healthcare plans, providers, the government, and consumers. As part of this initiative, CAQH has created a **Committee on Operating Rules for Information Exchange (CORE)**, which borrows from the banking industry's standards for one of the largest electronic payment systems in the world. Based on stakeholder input, CORE has set up standards and operating rules for streamlining processes between providers and healthcare plans. This system allows for real-time access to patient information, pre- and post-care. Established by DHHS, the Health Information Technology Standards Panel (HITSP) utilized the CORE platform in its first set of data standards. HITSP is working toward the national integration of both public and private healthcare data standards for sharing among all organizations. As part of the required data standards mandated by the Affordable Care Act, the CORE is being used for data exchange of EHRs to ensure compliance with the Health Insurance Portability and Accountability Act (HIPAA) and other standards. To date, there have been 200 CORE certifications obtained (CAQH, 2016).

OTHER APPLICATIONS

Enterprise Data Warehouse

Enterprise data warehouses (EDWs) are developed to provide information that helps organizations in strategic decision making. Data warehousing requires an integration of many computer systems across an organization. Older systems, often referred to as **legacy systems**, are difficult, but worthwhile, to integrate because they further support strategic decision making. Business EDWs collect numeric data to assess trends. Retail, banking, and manufacturing firms use EDWs because these industries usually have repetitive actions that can be categorized easily. For example, banks have savings accounts, CDs, Roth IRAs, money markets, etc. It is very easy to analyze that type of data. Healthcare transactions can occur in the hospital, in community health centers, and in physicians' offices, and each transaction is unique. Other patient healthcare data may not be numeric (Inmon, 2007). Written information, such as a physician's prognosis, needs to be integrated into a system. Therefore, a healthcare EDW that acknowledges these differences must be developed. One of the first healthcare systems to utilize an EDW was the Veterans Health Administration (VHA) (VHA, 2016).

The Centers for Medicaid and Medicare Services Enterprise Data Warehouse

In 2006, CMS, as a pilot study, developed the largest EDW in history to gather hospital, prescription, and physician data to analyze the claims data for Medicare and Medicaid. CMS felt that the integration of its data would enable the analysis of the large number of claims submitted by providers. It also assisted in identifying any potential fraud and abuse. It was determined that the EDW was successful, but CMS was concerned that it was a claims-oriented warehouse. Therefore, part of their EDW strategy is the Integrated Data Repository (IDR), which integrates data from CMS and its partners in a consistent, secure, multi-view environment that includes providers, patients, claims, drug information, and other data as needed (CMS, 2016a).

Radio Frequency Identification

Radio frequency identification (RFID) chips transmit data to receivers. Each of these chips is uniquely identified by a signal indicating where it is located. RFID has been used in business for inventory management by placing a chip on each of the pieces of inventory. Walmart was one of the first retailers to use RFID technology to manage its massive inventory. Recently, RFID technology is being used in many aspects of healthcare industry operations. RFID can be used for the following (GAO RFID, 2016):

- Tracking pharmaceuticals as they are shipped from the manufacturer to the customer
- Tracking pharmaceutical inventory in a healthcare facility
- Tracking wait time in emergency rooms
- Tracking the use of what is being used in surgeries
- Tracking costly medical equipment to ensure easy access
- Identifying providers in hospitals to ensure efficiency in care
- Identifying laboratory specimens to reduce medical errors
- Tracking patients, including infants, while they are hospitalized
- Tracking hazardous materials that pose a public health threat
- Tracking hand washing use to ensure employee compliance

The following are specific examples of how RFID technology is used in the healthcare industry:

- Wake Forest Baptist Medical Center (North Carolina) sews RFID tags into the seams of x-ray protection vests in an effort to reduce the time it takes to locate the vests for government inspections.
- Texas Health Harris Methodist Hospital uses RFID tags deployed to patients and staff to trace people who come into contact with patients with a contagious, potentially dangerous infection such as TB.
- Sanraku Hospital, a 270-bed hospital in Tokyo, uses a handheld reader with RFID tags in patient wristbands to match drugs with prescription information in electronic medical records (Balm, 2013).

APPLIED HEALTH INFORMATION TECHNOLOGY

The PhreesiaPad

Chaim Indig and Evan Roberts, both younger than 30 years old, spent a year examining the healthcare market. They felt, as entrepreneurs, that the healthcare industry was the best entry for them to start a business. They realized that patient check-in at doctors' offices was a problem. Backed by venture capital firms and with advice from medical professionals, they developed Phreesia-Pad, a wireless digital device with a touch screen keyboard that allows patients to enter their demographic information and the reason they are visiting the doctor. This point of service technology eliminates the need for patients to replicate their information each time they pay a visit to the doctor. The software automatically verifies the patient insurance information. If they have a copay or balance, they can pay with a credit or debit card. When the patient is finished, a report is automatically generated for the doctor to review before seeing the patient. This increases office efficiency, shortens visit rates, and reduces error rates. This information can also be uploaded to an EHR (Phreesia, 2016).

According to a study conducted by the Medical Group Management Association (MGMA), approximately 30% of patients leave their clinician's office without making any payment, and it takes practices an average of 3.3 billing statements before a patient's outstanding balance is paid in full. Phreesia is a tool that can rectify these financial issues (Leatherbury, 2012).

PatientPoint (Formerly Healthy Advice Network)

PatientPoint provides education to patients electronically while in the waiting room or an exam room. Health education information is customized with brand advertising messages displayed on digital flat screens in physicians' waiting rooms. There are 25-minute loops of brand materials that focus on prevention and management of disease. PatientPoint has programs in more than 31,000 locations. PatientPoint serves more than 70,000 healthcare providers and 750 hospitals nationwide, affecting 113 million patients and creating more than 586 million patient and caregiver exposures each year (PatientPoint, 2016).

MelaFind Optical Scanner

The **MelaFind optical scanner** is not used for definitive diagnosis but rather to provide additional information a doctor can use in determining whether or not to order a biopsy. The goal is to reduce the number of patients left with unnecessary biopsy scars, with the added benefit of eliminating the cost of unnecessary procedures. The MelaFind technology (MELA Sciences, Irvington, NY) uses missile navigation technologies originally paid for by the Department of Defense to optically scan the surface of a suspicious lesion at 10 electromagnetic wavelengths (Gidalovtiz, 2014).

Electronic Aspirin

A technology under clinical investigation at Autonomic Technologies, Inc. (Redwood City, California), **electronic aspirin** is a patient-powered tool for blocking pain-causing signals at the first sign of a headache. The system involves the permanent implant of a small nerve-stimulating device in the upper gum on the side of the head normally affected by the headache. When a patient senses the onset of a headache, he or she places a handheld remote controller on the cheek nearest the implant. The resulting signals block the pain-causing neurotransmitters (Intellitechaz, 2015)

Robotic Checkups

Through **robotic checkups**, medical robots can make rounds, checking on patients in different rooms and managing their individual charts and vital signs without direct human intervention. The RP-VITA Remote Presence Robot produced jointly by iRobot Corp. and InTouch Health is the first such autonomous navigation remote-presence robot to receive FDA clearance for hospital use. The device is a mobile cart with a two-way video screen and medical monitoring equipment, programmed to maneuver through healthcare facilities. This is an innovative method of telemedicine (iRobot, 2016).

Sapien Heart Valve

The **Sapien heart valve** is a life-saving alternative to open-heart surgery for patients who need a new valve but are at high risk for surgery. Manufactured by Edwards Life Sciences (Irvine, California), the Sapien has been available in Europe but was approved for use by the FDA in 2011. It is finding its first use in U.S. heart centers—where it is limited only to the highest at-risk patients. The Sapien valve is inserted by catheter from a small incision near the rib cage. The valve material is made of bovine tissue attached to a stainless-steel stent, which is expanded by inflating a small balloon in the valve space. Inserting the Sapien valve is a simpler procedure with much shorter hospitalizations and could have a positive impact on healthcare costs (Edwards Lifesciences Corporation, 2016).

Acuson P10

Siemens has introduced a pocket-sized ultrasound, **Acuson P10**, which can be used for traditional applications of diagnostic and screening tests. It is designed for quick and easy use in an emergency medicine, cardiology, ICU, and OB/GYN situation. In each of these situations, the device provides a quick view of anatomy and tissue. It can be used in outpatient areas, intensive care units, and rescue helicopters to provide instant information to make a diagnosis. The results can be viewed on the screen but can also be uploaded to a computer. This technology eliminates the need for the provider to send the patient to an imaging center (MNT, 2016a).

Piccolo Xpress Chemistry Analyzer

The size of a shoebox, the **Piccolo Xpress Chemistry Analyzer** is a compact, portable chemistry analyzer that delivers blood test results quickly.

The provider places the sample, such as blood, on a small disc and slides the disc into the Piccolo Xpress. The provider requests tests to be performed using its touch-screen display. The device then prints out a hardcopy report in approximately 12 minutes or transmits the information to an EHR. This technology expedites the provider's ability to diagnose a patient (Piccolo Xpress, 2016).

THE IMPORTANCE OF HEALTH INFORMATION TECHNOLOGY

A recent study focused on the implementation and management of IT in the hospital setting. Szydlowski and Smith (2009) interviewed six hospital CIOs (or their equivalents) and nurse managers to assess why they used HIT. The CIOs indicated they used HIT to streamline administrative processes in the organization. They all recognized the substantial cost to invest in HIT but understood that the investment was long term and that it would ultimately be very cost effective. The nurse managers focused on the ability to reduce medical errors as a result of HIT. They also indicated that having electronic patient data ultimately contributed to more efficient and effective clinical decision making. The barriers to successful implementation identified by both the CIOs and the nurse managers were inadequate training on HIT and the amount of time needed to become familiar with HIT. The concerns the CIOs indicate are also applicable to other healthcare providers such as physician offices and outpatient facilities.

From a consumer perspective, health information technology can mean safer care. Electronic health records can provide a more complete picture of a person's health status. E-prescribing may reduce medical errors because pharmacists will not have to interpret poor physician writing. Sharing medical information with other providers electronically may reduce the number of tests

a consumer could receive. In case of a disaster where paper records could be destroyed, having an electronic copy of consumer medical records could save a life (Alaska eHealth Network, 2016).

CONCLUSION

The healthcare industry has lagged behind other industries utilizing IT as a form of communicating important data. Despite that fact, there have been specific applications developed for HIT such as e-prescribing, telemedicine, e-health, and specific applied technologies such as the Patient-Point, MelaFind optical scanner, the PhreesiaPad, Sapien heart valve, robotic checkups, electronic aspirin, Acuson P10, and the Piccolo Xpress, which were discussed in this chapter. Healthcare organizations have recognized the importance of IT and have hired CIOs and CTOs to manage their data. However, healthcare consumers need to embrace an electronic patient record, which is the basis for the Microsoft HealthVault. This will enable patients nationwide to be treated effectively and efficiently. The patient health records can be integrated into the electronic health records. Having the ability to access a patient's health information could assist in reducing medical errors. As a consumer, utilizing a tool like HealthVault could provide an opportunity to consolidate all medical information electronically, so if there are any medical problems, the information will be readily available. The health navigator can play a role with the patient by assisting them with the use of technology in managing their health. Assisting them with using the Microsoft HealthVault to provide their medical records electronically may assist with their care. The predominant demographic who uses the healthcare system is the elderly. Although there has been an increase in their use of technology, many elderly patients are not tech savvy. This could be a prime opportunity for the health navigator to assist with patient care.

Summary

Vocabulary

Acuson P10

Artificial intelligence

Chief information officer (CIO)

Chief technology officer (CTO)

Committee on Operating Rules for Information Exchange (CORE)

Computerized physician order entry

Drug–drug interaction (DDI) alerts

E-health

Electronic aspirin

Electronic clinical decision support systems

Electronic health record (EHR)

Electronic medical record (EMR)

Electronic patient records

Enterprise data warehouse

E-prescribing

Expert system

Health informatics

Health information systems

Health information technology

HealthVault

Imaging informatics

Informatics

Information technology (IT)

Legacy systems

Meaningful use

Medical informatics

MelaFind optical scanner

National Alliance for Health Information Technology (NAHIT)

PatientPoint

Patient portal

Pharmacy benefit manager (PBM)

Piccolo Xpress Chemistry Analyzer

Primary Care Information Project (PCIP)

Radio frequency identification (RFID)

Robotic checkups

Sapien heart valve

Telehealth

Telemedicine

References

Alaska eHealth Network. (2016). Why is health information technology important to me? http://www.ak-ehealth.org/for-patients/why-is-health-information-technology-important-to-me/.

American Telemedicine Association. (2016). What is telemedicine? http://www.americantelemed.org/home.

American Telemedicine Association. (2016). Telemedicine case studies. http://hub.americantelemed.org/resources/telemedicine-case-studies.

Anderson, R., Rice, T., & Kominksi, G. (2007). *Changing the U.S. health care system.* San Francisco, CA: Jossey-Bass.

Appleby, C. (2008). G. Octo Barnett. Founder of the Laboratory of Computer Science. http://www.mghlcs.org/about/team/octobarnett/.

Ash, J., Gorman, P., Seshadri, V., & Hersh, W. (2004). Computerized physician order entry in U.S. hospitals: Results of a 2002 survey. *JAMIA, 11*(2): 95–99.

Avera eCare (2016). http://www.averaecare.org/ecare/who-we-are/about-avera-ecare/.

Balm, S., (201). 5 ways the healthcare industry is implementing RFID technology. http://medcitynews.com/2013/12/5-ways-hospitals-implementing-rfid-tags-emerging-trend-healthcare/.

Buchbinder, S., & Shanks, N. (2007). *Introduction to health care management.* Sudbury, MA: Jones and Bartlett Publishers.

Centers for Medicare and Medicaid Services (CMS). (2016a). CMS Integrated Data Repository (IDR). http://www.cms.gov/Research-Statistics-Data-and-Systems/Computer-Data-and-Systems/IDR.

CMS. (2016b). Electronic prescribing (eRx) incentive program. http://www.cms.gov/Medicare/Quality-Initiatives-Patient-Assessment-Instruments/ERxIncentive/index.html?redirect=/erxincentive.

CMS. (2016c). Meaningful use. https://www.cms.gov/Regulations-and-Guidance/Legislation/EHRIncentivePrograms/index.html?redirect=/ehrincentiveprograms/.

CMS. (2016d). Medicare and Medicaid EHR incentive program basics. http://www.cms.gov/Regulations-and-Guidance/Legislation/EHRIncentivePrograms/Basics.html.

Coiera, E. (2003). *The guide to health informatics* (2nd ed.). London: Hodder Arnold.

Council for Affordable Quality Health Care (CAQH). (2016). What are operating rules? http://www.caqh.org/CORE_rules.php.

Daigrepont, J., & McGrath, J. (2011). EHR critical success factors. In *Complete guide and toolkit to successful EHR adoption* (pp. 13–21). Chicago, IL: HIMSS.

Department of Health and Human Services (DHHS). (2016). Health information technology. https://www.healthit.gov/.

eJobDescription. (2016). Chief information officer job description. http://www.ejobdescription.com/CIO_Job_Description.html.

Edwards Lifesciences Corporation. (2016). Edwards Sapien transcatheter heart valve. http://www.edwards.com/products/transcathetervalve/Pages/THVcategory.aspx.

Federal Trade Commission. (2016). FTC and DOJ issue report on competition and health care. https://www.ftc.gov/tips-advice/competition-guidance/industry-guidance/health-care.

Gamble, M. (2012). 5 legal issues surrounding electronic medical records. http://www.beckershospitalreview.com/legal-regulatory-issues/5-legal-issues-surrounding-electronic-medical-records.html.

GAO RFID. (2016). RFID for healthcare industry. http://gaorfid.com/healthcare-rfid-solutions/.

Goldstein, M., & Blumenthal, D. (2008). Building an information technology infrastructure. *J Law Med Ethics*, 709–715.

Gidalevitz, Y. (2014). Reduce the number of melanoma skin cancer biopsies with MelaFind in your #MEDTECHTOOLBOX. https://www.fortis.edu/blog/healthcare/reduce-the-number-of-melanoma-skin-cancer-biopsies-with-melafind-in-your-medtechtoolbox/id/3062.

Harris, C. (2008). C. Martin Harris, CIO, Cleveland Clinic. *Health Management Technology*, 29(7): 10.

HealthVault. (2016). Overview. https://www.healthvault.com/us/en/overview.

HIT. (2016). https://www.healthit.gov/patients-families/blue-button/about-blue-button.

iMedicalApps. (2016). Cleveland Clinic pilots Microsoft Health-Vault. http://www.imedicalapps.com/2010/03/microsoft-healthvault-community-connect-cleveland-clini/.

Inmon, B. (2007). Data warehousing in a health care environment. The Data Newsletter. http://tdan.com/print/4584.

Institute of Medicine (IOM). (2001). Crossing the quality chasm: A new health system for the 21st century. http://www.nationalacademies.org/hmd/Reports/2001/Crossing-the-Quality-Chasm-A-New-Health-System-for-the-21st-Century.aspx.

Intellitechaz (20156). Three innovations in medical practice. http://www.intellitechaz.com/blog/category/electronic-aspirin/.

iRobot. (2016).InTouch Health and iRobot announce first customers to install RP-VITA, the new face of telemedicine. http://www.irobot.com/us/Company/Press_Center/Press_Releases/Press_Release.aspx?n=050613

Leatherbury, L. (2012). Phreesia increases productivity, improves collections for medical practices. South Florida Hospital News. http://southfloridahospitalnews.com/page/Phreesia_Increases_Productivity_Improves_Collections_for_Medical_Practices/7158/1/.

Leung, L. (2008). Internet embeddedness: Links with online health information seeking, expectancy value/quality of health information websites, and Internet usage patterns. *Cyber Psychology & Behavior*, 11(5): 565–569.

MNT. (2016a). ACUSON P10 crosses healthcare boundaries: Handheld pocket ultrasound carries out essential obstetric scanning in Tanzania. http://www.medicalnewstoday.com/articles/114511.php.

MNT. (2016b). The National Alliance for Health Information Technology explores next set of strategic initiatives. http://www.medicalnewstoday.com/articles/101878.php.

Murer, C. (2007). EHRS: Issues preventing widespread adoption. *Rehab Management*, 20, 38–39.

Murphy, J., Malone, D., Olson, B., Grizzle, A., Armstrong, E., & Skrepnek, G. (2009). Development of computerized alerts with management strategies for 25 serious drug-drug interactions. *Am J Health Syst Pharm*, 66, 38–44.

New York City Department of Health and Mental Hygiene (DOHMH). (2016). EHR expansion initiative. https://www.health.ny.gov/health_care/medicaid/program/update/2016/2016-09.htm.

Open Clinical. (2016). Health informatics. http://www.openclinical.org/healthinformatics.html.

Oz, E. (2009). *Management information systems*. Mason, OH: Cengage Learning.

PatientPoint. (2013). About us. http://www.patientpoint.com/aboutus/formerly-healthy-advice.aspx.

HIT. Patient Portals. https://www.healthit.gov/providers-professionals/faqs/what-patient-portal.

Perreault, L., & Metzger, J. (1999). A pragmatic framework for understanding clinical decision support. *JHIM*, 13(2): 5–21.

Phreesia. (2016). Phreesia news. http://www.phreesia.com/news.asp.

Piccolo Xpress. (2016). Overview. http://www.piccoloxpress.com/products/piccolo/overview.

Robeznieks, A. (2013). Pediatricians offer model for kids' EHRs. http://www.modernphysician.com/article/20130404/MODERNPHYSICIAN/304049975.

Shields, A., Shin, P., Leu, M., Levy, D., Betancourt, R., Hawkins, D., & Proser, M. (2007). Adoption of health information technology in community health centers: Results of a national survey. *Health Aff*, 26(3): 1373–1383.

Singer, J. (2013). EHRs are a tool not a solution: The NYC primary care information project. http://healthaffairs.org/blog/2013/03/13/ehrs-are-a-tool-not-a-solution-the-nyc-primary-care-information-project.

Surescripts. (2012). National Progress Report on EPrescribing and Safe-Rx Rankings. http://www.surescripts.com/about-e-prescribing/progress-reports/national-progress-reports#downloads.

Szydlowski, S., & Smith, C. (2009). Perspectives from nurse leaders and chief information officers on health information technology implementation. *Hospital Topics: Research and Perspectives on Healthcare*, 87(1): 3–9.

Valerius, J. (2007). The electronic health record: What every information manager should know. *Information and Management Journal*, 4(1): 56–59.

Ventres, W., & Shah, A. (2007). How do EHRs affect the physician patient relationship? *American Family Physician*, 75(9), 1385–1390.

Vreeman, D., Taggard, S., Rhine, M., & Worrell, T. W. (2006). Evidence for electronic health record systems in physical therapy. *Physical Therapy*, 86(3): 434–446.

Walker, J. M. (2013). Using the EHR to transform healthcare. http://www.ehcca.com/presentations/hitsymposium/walker_2a.pdf.

About telemedicine? (2016). https://www.americantelemed.org/about/about-telemedicine

Whitman, J. C., & David, S. (2007). Effectively integrating your EMR/EHR initiative. *The Physician Executive*, 33(5): 56–59.

Student Activity 8-1

In Your Own Words

Based on this chapter, please provide an explanation of the following concepts in your own words. DO NOT RECITE the text.

Computerized physician order entry (CPOE) systems

Electronic health records

Enterprise data warehouse

Expert systems

Health information technology

Legacy systems

PatientPoint

PhreesiaPad

Radio frequency identification

Student Activity 8-2

Complete the following case scenarios based on the information provided in the chapter. Your answer must be IN YOUR OWN WORDS.

Real-Life Applications: Case Scenario One

As one of four physicians, you all are interested in implementing an EHR system. You heard there was an excellent project in New York City that has successfully implemented a system.

Activity

You schedule a visit to New York City to visit their project. You prepare a report for your physicians on the results of their project.

Case Scenario Two

As a new physician, one of your goals is to increase access to providing health care in the rural areas of your state. You have heard that telemedicine may be an opportunity for you.

Activity

You perform research on the advantages and disadvantages of telemedicine for your practice.

Case Scenario Three

You were just promoted to CIO of your hospital. One of your goals is to improve the efficiencies of hospital operation. You heard that RFID is a viable option.

Activity

Perform research on RFID technology and its application to the healthcare industry. Select three types of RFID applications that will work for your hospital and develop a report for your CEO.

Case Scenario Four

An elderly relative heard you were starting a job as a health navigator for the elderly. Your relative is interested in understanding how technology can improve the management of her health care.

Activity

Discuss the Microsoft HealthVault with your relative and explain how it may be helpful with her care.

Student Activity 8-3

Internet Exercises

- Visit each of the websites listed here.
- Name the organization.
- Locate its mission statement on the website.
- Provide a brief overview of the activities of the organization.
- How does this organization participate in the U.S. healthcare system?

Websites

http://www.aap.org

Organization Name
Mission Statement
Overview of Activities
Importance of Organization to U.S. Health Care

http://www.patientpoint.com

Organization Name
Mission Statement
Overview of Activities
Importance of Organization to U.S. Health Care

http://www.healthdatamanagement.com

Organization Name
Mission Statement
Overview of Activities
Importance of Organization to U.S. Health Care

http://www.nationalehealth.org

Organization Name
Mission Statement
Overview of Activities
Importance of Organization to U.S. Health Care

http://www.phreesia.com

Organization Name
Mission Statement
Overview of Activities
Importance of Organization to U.S. Health Care

http://www.healthvault.com

Organization Name
Mission Statement
Overview of Activities
Importance of Organization to U.S. Health Care

Student Activity 8-4

Discussion Questions

The following are suggested discussion questions for this chapter.

1. What is radio frequency identification? Using the textbook and the Internet, discuss three ways this technology applies to healthcare.
2. What is PatientPoint? Do you think this is an effective way to educate patients? Defend your answer.
3. What is electronic aspirin? What are the advantages and disadvantages of this new product? Would you use this product? Defend your answer.
4. What are two advantages and two disadvantages of EHR? What is meaningful use? What are the barriers to implementing an EHR system?
5. What is the Primary Care Information Project? Do you think it has been successful? Why or why not?
6. If you were an IT Health Navigator, describe your role with your patient.

Student Activity 8-5

Current Events

Perform an Internet search and find a current events topic that relates to this chapter. Provide a summary of the article and the link to the article and explain how the article relates to the chapter.

CHAPTER 9

Navigating Healthcare Law

LEARNING OBJECTIVES

The student will be able to:

- Describe the legal relationship between patient and provider.
- Apply civil and criminal liability concepts to healthcare providers and consumers.
- Analyze six employment laws and their importance to the healthcare workplace.
- Define and discuss the different contracts between a patient and healthcare provider.
- Discuss the role of a health navigator with patient legal rights.
- Discuss the importance of the original Patient Bill of Rights.

DID YOU KNOW THAT?

- The Ethics in Patient Referral Act of 1989 was passed because providers were referring patients to medical services in which they or family members had a financial interest.
- *Qui tam* provisions, a concept used in antitrust law, is Latin for *he who sues*. This provision enables individuals to sue providers for fraudulent activity against the federal government, recovering a portion of the funds to be returned to the government.
- In response to the Affordable Care Act antifraud initiatives, more than 15,000 Medicare providers were expelled from the system for fraudulent activity.
- According to civil law, a surgeon performing surgery without consent could be considered assault and battery.
- The most important relationship in the healthcare system is the relationship between the

patient—the healthcare consumer—and the provider, which could be a physician or an organization such as a clinic or hospital in which the physician has a relationship.

- Defensive medicine occurs when clinicians order more tests and provide more services than necessary to protect themselves from malpractice lawsuits.

INTRODUCTION

To be effective, healthcare managers must understand basic legal and ethical principles that influence the work environment, including the legal relationship between the organization and the consumer—the healthcare provider and the patient. The basic concepts of civil and criminal healthcare law, tort reform, employment-related legislation, safety in the workplace, and the legal relationship between the provider and the patient will be discussed in this chapter.

BASIC CONCEPTS OF HEALTHCARE LAW

The healthcare industry is one of the most heavily regulated industries in the United States. Those who provide, receive, pay for, and regulate healthcare services are affected by the law (Miller, 2006). **Law** is a body of rules for the conduct of individuals and organizations. Law is created so there is a minimal standard of action required by individuals and organizations. **Public law** enforces relationships between entities and the government, and **private law** deals with issues among individual. Public law is created by federal, state, and local governments. As the judiciary system interprets previous legal decisions regarding a case, creates **common law** (Pozgar, 2014). The minimal standard for action is federal law, although state law may be more stringent. Legislative bodies such as the Congress create laws called **statutes**. Both common law and statutes are then interpreted by administrative agencies in developing **rules and regulations** that interpret the law. Both civil and criminal laws affect the healthcare industry.

Criminal law, an example of public law, is concerned with actions that are illegal based on court decisions. In order to convict someone of a criminal activity, guilt has to be proven without a reasonable doubt. The most common types of criminal law infractions would be Medicare and Medicaid fraud (Miller 2006). **Civil law**, an example of private law, focuses on the wrongful acts against individuals and organizations based on contractual violations. **Torts**, derived from the French word for *wrong*, is a category in civil law of wrongful acts that do not involve a preexisting contract. Proving a civil infraction does not require as much evidence as in a criminal case. Several different types of violations can apply to health care. There are two basic healthcare torts: (1) negligence, which involves the unintentional or omission of an act that would contribute to the positive health of a patient, and (2) intentional torts, such as assault and battery or invasion of privacy (Pozgar, 2014).

An example of **negligence** would be if a provider does not give appropriate care or withholds care that results in damages to the patient. In the healthcare industry, **intentional torts** such as assault and battery would be a surgeon performing surgery on a patient without his or her consent (Bal, 2009). Invasion of privacy would be the violation of patients' health records. Privacy issues relating to patient information is a major issue in the healthcare industry. These activities are categorized under the term *medical malpractice*.

According to the *American Heritage Dictionary* (2000), **medical malpractice** is the "improper or negligent treatment of a patient by a provider which results in injury, damage, or loss" (p. 1060). According to the Institute of Medicine's (IOM) landmark report *To Err Is Human*, medical malpractice has resulted in approximately 80,000–100,000 deaths per year. Unfortunately, recent research indicates that this data is low. Preventable medical errors are the third-leading cause of death in the United States, with estimates of more than 400,000 cases, despite the many patient safety standards that have been implemented to lower this estimate (McCann, 2014). Disputes over improper care of a patient have hurt both the providers and patients. Patients have sued physicians because they feel their provider has not delivered the proper level of care compared to the standard of care in the industry.

To prove negligence, four legal elements must be proven: (1) a professional duty owed to the patient as determined by the standard of care, (2) breach of such duty, (3) injury caused by the breach, and (4) proven causation between the action and the injury. There are four types of damages considered: (1) economic damages, a fixed price based on a loss of an object, (2) non-economic damages, not a fixed amount, including pain and suffering from the negligence, (3) compensatory damages, including both economic and non-economic damages, and (4) punitive damages, which are uncommon, intended to punish the defendant (Pozgar, 2014).

TORT REFORM DISCUSSION

As a result of the number of malpractice claims in the United States, malpractice insurance premiums have increased. This has resulted in the concept of **defensive medicine**, which means that providers often order more tests and provide more services than necessary to protect themselves from malpractice lawsuits. Surveys of physicians over the years reveal more than 70% of physicians admit to defensive medicine practices because they are afraid of litigation (Sekhar & Vyas, 2013). Historically, there have been continued malpractice insurance crises during the 1970s,

1980s, and, most recently, the beginning of this century (Danzon, 1995). The issues in the 1970s led to joint underwriting measures that required insurance companies to offer medical malpractice if the physician purchased other insurance. In some states, compensation funds were established to offset large award settlements. The level of malpractice suits lessened but the amount of awards were still huge. During the mid-1980s, the premiums were rising again—nearly 75%. It was determined that any initiatives established in the 1970s were not effective (Rosenbach & Stone, 1990). A third malpractice insurance crisis occurred in the 2000s. Issues with obtaining medical malpractice insurance in several states have increased, forcing physicians to join underwriting associations, which can charge exorbitant premiums.

As a result of the recent malpractice insurance crisis, more states have adopted statutory caps on monetary damages that a plaintiff can recover in malpractice claims. States felt that a cap on monetary damages would have the most impact on malpractice insurance premiums because the less an insurance company has paid out in insurance claims, the less the insurance company would have to raise insurance rates. More than half of the states have established caps on awards. For example, Florida, Kansas, Maryland, Massachusetts, Michigan, North Carolina, and Texas have established **non-economic damages** for different medical cases. An example of a noneconomic damage policy is Texas, which has implemented the following:

- A per-claimant **$250,000** cap on non-economic damages in medical malpractice cases against a physician or healthcare provider
- For a single healthcare institution, a per-claimant **$250,000** cap on non-economic damages
- For multiple healthcare institutions, an overall cap of **$500,000** per claimant for non-economic damages, and no single institution can be on the hook for more than **$250,000** in non-economic damages, per claimant.

As stated earlier, noneconomic damages include compensation for losses such as pain and suffering and emotional distress. Non-economic damages are said to be more "subjective," which is why many states have set caps for this type of damage (NOLO, 2016).

Many legal factors have contributed to the increase in claims. Voluntary hospitals are no longer exempt from malpractice suits. The fact that employers now have to take responsibility for their employees' wrongdoing also has increased claims. The concept of informed consent for the patient has expanded and increased claims. The acceptable **standard of care**, once strictly based on a locality rule, has now become a state or national standard, and this also has resulted in increased claims (Pozgar, 2014). Statutes specifying the acceptable standard of care in a malpractice suit in a local setting were replaced by a national or state standard. This increased the ability to locate expert witnesses that would testify at a trial regarding the standard of care given to the plaintiff.

Some physicians are leaving private practice because they can no longer afford the premiums. They are now in administrative positions at all levels of government, are academicians, or are teaching at medical universities. The malpractice insurance issues have forced many states to review their malpractice guidelines. Some states' tort reform, which has imposed limits on the amount awarded, continues to cause controversy. However, recent federal studies have indicated that imposing caps on awards may be an effective method to reduce malpractice costs and to discourage frivolous lawsuits. In addition, the U.S. Supreme Court ruled that any awards must be included in an individual's taxed income (Miller, 2006).

THE ROLE OF THE HEALTH NAVIGATOR

The health navigator can play an instrumental role in helping people to understand their legal rights as a patient. Patients may or may not understand that the relationship with the provider is a legal relationship and they have rights that must be respected. The concept of the Patient

Bill of Rights that outlines the patient rights of autonomy in their health care may or may not be adhered to by a provider. The patient navigator can help the patient be empowered in recognizing their right to refuse treatment, their right to question their provider, and the right to be clearly informed about their patient care. The health navigator should be familiar with healthcare law to ensure that the patient is treated within his or her legal rights. For example, a provider cannot abandon a patient. There are regulations in place to ensure that cannot occur. The patient may not be aware of that rule. There are 44,000–99,000 medical deaths each year due to medical errors that could have been prevented by improved communication. A health navigator could play a role to ensure that protocols are followed.

THE LEGAL RELATIONSHIP BETWEEN THE PROVIDER AND CONSUMER

The most important relationship in the healthcare system is the relationship between the patient—the healthcare consumer—and his or her provider, which could be a physician or an organization such as a clinic or hospital where the physician has a relationship. The provider–consumer relationship can be considered a contract, which is an agreement, either oral or written, between two or more parties that designate legally enforceable activities (Pozgar, 2016). A physician can establish a contractual relationship with a patient in three ways: (1) establishing a **contractual relationship to care for a designated population**, (2) establishing an express contract with a patient under mutual agreement, and (3) establishing a relationship under an implied contract (Laws, 2016).

In order for a contract to exist, it must have four components: (1) agreement between two parties, (2) both parties must be competent to consent to the agreement, (3) the agreement must be of value, and (4) the agreement must be legally enforceable. If any of these components are missing, the parties are not bound by the agreement to comply with the terms (Buchbinder & Shanks, 2007). This chapter will discuss several types of contracts as they pertain to health care.

A contract to care for a designated population is indicative of a health maintenance organization (HMO) or managed care contract. A physician is contractually required to care for those member patients of a managed care organization. The physicians may sign contracts to provide care for hospitals, schools, or long-term care facilities that have designated populations (Miller, 2006).

An **express contract** is a simple contract—a mutual agreement of care between the physician and patient. The physician may define the limitations of the contract, including the parameters of care. The physician may decide only to practice in a certain geographic area or only provide services in a certain specialty. An implied contract can be implied from a physician's actions. If a physician casually gives advice regarding medical treatment, there is **an implied contract** (Laws, 2016). The relationship between a patient and hospital, a **contractual right to admission**, can be considered a contract if a hospital has contracted to treat certain members of an organization, such as a managed care organization; if so, the hospital is required to treat those members. A second example of this type of contractual right to admission is if governmental hospitals, such as county hospitals, are required to provide care for patients regardless of ability to pay (Miller, 2006).

How Does a Relationship with a Provider End?

According to the American Medical Association (AMA), once a patient and physician relationship has started, the physician is legally and ethically obligated to continue the relationship until the patient no longer requires their care. There may be a practical reason for a relationship to end such as geographic relocation or change of healthcare insurance. If a patient becomes noncompliant and abusive, the physician has the right to end a relationship. However, to protect the physician from being accused of **patient abandonment**, the physicians must take steps to properly end the relationship. If a patient withdraws from the relationship with the provider, then the physician no longer has a duty to provide follow up. Also, if medical care is no longer needed, the relationship naturally is completed. If a patient is transferred to another provider, the provider then establishes a relationship with the new patient. However, a physician could withdraw from a relationship by giving sufficient notice of withdrawal or providing the patient with a referral. However, if a physician withdraws from a relationship without sufficient reason, the provider may be liable for breach of contract or patient abandonment. The AMA (2016) provides the following five steps for a physician to terminate a relationship:

1. Giving the patient written notice, preferably by certified mail
2. Providing the patient with a specific reason for termination
3. Continuing to provide care for a reasonable period of time so the patient can find other care
4. Providing assistance to the patient to find other care
5. Offering to transfer all medical records with patient permission

HEALTHCARE-RELATED LEGISLATION

Healthcare Consumer Laws

Other legislative acts will be discussed thoroughly throughout the text; however, the following acts directly affect how health care is provided to consumers.

Hill–Burton Act

The **Hill–Burton Act of 1946** was passed because the federal government recognized the lack of hospitals in the United States during the 1940s. The Hospital Survey and Construction Act, more commonly known as the Hill–Burton Act provided for federal grants to states for hospital construction to ensure there were 4.5 beds per 1,000 people (Shi & Singh, 2008). This act had a huge influence on creating more hospitals nationally. If a hospital received federal funds from the Hill–Burton Act, it agreed to a community service requirement, so that any person residing in the area of the hospital could not be denied treatment in the portion of the hospital financed by the Hill–Burton Act. Exceptions to

this service required included lack of needed services, unavailability of the services needed, or the patient's ability to pay. The program stopped providing funds in 1997, but about 150 healthcare facilities nationwide are still obligated to provide free or reduced-cost care. Since 1980, more than $6 billion in uncompensated services have been provided to eligible patients through Hill–Burton. Hospitals that are under the Hill–Burton Act are required to post notices about the program in their area of admission. These notices must be easy to read and in languages appropriate to the community (HRSA, 2016).

Emergency Medical Treatment and Active Labor Act

The **Emergency Medical Treatment and Active Labor Act (EMTALA)** of 1986, enforced by the Centers for Medicare and Medicaid Services (CMS) and the Office of Inspector General (OIG), requires Medicare participants to receive emergency care from a hospital or medical entity that provides dedicated emergency services. This was passed as part of the **Consolidated Omnibus Budget Reconciliation Act of 1985 (COBRA)**. This requirement is a type of fiduciary duty that means the healthcare provider or organization is obligated to provide care to someone who has placed his or her trust in them (CMS, 2016). This law is also called the "antidumping" statute because, prior to the enactment of this law, many hospitals dumped Medicare patients. Penalties for violating EMTALA include the following:

1. A hospital can be fined from $25,000–$50,000 per violation.
2. Hospitals can be excluded from the Medicare program.
3. Physicians can be fined up to $50,000 per violation.
4. Physicians can be excluded from Medicare/Medicaid.

The original act was amended in 2000 and 2006 to strengthen the law. CMS issued guidelines that further explained the act. This legislation protects consumers to ensure they receive appropriate emergency care when they present themselves to regulated hospitals and medical organizations (CMS, 2016).

Children's Health Insurance Program

The **Children's Health Insurance Program (CHIP)** was enacted under the Balanced Budget Act of 1997, is Title XXI of the Social Security Act, and is jointly financed by federal and state funding and administered by the states and CMS. The purpose of this program is to provide coverage for low-income children younger than the age of 19 who live above the income-level requirements of Medicaid. As an incentive for states to expand their coverage programs for children, Congress created an "enhanced" federal matching rate for CHIP that is generally about 15 percentage points higher than the Medicaid rate—averaging 71% nationally. For example, if a state has a 50% match rate for Medicaid, they may have a 65% match rate for CHIP (Financing, 2016). Children cannot be eligible for Medicaid or be covered by private health insurance (National Health Law Program, 2016). Approximately 8 million children who are uninsured and ineligible for public assistance have been positively affected by this program. Children who are eligible for state health benefit plans are not eligible for CHIP. Studies have indicated that this program has improved access to health insurance for children (Kaiser Family Foundation, 2016).

Benefits Improvement and Protection Act

The **Benefits Improvement and Protection Act of 2000 (BIPA)**, formally called the Medicare, Medicaid, and CHIP Benefits Improvement and Protection Act, modifies Medicare payment rates for many services. It also adds coverage for preventive and therapeutic service. It increases federal funding to state programs. From a healthcare consumer perspective, it protects Medicare beneficiaries by granting them the ability to appeal provider termination of services (BIPA, 2016). It requires providers to issue a written notice to the patient that coverage has been terminated, giving an end date for the termination. The patient has the right to appeal the decision.

The **HIPAA National Standards of 2002** or the HIPAA **Privacy Rule** is to further protect patient's personal medical records and other personal health information maintained by healthcare providers, hospitals, insurance companies, and health plans. It gives patients new rights to access of their records, restricts the amount of patient information released, and establishes new restrictions to researchers' access (U.S. Department of Health & Human Services, 2016a).

ANTITRUST LAWS

The purpose of **antitrust law** is to protect the consumer by ensuring there is a market driven by competition so the consumer has a choice for health care. In a sense, antitrust laws protect the competition so the consumer has a choice. Antitrust laws apply to most healthcare organizations. There are antitrust laws at the both federal and state levels. Four main federal antitrust laws will be discussed in this chapter: the Sherman Antitrust Act, the Clayton Act, the Federal Trade Commission Act, and the Robinson–Patman Act (the amendment to the Clayton Act). These acts are important to know because they were developed to protect the healthcare consumer and those who provide healthcare services.

The **Sherman Act of 1890** focuses on eliminating **monopolies**, which are healthcare organizations that control a market so that the consumer has no choice in health care. It also targets **price fixing** among competitors; price fixing prohibits the consumer from paying a fair price because competitors establish a certain price (by either increasing or lowering prices) among themselves to stabilize the market. Healthcare facilities also may have an agreement on **market division**. This illegal action occurs when one or more health organizations decide which type of services will be offered at each organization. **Tying** refers to healthcare providers that will only sell a product to a consumer who will also buy a second product from them. **Boycotts** also are illegal according to this act. When healthcare providers have an agreement to not deal with anyone outside their group, which is considered interfering with the consumers' rights to choose. **Price information** exchange of services between providers also can be illegal (Miller, 2006). Healthcare providers are protected under the act if it has been determined that hospitals have exclusive contracts with certain providers, which excludes other providers from use of the hospital. This could be a violation of the act. Violations of the act are considered federal crimes.

The **Clayton Act of 1914** was passed to supplement the Sherman Act, as amended by the Robinson–Patman Act, which issues further restrictions on mergers and acquisitions. With the increasing development of hospital chains, this act has focused on hospitals. There are no criminal violations of the Clayton Act, unlike the Sherman Act. Any organization considering a merger or acquisition above a certain size must notify both the Antitrust Division of the DOJ and FTC. The act also prohibits other business practices that, under certain circumstances, may harm competition. The act also allows individuals to sue for three times their actual damages plus legal costs.

The **Hart–Scott–Rodino Antitrust Improvement Act of 1976**, as an amendment to the Clayton Act, ensures those hospitals and other entities that entered mergers, acquisitions, and joint ventures must notify DOJ and FTC before any final decisions are made. This is a requirement for any hospitals with more than $100 million in assets acquiring a hospital with more than $10 million in assets (Buchbinder & Shanks, 2007). The Department of Justice and Federal Trade Commission will make the final decision on these proposals. This ensures there will not be any type of monopoly within a certain geographic area.

The Federal Trade Commission and the Department of Justice are the federal agencies that enforce antitrust violations. The **Federal Trade Commission (FTC)**, established in 1914 by the **Federal Trade Commission Act**, is one of the oldest federal agencies and is charged with the oversight of commercial acts and practices. Two major activities of the FTC are to maintain free and fair competition in the economy and to protect consumers from misleading practices. They may issue "cease and desist orders"

to companies to ensure they stop their practices until a court decides what the company may do (Carroll & Buchholtz, 2015). The **Department of Justice (DOJ)**, headed by the U.S. Attorney General, was established in 1870 to handle U.S. legal issues, including the enforcement of federal laws. The DOJ and FTC collaborate on antitrust law enforcement (FTC, 2016).

INFORMED CONSENT

The concept of **informed consent** is based on the patient's right to make an informed decision regarding medical treatment. It is a legal requirement in all 50 states. It is more than a patient signing an informed consent form—it is the communication between the provider and patient regarding a specific medical treatment. The provider is responsible for discussing the following information with the patient: the diagnosis if it has been established; the nature of a proposed treatment or operation, including the risks and benefits, any alternatives, and the risks and benefits of the alternatives; and the risks and benefits of not agreeing to the procedure or treatment (AMA, 2016). If a patient did not provide informed consent for a procedure or treatment, it is considered a case of negligence. It is the duty of the physician to provide sufficient information to the patient to enable the patient to evaluate the proposed treatment before giving consent. The patient must understand the information or it is not considered an informed consent.

A medical emergency may eliminate the need for an informed consent. If a patient cannot clinically give consent to a lifesaving medical treatment, **statutory consent** may be considered which presumes a reasonable person would give consent to the lifesaving procedure. Consent may be implied in nonemergency situations. If a patient volunteers for a procedure, implying consent, without an oral or written verification, could be considered an informed consent (Pozgar, 2016)

Informed consent is a basic patient right. It is important that the physician provides information that the patient clearly understands so the patient can evaluate the risks and benefits of the intervention.

PATIENT BILL OF RIGHTS

The **Patient Self-Determination Act of 1990** requires hospitals, nursing homes, home health providers, hospices, and managed care organizations that provide services to Medicare- and Medicaid-eligible patients to supply information on patient rights to patients upon admission. It applies to virtually every type of healthcare facility. The facility must provide adult patients with written information, under the state law, about making healthcare decisions. Based on the concept of informed consent, in 1972 the Board of Trustees of the American Hospital Association developed a Patient Bill of Rights. The **Patient Bill of Rights** states that the patient has the right to all information from this provider regarding any testing, diagnoses, and treatments. This information must be provided to the patient in terms that the patient will be able to understand (Rosner, 2004). Eligible health organizations will have the Patient Bill of Rights displayed.

HEALTHCARE FRAUD

The most common type of criminal violation in the healthcare industry is healthcare fraud, which typically involves illegal acts for financial gain. Fraud can be perpetrated by many healthcare stakeholders: by multi-state organized crimes rings that improperly bill Medicare for $40 million dollars of home health care, by a single physician who brings in an extra $20,000 a year by regularly "up-coding" office procedures (upgrading simple procedures to a more complicated procedure to increase billing), and by healthcare systems who systematically defraud Medicare of hundreds of millions of dollars (Mahar, 2016). Healthcare fraud costs the healthcare system and its stakeholders $80 billion annually. The FBI is responsible for investigating healthcare fraud. The Department of Justice and Human Services Medicare Fraud Strike Force is designed to combat fraud (OIG, 2016). The centerpiece for fraud recovery is the False Claims Act, enacted in 1863. The **False Claims Act (FCA)**, also known as the Lincoln law, was originally passed to protect the federal government against defense contractors during the Civil War. The False Claims Act has been amended several times throughout the years; however, in the 1990s, the act focused on healthcare fraud, most notably Medicare and Medicaid fraud. The False Claims Act of 1995 imposes criminal penalties on anyone who tries to present fictitious claims for payment to the federal government. It is one of the most powerful government tools to combat healthcare fraud. This act also provides financial incentives for whistleblowers, allowing employees to blow the whistle about contractor fraud against the federal government. Private plaintiffs fulfilling this role are pursuant to the *qui tam* provisions of the act, which means "he who sues." The Deficit Reduction Act of 2005 introduced additional incentives for states to crack down on healthcare fraud by giving the states additional incentives under their own fraud law. The *qui tam* provisions allow whistleblowers to receive between 15% and 25% of proceeds in the case. As a result of the financial incentive program, the federal government has received billions in returned funds (Carroll & Buchholtz, 2009).

The Fraud Enforcement and Recovery Act of 2009 (FERA) and the Affordable Care Act (ACA) of 2010 further strengthened the False Claims Act. The FERA expanded potential liability for false claims by applying the FCA to a broader range of transactions, reducing the proof required to establish illegal activities, and expanding the pool of potential whistleblowers that may bring retaliation claims. The Affordable Care Act provided an additional $350 million over 10 years to help fund new initiatives to fight fraud. It also called for more stringent federal sentencing guidelines for healthcare fraud (Mahar, 2016).

Medicare Fraud Strike Force

Established in 2007, the Task Force uses both federal and local law enforcement agencies to combat healthcare fraud. As of September 2015, the Task Force has indicted nearly 2,000 individuals and recouped $1.8 billion. In September 2015, they caught 200 individuals who defrauded Medicare and Medicaid by more than $700 million. In 2016, they have recouped to date more than $200 million from nine different fraud schemes (OIG, 2016).

Ethics in Patient Referral Act of 1989

The Stark laws (named after Representative Pete Stark who authored the legislation), also known as the **Physician Self-Referral Laws** or the **Ethics in Patient Referral Act of 1989**, prohibit physicians, including dentists and chiropractors, from referring Medicare and Medicaid patients to other providers for **designated health services** in which they have a financial interest. These laws directly prohibit many referrals that may increase a provider or family members' financial interest. Designated health services include clinical laboratory services, outpatient prescription drug services, physical and occupational therapy, and imaging services such as magnetic resonance imaging (MRI), and the like. The statute became effective on January 1, 1995, but the regulations interpreting the statute were not released until January 4, 2001 (Gosfield, 2003). Additional Stark amendments expanded the types of services to which a physician could not refer Medicare and Medicaid patients if the physician or a family member has a financial interest. These regulations protect consumers by ensuring they will receive objective referrals for health services.

Fraud in the healthcare industry is easy to commit for several reasons. The government system assumes providers are trustworthy; it is easy to obtain a government issued provider number for Medicare and Medicaid; perpetrators believe it is easy to escape notice when committing fraud; and the penalties are low. As a result of these factors, some Medicare providers sell access to their program ID number. The ACA antifraud initiatives should help to reduce these fraudulent activities (Mahar, 2016).

EMPLOYMENT-RELATED LEGISLATION

As part of healthcare law, it is important to be familiar with the impact of employment-related healthcare legislation. Employment law was passed to ensure that both the employers and employees are aware of their rights in the workplace. The following section outlines major employment-related legislation that influences the healthcare industry.

Civil Rights Act of 1964, Title VII

The landmark **Civil Rights Act of 1964, Title VII**, prohibits discrimination based on race, sex, color, religion, and national origin. Discrimination means making distinctions among people who are different. This legislation is the key legal piece to equal opportunity employment. Two components to this legislation, which will be discussed later, are disparate treatment and disparate impact. It applies to employers with 15 or more employees. This act is enforced by the Equal Employment Opportunity Commission (EEOC).

The Civil Rights Act of 1964, Title VII, created a concept of protected classes to protect these groups from employment discrimination of compensation, conditions, or privileges of employment. The protected classes include sex, age, national origin, race, and religion. A major current issue under the purview of discrimination legislation is sexual harassment. According to the EEOC, **sexual harassment** is defined as unwelcome sexual conduct that has a negative impact on the employee. There are two kinds of sexual harassment: (1) quid pro quo sexual harassment, which occurs when sexual activities occur in return for an employment benefit, and (2) hostile environment sexual harassment, which occurs when the behavior of coworkers is sexual in nature and creates an uncomfortable work environment. Sexual harassment that occurs with the creation of a hostile work environment is more prevalent than quid pro quo sexual harassment. Several court case judgments indicate that repeated suggestive joke telling and lewd photos on display can be legally constituted as a hostile work environment. In the healthcare industry, nurses experience sexual harassment from colleagues, physicians, and patients.

Civil Rights Act of 1991

Title VII only allowed damages for back pay. The **Civil Rights Act of 1991** enables individuals to receive both **punitive damages**, which are damages that punish the defendant, and **compensatory damages** for financial or psychological harm. This act applies to employers with 15 or more employees. The amount of the damages is based on the size of the company: $50,000 for employers with 15 to 100 employees; $100,000 for companies with 101 to 200 employees; $200,000 for employers with 201 to 500 employers; and $300,000 for employers with more than 500 employees. This act is enforced by the EEOC.

The 1991 law extended the possibility of individuals collecting damages related to sex, religious, or disability-related discrimination. Organizations had developed a policy of adjusting scores on employment tests so a certain percentage of a protected class would be hired. This amendment to Title VII specifically prohibits quotas, which are diversity goals to increase the number of protected class in a work force (Gomez-Mejia, Balkin, & Cardy, 2012).

Age Discrimination in Employment Act of 1967

The **Age Discrimination in Employment Act of 1967** protects employees and job applicants 40 years and older from discrimination as it applies to hiring, firing, promotion, layoffs, training, assignments, and benefits. Older employees file lawsuits for age discrimination in job termination. It applies to employers with 20 or more employees and is enforced by the EEOC.

During difficult economic times, older employees file complaints with the EEOC because of their termination. In November 2010, Hawaii Professional Homecare Services was sued by the EEOC because the owner fired a 54-year-old female employee; the owner called the employee a "bag of old bones" and said she sounded old over the phone and so did not want her representing the company (U.S. EEOC, 2010).

Older Workers Benefit Protection Act of 1990

The **Older Workers Benefit Protection Act of 1990** amended the Age Discrimination in Employment Act. Its goal was to ensure that older workers' employee benefits were protected and that organizations provide the same benefits to both younger and older workers. The act also gives employees time to decide if they would accept early retirement options and allows employees to change their mind if they have signed a waiver for their right to sue. The act is enforced by the EEOC.

Rehabilitation Act of 1973

The **Rehabilitation Act of 1973** applies to organizations that receive financial assistance from federal organizations, including the Department of Health and Human Services, from discriminating against individuals with disabilities from receiving employee benefits and job opportunities. These organizations and employers include many hospitals, nursing homes, mental health centers, and human service programs. Employers with 50 or more employees and federal contracts of $50,000 or greater must submit written affirmative action plans. The PPACA amends this act by requiring all healthcare manufacturers to redesign medical equipment so they can accommodate individuals with disabilities. Healthcare provider locations also must be accessible to those with disabilities. This act is enforced by the Office of Federal Contract Compliance Programs (OFCCP).

Equal Pay Act of 1963

The **Equal Pay Act of 1963**, enforced by the U.S. Department of Labor, amended the Fair Labor Standards Act. It mandates that all employers award pay fairly to both genders if it is determined their jobs have equal responsibilities and require the same skills. It can be difficult to assess whether two employees are performing the exact same job. One employee may have additional duties, which would affect pay. The current trend in business is pay for performance so some employees may earn more if they perform better. However, research consistently states that women earn less than men. An individual who alleges pay discrimination may file a lawsuit without informing the EEOC.

Executive Orders 11246, 11375, and 11478

The President of the United States, for federal agency directions, writes Executive Orders. **Executive Orders 11246 (1965), 11375 (1967) and 11478 (1969)** focus on discrimination issues and require affirmative action based on these factors. These orders focus on both federal contractors and employers with 50 or more employees.

An **affirmative action plan** is a strategy that encourages employers to increase the diversity of their workforce by hiring individuals based on race, sex, and age. These potential employees must be qualified for the job. Although an affirmative action plan encourages hiring protected class candidates, an employer cannot set quotas for this process. They can develop strategies to encourage applications by diverse candidates.

An employer who develops an affirmative action plan must perform an analysis of the demographics of the current workforce compared to the eligible pool of qualified applicants. The employer also must calculate the percentage of those protected classes in the qualified applicants. The percentages are compared to determine if there was an underrepresentation of diverse employees in the organization. If it is determined the current workforce is not diverse, then an employer develops a timetable to hire diverse employees that also includes a recruitment plan.

Pregnancy Discrimination Act of 1978

An amendment to Title VII of the Civil Rights Act of 1964, the **Pregnancy Discrimination Act of 1978**, protects female employees who are discriminated against based on pregnancy-related conditions, which constitutes illegal sex discrimination. A pregnant woman must be treated like anyone with a medical condition. For example, an organization must allow sick leave for pregnant women with morning sickness if they also allow sick leave for other nausea illnesses (Gomez-Mejia, Balkin, & Cardy, 2012). This act applies to employers with at least 15 employees and is enforced by EEOC.

Americans with Disabilities Act of 1990

The **Americans with Disabilities Act of 1990 (ADA)** focuses on individuals who are considered disabled in the workplace. There are three sections: Section I contains employment limitations, Section II, and Section III target local government organizations, hotels, restaurants, and grocery stores. This act applies to employers who have 15 employees or more and is enforced by the EEOC. According to the law, a disabled person is someone who has a physical or mental impairment that limits the ability to hear, see, speak, or walk. The act was passed to ensure that those individuals who had a disability but who could perform primary job functions were not discriminated against. According to the act, disabilities included learning, mental, epilepsy, cancer, arthritis, mental retardation, AIDS, asthma, and traumatic brain injury. From a healthcare standpoint, a nursing home cannot refuse to admit a person with AIDS that requires a nursing service if the hospital has that type of service available (DOL, 2016). Alcohol and other drug abuses are not covered under the ADA. Individuals who are morbidly obese can be considered disabled if the obesity was related to a physical cause.

Title I of the ADA states that employment discrimination is prohibited against individuals with disabilities who can perform essential functions of a job with or without reasonable accommodation. *Essential functions* are job duties that must be performed to be a satisfactory employee. *Reasonable accommodation* refers to employers that take reasonable action to accommodate a disabled individual such as providing special computer equipment or furniture to accommodate a physical limitation. The reasonable accommodation should not cause undue financial hardship to the employer.

Individuals with disabilities have mental or physical limitations such as walking, speaking, breathing, sitting, seeing, and hearing. **Intellectual disabilities** refer to an IQ of less than 70–75, the disability occurred before 18 years of age, and issues with social skills. Intellectual disabilities must significantly limit major life activities such as walking, seeing, hearing, thinking, speaking, learning, concentrating, and working. The ADA amendments of 2008 expanded living activities to include bodily functions such as bladder, circulatory, neurological, and digestive functions.

Role of Equal Employment Opportunity Commission (EEOC)

The Equal Employment Opportunity Commission was created by Title VII of the Civil Rights Act of 1964. It is responsible for processing complaints, issuing regulations, and collecting information from employers.

Processing Complaints

If an individual feels discriminated against, he or she files a complaint with the EEOC who, in turn, notifies the employer. The employer is responsible for safeguarding any written information regarding the complaint. The EEOC then investigates the complaint to determine if the employer did violate any laws. If a violation was found, the EEOC uses conciliation or negotiation to resolve the issue without going to court. If conciliation is not successful, litigation or going to trial is the next step. Most employers prefer to avoid litigation because it is costly and damages their reputation. Most cases are resolved by conciliation.

Issuing Regulations

The EEOC is responsible for developing regulations for any EEOC law and its amendments. They have written regulations for the ADA, ADEA, and Equal Pay Act. They also issue guidelines for different issues such as sexual harassment and affirmative action.

Information and Education

The EEOC acquires information from employers regarding their practices. Employers with 100 or more employees must file an EEO-1 report that reflects the number of women and minorities who hold positions. This report is used to assess any potential discrimination trends. The EEOC also provides written and electronic media education on discrimination to employers. They send this information to the HR departments, which disseminates the information with training classes.

These pieces of legislation focus on equal employment opportunity in the workplace. These laws ensure that protected classes, as outlined in the Civil Rights Act of 1964, are provided opportunities for equal employment without bias or discrimination. In addition to this landmark legislation, the Age in Discrimination Act, Older Worker Benefit Protection Act, and the Americans with Disabilities Act establish standards for treating individuals who are older than 40 years and those individuals who have a disability are also treated fairly in their terms of employment. Both the Age in Discrimination Act and the Americans with Disabilities Act were further strengthened by the passage of the Lilly Ledbetter Fair Pay Act regarding pay discrimination. In addition, the Pregnancy Discrimination Act and the Equal Pay Act target discrimination against women. Despite the amount of antidiscrimination legislation, discrimination continues to exist in the work environment.

Occupational Safety and Health Act of 1970

The **Occupational Safety and Health Act of 1970** is also important to the healthcare industry because of the high incidence of employee injury. There is a higher risk of exposure to workplace hazards such as airborne and blood-borne infectious diseases, physical injuries from lifting patients, and needle-stick injuries. This law was passed to ensure that employers have a **general duty** to provide a safe and healthy work environment for their employees, which are very important for the healthcare industry because of potential exposure to bacteria, viruses, and contaminated fluids.

Employers also are required to inform employees of potential hazardous conditions and OSHA standards. Posters and other materials are posted for employees' education. The Occupational Safety and Health Administration (OSHA) is responsible for enforcing these provisions. The National Institute for Occupational Safety and Health (NIOSH) was established as part of this act to provide research to support the standards. OSHA enforces the **Hazard Communication Standard** that requires companies to label hazardous materials. Information is contained on **Safety Data Sheets (SDSs)** that are provided to employees via the Internet or on site. OSHA also has issued a standard for exposure to human immunodeficiency virus (HIV), hepatitis B virus (HBV), and other blood-borne pathogens. This standard is crucial to the healthcare industry because of increased risk of exposure by nurses and laboratory workers.

OSHA has also developed standards for **personal protective equipment (PPE)**, which require equipment for exposure to hazardous materials or working conditions. Companies also must maintain records of employee accidents. OSHA provides workers with the rights to receive training, keep a copy of their medical records, and request OSHA inspections of their workplace (Occupational Safety & Health Administration, U.S. Department of Labor, 2016a).

OSHA also has developed standards for **ergonomics**, which is the study of working conditions that affect the physical condition of employees. Studies indicate that repetitive motion can create employee injuries. A common disorder is **carpal tunnel syndrome**, which is a wrist injury common to repetitive hand motion that takes place in jobs such as grocery cashiers and computer users. Employers can provide ergonomic friendly equipment and guidelines for ergonomic actions to eliminate these types of injuries. Ergonomic equipment and actions are important to the healthcare industry because many workers often lift patients to and from beds, operating tables, and wheelchairs (Occupational Safety & Health Administration, U.S. Department of Labor, 2016b).

Immigration Reform and Control Act (1988)

The **Immigration Reform and Control Act of 1988 (IRCA)** requires employers with one or more employees to verify that all job applicants are U.S. citizens or authorized to work in the United States. Most employees are only aware of this legislation because of the I-9 form all new employees must complete. There are three categories—A, B, and C—on the form. Category A establishes identity and eligibility to work such as a passport, Permanent Resident Card, or Permanent Alien Registration Receipt Card. Category B establishes

identity of the individual. Acceptable proof of identity includes a driver's license or other types of identification cards with photographs. Category C focuses on eligibility of an employee to work. Documentation includes a social security card or birth certificate. If an employee cannot provide this information, he or she must provide documentation in both Category B and Category C. This prohibits any company from hiring illegal aliens and penalizes employers who hire illegal aliens. However, immigrants with special skill sets or those who can satisfy a labor shortage in the United States, such as nurses, will be permitted to work in the United States. This act is enforced by the U.S. Department of Labor.

OTHER EMPLOYMENT-RELATED LEGISLATION

The **Consumer Credit Protection Act (Title III) of 1968** prohibits employers from terminating an employee if the individual's earnings are subject to garnishment due to debt issues. This act also limits the weekly garnishment amount from their pay and is enforced by the Federal Deposit Insurance Corporation (FDIC).

The **Drug Free Workplace Act of 1988** requires any employers who receive federal grants or who have a federal contract of $25,000 or greater to certify that they operate a drug-free workplace. They are required to provide education to their employees about drug abuse. Many employers now offer drug testing. The act is enforced by the U.S. Department of Labor.

According to the **Worker Adjustment and Retraining Notification Act of 1989**, employers who have 100 employees or more must give their employees 60 days notice of layoffs and business closings. This act is enforced by the U.S. Department of Labor.

The **Employee Retirement Income Security Act of 1974 (ERISA)** regulates pension and benefit plans for employees, including medical and disability benefits. It protects employees because it forbids employers from firing an employee so that they cannot collect under their medical coverage. Employees may change the benefits provided under their plan, but employers cannot force an employee to leave so that the employer does not have to pay the employee's medical coverage.

The **Consolidate Omnibus Budget Reconciliation Act of 1986 (COBRA)**, an amendment to ERISA, was passed to protect employees who lost or changed employers so they could keep their health insurance if they paid 102% of the full premium (Anderson, Rice, & Kominski 2007). The act was passed because, at the time, people were afraid to change jobs, resulting in the concept of **job lock** (Emanuel, 2008). With the establishment of the Healthcare Insurance Marketplace, individuals may find more affordable health insurance plan options rather than using the COBRA option.

The **Health Insurance Portability and Accountability Act of 1996 (HIPAA)** was passed to promote patient information and confidentiality in a secure environment. The *Standards for Privacy of Individually Identifiable Health Information* (**Privacy Rule**) establishes, for the first time, a set of national standards for the protection of certain health information. The major goal of the Privacy Rule is to assure that individuals' health information is properly protected while allowing the flow of health information needed to provide and promote high-quality health care of the patient and to protect the public's health and well-being. There are two exceptions to the privacy rule: if the patient requests the disclosure of their information or there is an investigation. This act is enforced by the Department of Health and Human Services' Office for Civil Rights and the Department of Justice.

The **Health Information Technology for Economic and Clinical Health Act of 2009 (HITECH)** became effective September 23, 2009; this act amends HIPAA by requiring stricter notification protocols for breach of any patient information. The notification must occur within 60 days of the breach and the media also must be informed of the breach. These new rules apply to any associates of the health organizations. In addition to the Privacy Rule, the **Security Rule**, which applies to e-PHI or electronic patient information, was implemented. The Security Rule

was developed because of the increased use of electronic patient records. These new rules also apply to any associates of the health plans. It also increased HIPAA's civil and criminal penalties for violating consumer privacy regarding their health information. Civil penalties were increased to $1,500,000 per calendar year, which was a huge increase in the original penalty cap of $25,000. The criminal penalties of up to $50,000–$250,000 and 10 years of incarceration remained the same.

Releasing patient information is more complex because of the introduction of information technology to the healthcare industry. For example, patient information may be faxed as long as only necessary information is transmitted and safeguards are implemented. Physicians also may communicate via email as long as safeguards are implemented.

Employee wellness programs, which can include promotion of exercise, health risk appraisals, disease management, and healthcare coaching, have become a popular employee benefit. However, there have been legal issues surrounding the implementation of wellness programs in the workplace because they discriminate based on the health conditions of employees. HIPAA states that wellness programs that are part of a group health plan must be designed to promote health and cannot be a subterfuge discriminating against an employee based on a health condition. Many wellness programs also offer incentives for wellness-program performance. The incentive program must be designed so that all employees may participate in the incentive program regardless of health conditions, which means the incentive/rewards program must be flexible to adapt to employees who want to participate but may be restricted based on a health condition (DOL, 2016).

The **Family Medical Leave Act of 1993 (FMLA)** requires employers with 50 or more employees within a 75-mile radius who work more than 25 hours per week and who have been employed more than 1 year to provide up to 12 work weeks of unpaid leave, during any 12-month period, to provide care for a family member or the employee him- or herself. This benefit also can include post childbirth or adoption. Employers must provide healthcare benefits, although they are not required to provide wages. This benefit does not cover the organization's 10% highest-paid employees. The employer also is supposed to provide the same job or a comparable position upon the return of the employee. The Department of Labor announced a final rule in 2015 to amend the term of "spouse" to include legal same-sex marriage spouses (DOL, 2016).

Releasing patient information is more complex because of the introduction of information technology to the healthcare industry. For example, patient information may be faxed as long as only necessary information is transmitted and safeguards are implemented. Physicians also may communicate via email as long as safeguards are implemented.

The **Mental Health Parity Act of 1996** defines the equality or parity between lifetime and annual limits of health insurance reimbursements on both mental health and medical care. Unfortunately, the act did not require employers to offer mental health coverage, it did not impose limits on deductibles or coinsurance payments, nor did it cover substance abuse. This federal legislation spurred several states to implement their own parity legislation (Anderson, Rice, & Kominski, 2007). The Wellstone Act or the **Mental Health Parity and Addiction Equity Act of 2008** amends the Mental Health Parity Act of 1996 to include substance abuse treatment plans as part of group health plans.

The **Genetic Information Nondiscrimination Act of 2008** prohibits U.S. insurance companies and employers from discriminating based on information derived from genetic tests. Genetic information includes information about an individual's genetic tests and the genetic tests of an individual's family members, as well as information about the manifestation of a disease or disorder in an individual's family members (i.e. family medical history). Family medical history is included in the definition of genetic information because it is often used to determine whether someone has an increased risk of getting a disease, disorder, or condition in the future. Genetic information also includes the following: an individual's request for, or receipt of, genetic services; the participation in clinical research that includes genetic

services by the individual or a family member of the individual; the genetic information of a fetus carried by an individual or by a pregnant woman who is a family member of the individual; and the genetic information of any embryo legally held by the individual or family member using an assisted reproductive method. Specifically, it forbids insurance companies from discriminating through reduced coverage or price increases. It also prohibits employers from making adverse employment decisions based on a person's genetic factors (EEOC, 2016a).

The **Lilly Ledbetter Fair Pay Act of 2009 (FPA)**, an amendment to Title VII of the Civil Rights Act of 1964, provides protection for unlawful employment practices related to compensation discrimination. This act also applies to claims under the Age Discrimination Act of 1967 and the Americans with Disabilities Act of 1990. It was named after Lilly Ledbetter, an employee of Goodyear Tire and Rubber Company who found out near her retirement that her male colleagues were paid more than she was. The Supreme Court ruled that she should have filed a suit within 180 days of the date that Goodyear paid her less than her peers. This act allows the statute of limitations to restart every 180 days from the time the worker receives a paycheck (EEOC, 2016b).

To avoid litigation, Sedhom (2009) suggests the implementation of a program coordinated by senior management and HR to help protect employers from being accused of unfair employment practices. The following summarizes the steps of the program:

1. Establish compensation criteria.
2. Develop pay audits and document these audits for several years.
3. Document retention processes related to pay.
4. Train managers on providing objective performance evaluations.
5. Develop and implement a rigorous statistical analysis of pay distributions.

The Patient Protection and Affordable Care Act of 2010 (ACA) has had a major impact on the U.S. healthcare system. Therefore, a separate chapter in this book has been devoted to the act and its mandates. A brief summary of the ACA is included in this chapter.

The **Patient Protection and Affordable Care Act (PPACA)** or as it is commonly called, the **Affordable Care Act (ACA)**, and its amendment, the **Healthcare and Education Affordability Reconciliation Act of 2010**, was signed into law on March 23, 2010, by President Barack Obama. The goal of the act is to improve the accessibility and quality of the U.S. healthcare system. Nearly 50 healthcare reform initiatives resulting from this legislation are being implemented during 2010–2017 and beyond. The passage of this complex landmark legislation has been very controversial and continues to be contentious today.

There were national public protests and a huge division among the political parties regarding the components of the legislation. People, in general, agreed that the healthcare system needed some type of reform, but it was difficult to develop common recommendations that had majority support. Criticism, in part, focused on the increased role of government in implementing and monitoring the healthcare system. Proponents of healthcare reform reminded people that Medicare is a federal government entitlement program because when individuals reach 65 years of age, they can receive their health insurance through this program. Millions of individuals are enrolled in Medicare. Medicaid is a state-established government public welfare insurance program based on income for millions of individuals, including children, that provides health care for its enrollees.

On October 1, 2013, the federal government was shut down because there were elected politicians who do not want the Affordable Care Act to proceed further. These politicians refused to approve a bill that would continue financial operations of the U.S. government. They attempted to include defunding portions of the Affordable Care Act as part of the federal government funding bill. Government functions resumed on October 17, 2013, after the Continuing Appropriations Act of 2014 was signed by Congress. Poll results indicate that public approval ratings of Congress declined significantly during the shutdown (Newport, 2013).

The one implementation that has been generally supported is increasing the dependent coverage of health insurance from age 25 until age 26, even if the child is not living with his or her parents, is not declared a dependent on the parents' tax return, or is no longer a student. This would not apply to individuals who have employer-based coverage (DOL, 2013). Another positive mandate, also implemented in July 2010, was the establishment of a Web portal, www.healthcare.gov, to increase consumer awareness about individuals' eligibility for specific healthcare insurance.

In addition to the two reforms discussed in the previous paragraphs, the following are selected major reforms that were also implemented in 2010:

- Elimination of lifetime and annual caps on healthcare reimbursement
- Granting assistance for the uninsured with preexisting conditions
- Creation of a temporary reinsurance program for early retirees

In the past, health insurance companies would establish an annual or lifetime cap of reimbursement for the use of healthcare insurance. These would be eliminated. Health insurance companies also would no longer be permitted to drop individuals and children with certain conditions or not to provide insurance to individuals with preexisting conditions. The government would provide assistance in securing health insurance for these high-risk individuals.

The following are selected major ACA reforms that have been implemented:

- Insurance companies will be prohibited from setting insurance rates based on health status, medical condition, genetic information, or other related factors
- Establishment of a Health Insurance Marketplace Exchange, which is a marketplace where consumers can obtain information and buy health insurance. If the state opts not to establish a marketplace, individuals can use the federal marketplace website to obtain insurance.
- Most individuals must maintain minimum essential healthcare coverage or pay a fine

In the past, there were issues with health insurance companies denying coverage based on health status or other conditions. Premiums now will be based on family type, geography, tobacco use, and age. In addition, each state will establish Health Insurance Marketplace Exchanges to assist consumers with obtaining health insurance. If the state chooses not to establish a state-run operation, residents of the state will use the federal government website. The information will be provided to consumers in a standardized format so they can compare the plans. Plans and cost will vary based on level of coverage. There are exceptions based on circumstances. By 2014, most consumers were responsible for obtaining health insurance or to pay a penalty that will increase each year they do not obtain health insurance coverage (Niles, 2010). According to an analysis by the Kaiser Family Foundation, as of the end of the third open enrollment under the Affordable Care Act (ACA) (2016), 12.7 million people had signed up for coverage in the health insurance marketplaces, up from 11.7 million in 2015 and 8.0 million in 2014. Recent data indicates there will be attrition due to people not paying their premium, having their coverage terminated due to inconsistencies on their applications, or others receiving health insurance with an employer. Actual enrollment may be closer to 10 million, which meets the HHS target (Levitt, Claxton, Demico, & Cos, 2016). As of this writing, there is a change in the administration which may result in the repeal of some initiatives established by the Affordable Care Act.

CONCLUSION

To be an effective healthcare manager, it is important to understand basic legal principles that influence the work environment, including the legal relationship between the organization and the consumer—the healthcare provider and the patient. As both a healthcare manager and healthcare consumer, you must be familiar with the different federal and state laws that affect the healthcare organization. It is also important that you understand the differences between civil and criminal law and the penalties that may be imposed for breaking those laws. Both federal and state laws have been enacted and policy has been implemented to protect both the healthcare provider and the healthcare consumer. New laws have been passed and older laws have been amended to reflect needed changes regarding health care to continue to protect its participants from both a patient and an employee/employer perspective. The role of the health navigator can be crucial to a patient and provider relationship. A navigator certainly does not replace an attorney but can provide guidance to the patient. The healthcare industry is the most heavily regulated industry with many rules and regulations that a patient may not understand.

Summary

© Jim Barber/Shutterstock

Vocabulary

Affirmative action plan
Affordable Care Act of 2010 (ACA)
Age Discrimination in Employment Act of 1967
Americans with Disabilities Act of 1990 (ADA)
Antitrust law

Benefits Improvement and Protection Act of 2000 (BIPA)
Boycotts
Carpal tunnel syndrome
Children's Health Insurance Program (CHIP)
Civil law

Civil Rights Act of 1964, Title VII

Civil Rights Act of 1991

Clayton Act of 1914

Common law

Compensatory damages

Contractual relationship to care for a designated population

Contractual right to admission

Consolidated Omnibus Budget Reconciliation Act of 1985 (COBRA)

Consumer Credit Protection Act (Title III) of 1968

Criminal law

Defensive medicine

Department of Justice (DOJ)

Designated health services

Drug Free Workplace Act of 1988

Employee wellness programs

Emergency Medical Treatment and Active Labor Act (EMTALA)

Employee Retirement Income Security Act of 1974 (ERISA)

Equal Pay Act of 1963

Ergonomics

Ethics in Patient Referral Act of 1989

Executive Orders 11246 (1965), 11375 (1967), and 11478 (1969)

Express contract

False Claims Act (FCA)

Family Medical Leave Act of 1993 (FMLA)

Federal Trade Commission (FTC)

Federal Trade Commission Act

General duty

Genetic Information Nondiscrimination Act of 2008

Hart–Scott–Rodino Antitrust Improvement Act of 1976

Hazard Communication Standard

Healthcare and Education Affordability Reconciliation Act of 2010

Health Information Technology for Economic and Clinical Health Act of 2009 (HITECH)

Health Insurance Portability and Accountability Act of 1996 (HIPAA)

Hill–Burton Act of 1946

HIPAA National Standards of 2002

Immigration Reform and Control Act of 1988 (IRCA)

Implied contract

Informed consent

Intellectual disabilities

Intentional torts

Job lock

Law

Lilly Ledbetter Fair Pay Act of 2009 (FPA)

Market division

Medical malpractice

Mental Health Parity Act of 1996

Mental Health Parity and Addiction Equity Act of 2008

Monopolies

Negligence

Non-economic damages

Occupational Safety and Health Act of 1970

Older Workers Benefit Protection Act of 1990

Patient abandonment

Patient Bill of Rights

Patient Protection and Affordable Care Act of 2010 (PPACA)

Patient Self-Determination Act of 1990

Personal protective equipment (PPE)

Privacy Rule

Private law

Physician Self-Referral Laws

Pregnancy Discrimination Act of 1978

Price fixing

Price information exchange

Public law

Punitive damages

Qui tam

Rehabilitation Act of 1973

Rules and regulations

Safety Data Sheets (SDSs)

Security Rule

Sexual harassment

Sherman Act of 1890

Standard of care

Statutes

Statutory consent

Torts

Tying

Worker Adjustment and Retraining Notification Act of 1989

References

Akhbari, K. (2012). What is medical malpractice? http://www.legal
match.com/law-library/article/medical-malpractice.html.

American Heritage Dictionary. (2000). *Medical malpractice*. Boston,
MA: Houghton Mifflin.

American Medical Association (AMA). (2016). Ending the patient-phy-
sician relationship. http://www.ama-assn.org//ama/pub/physician
-resources/legal-topics/patient-physician-relationship-topics
/ending-patient-physician-relationship.page#

Anderson, R., Rice, T., & Kominksi, G. (2007). *Changing the U.S. health
care system*. San Francisco, CA: Jossey-Bass.

Bal, B. (2009). An introduction to medical malpractice in the United
States. *Clinical Orthopedics and Related Research, 467*(2): 339–347.

BIPA (2016). https://www.ruralcenter.org/tasc/resources/medicare
-medicaid-and-schip-benefits-improvement-and-protection-act
-2000-bipa.

Buchbinder, S., & Shanks, N. (2007). *Introduction to health care management*. Sudbury, MA: Jones and Bartlett Publishers.

Budnick, N. (2013). John Kitzhaber recommends reform for Oregon
medical malpractice laws. http://www.oregonlive.com/health
/index.ssf/2012/07/john_kitzhaber_rolls_out_his_r.html.

Carroll, A., & Buchholtz, A. (2009). *Business & society: Ethics and
stakeholder management* (7th ed.). Mason, OH: South-Western
/Cengage Learning.

Centers for Medicare and Medicaid Services (CMS). (2016). Emergency
Medical Treatment & Labor Act (EMTALA). http://www.cms.hhs
.gov/EMTALA.

Clayton Act, 15 U.S.C. §§ 12–27 (1914).

Congressional Budget Office. (2001). H.R. 5661, Medicare, Medicaid,
and SCHIP Benefits Improvement and Protection Act of 2000
(Incorporated in H.R. 4577, the Consolidated Appropriations Act):
Cost estimate. http://www.cbo.gov/publication/13285.

Danzon, P. (1995). *Medical malpractice: Theory, evidence, and public
policy*. Cambridge, MA: Harvard University Press.

Degnan, J. M., & Scoggin, S. A. (July, 2007). Medical defense and health
law. *IADC Committee Newsletter, 9*.

Draschler, D. (2010). Notes on: Year one of the Lilly Ledbetter Fair Pay
Act. *Labor Law Journal*, 102–106.

Equal Employment Opportunity Commission (EEOC). (2016a).
Genetic information discrimination. http://www.eeoc.gov/laws
/types/genetic.cfm.

EEOC (2016b). Equal Pay Act of 1963 and Lilly Ledbetter Fair Pay
Act Of 2009. http://www.eeoc.gov/eeoc/publications/brochure
-equal_pay_and_ledbetter_act.cfm.

Emanuel, E. (2008). *Health care guaranteed*. New York, NY: Public
Affairs.

Federal Trade Commission (FTC). (2016). About the FTC. http://www
.ftc.gov/ftc/about.shtm.

Gomez-Mejia, L., Balkin, D., & Cardy, R. (2012). *Managing human
resources*. Upper Saddle River, NJ: Pearson: 100–125.

Gosfield, A. G. (2003). The stark truth about the STARK law: Part I. *Fam
Pract Manag, 10*(10): 27–33. http://www.aafp.org/fpm/2003/1100
/p27.html.

Hickman, J., Gilligan, M., & Patton, G. (2008). FMLA and benefit obligations: New rights under an old mandate. *Benefits Law Journal,
21*(3): 5–16.

Kaiser Family Foundation. (2016). Total number of children ever
enrolled in CHIP annually. http://kff.org/other/state-indicator
/annual-chip-enrollment 0.

Kaiser Family Foundation. http://kff.org/private-insurance/issue-brief
/assessing-aca-marketplace-enrollment/?utm_campaign=KFF
-2016-March-Assessing-ACA-Enrollment&utm_source=hs
_email&utm_medium=email&utm_content=26937070&_hsenc
=p2ANqtz-96gsGlUVGkTGyZoOE7KdOa9wSOhSwJ1YEvYskNAw5

_mm__UJo393VFNIRbnIYzmOT7B4hZZ8LFklcecv8d-yz5yxv5kQ&
_hsmi=26937070.

Kesselheim, A., & Studdert, D. (2008). Whistleblower-initiated enforcement actions against health care fraud and abuse in the United
States, 1996–2005. *Ann Intern Med, 149*(5): 342–349.

Laws. (2013). Express and implied contracts from a physician. (2013).
http://malpractice.laws.com/professional-patient-relationship/
express-implied-contracts-from-a-physician.

Levitt, L., Claxton, L., Damico, G., & Cox, C. (2016). Assessing ACA
marketplace enrollment.

Mahar, M. (2016). Taking on the "epidemic" of health care fraud.
Healthcare IT News. http://www.theihcc.com/en/communities
/policy_legislation/taking-on-the-epidemic-of-health-care-fraud
_gs3lc2x7.html.

McCann, E. (2014). Deaths by medical mistakes hit records.
http://www.healthcareitnews.com/news/deaths-by-medical
-mistakes-hit-records.

Medicaid.gov. Financing. (2016). https://www.medicaid.gov/chip
/financing/financing.html.

MedicineNet. (2016). Definition of defensive medicine. http://www
.medicinenet.com/script/main/art.asp?articlekey=33262

Memmott, S., & Makwana, K. (2007). Beware the whistleblower
within—Recent False Claims Act settlements remind industry
that almost anyone can be a whistleblower. *Journal of Health Care
Compliance, 9*, 47–65.

Miller, R. (2006). *Problems in health care law* (9th ed.). Sudbury, MA:
Jones and Bartlett Publishers.

Moran, A. (2008). Wellness programs: What's permitted? *Employee Relations Law Journal, 34*(2): 111–116.

Moseley, G. (2015). *Managing legal compliance in the health care industry*. Burlington, MA: Jones and Bartlett Learning.

National Human Genome Research Institute. (2016). http://www
.genome.gov/About/.

Newport, F. (2013). Congress' job approval falls to 11% amid gov't shutdown: Americans' approval of their own representative averages
44%. http://www.gallup.com/poll/165281/congress-job-approval
-falls-amid-gov-shutdown.aspx

Niles, N. (2010). *Basics of the U.S. health care system*. Sudbury, MA:
Jones and Bartlett Publishers: 247–259.

Noe, R., Hollenbeck, J., Gerhart, B., & Wright, P. (2011). *Fundamentals
of human resource management* (4th ed.). Boston, MA: McGraw
Hill-Irwin.

Occupational Safety & Health Administration, U.S. Department
of Labor. (2016a). Ergonomics. http://www.osha.gov/SLTC
/ergonomics.

Occupational Safety & Health Administration, U.S. Department of
Labor. (2016b). Workers. http://www.osha.gov/workers.html.

Office of Technology Assessment. (1993). Impact of legal reforms on
medical malpractice cost, (OTA-BP-H-19). Washington, DC: U.S.
Government Printing Office.

Office of Inspector General (OIG), U.S. Department of Health and
Human Services. (2016). http://oig.hhs.gov/fraud/strike-force/.

Pho, K. (2012). Patient centered medical malpractice reform in New
Hampshire. http://www.kevinmd.com/blog/2012/04/patient
-centered-medical-malpractice-reform-hampshire.html.

Ringholz, J. (2005). An outline of the basic requirements of EMTALA,
as it relates to compliance. *Journal of Health Care Compliance*,
35–36.

Rosenbach, M., & Stone, A. (1990). Malpractice insurance costs and
physician practice—1981–1986. *Health Aff, 9*, 176–185.

Rosner, F. (2004). Informing the patient about a fatal disease: From
paternalism to autonomy—The Jewish view. *Cancer Investigation,
22*(6): 949–953.

Sekhar, M. & Vyas, N., (2013). Defensive medicine: A bane to healthcare. *Ann Med Health Sci Res.* 2013, Apr–Jun; *3*(2): 295–296.

Sedhom, S. (2009). Reacting to the Lilly Ledbetter Fair Pay Act: What every employer needs to know, *Employee Relations Law Journal, 35*(3): 3–8.

Shi, L., & Singh, D. (2008). *Essentials of the U.S. health care delivery system.* Sudbury, MA: Jones and Bartlett Publishers.

Sultz, H., & Young, K. (2006). *Health care USA: Understanding its organization and delivery* (5th ed.). Sudbury, MA: Jones and Bartlett Publishers.

U.S. Legal. (2016). Noneconomic damages law and legal definition. http://definitions.uslegal.com/n/non-economic-damages.

U.S. Department of Health & Human Services. (2016a). Health information privacy. http://www.hhs.gov/ocr/privacy/hipaa/administrative.

U.S. Department of Health & Human Services. (2016b). Medical treatment in Hill Burton funded healthcare facilities. http://www.hrsa.gov/gethealthcare/affordable/hillburton/.

U.S. Department of Labor. (2016). Young adults and the Affordable Care Act: Protecting young adults and eliminating burdens on families and businesses. http://www.dol.gov/ebsa/newsroom/fsdependent coverage.html.

U.S. Department of Labor (DOL). (2016). Nondiscrimination and wellness programs in health coverage in the group market: Rules and regulations. http://www.dol.gov/ebsa/Regs/fedreg/final/2006009557.htm.

U.S. Equal Employment Opportunity Commission (EEOC). (2010). EEOC sues Hawaii healthcare professionals for age discrimination. http://www.eeoc.gov/eeoc/newsroom/release/9-28-10.cfm.

Student Activity 9-1

In Your Own Words

Based on this chapter, please provide an explanation of the following concepts in your own words as they apply to healthcare law. DO NOT RECITE the text.

Affirmative action plan

Civil law

Criminal law

Defensive medicine

Job lock

Privacy Rule

Qui tam

Standard of care

Torts

Student Activity 9-2

Complete the following case scenarios based on the information provided in the chapter. Your answer must be IN YOUR OWN WORDS.

Real-Life Applications: Case Scenario One

As a new healthcare administrator, you are in charge of orientation for four new employees regarding employment law. There is one female, one disabled person, one African American, and one Muslim individual. You feel it is important to emphasize laws that were passed to protect employees from discrimination.

Activity

Select the laws you feel are the most important to the new employees. Provide a brief description of each law and its impact on the new employees.

Case Scenario Two

Your physician has informed you that she can no longer be your primary care provider. Her office manager called to tell you there would be a letter sent to you confirming that change. You are confused because you did not request this change. You ask your health navigator for assistance with this matter.

Activity

You and your health navigator perform research on how a physician is required to end a relationship and develop a letter to your physician stating your findings.

Case Scenario Three

Your cousin is involved in a lawsuit. He is the claimant of the case. You were very surprised and you asked him to give you a summary of the problem. He mentioned the words "non-economic damages," "standard of care," and "medical malpractice." You are not sure what these words mean, so you decide to do some research on them.

Activity

Research these three terms and provide specific "real-world" examples of the application of these terms.

Case Scenario Four

You just joined a company and one of the benefits was an employee wellness program. You are not sure what type of program it was and whether you would use the program.

Activity

Perform research on different types of employee wellness programs and discuss the relationship between employee wellness programs and the HIPAA law.

Student Activity 9-3

Internet Exercises

- Visit each of the websites listed here.
- Name the organization.
- Locate its mission statement on the website.
- Provide a brief overview of the activities of the organization.
- How does this organizations participate in the U.S. healthcare system?

Websites
https//:www.justice.gov

Organization Name
Mission Statement
Overview of Activities
Importance of Organization to U.S. Health Care

http://www.americanbar.org

Organization Name
Mission Statement
Overview of Activities
Importance of Organization to U.S. Health Care

http://www.healthlaw.org

Organization Name
Mission Statement
Overview of Activities
Importance of Organization to U.S. Health Care

http://www.eeoc.gov

Organization Name
Mission Statement
Overview of Activities
Importance of Organization to U.S. Health Care

http://www.medicalmalpractice.com

Organization Name
Mission Statement
Overview of Activities
Importance of Organization to U.S. Health Care

http://www.hg.org/health-law.html

Organization Name
Mission Statement
Overview of Activities
Importance of Organization to U.S. Health Care

Student Activity 9-4

Discussion Questions

The following are suggested discussion questions for this chapter.

1. Discuss the concepts of negligence and intentional torts and give examples of these in the healthcare industry.
2. What is tort reform? Do you believe tort reform is necessary? Why or why not?
3. Name and discuss three employment-related pieces of legislation that you feel are very important and explain why.
4. What is an affirmative action plan? Research on the Internet and discuss with your classmates the issues regarding this type of plan.
5. What is defensive medicine? Do you think physicians really do this? Research on the Internet and locate current information on this topic to share with your classmates.

Student Activity 9-5

Current Events

Perform an Internet search and find a current events topic that relates to this chapter. Provide a summary of the article and the link to the article and explain how the article relates to the chapter.

CHAPTER **10**

Navigating Healthcare Ethics

LEARNING OBJECTIVES

The student will be able to:

- Discuss the concept of ethics and its application to healthcare organizations.
- Define the four basic models of healthcare provider behavior.
- Define and discuss the four ethical models of a physician–patient relationship.
- Discuss how the health navigator can play a role in health ethics as it applies to a patient.
- Discuss the ethical dilemmas of organ transplants.
- Describe five different types of genetic testing.

DID YOU KNOW THAT?

- The concept of *bioethics* evolved as a result of the Nazi's human experimentation in World War II prisoner camps.
- Each day 18 people die waiting for an organ transplant.
- Xenotransplantation, which is transferring organs from one species to another, was first performed in 1984 when Baby Fae, a five-pound infant, received the heart of a baboon.
- The term euthanasia comes from the Greek language and means *good death*.
- As the cost of U.S. medical procedures has increased, medical tourism is becoming popular as more citizens travel overseas for medical procedures because the procedures are less expensive overseas.
- Workplace bullying is common in the healthcare industry.

INTRODUCTION

Legal standards are the minimal standard of action established for individuals in a society. Ethical standards are considered one level above a legal action because individuals make a choice based on what is the "right thing to do," not what is required by law. There are many interpretations of the concept of ethics. Ethics has been interpreted as the moral foundation for standards of conduct (Taylor, 1975). The concept of **ethical standards** applies to actions that are hoped for and expected by individuals. Actions may be considered legal but not ethical. There are many definitions of ethics but, basically, **ethics** is concerned with what are right and wrong choices as perceived by society and its individuals.

The concept of ethics is tightly woven throughout the healthcare industry. It has been dated back to Hippocrates, the father of medicine, in the 4th century BC, and evolved into the Hippocratic Oath, which is the foundation for the ethical guidelines for patient treatment by physicians. In 1847, the American Medical Association (AMA) published a *Code of Medical Ethics* that provided guidelines for the physician–provider relationship, emphasizing the duty to treat a patient (AMA, 2013a). To this day, physicians' actions have followed codes of ethics that demand the **duty to treat** (Wynia, 2007).

Applying the concept of ethics to the healthcare industry has created two areas of ethics: medical ethics and bioethics. **Medical ethics** focus on the decisions healthcare providers make on the patient's medical treatment. Euthanasia or physician-assisted suicide would be an example of a medical ethic. A **living will** is a legal document that outlines the wishes of the individual's medical treatment. This tool is helpful to the caregivers of the patient because it avoids any confusion about what type of end-of-life care the patient wants or does not want such as hydration or nutrition. An **advance directive**, in some states called a **durable power of attorney**, is an order that patients give to providers to ensure that, if they are terminally ill and incompetent to make a decision, certain measures will not be taken to prolong that patient's life. An advance directive should be inserted into the patient records. A living will focuses on life-sustaining decisions if the patient's death is imminent. The advance directive provides more options for life-sustaining decisions and end-stage decisions (Pozgar, 2016). If advance directives are not provided, the ethical decision of when to withdraw treatment may be placed on the family and provider. These issues are legally defined, although there are ethical ramifications surrounding these decisions.

This chapter will also discuss **bioethics**. This field of study is concerned with the ethical implications of certain biologic and medical procedures and technologies, such as cloning; **alternative reproductive methods**, such as in vitro fertilization; organ transplants; genetic engineering; and care of the terminally ill (Adelaide Center for Bioethics and Culture, 2013). Additionally, the rapid advances in medicine in these areas raise questions about the influence of technology on the field of medicine (Coleman, Bouesseau, & Reis, 2008).

It is important to understand the impact of ethics in different aspects of providing health care. Ethical dilemmas in health care are situations that test a provider's belief and what the provider should do professionally. Ethical dilemmas are often a conflict between personal and professional ethics. A **healthcare ethical dilemma** is a problem, situation, or opportunity that requires an individual, such as a healthcare provider, or an organization, such as a managed care practice, to choose an action that could be unethical. A decision-making model is presented that can help resolve ethical dilemmas in the healthcare field (Niles, 2013). This chapter will discuss ethical theories, codes of healthcare conduct, informed consent, confidentiality, special populations, research ethics, ethics in public health, end-of-life decisions, genetic testing and profiling, and biomedical ethics, which focuses on technology use and health care.

HEALTHCARE STAKEHOLDER MANAGEMENT MODEL

A **stakeholder** is an individual or group that has an interest in an organization or activity. A stakeholder should not be confused with a "shareholder," who has a financial interest in an organization. The concept of **stakeholder management** focuses on the relationship between organizations and all of their constituents, including shareholders, and how management recognizes the different expectations of each group. For example, customer stakeholders would have an interest in an organization where they purchase a product or a service. For some organizations, the government is an important stakeholder because the government regulates the organization's activities. Managing the interests of all of the stakeholders is a challenge for management, particularly in the healthcare industry. The pressure that stakeholders may impose on managers can affect their ethical decision-making process (Carroll & Buchholtz, 2008).

The basic stakeholder relationship in the healthcare industry is the relationship between the physician/clinician and the patient. However, Oddo (2001) has proposed that there are several other stakeholders that play a role in their relationship. Patients will have relationships that affect their interaction with the physician. The physician also has relationships with other stakeholders who have expectations of the physician. For example, the patient will have family and friends as well as a health insurance company or the government that is paying for the health procedure. The family and friends have expectations that the physician will cure their friend or family member. They have an emotional relationship. The health insurance company's relationship with the patient is professional. The physician's stakeholder relationships are more complex. They may be a part of a managed care facility or have admitting privileges at a hospital so they have the relationship with that entity and the entity might have expectations of how they will treat the patient. Physicians also are affected by health insurance companies who want them to treat the patient according to standardized diagnostic procedures. Drug companies have an interest in the physician because they want the provider to use their products. All of these stakeholders have expectations based on the simple relationship between the patient and provider. When these stakeholders place undue pressure on this relationship, the decision-making process of the provider may not always place the patient first, although, as stated previously, the provider is ethically bound to treat the patient.

BASIC CONCEPTS OF ETHICS IN THE HEALTHCARE WORKPLACE

Ethical standards are considered one level above legal standards because individuals make a choice based on what is the "right thing to do," not what is required by law. There are many interpretations of the concept of ethics. Ethics has been interpreted as the moral foundation for standards of conduct (Taylor, 1975). The concept of *ethical standards* applies to actions that are hoped for and expected by individuals. There are many definitions of ethics but, basically, ethics is concerned with what are right and wrong choices as perceived by society and its individuals. Ethical dilemmas are often a conflict between personal and professional ethics. A healthcare dilemma occurs when the ethical reasoning of the decision maker conflicts with the ethical reasoning of the patient and the institution. Dilemmas often are resolved through applying the guidelines provided by codes of medical ethics of medical

associations or healthcare institutions or using ethical decision-making models.

HEALTHCARE CODES OF ETHICS

As a result of many public ethical crises that have occurred, particularly in the business world, many organizations have developed a **code of ethics**, which are written guidelines for industry participants' actions. Codes of ethics provide a standard for operation so that all participants understand that if they do not adhere to this code, there may be negative consequences. The healthcare industry is no different.

Physicians have been guided by many healthcare codes of ethics. The American Medical Association created a code of ethics for physicians in 1847. This code was revised and adopted in 2001. Each healthcare professional has a code of conduct. The **American Nurses Association (ANA)** established a code for nurses in 1985, which was revised in 1995 and then again in 2001 (ANA, 2013). Healthcare executives have a code of ethics that was established in 1941 that discusses the relationship with their stakeholders. The **American College of Healthcare Executives (ACHE)** represents 30,000 executives internationally who participate in the healthcare system (ACHE, 2013). It also offers ethical policy statements on relevant issues such as creating an ethical culture for employees. In addition, the organization offers an ethics self-assessment tool that enables employees to target potential areas of ethical weakness. Many hospitals have established a code of ethics, which may help providers when they are dealing with medical situations, such as organ donations.

The **Advanced Medical Technology Association (AdvaMed)**, an industry association that represents medical products, also has developed a code of ethics that addresses interactions with healthcare professionals who are potential customers of their products. Their ethical issues are similar to the pharmaceutical industry because the industry encourages the use of medical devices by providing physicians with incentives such as gifts or paying for healthcare providers' travel to medical conferences (Advanced Medical Technology Association, 2013).

How to Develop a Code of Ethics

A code of ethics must be written clearly, so that employees at all organizational levels can utilize it. If a certain employee category needs a specific code of ethics, then a written code should be specifically developed for that category. The code must be current in laws and regulations. Driscoll and Hoffman (2000) recommend the following outline for developing a code of ethics:

1. Memorable Title
2. Leadership Letter
3. Table of Contents
4. Introduction
5. Core Values of the Organization
6. Code Provisions
7. Information and Resources

The code of ethics must be a user-friendly resource for the organization. It should be updated to include current laws and regulations. The language should be specific as to what the organization should expect from its employees, and training should be provided on the code of ethics so employees understand the organization's expectations.

WORKPLACE BULLYING

In 1992, Andrea Adams, a BBC journalist, coined the term **workplace bullying**, describing an ongoing harassing workplace behavior between employees that results in negative health outcomes for the targeted employees (Adams, 1992). Workplace bullying is receiving increased attention worldwide as a negative organizational issue. It is considered a serious and chronic workplace stressor that can lead to diminished work productivity and work quality (Hoel, Faragher, & Cooper, 2004). The negative behavior is considered bullying if it is repeated over an extended period of time. It can occur between colleagues, supervisors, or supervisees, although the bully often is the supervisor. Definitions also include negative verbal or nonverbal behavior such as snide comments, verbal or physical threats, or items being thrown. Employees also have reported less-aggressive behavior such as demeaning their work or gossiping about them on a continual basis. The literature has reported an increased incident of bullying reported in healthcare organizations and in academe (Ayoko, Callan, & Hartel, 2003; Vartia, 2001; Djurkovic, McCormack, & Casimir, 2008).

Workplace Bullying in Healthcare

Workplace bullying has been reported as common in health care. Specifically, there are bullying issues between physicians and nurses. The Center for American Nurses, American Association of Critical-Care Nurses, International Council of Nurses, and National Student Nurses Association all have issued statements regarding the need for healthcare organizations to eliminate bullying in the healthcare workplace. Often, verbal abuse also occurs towards nurses by physicians, patients, and their families. **Lateral violence** also occurs in health care, which is defined as "nurse to nurse" aggression, demonstrated by both verbal and nonverbal behavior (American Nurses Association, 2011).

Legal Implications of Workplace Bullying

There is no federal legislation in the United States that forbids workplace bullying. New York is the only state that has enacted legislation that forbids this type of behavior in the workplace. However, there are two federal laws that can be applied in workplace bullying: The Occupational Safety and Health Act of 1970 (OSHA) and Title VII of the Civil Rights Act of 1964. The OSHA Act of 1970 states that employers must provide a safe and healthful working environment for their employees. Under Title VII of the Civil Rights Act, if a protected class employee (gender, religion, ethnicity, etc.) is bullied by another employee, the action can be illegal based on the concept of a hostile work environment, which is illegal under sexual harassment.

Recommendations to Eliminate Workplace Bullying

To date, there is no federal legislation that specifically addresses workplace bullying. In order to reduce its prevalence, employers should implement policies to eliminate this behavior. The following are recommendations for organizations, including health care, to eliminate workplace bullying (LaVan & Martin, 2007):

1. Adopt a policy of zero tolerance for workplace bullying and develop measures to discipline bullies in the workplace.
2. Create an organizational culture that focuses on a positive work environment enabling all individuals to pursue their careers.
3. Reward behaviors that encourage teamwork and collaboration among employees and their supervisors.
4. Develop an educational program for all employees on what constitutes workplace bullying.

Workplace bullying continues to be a pervasive organizational problem worldwide. In the United States, the Workplace Bullying Institute has developed a Healthy Workplace Bill that precisely defines workplace bullying and extends protection to employees against this type of behavior. The bill has been introduced in 14 states since 2003. There is no specific federal legislation against bullying, so workplace bullying will continue to be legal unless legislation is enacted. It is important that workplace bullying educational programs and organizational policies be implemented to ensure that employees are protected against this type of negative behavior. The results can be devastating from both an organizational and individual level.

In 2008, **The Joint Commission** developed a standard for workplace bullying called "intimidating and disruptive behaviors in the workplace." They issued the following statement:

Intimidating and disruptive behaviors can foster medical errors, contribute to poor patient satisfaction and to preventable adverse outcomes, increase the cost of care, and cause qualified clinicians, administrators, and managers to seek new positions in more professional environments. Safety and quality of patient care is dependent on teamwork, communication, and a collaborative work environment. To assure quality and to promote a culture of safety, health care

organizations must address the problem of behaviors that threaten the performance of the healthcare team. (The Joint Commission, 2008, p. 1)

Two leadership standards are now part of The Joint Commission's accreditation provisions: The first requires an institution to have "a code of conduct that defines acceptable and disruptive and inappropriate behaviors." The second requires an institution "to create and implement a process for managing disruptive and inappropriate behaviors" (Yamada, 2004).

A recent Joint Commission study found that more than 50% of nurses have suffered some type of bullying with 90% observing some type of abuse. The standard focused on the impact these types of behavior have on patient care quality. The Joint Commission requires healthcare institutions to create a code of conduct that defines appropriate behavior and has a system in place to manage inappropriate behavior such as workplace bullying. In 2016, the Joint Commission developed the resource center in response to statistics showing higher rates of workplace violence in health care compared to other settings (the Joint Commission, 2016).

The Center for Professional Health at the Vanderbilt University Medical Center has developed a program for treating and remediating disruptive behaviors by physicians. Nurses' unions also are developing education programs on workplace bullying (Minding the Workplace, 2009).

ETHICS AND THE DOCTOR–PATIENT RELATIONSHIP

The foundation of health care is the relationship between the patient and physician. In 2004, the **American College of Physicians and Harvard Pilgrim Health Care Ethics Program** developed a statement of ethics for managed care. The following is a summary of the statements (Povar et al., 2004):

- Clinicians, healthcare plans, insurance companies, and patients should be honest in their relationship with each other.

- These parties should recognize the importance of the clinician and patient relationship and its ethical obligations.
- Clinicians should maintain accurate patient records.
- All parties should contribute to developing healthcare policies.
- The clinician's primary duty is the care of the patient.
- Clinicians have the responsibility to practice effective and efficient medicine.
- Clinicians should recognize that all individuals, regardless of their position, should have health care.
- Healthcare plans and their insurers should openly explain their policies regarding reimbursement of types of health care.
- Patients have a responsibility to understand their health insurance.
- Health plans should not ask clinicians to compromise their ethical standards of care.
- Clinicians should enter agreements with healthcare plans that support ethical standards.
- Confidentiality of patient information should be protected.
- Clinicians should disclose conflicts of interest to their patients.
- Information provided to patients should be clearly understood by the patient.

This statement was developed as a result of the continued economic and policy changes in the healthcare industry. It provided guidelines to healthcare practitioners, healthcare organizations, and the healthcare insurance industry about ethical actions in the changing healthcare environment.

PHYSICIAN–PATIENT RELATIONSHIP MODEL

To understand the physician–patient relationship, several different models can be applied. Veatch (1972) identified four models that apply to the doctor–patient relationship: engineering model, priestly model, contractual model, and collegial model.

The **engineering model** focuses on patients and their power to make decisions about their health care. The provider gives the patient all of the necessary information to make a decision. The provider empowers the patient with knowledge to make a decision. The **priestly model** assumes the doctor will make the best decisions for the patient's health. The patient assumes a passive role, giving the provider great power in the decision-making process. This is a traditional relationship that often would occur between the elderly and physicians because they were taught to revere the medical world. The **contractual model**, based on a legal foundation, assumes there is an agreement between the two parties, assuming mutual goals. It is a relationship between the two parties with equal power. The patient understands the legal ramifications of the relationship. The **collegial model** assumes trust between the patient and doctor and that decision making is an equal effort (Veatch, 1972). These models are dependent on the type of relationship a patient expects with his or her practitioner. In each model, ethics plays a role in the relationship. Although the provider may play different roles in each of these models, the underlying foundation is assuming that the doctor's actions are ethical and represent the best interest of the patient.

According to Beauchamp and Childress (2001) and Gillon (1994), the role of ethics in the healthcare industry is based on five basic values that all healthcare providers should observe:

- **Respect for autonomy**: Decision making may be different and healthcare providers must respect their patients' decisions even if they differ from their own.
- **Beneficence**: The healthcare provider should have the patient's best interests when making a decision.
- **Nonmalfeasance**: The healthcare provider will cause no harm when taking action.
- **Justice**: Healthcare providers will make fair decisions.
- **Dignity**: Patients should be treated with respect and dignity.

Each of these principles will be discussed in depth because these concepts are important to understanding the role of ethics in the healthcare industry. **Autonomy**, which is defined as self-rule, is an important concept to healthcare because it is applied to **informed consent**, which requires a provider to obtain the approval of a patient who has been provided adequate information to make a decision regarding intervention. Informed consent is a legal requirement for medical intervention. As part of the autonomy concept, it is important that providers respect the decision of their patient even if the patient's decisions do not agree with the provider's recommendation. For example, a woman who has been diagnosed with a very advanced stage of melanoma (skin cancer) was told by her provider that she could enroll her in an experimental program that would give her two to three months to live. The intervention is very potent with severe side effects. The woman decided to try a homeopathic medicine to attack her disease. The doctor was not in agreement with the woman's choice but respected her decision. She told the patient she would provide assistance with pain medication, if needed. This situation is an excellent example of autonomy in medicine.

Beneficence in the healthcare industry means that the best interest of the patient should always be the first priority of the healthcare provider and healthcare organizations. Nonmalfeasance further states that healthcare providers must not take any actions to harm the patient. As discussed in the paragraph on autonomy, this concept appears to be very easy to understand; however, there may be an interpretation between the provider and the patient as to what is best for the patient. For example, Jehovah's Witnesses, a religious sect, do not believe in blood transfusions and will not give consent during an operation for a transfusion to occur, despite the procedure's ability to possibly save a life (Miller, 2006). The provider has been trained to believe in beneficence and malfeasance. However, from the providers' point of view, if they respect the wishes of the patient and family, they will be potentially harming their patient.

Justice or fairness in the healthcare industry emphasizes that patients should be treated equally and that health care should be accessible to all. Justice should be applied to the way healthcare services are distributed, which means that healthcare services are available to all individuals. Unfortunately, in the United States, the healthcare system does not provide accessibility to all of its citizens. Access to health care often is determined by the ability to pay either out of pocket or by an employer- or government-sponsored program. In countries with universal healthcare coverage, justice in the healthcare industry is more prevalent. With an estimated 36 million uninsured in the United States in 2014, one can say that justice has not prevailed in the healthcare industry (Centers for Disease Control and Prevention, 2016).

PHARMACEUTICAL MARKETING TO PHYSICIANS

Drug companies have a long-standing direct marketing relationship with physicians. Over the past two decades, this relationship has received more scrutiny because of its appearance of unethical behavior. The pharmaceutical companies provide free samples and information to physicians because the companies want the provider to use their products. Although providers deny that these "perks" influence their decisions in choosing drugs, federal legislation—the **Physician Payment Sunshine Act**—was passed in 2010 as part of the Affordable Care Act (effective August 2013). This act requires manufacturers of drugs, medical devices, and other healthcare products who have relationships with Medicare and Medicaid providers and CHIP programs to submit reports annually listing any payments and items of value they give to providers. They also must report ownership interests held by physicians and their families (AMA, 2013b). In 2002 and updated in 2009, the **Pharmaceutical Research and Manufacturers of America (PhRMA)** implemented a new code of conduct governing physician–industry relationships (PhRMA, 2013). The code discourages gifts to physicians and other monetary rewards, emphasizing the relationship should focus on enhancing the quality of treatment of the patient. It emphasizes ethical marketing to the physicians. These types of codes of conducts will provide guidelines for the relationship between the provider and the companies, thereby providing more accountability for the use of certain prescriptions by providers. This type of relationship can test the ethical relationship between the provider and patient.

DECISION MODEL FOR HEALTHCARE DILEMMAS

Healthcare dilemmas require guidelines to process a solution to the dilemma. Codes of ethics and HR training can assist with a solution. Employee training can include a decision-making model that will assist the individual to process the steps in resolving the situation. The PLUS ethical decision-making model consists of (Ethics Resource Center, 2009):

1. Identification of the dilemma
2. Identification of the conflicting ethics of each party
3. Identification of alternatives to a solution
4. Identification of the impact of each alternative
5. Selection of the solution

Application of the Decision-Making Model

Healthcare Dilemma (discussed earlier): An oncologist has a patient with an advanced stage of melanoma (skin cancer). Prognosis: three to six months to live. The oncologist has developed an experimental treatment program that has severe side effects but may give the patient an additional six months. The patient prefers alternative remedies for medical treatment such as homeopathic solutions (natural remedies).

Step 1: *Define the problem*. This is the most important part of the process. This step should define the problem and the ultimate outcome of the decision-making process. Application: The problem is the differing views of treatment by both the physician and the patient. The physician does not believe in homeopathic remedies. The ultimate outcome of the decision-making process is to prolong the life of the patient, if possible.

Step 2: *Identify the alternative(s) to the problem.* List the possible alternatives to the desired outcome. Attempt to identify at least three, but five are preferred.

Alternative 1: Patient accepts experimental treatment program.

Alternative 2: Patient rejects experimental treatment program.

Alternative 3: Physician researches homeopathic remedies for patient.

Alternative 4: Physician refuses to research homeopathic remedies for patient.

Alternative 5: Patient seeks other medical advice from different physician.

Alternative 6: Physician refers patient to physician who is an expert in homeopathic medicine.

Step 3: *Evaluate the identified alternatives.* Discuss the positive and negative impact of each alternative.

Alternative 1: Patient accepts experimental treatment program.

Positive: Patient's cancer is eradicated or is in remission.

Negative: Treatment has no impact on cancer. Patient dies.

Alternative 2: Patient rejects experimental treatment program.

Positive: Cancer goes into remission.

Negative: Patient dies shortly.

Alternative 3: Physician researches homeopathic remedies for patient.

Positive: Physician finds a homeopathic remedy that can be used in conjunction with experimental program. Patient accepts treatment. Cancer is eradicated or goes into remission.

Negative: Physician finds no homeopathic solution that can be used in conjunction with experimental program. Patient refuses treatment. Patient dies shortly.

Alternative 4: Physician refuses to research homeopathic remedies for patient.

Positive: Patient believes in physician and agrees to try experimental program. Program is successful.

Negative: Patient cuts ties with physician. Receives no treatment and dies shortly.

Alternative 5: Patient seeks other medical advice from different physician.

Positive: Patient finds a physician who agrees with homeopathic remedies. Patient accepts homeopathic remedies and cancer is eradicated or goes into remission.

Negative: Patient does not find a physician who would help her and dies quickly, trying to find someone.

Alternative 6: Physician refers patient to physician who is expert in homeopathic medicine.

Positive: Patient is treated with a homeopathic solution that prolongs her life.

Negative: Patient is treated with a homeopathic solution that does not prolong her life.

Step 4: *Make the decision.* In the healthcare industry, the decision must include the patient's best interest and his or her values, which can be conflicting at times. However, patients have the right to make an informed decision about their health. In this instance, alternative 6 is chosen, because the patient believes in homeopathic medicine. The physician who does not believe in natural remedies respected the patient's beliefs, which differed from hers, but she still wanted to help the patient. The physician wanted to be involved in the patient care by supporting the beliefs of her patient.

Step 5: *Implement the decision.* Once the decision is made, the physician actually finds a physician referral that would help her patient. The primary physician said she would provide any assistance with pain medication if needed.

Step 6: *Evaluate the decision.* The patient accepted the referral of the new physician and entered a homeopathic treatment program. The patient lived three more years with a high quality of life.

This decision-making model is an excellent method of resolving many types of healthcare dilemmas. This model can be utilized in employee training on ethical issues in the healthcare workplace.

ROLE OF THE HEALTH NAVIGATOR IN ETHICAL DILEMMAS

The health navigator can play an important patient advocate role when dealing with ethical dilemmas. This is pertinent particularly to the relationship between the patient and clinician. The issue with autonomy and beneficence between the two stakeholders can be difficult. The patient has the absolute right to make a healthcare decision even if the clinician does not agree it may the best decision for the patient. Autonomy focuses on respect for the patient and beneficence focuses on doing the best for the patient's health. The two may conflict if the patient feels differently. The health navigator can be a mediator between the physician and the patient to resolve any issues. Encouraging the patient to develop advance directives so caregivers and their physicians understand and respect their wishes can be very important.

ETHICS AND PUBLIC HEALTH

In contrast to the bioethicist view of the physician–patient relationship, ethical analysis has expanded to public health. There are several ethics in public health that focus on the design and implementation of measures to monitor and improve the community's health (Coleman et al., 2008). Issues in public health include inaccessibility to health care for certain populations, response to bioterrorism, research in developing countries, health promotion and its infringement on an individual's lifestyle choices, and public health's response to emergencies. The concept of **paternalism** and public health is the concern that individual freedom will be restricted for the sake of public health activities because the government infringes on individual choices for the sake of protecting the community (Ascension Health, 2016).

The **Nuffield Council on Bioethics**, based in Great Britain, has proposed a stewardship model that outlines the principles public health policy makers should utilize globally. This model addresses the issues of paternalism in public health. The **stewardship model** states that public health officials should achieve the stated health outcomes for the population while minimizing restrictions on people's freedom of choice.

The focus of public health is to reduce the population's health risks from other people's actions such as drunk driving, smoking in public places, environmental conditions, inaccessibility to health care, and maintaining safe working environments. While promoting a healthy lifestyle, according to the Nuffield Council on Bioethics, it is also important that public health programs do not force people into programs without their consent or introduce interventions that may invade people's privacy. The Council also introduces the concept of an intervention ladder that establishes a ranking of the type of public health intervention introduced, which may minimize people's choices. The higher the intervention moves up the ladder, the more justification is required for the action (Nuffield Council on Bioethics, 2016).

Childress, Faden, and Gaare (2002) specify five justifications for public health interventions that infringe on individual choices. The criteria are: (1) effectiveness, (2) need, (3) proportionality, (4) minimal infringement, and (5) public education. **Effectiveness** is essential to demonstrate that the public health efforts were successful and, therefore, it was necessary to limit individual freedom of choice. The need for a public health intervention must be demonstrated to limit individual freedom. If the **proportionality** of the public health intervention outweighs freedom of choice, then the intervention must be warranted. If the public health intervention satisfies effectiveness, need, and proportionality, the least restrictive intervention or **minimal infringement** on individual freedoms should be considered first. Lastly, public health must provide **public education** to explain the interventions and why the infringement on individual choices is warranted. For example, bioterrorism is now a viable threat. If it has been determined that a public health threat exists as a result of some biological weapons, then mandatory blood tests, possible quarantines, and other measures that would infringe on individual freedom of choice must be implemented (Buchanan, 2008).

Another ethical public health issue is the duty of practitioners to treat individuals during a public health crisis. If there is a natural disaster, what is the duty to treat during a time of crisis? During Hurricane Katrina, several healthcare professionals volunteered to stay behind in a local hospital. Unfortunately, several patients in the hospital died, and the providers were accused of murdering their patients. As a result of this incident, many professionals are now wary of volunteering during a crisis. From their perspective, if they commit to an ethical reaction, they may be rewarded with a criminal liability. There are civil liability protections that differ from state to state, such as Good Samaritan laws. Physicians practicing in free clinics are protected by federal law. Federal lawmakers should pass legislation that protects these healthcare professionals during public health emergencies (Wynia, 2007).

ETHICS IN RESEARCH

Conducting research involving human subjects requires the assessment of the risks and benefits to the human subjects, which must be explained clearly to them before they consent to participate in the research is given. The principles of ethical research are outlined in **Institutional Review Boards (IRBs)**. An IRB is a group that has been formally designated to review and monitor biomedical research involving human subjects. An IRB has the authority to approve, require modifications in (to secure approval), or disapprove research. This group review serves an important role in the protection of the rights and welfare of human research subjects (Food and Drug Administration [FDA], 2013). Any organization that performs research should develop an IRB. The ethical component of an IRB is to protect the participants of the study. IRBs require the researchers to maximize the benefits and minimize the risks to the participant and explain these assessments clearly. It is important that the IRB does not approve a study that imposes significant risks on the subjects.

Assuming the study clears the IRB's assessment of risks and benefits, it is important for subjects to understand the study and its impact on them. Informed consent, as it relates to treatment, is one of the basic ethical protections for human-subject research. It is designed to protect human subjects and increase autonomy. Informed consent protects human subjects because it allows the individual to consider personal issues before participating in medical research. Informed consent increases autonomy because it provides individuals with the opportunity to make a choice to exercise control over their lives (Mehlman & Berg, 2008). Research informed consent requires the disclosure of appropriate information to assist the individual in project participation.

Both the Department of Health and Human Services (HHS) and FDA have outlined common rule regulations that comprise the elements of informed consent. **Common rule** elements include a written statement that includes the purpose and duration of the study, the procedures and if they are experimental, any foreseen risks and potential benefits, and any alternative procedures that may benefit the subject (FDA, 2013; Korenman, 2009). Additional requirements are needed for children, pregnant women, people with disabilities, mentally disabled people, prisoners, etc. The IRB must provide guidelines for parents that have children who participate in research and for those subjects that may be mentally disabled who could be unduly influenced (Mehlman & Berg, 2008).

BIOETHICAL ISSUES

Designer or Donor Babies

Alternative reproductive methods are methods of conception that parents use to have children, such as in vitro fertilization, which means that the embryo is fertilized in a clinic using the sperm from the father. For couples who choose in vitro fertilization, **preimplantation genetic diagnosis (PGD)** can be performed to test the embryo for tissue compatibility with siblings prior to being transplanted into the mother. Then, if one of the siblings becomes ill, the "designer baby" can save his or her life by providing bone marrow

transplants. If it is determined that the embryo is not compatible, it could be destroyed. This procedure is considered controversial because many people consider the embryo early human life. Secondly, it raises the issue about whether the physicians and parents are "playing God" by determining whether the embryo should be saved. Does this type of control dehumanize **procreation** or creation of life? Another issue is what impact this would have on a child who may eventually become aware that s/he was created to save a sibling (Dayal & Zarek, 2008).

Cloning

All human beings possess **stem cells**, which are "starter" cells for the development of body tissue that has yet to be formed into specialized tissues for certain parts of the body (Sullivan, 2006). The term **cloning** applies to any procedure that creates a genetic replica of a cell or organism. There are two major types of cloning: **reproductive cloning**, which creates cloned babies, and **therapeutic cloning**, also called **research cloning**, which uses the same process but focuses on replicating sources for stem cells to replaced damaged tissues. The most famous reproductive clone was Dolly, the sheep that was cloned in 1996 from an adult cell (Baylis, 2002). Several countries have banned cloning for reproductive purposes but have been more lenient in therapeutic cloning. There are several ethical issues regarding cloning. Researchers worldwide have attempted human cloning with no success. Some feel that cloning humans is unnatural and "playing God" rather than allowing procreation to progress naturally. Some people, however, have cloned their beloved pets, and this has created an uproar. People are highly focused on the reproductive cloning issues rather than the potential research success of cloning that could result in effective treatment of many diseases. However, therapeutic cloning also is considered unethical because it involves destroying embryos to obtain healthy stem cells for research.

Research has focused on stem cells that could replace damaged body tissues from spinal injuries or cure diseases such as Parkinson's disease. These stem cells could be derived from surplus human embryos that are stored at in vitro fertilization clinics and were not used for fertility procedures. The ethical issue, similar to the designer baby issues, is that, in order to use the stem cells, they would be destroying human embryos for research purposes because embryos are considered human life by many people. The issue in both cases also is what should happen to the excess embryos that are stored in clinics? Studies have indicated there may be an estimated 400,000 embryos stored in U.S. clinics that may eventually be destroyed (The Coalition of Americans for Research Ethics, 2013). Could these embryos be used to develop therapies and cures for disease?

Genetic Testing

Genetic testing is carried out on populations based on age, gender, or other risk factors to determine if they are at risk for a serious genetic disease or if they have a carrier gene that they may pass on to their children. Genetic tests may be analyzed from bodily tissue, including blood, cells from the mouth, saliva, hair, skin, tumors, or fluid surrounding the fetus during pregnancy (National Human Genome Research Institute [NHGRI], 2016). The specimen is analyzed by a laboratory. There are several types of tests:

- **Diagnostic testing** is used to identify the disease when a person is exhibiting symptoms.
- **Predictive and asymptomatic testing** (no symptoms) is used to identify any gene changes that may increase the likelihood of a person developing a disease.
- **Carrier testing** is used to identify individuals who carry a gene that is linked to a disease. The individual may exhibit no symptoms but may pass the gene to offspring who may develop the disease or carry the gene themselves.
- **Prenatal testing** is offered to identify fetuses with potential diseases or conditions.
- Newborn screening is performed during the first one to two days of life to determine if the child has a disease that could affect its development.

- **Pharmacogenomic testing** is performed to assess how medicines react to an individual's genetic makeup.
- **Research genetic testing** focuses on how genes affect disease development.

The **Human Genome Project**, a long-term government-funded project completed in 2003, identified all of the 20,000–25,000 genes found in human DNA. Researchers catalogued these genes, which made it easier to quickly determine the genes an individual possesses. As a result of genetics research, several genes have been identified as markers of prediction of diseases such as breast cancer, colon cancer, cystic fibrosis, and Down syndrome in fetuses (Oak Ridge National Laboratory [ORNL], 2016).

Although information gained from genetic testing is important to individuals and their families, there are several ethical issues regarding genetic testing. If employers were aware of this information, would they use it to discriminate against employees? Would parents decide against having a child because of a result of a genetic test? How accurate are the genetic tests? There are no regulations regarding genetic tests, so individuals and families may make decisions based on faulty laboratory tests. It is important that genetic testing be provided in conjunction with genetic counseling to ensure that individuals understand the results. Recently, private companies have developed home kits for genetic testing. This type of information without discussion with a genetic counselor or physician may have repercussions because an individual may make decisions based on lack of comprehension.

Euthanasia: Treating the Terminally Ill

End-of-life issues of a patient can be an ethical challenge. Healthcare providers may find this difficult to understand because they have been trained to save lives. **Euthanasia**, or assisting a patient with ending his or her life, is the term most often associated with end-of-life issues. From the Greek word meaning *good death*, this practice may seem unethical because it involves allowing an individual to die. Letting a patient die may be morally justifiable if it has been determined that any medical intervention is completely futile. There are two major types of euthanasia: voluntary and nonvoluntary. **Voluntary euthanasia** is assisting a patient with ending his or her life at the patient's request. **Nonvoluntary euthanasia** means ending the life of an incompetent patient usually at the request of a family member. The two most famous nonvoluntary euthanasia cases are Karen Quinlan and Terri Schiavo. In 1975, the New Jersey Supreme Court granted Ms. Quinlan's father the right to remove his daughter's respirator, which resulted in her death 10 years later. She had remained in a coma or persistent vegetative state for 10 years. Because she was not able to make the decision herself, the judge granted her father the right to limit any medical interventions to continue her life. Terri Schiavo suffered a heart attack in 1990 and remained in a coma on a feeding tube until 2005, when the Florida Supreme Court allowed her husband to remove her feeding tube despite her parent's protests (University of Miami Ethics Programs, 2016).

There is confusion regarding the difference between euthanasia and physician-assisted suicide. **Physician-assisted suicide** refers to the physician providing the means for death, most often with a prescription. The patient, not the physician, will ultimately administer the lethal medication. Euthanasia generally means that the physician would act directly, for instance by giving a lethal injection, to end the patient's life.

Although euthanasia is illegal in all states except Oregon, Washington (2008), Vermont (2013), and California (2016) (physician-assisted suicide), it is important to examine end-of-life issues because many of us will face them ourselves or with a loved one. The **Oregon Death with Dignity Act (ODWDA)** was passed in 1994 and became effective in 1997. Since 1997, when data on these occurrences began to be maintained, each year there are more physician-assisted suicides. During 2015, 218 people received prescriptions for lethal medications under the provisions of the Oregon DWDA, compared to 155 during 2014. As of January 27, 2016, the Oregon Public Health Division had received reports of 132 people who had died during 2015 from ingesting

the medications prescribed under DWDA. Since the law was passed in 1997, a total of 1,545 people have had prescriptions written under the DWDA, and 991 patients have died from ingesting the medications (ODWDA, 2015 data summary, 2016). **Figure 10-1** is a copy of the patient request form for physician-assisted suicide in Oregon.

The Washington mandate, effective 2009, was modeled after the Oregon law. In both states, the patient needs to be deemed terminal by two physicians. If physicians have doubts about a patient's mental state, a mental health professional will be consulted. The patient must make an oral and witnessed written request and another request 15 days later. The physicians must inform the patient about hospice and palliative care options (O'Reilly, 2009). In 2015, medication was dispensed to 213 individuals (defined as 2015 participants):

- Prescriptions were written by 142 different physicians.
- Medications were dispensed by 49 different pharmacists.

Of the 213 participants in 2015:

- 202 are known to have died.
- 166 died after ingesting the medication.
- 24 died without having ingested the medication.
- For the remaining 12 people who died, ingestion status is unknown.
- For the eleven participants not included among those known to have died, the state health department has received no documentation that indicates death has occurred.

Since the last Death with Dignity report was published on July 28, 2015, the department received additional information on participants from prior years. As of March 25, 2016, 172 of the 176 participants in 2014, 169 of the 173 participants in 2013, 121 of the 121 participants in 2012, 102 of the 103 participants in 2011, 87 of the 87 participants in 2010, and 64 of the 65 participants in 2009 had died. The status of the four remaining participants in 2014, the four remaining participants 2013, the one remaining participant in

FIGURE 10-1 Oregon Patient Request Form

REQUEST FOR MEDICATION
TO END MY LIFE IN A HUMANE AND DIGNIFIED MANNER

I, _____, am an adult of sound mind.

I am suffering from _____, which my attending/prescribing physician has determined is a terminal disease and which has been medically confirmed by a consulting physician.

I have been fully informed of: my diagnosis; prognosis; the nature of medication to be prescribed and potential associated risks; the expected result; and feasible alternatives, including comfort care, hospice care and pain control.

I request that my attending/prescribing physician prescribe medication that will end my life in a humane and dignified manner and also contact any pharmacist to fill the prescription.

Initial One

[____] I have informed my family of my decision and taken their opinions into consideration.

[____] I have decided not to inform my family of my decision.

[____] I have no family to inform of my decision.

I understand that I have the right to rescind this request at any time.

I understand the full import of this request, and I expect to die when I take the medication to be prescribed.

I make this request voluntarily and without reservation, and I accept full moral responsibility for my actions.

I further understand that although most deaths occur within three hours, my death may take longer and my physician has counseled me about this possibility.

Signature:	County of Residence:	Date:

DECLARATION OF WITNESSES

By *initialing* and *signing* below, we declare that the person making and signing the above request:

Witness 1   Witness 2

[__] [__] 1. Is personally known to us or has provided proof of identity;

[__] [__] 2. **Signed this request in our presence on the date following the person's signature;**

[__] [__] 3. Appears to be of sound mind and not under duress, fraud or undue influence;

[__] [__] 4. Is not a patient for whom either of us is the attending physician.

Printed Name: Witness 1	Signature:	Date:
Printed Name: Witness 2	Signature:	Date:

NOTE: One witness shall not be a relative (by blood, marriage or adoption) of the person signing this request, shall not be entitled to any portion of the person's estate upon death and shall not own, operator be employed at a health care facility where the person is a patient or resident. If the patient is an inpatient at a long-term health care facility, one of the witnesses shall be an individual designated by the facility.

PLEASE MAKE A COPY OF THIS FORM TO KEEP IN YOUR HOME

Copies of this form are available at:
http://public.health.oregon.gov/ProviderPartnerResources/EvaluationResearch/DeathwithDignityAct/Pages/pasforms.aspx

Rev. 02/14

Oregon Patient Request Form. Retrieved from https://public.health.oregon.gov/ProviderPartnerResources/EvaluationResearch/DeathwithDignityAct/Documents/pt-req.pdf

2011, and the one remaining participant in 2009 remains unknown. These participants may have died, but no documentation of the death has been received (Washington Department of Health, 2016). A survey of terminal patients showed they requested the prescriptions because they felt they were becoming a burden on their families, losing their independence, and losing the ability to enjoy life (Washington State Department of Health, 2012).

This has been a controversial piece of legislation that has generated commentary throughout the country and worldwide. Healthcare providers who support euthanasia feel that (1) it is an opportunity to relieve the pain a patient is experiencing at the end of his or her life; (2) it is an example of autonomy in life by allowing a person to choose when he or she will die; and (3) it allows an opportunity to be released a person from a life that no longer has quality. Healthcare providers who believe that euthanasia is unethical believe that (1) it devalues the concept of life, (2) it may merely be an opportunity to contain medical costs for both the families and health insurance companies and, most importantly, and (3) a provider should not be directly involved in killing a patient (Sullivan, 2005). The opponents of euthanasia also believe that a physician cannot, with medical certainty, tell patients that they will die within six months. The patient's emotional state and response to medication may alter that prognosis.

Dr. Jack Kevorkian and Dr. Phillip Nitschke

It is important to mention two physicians who have strongly supported euthanasia throughout the years. U.S. physician Dr. Jack Kevorkian, or Dr. Death as he was called, had provided assisted-suicide services to at least 45 ill patients. In 1989, he developed a suicide machine that allowed patients to administer a lethal injection of medication to themselves. In 1997, the U.S. Supreme Court ruled that individuals who want to kill themselves, but are physically unable to do so, have no constitutional right to end their lives. Dr. Kevorkian was sentenced to 10–25 years in prison that same year. He was paroled in 2007 because he

was in failing health, and he died in 2011 (Notable Names Database, 2016).

Australian physician Dr. Phillip Nitschke travels internationally presenting "how to commit suicide" clinics. Several years ago, he created a concoction from household ingredients that he calls the "Peaceful Pill." He believes that if there is a right to life, there is also a right to die, and that individuals should have the right to choose to end their own life. He does not restrict this right to just the terminally ill. He also believes that the depressed, the elderly, and the grieving should have the right to end their lives (Exit International, 2016).

Transplantation

Transplantation is the general procedure of implanting a functional organ from one person to another. This procedure can include simple blood transfusions or complicated procedures such as heart and lung transplants and bone marrow transplants. Organ transplants are becoming a more common approach to the treatment of diseased organs, making organ donations important to saving lives. Many patients have a significant chance for long-term survival because of impressive gains in the field (Burrows, 2004; Woloschak, 2003). Organs can be harvested from a living or dead person. There are two major ethical and legal issues associated with organ transplants between humans, including (1) the decision-making process for who receives the organ and (2) financial remuneration from selling organs, which has resulted in a black market for buying and selling organs. By 1990, many countries and the World Health Organization have issued similar bans. The Ethics Committee of the Transplantation Society issued a policy statement further supporting the ban on illegally buying and selling organs (Friedman & Friedman, 2006).

Who Should Receive the Organ?

According to the **United Network for Organ Sharing (UNOS)**, since 1984, as a result of the passage of the National Organ Transplant Act, it is illegal in the United States to buy and sell organs, which has resulted in 22 people dying daily because of lack of available organs. In 2016, 13,550 transplant operations occurred and 120,000 are people waiting for an organ. Of those 13,500 operations, 43% of the patients who received the transplants were between 50 and 64 years of age with 18% older than 65 years of age (UNOS, 2016). Ethical questions arise when deciding who will receive an organ. In the United States, there is an organ waiting list. Should the sickest recipient waiting on the organ list receive the organ, or should the patient who may live longer receive it? Under the current UNOS, patients awaiting a transplant are assigned a priority based on medical need. If a patient is waiting for a heart transplant, the patient who is on life support or is in intensive care has first priority. Kidneys are allocated based on a point system maintained by UNOS. Liver transplants also include guidelines on alcohol abuse, which often destroys livers. UNOS guidelines require six months of sobriety prior to a transplant. Should the alcoholic receive a liver transplant at all? Some organ transplant centers will not provide any liver transplants to alcoholics (Giuliano, 1997).

A recent trend over the last decade is transplanting organs in the elderly. The ethical dilemma for a surgeon is whether to transplant an organ in an older patient rather than trying to save the life of a younger patient. Studies have indicated that survival rates for elderly lung recipients are acceptable—a 73.6%, 3-year survival rate compared to 74.2% for younger patients (Davis, 2008). However, does the surgeon opt to shorten the life of a younger patient in order to give an additional three years of life to an elderly patient who already has lived a full life?

Consent for Organ Donations

As stated in a previous paragraph, organ donations also may occur when a person dies. Depending on the state of residence, individuals may enroll in a program that gives permission for organ harvest when they die, alleviating the pressure on families of having to make that decision. However, in some states, permission is required by the family, which places pressure on them. Some families feel it is unethical to donate their family

member's body for science because of religious or personal philosophical reasons.

In the United States, consent to donate an organ must be actively received from the family before the transplantation procedure can be performed. In other parts of the world, countries use **presumed consent**, which means that if a parent does not actively oppose the transplantation, the procedure automatically occurs. As a result of presumed consent, those countries receive significantly more donations (Burrows, 2004). Is it an ethical policy to assume the family will consent to organ donations? Oftentimes, a family is frozen with grief and cannot make a coherent decision.

Organ Transplants from Family Members

Often, organ transplants may occur between two family members because it has been determined that the compatibility is very high, which would result in less risk for an organ to be rejected. An ethical issue with this situation is the pressure a family member feels from other family members to agree to give an organ to another member. Most parents would gladly donate an organ to their sick offspring. What about siblings who don't like each other? Should they feel compelled to give an organ? Are they being pressured by other family members to go into surgery? The donors also are at risk. Any time surgery is performed there is a risk to the individual. Should physicians provide a "medical excuse" to the potential family donor as a way to rationalize the decision not to give their organ to a family member? The family member should not be coerced or forced to have the surgery.

Financial Payoff for Organ Donations

Living donor organ transplantation is the only field in medicine in which two individuals are ultimately involved—the person donating the organ and the person receiving the organ. Because of the success of organ transplantation, more treatments are focusing on this alternative. As stated previously, the statistics indicate that the need for organ donations far outstrips the number of donors. In the United States, 17 states offer a tax incentive to donate organs or marrow. These include Arkansas, Georgia, Idaho, Iowa, Louisiana,

Maryland, Massachusetts, Minnesota, Mississippi, New Mexico, New York, North Dakota, Ohio, Oklahoma, South Carolina, Utah, Virginia, and Wisconsin. For example, residents of Louisiana who donate are allowed to take a tax credit of up to $10,000 on their state income taxes for travel, lodging, and lost wages related to the donation process.

The American Transplant Foundation has a Patient Assistance Program that offers two types of grants: one for living donors and one for transplant recipients. This program is designed to provide lifesaving monetary assistance for the most vulnerable patients with significant financial hardship. The goal is to provide support so the recipients won't have financial hardship. This is the only program of its kind available nationwide that provides emergency financial assistance grants to transplant recipients and living organ donors, regardless of their legal status (American Transplant Foundation, 2016).

As a result of the increasing need for organs, a **black market**, which is an illegal form of commerce, has developed for the buying and selling of organs. The trade has risen to such a level that around 10,000 black market operations take place annually worldwide—more than one an hour. In India, around 2,000 people are thought to illegally sell their kidneys each year for $2,000 each. A recent documentary claims that Chinese hospitals are harvesting up to 11,000 organs from political prisoners without anesthetic every year, even though there are only 37 registered organ donors in China (Tomlinson, 2015).

Because healthcare costs are so much higher in the United States, the concept of **medical tourism** or "medical value travel" has evolved. Organ transplants can cost $100,000 in the United States, but they cost considerably less overseas. IndUShealth and Global Health Administrators, Inc., have collaborated with insurance companies to arrange for U.S. residents to obtain medical treatment in India. United Group Programs offers living and deceased organ donor transplants from foreign countries such as Thailand (Bramstedt & Xu, 2007). Medical tourism has become so popular that the first medical tourism association

was formed. The Medical Tourism Association, also referred to as the Medical Travel Association (MTA), is the first membership-based international nonprofit trade association for the medical tourism and global healthcare industry comprised of international hospitals, healthcare providers, medical travel facilitators, insurance companies, and other affiliated companies and members with the common goal of promoting quality healthcare worldwide (Medical Tourism Association, 2013). Although these programs are cost-effective, concerns about follow-up care or complications may determine the effectiveness of these medical value plans. Are these programs ethical? Are insurance companies focusing on cost rather than safety of the patient? Is the patient fully aware of the risk of these types of options?

Xenotransplantation

Another type of transplantation is **xenotransplantation**, which is the transfer of organs from one species to another. This has evolved as a result of the shortage of human organs available for donation. The first xenotransplantation was the transfer of a baboon heart into a five-pound infant in 1984. Baby Fae survived three weeks before the baboon heart was rejected (Ascension Health, 2013). Since that time, several other xenotransplants have occurred using pig livers and hearts. Pigs are the preferred choice for xenotransplantation. There have been few successful xenotransplants because of the high risk of rejection.

Although xenotransplantation is promising, the ethical dilemma is that we are killing animals for these procedures, which are considered experimental. Is there a difference between killing animals for food and killing them for organ transplants? Although ultimately we may be saving lives, for some individuals, xenotransplantation is not ethical. Another issue is the contraction of animal disease to humans. If xenotransplantation is to be successful, it is important that the animals be screened for any diseases humans may contract such as rabies and viruses. The Food and Drug Administration is responsible for regulating xenotransplantation activities.

CONCLUSION

This chapter discusses the many ethical issues involving the healthcare industry and its stakeholders. There are two components of ethics in health care: medical ethics, which focus on the treatment of the patient, and bioethics, which focus on technology and how it is utilized in health care. The most important stakeholder in health care is the patient. The most important relationship with this stakeholder is the healthcare provider. This relationship is affected by the other stakeholders in the industry, including the government who regulates healthcare provider activities, the insurance companies who interact with both provider and patient, and healthcare facilities, such as hospitals or managed care facilities, where the physician has a relationship. All of these stakeholders can influence how a healthcare provider interacts with the patient because they have an interest in the outcome. For that reason, many organizations that represent these stakeholders have developed codes of ethics to provide guidance for ethical behavior. Codes of ethics for the physicians and other healthcare providers, nurses, pharmaceutical companies, and medical equipment companies emphasize how these stakeholders should interact with both the healthcare providers and patients. These codes of conduct also apply to the relationship among employees in a healthcare facility. The issue of workplace bullying has been a continuing problem. The Joint Commission issued a statement and guidelines for workplace behavior in the healthcare industry. It indicated that this type of behavior can be destructive, resulting in medical errors.

Another major area of ethics is the treatment of patients who are dying. Euthanasia, including physician-assisted suicide, illegal in all states but Oregon, Washington, and most recently, Vermont, has been a controversial issue for years. Supporters of euthanasia believe it is the individual's right to choose when they want to end their life and they should have assistance from a physician, if needed. Opponents believe it is unethical because it is the responsibility of a physician to save a life, not to take a life. This issue is tied into advance directives that a patient gives to the provider requesting that certain treatments be administered or not. If the patient is incompetent, advanced directives provide guidance on how the provider should treat the patient at the end of his or her life. The role of the health navigator can be instrumental in ensuring patient's wishes are respected by caregivers and physicians.

Another area of ethical discussion is organ transplantation. There are not enough organ donors in the United States to fulfill demand, thereby creating a long waiting list. With limited supply, the ethical dilemma of organ transplants is how to determine who should receive an organ. For example, the famous New York Yankee baseball player, Mickey Mantle, a long-time alcoholic, received a liver transplant. He needed a liver transplant as a result of his alcoholism. There was a public outcry because people believed he received the liver because he was famous. Although the doctors explained that was not the case, people were upset because they felt his addiction caused the liver failure. Why should he receive a new liver after he damaged his first one? As a result of designer or donor babies, children must be included in the transplant discussion. Should parents have another child specifically to save their other child's life? Children designated as donor babies may have emotional issues because they will eventually be aware that they were created specifically for their sibling's transplant needs.

When Dolly the sheep was cloned in 1995, she created an international furor. There are diametrically opposed views on cloning. Opponents feel that cloning turns the natural procreation process into a scientific experiment. Supporters feel the scientific community has provided an opportunity to recreate a specimen, at will, with the desired genes.

And, finally, it is necessary to address the ethical foundation of our healthcare system. Although the Affordable Care Act has decreased the number of uninsured in the United States, there are still millions of underinsured and uninsured citizens in the United States. The United States is the only industrialized nation that has no universal healthcare coverage. Other nations have stated that health care is a right, not a privilege. Is it unethical for the United States to have a system that does not provide for all citizens? The recent legal battles over the implementation of the individual mandate to purchase health insurance indicate the various attitudes toward access to healthcare insurance for most citizens. This text cannot provide answers to ethical situations because ethics are viewed differently by each individual. This chapter can only provide questions for readers so they can assess their ethical viewpoint as it relates to the healthcare industry.

Summary

© Jim Barber/Shutterstock

Vocabulary

Advance directives

Advanced Medical Technology Association (AdvaMed)

Alternative reproductive methods

American College of Healthcare Executives (ACHE)

American College of Physicians and Harvard Pilgrim Health Care Ethics Program

American Nurses Association

Autonomy

Beneficence

Bioethics

Black market

Carrier testing

Cloning

Code of ethics

Collegial model

Common rule

Contractual model

Diagnostic testing

Dignity

Durable power of attorney

Duty to treat

Effectiveness

Engineering model

Ethical standards

Ethics

Euthanasia

Genetic testing

Healthcare ethical dilemma

Human Genome Project

Informed consent

Institutional Review Boards (IRBs)

Justice

Lateral violence

Living will

Medical ethics

Medical tourism

Minimal infringement

Nonmalfeasance

Nonvoluntary euthanasia

Nuffield Council on Bioethics

Oregon Death with Dignity Act (DWDA)

Paternalism

Preimplantation genetic diagnosis (PGD)

Pharmaceutical Research and Manufacturers of America

Pharmacogenomic testing

Physician-assisted suicide

Physician Payment Sunshine Act

Predictive and asymptomatic testing

Prenatal testing

Presumed consent

Priestly model

Procreation

Proportionality
Public education
Reproductive cloning
Research cloning
Research genetic testing
Respect for autonomy
Stakeholder
Stakeholder management

Stem cells
Stewardship model
Therapeutic cloning
Transplantation
United Network for Organ Sharing (UNOS)
Voluntary euthanasia
Workplace bullying
Xenotransplantation

References

Adams, A. (1992). *Bullying at work*. London: Virago Press: 1–20.

Adelaide Center for Bioethics and Culture. (2013). Healthcare. http://www.bioethics.org.au/Resources/Resource%20Topics/Healthcare.html.

Advanced Medical Technology Association (AdvaMed). (2013). Code of ethics. http://advamed.org/issues/code-of-ethics.

American College of Healthcare Executives (ACHE). (2013). About ACHE. http://www.ache.org/aboutache.cfm.

American Medical Association (AMA). (2013a). Code of Medical ethics. https://www.ama-assn.org/about-us/code-medical-ethics.

American Medical Association (AMA). (2013b). Physician financial transparency reports (Sunshine Act). https://www.ama-assn.org/ama/pub/advocacy/topics/sunshine-act-and-physician-financial-transparency-reports.page.

American Nurses Association (ANA). (2011). Lateral violence and bullying in nursing. http://nursingworld.org/Mobile/Nursing-Factsheets/lateral-violence-and-bullying-in-nursing.html.

American Nurses Association (ANA). (2013). Ethics. http://www.nursingworld.org/MainMenuCategories/EthicsStandards.aspx.

American Transplant Foundation. (2013). Tax incentives and organ donation. http://www.americantransplantfoundation.org/2012/11/tax-incentives-and-organ-donation/.

Ascension Health. (2013). Healthcare ethics. http://www.ascensionhealth.org/ethics/public/cases/case4.asp.

Ayoko, O., Callan, V., & Hartel, C. (2003). Workplace conflict, bullying and counterproductive behaviors. *International Journal of Organizational Analysis*, 11, 283–301.

Baylis, F. (2002). Human cloning: Three mistakes and an alternative. *J Med Philos*, 27(3): 319–337.

Beauchamp, T., & Childress, J. (2001). *Principles of biomedical ethics* (5th ed.). Oxford: Oxford University Press.

Berman, R. (2005). Lethal legislation. *Robert Kennedy School Review*, 6, 13–18.

Bilefsky, D. (2013, April 29).Five are convicted in Kosovo organ trafficking. *New York Times*. http://www.nytimes.com/2013/04/30/world/europe/in-kosovo-5-are-convicted-in-organ-trafficking.html?_r=0.

Bramstedt, K., & Xu, J. (2007). Checklist: Passport, plane ticket, organ transplant. *American Journal of Transplantation*, 7, 1698–1701.

Buchanan, D. (2008). Autonomy, paternalism and justice: Ethical priorities in public health. *Am J Public Health*, 98, 15–21.

Burkett, L. (2007). Medical tourism. Concerns, benefits, and the American legal perspective. *J Leg Med*, 28, 223–245.

Burrows, L. (2004). Selling organs for transplantation. *Mt Sinai J Med*, 71(4): 251–254.

Campbell, E. (2007). Doctors and drug companies—Scrutinizing influential relationships. *N Engl J Med*, 357(18): 1796–1797

Carroll, A., & Buchholtz, A. (2008). *Business & society: Ethics and stakeholder management* (7th ed.). Mason, OH: Southwestern/Cengage Learning.

Centers for Disease Control and Prevention (CDC). (2013). Health insurance coverage. http://www.cdc.gov/nchs/fastats/hinsure.htm.

Childress, J., Faden, R., & Gaare, R. (2002). Public health ethics: Mapping the terrain. *J Med Ethics*, 30, 170–178.

The Coalition of Americans for Research Ethics. (2013). Do no harm. http://www.stemcellresearch.org.

Coleman, C., Bouesseau, M., & Reis, A. (2008). The contribution of ethics to public health. *Bulletin of the World Health Organization*, 86(8): 578–589.

Davis, R. (2008). More elderly having transplantation surgery. http://www.usatoday.com/news/health/2008-02-04-transplant_N.htm.

Dayal, M., & Zarek, S. (2008). Preimplantation genetic diagnosis. http://emedicine.medscape.com/article/273415-overview.

Death with Dignity Act, O.R.S. 127.800–995 (1994). http://public.health.oregon.gov/ProviderPartnerResources/EvaluationResearch/DeathwithDignityAct/Pages/index.aspx.

Djurkovic, N., McCormack, D., & Casimir, G. (2008). Workplace bullying and intention to leave: The modernizing effect of perceived organizational support. *Human Resource Management Journal*, 18(4): 405–420.

Ethics Resource Center. (2009). The PLUS decision making model. http://www.burtbertram.com/teaching/ethics/Article_02-PLUS_DecisionMakingModel.pdf

Exit International. (2016). Voluntary euthanasia and assisted suicide information by Exit International. http://www.exitinternational.net.

Food and Drug Administration (FDA). (2016). Information sheet guidance for institutional review boards (IRBs), clinical investigators, and sponsors. http://www.fda.gov/oc/ohrt/irbs/facts.html#IRBOrg.

Friedman, E., & Friedman, A. (2006). Payment for donor kidneys: Pros and cons. *International Society of Nephrology*, January, 960–962.

Gillon, R. (1994). Principles of medical ethics. *BMJ*, 309, 184.

Giuliano, K. (1997). Organ transplants: Tackling the tough ethical questions. *Nursing*, 27, 34–40.

Hoel, H., Faragher, B., & Cooper, C. (2004). Bullying is detrimental to health but all bullying behaviors are not necessarily equally damaging. *British Journal of Guidance & Counseling*, 32(3): 367–387.

The Joint Commission (2008). Joint Commission launches online resource center to prevent workplace violence. https://www.jointcommission.org/the_joint_commission_launches_online_resource_center_to_prevent_workplace_violence_in_health_care/

The Joint Commission. (2008, July 9). Behaviors that undermine a culture of safety. *Sentinel Event Alert*, 40. http://www.jointcommission.org/assets/1/18/SEA_40.PDF.

Keashly, L. (2001). Interpersonal and systemic aspects of emotional abuse at work: The target's perspective. *Violence and Victims*, 16, 233–268.

Korenman, S. G. (2009). Teaching the responsible conduct of research in humans. http://ori.hhs.gov/education/products/ucla/chapter2/page04b.htm.

LaVan, H., & Martin, W. (2007). Bullying in the U.S. workplace: Normative and process-oriented ethical approaches. *Journal of Business Ethics, 83,* 147–165.

Medical Tourism Association (MTA). (20136). About the MTA. http://www.medicaltourismassociation.com/en/about-the-MTA.html.

Mehlman, M., & Berg, J. (2008). Human subjects' protections in biomedical enhancement research: Assessing risk and benefit and obtaining informed consent. *Journal of Law, Medicine & Ethics, 36*(3): 546–559.

Miller, R. (2006). *Problems in health care law* (9th ed.). Sudbury, MA: Jones and Bartlett Publishers.

Minding the Workplace. (2009). Workplace bullying in healthcare I: The Joint Commission standards. http://newworkplace.wordpress.com/2009/12/15/workplace-bullying-in-healthcare-i-the-joint-commission-standards/.

Morgan, S., Harrison, T., Long, S., Afiffi, W., Stephenson, M., & Reichert, T. (2005). Family discussions about organ donations: How the media influences opinions about organ donations. *Clin Trans, 19,* 674–682.

National Human Genome Research Institute. (2016). Regulation of genetic tests. http://www.genome.gov/10002335

Niles, N. (2011). *Basics of the U.S. health care system.* Burlington, MA: Jones and Bartlett Learning.

Niles, N. (2013). *Basic concepts of health care human resource management.* Burlington, MA: Jones and Bartlett Learning: 50.

Notable Names Database. (2016). Jack Kevorkian. http://www.nndb.com/people/272/000023203/.

Nuffield Council on Bioethics Report. (2016). Public health: Ethical issues guide to the report. http://nuffieldbioethics.org/project/public-health/.

Oak Ridge National Laboratory (ORNL). (2016). Human Genome Project information. http://www.ornl.gov/sci/techresources/Human_Genome/home.shtml.

Oddo, A. (2001). Health care ethics: A patient-centered decision model. *Journal of Business Ethics, 29,* 126.

Oregon Death with Dignity Act: 2015 Data Summary. (2016). http://www.healthoregon.org/dwd.

O'Reilly, K. B. (2009). Five people die under new Washington physician-assisted suicide law. http://www.amednews.com/article/20090706/profession/307069977/7.

Organ Procurement and Transplantation Network, Health Resources and Services Administration, U.S. Department of Health & Human Services. (2013). Donors recovered in U.S. by donor type. http://optn.transplant.hrsa.gov/latestData/viewDataReports.asp.

Peng, T. (2008). Should drug companies reveal payments to doctors? http://www.newsweek.com/id/160894?from=rss?nav=slate.

Pharmaceutical Research and Manufacturers of America (PhRMA). (2016). About PhRMA. http://www.phrma.org/about.

Povar, C., Blumen, H., Daniel, J., Daub, S., Evans, L., Holm, R.,… Campbell, A. (2004). Ethics in practice: Managed care and the changing health care environment. *Ann Intern Med.* (2004 Jul. 20);*141*(2): 131–136.

Pozgar, G., (2016). *Legal and ethical issues for health professionals.* Burlington, MA: Jones and Bartlett Learning: 121–155.

Scheper-Hughes, N. (2003). Keeping an eye on the global traffic in human organs. *Lancet, 361,* 1645–1648.

Sullivan, D. (2005). Euthanasia versus letting die: Christian decision-making in terminal patients. *Ethics and Medicine, 21*(2): 109–118.

Sullivan, D. (2006). Stem cells 101—An audio/MP3 version. http://www.bioethics.com/?page_id=533.

Sultz, H., & Young, K. (2006). *Health care USA: Understanding its organization and delivery* (5th ed.). Sudbury, MA: Jones and Bartlett Publishers.

University of Miami Ethics Programs. (2016). Schiavo timeline, part 1. http://www.miami.edu/index.php/ethics/projects/schiavo/schiavo_timeline/.

Taylor, P. (1975). *Principles of ethics: An introduction to ethics* (2nd ed.). Encino, CA: Dickinson.

Tomlinson, S. (2015). Inside the illegal hospitals performing thousands of black market organ transplants for $200,000 a time. http://www.dailymail.co.uk/news/article-3031784/Inside-illegal-hospitals-performing-thousands-black-market-organ-transplants-year-200-000-time.html.

United Network for Organ Sharing (UNOS). (2016). Homepage. http://www.unos.org.

Vartia, M. (2001). Consequences of workplace bullying with respect to the well-being of its targets and the observers or bullying. *Scandinavian Journal of Work Environment and Health, 27,* 63–59.

Veatch, R. (1972). Medical ethics: Professional or universal. *Harvard Theological Review, 65,* 531–559.

Washington State Department of Health. (2016). Washington State Department of Health 2015 Death with Dignity Act Annual Reports. http://www.doh.wa.gov/YouandYourFamily/IllnessandDisease/DeathwithDignityAct/DeathwithDignityData.

Wazana, A. (2000). Physicians and the pharmaceutical industry: Is a gift ever just a gift? *JAMA, 283,* 373–380.

Woloschak, G. (2003). Transplantation: Biomedical and ethical concerns raised by the cloning stem cell debate. *Zygon, 8,* 599–704.

Wynia, M. (2007). Ethics and public health emergencies: Encouraging responsibility. *The American Journal of Bioethics, 7,* 1–4.

Xue, J., Ma, J., & Louis, T. (2001). Forecast of the number of patients with end-stage renal disease in the United States to the year 2010. *JASN, 12,* 2753–2758.

Yamada, D. C. (2004). Crafting a legislative response to workplace bullying. *Employee Rights and Employment Policy Journal, 8,* 475. http://ssrn.com/abstract=1303725

Student Activity 10-1

In Your Own Words

Based on this chapter, please provide an explanation of the following concepts in your own words. DO NOT RECITE the text.

Autonomy

Institutional Review Boards

Medical tourism

Paternalism

Presumed consent

Stem cell

Stewardship model

Therapeutic cloning

Transplantation

Xenotransplantation

Student Activity 10-2

Real-Life Applications: Case Scenario One

A friend from high school moved into your neighborhood, who is pregnant with her third child. She told you that her eldest child was very ill and required a bone marrow transplant. There were no matching donors on the national list. She and her husband decided to have a baby that could be used to save her other child. She asked what you thought of her actions. Before making any statements that could hurt your friend, you decide to do some research on the topic.

Activity

(1) Explain this type of procedure and what the procedure entails, (2) identify any ethical issues associated with this type of procedure, and (3) provide an opinion on this procedure—would you do it or not and why?

Case Scenario Two

You need a back operation but cannot afford your cost share of the operation. You have heard that other countries may offer less expensive medical procedures. You decide to investigate this option.

Activity

Perform an Internet search and use textbook information on medical tourism. Locate two countries that offer lower cost surgeries. Write a report and submit to the class.

Case Scenario Three

One of your best friends is on the waiting list for a new liver. According to current research, there is a huge waiting list for organ donations. Several states have offered tax incentives to encourage organ donation. You are unsure of how to encourage her to be optimistic.

Activity

You decide to do research on tax incentives in the different states and other options to encourage organ donation.

Case Scenario Four

You and your parents were discussing physician assisted and whether it was an ethical procedure. Your parents did not believe in it but you feel it is an option depending on the circumstance. You think of your great grandmother who is terminally ill but is in pain. She has requested information about physician-assisted suicide and wants to create an advance directive. You have a friend who is being trained as a health navigator and asks for her advice.

Activity

Using the textbook and the Internet, research both the pros and cons of physician-assisted suicide and how the health navigator can assist with this ethical question.

Student Activity 10-3

Internet Exercises

- Visit each of the websites listed here.
- Name the organization.
- Locate its mission statement on the website.
- Provide a brief overview of the activities of the organization.
- How does this organizations participate in the U.S. healthcare system?

Websites

http://www.nursingworld.org

Organization Name
Mission Statement
Overview of Activities
Importance of Organization to U.S. Health Care

http://www.thehastingscenter.org

Organization Name
Mission Statement
Overview of Activities
Importance of Organization to U.S. Health Care

http://www.phRMA.org

Organization Name
Mission Statement
Overview of Activities
Importance of Organization to U.S. Health Care

http://www.procon.org

Organization Name
Mission Statement
Overview of Activities
Importance of Organization to U.S. Health Care

http://www.ornl.gov

Organization Name
Mission Statement
Overview of Activities
Importance of Organization to U.S. Health Care

http://stemcells.nih.gov

Organization Name
Mission Statement
Overview of Activities
Importance of Organization to U.S. Health Care

Student Activity 10-4

Discussion Questions

The following are suggested discussion questions for this chapter.

1. If you were going to develop a code of ethics for this class, what behavior components should be included?
2. Do you think human beings should be cloned? Defend your answer.
3. What is your definition of ethics? What do you think are some unethical situations in the healthcare industry?
4. What is workplace bullying? Have you witnessed this behavior in the workplace? Do you consider this behavior unethical? Defend your answer.
5. What is voluntary euthanasia? Do you believe there should be national legislation to make it legal in all states? Defend your answer.

Student Activity 10-5

Current Events

Perform an Internet search and find a current events topic that relates to this chapter. Provide a summary of the article and the link to the article and explain how the article relates to the chapter.

CHAPTER **11**

Navigating Mental Health Issues

LEARNING OBJECTIVES

The student will be able to:

- List and discuss five alternative approaches to mental health care.
- Discuss how a health navigator can help a patient with mental health services.
- Discuss at least five liability issues surrounding mental health professionals.
- Define mental health behavioral companies and discuss their relationship to mental health care.
- Discuss mental health issues in high-risk populations.
- Define and discuss why posttraumatic stress disorder (PTSD) occurs.
- Evaluate the importance of the National Institute for Mental Health and the American Psychological Association (APA) to mental health care.

DID YOU KNOW THAT?

- Surveys indicate that one in four Americans suffer from a mental disorder in any one year.
- Half of all lifetime mental health illnesses begin by age 14; three-quarters occur by age 24.
- The annual economic, indirect cost of mental illness is estimated to be $79 billion.
- More than 50% of students with a mental disorder at age 14 and older drop out of high school—the highest drop-out rate of any disability group.
- Mental health ranks second to heart disease as a limitation on health and productivity.

INTRODUCTION

According to the World Health Organization, mental wellness or mental health is an integral and essential component of health. It is a state of well-being in which an individual can cope with normal stressors, can work productively, and is able to contribute to his or her community. Mental health behavioral disorders can be caused by biological, psychological, and personality factors. By 2020, behavioral health disorders will surpass all physiological diseases as a major cause of disability worldwide (World Health Organization, 2016). Mental disorders are the leading cause of disability in the United States. Mental illnesses can affect individuals of any age, race, religion, or income. According to SAMHSA's 2014 National Survey, an estimated 43.6 million (18.1%) Americans ages 18 and up experienced some form of mental illness. In the past year, 20.2 million adults (8.4%) had a substance use disorder. According to recent estimates, mental illnesses account for 21.3 percent of all years lived with disability in the United States (SAMSHA, 2014). An estimated 9.6 million American adults suffer from a serious mental illness (SMI) in which the ability to function in daily life is significantly impaired. Mental illness ranks as the third most costly medical condition in terms of overall healthcare expenditure, behind heart conditions and traumatic injury (NIMH, 2016). Anxiety disorders are the most common type of mental disorder, followed by depressive disorders. Different mental disorders are more likely to begin and occur at different stages in life and are thus more prevalent in certain age groups. Lifetime anxiety disorders generally have the earliest age of first onset, most commonly around age six (SAMHSA, 2016).

Although mental health is a disease that requires medical care, its characteristics set it apart from traditional medical care. U.S. Surgeon General David Satcher released a landmark report in 1999 on mental health illness, *Mental Health: A Report of the Surgeon General*. The Surgeon General's report on mental health defines **mental disorders** as conditions that alter thinking processes, moods, or behavior that result in dysfunction or stress. It can be psychological or biological in nature. The most common conditions include **phobias**, which are excessive fear of objects or activities; substance abuse; and affective disorders, which are emotional states such as depression. Severe mental illness would include schizophrenia, major depression, and psychosis. Obsessive–compulsive disorders (OCD), mental retardation, Alzheimer's disease, and dementia also are considered mentally disabled conditions. According to the report, mental health ranks second to heart disease as a limitation on health and productivity (U.S. Public Health Service, 1999). People who have mental disorders often exhibit feelings of anxiety, or may have hallucinations or feelings of sadness or fear that can limit normal functioning in their daily life. Because the cause or etiology of mental health disorders is less defined and less understood compared to traditional medical problems, interventions are less developed than other areas of medicine (Anderson, Rice, & Kominski, 2007). This chapter will provide a discussion on the following topics: the history of the U.S. mental healthcare system, a background of healthcare professionals, mental healthcare law, insurance coverage for mental health, barriers to mental health care, the populations at risk for mental disorders, the types of mental health disorders as classified by the American Psychiatric

Association's *Diagnostic and Statistical Manual of Mental Disorders (DSM)*, liability issues associated with mental health care, an analysis of the mental healthcare system, and guidelines and recommendations to improve U.S. mental health care. The role of the health navigator also will be discussed.

THE ROLE OF THE HEALTH NAVIGATOR IN MENTAL HEALTH

A health navigator can play an integral role in mental health care. Many individuals go undiagnosed because of the patient's fear of being diagnosed with a mental health disorder. They are afraid to tell their family or friends about this type of medical issue A physician who does not specialize in mental illness may misdiagnose a condition. Health navigators with experience in mental health care can be a valuable liaison with mental healthcare facilities. Navigators may assist with communication with families or the patient's clinicians. They can provide education regarding mental illness. Because mental health care may involve both personal and professional resources, a health navigator could be a coordinator for the individual's care.

HISTORY OF U.S. MENTAL HEALTH CARE

Over the past three centuries, the mental health system has consisted of a patchwork of services that has become very fragmented (Regier et al., 1993). Initially, mentally ill individuals were relegated to care by their families. State governments then built **insane asylums**, later known as hospitals. In the mid-1700s, the state of Pennsylvania opened a hospital in Philadelphia where the mentally ill were housed in the basement. During this period, Virginia was the first state to build an asylum in its capital city of Williamsburg. If the mentally ill were not cared for by their families or sent to an asylum, they were found in jails or almshouses. It was not until the 1800s that the mentally ill were treated with sensitivity. This **moral treatment** approach was used in Europe earlier with success. Mental health patients in hospitals were treated while participating in work and educational activities.

Dorothea Dix and Horace Mann were the first mental health reformers in the United States. They crusaded for this moral movement by convincing the public that some mentally ill patients can be treated in a controlled environment outside the confines of an asylum. Asylums should be focused on housing mentally ill individuals who have untreatable chronic conditions. During this period, more states built more asylums, which became overcrowded. It is important to note that the local governments were responsible for funding the care of the asylum residents, which resulted in deteriorating conditions and exposure of the patients to inhumane treatment. State care acts were passed that mandated state funding for treatment between 1894 and World War I. Asylums were renamed mental hospitals. Psychiatric units were also opened in general hospitals to promote mental health as part of general health care (Regier et al., 1993).

After World War I, many war veterans returned home with mental disorders, or what is now known as PTSD (posttraumatic stress disorder), because of their war experiences. It was not until the 1930s that medications became available. However, other controversial treatments, such as **electrotherapy**, were used. Brain surgery or lobotomies also became a method to treat the mentally ill. World War II further focused the government on mental health issues, and the National Institute of Mental Health was created. Government funding was awarded for mental health training and research. The Department of Veterans Affairs (VA) established psychiatric hospitals and clinics. During this period, most health care focused on inpatient services. The VA also developed mental health disorder categories in order to improve treatment of war veterans. By the mid-1950s, more than 500,000 mental health patients were being treated in government mental health hospitals. In 1952, the **American Psychiatric Association** published the first *DSM*, which was coordinated with the World Health Organization's (WHO) International Classification of Disease (American Psychiatric Association, 2016a) to encourage acceptance of mental health disorders.

Finally, the first psychoactive medication was developed that allowed outpatient treatment of mentally disabled patients. In 1955, the **U.S. Commission on Mental Health** was established. It investigated the quality of mental hospitals and allocated funding for outpatient facilities. As more **psychotropic medications** were developed, which are medications used for depression, Congress provided more funding allocations for community-based services. Medicaid, Medicare, Supplemental Security Income (SSI), Social Security, and Disability insurance became accessible for mental health care (Grob, 1983, 1994; Sultz & Young, 2006).

During the 1960s and 1970s, community mental health centers were developed and supported by the federal government. Most of the funding focused on the less severe mentally ill who could live normally with outpatient services. In the late 1970s, President Carter appointed a Presidential Committee on Mental Health, which had limited success; however, Medicaid payments for outpatient mental health services were increased. By 1990, most mental health services were offered as outpatient services. Research in the 1990s indicated that the reason people did not seek assistance for mental health disorders is their shame and embarrassment. The Mental Health Parity Act was passed in 1996 to ensure there was adequate coverage for mental health illnesses and that annual lifetime reimbursement limits on mental health services were similar to other medical benefits.

In 2002, President George W. Bush established the **New Freedom Commission on Mental Health** that was charged with implementing an analytical study on the U.S. mental health service system and developing recommendations to improve the public mental health system that could be implemented at the federal, state, and local levels. This was the first study performed since 1978 when President Jimmy Carter's Mental Health Commission's report was published. In 2003, the Commission issued a final report that contained nearly 20 recommendations that focused primarily on mental illness recovery, including a comprehensive approach to mental health care, such as the screening of mental illness for children and other high-risk populations (APA, 2003).

The **Mental Health Parity and Addiction Equity Act of 2008** further supported mental health care by requiring insurance plans to offer mental health benefits and cost sharing similar to those of traditional medical benefits. Over the past 15 years, increased funding has improved the quality of mental health services. As with the 1996 act, there were loopholes that reduced the effectiveness of the 2008 act. The Obama administration recognized the importance of funding mental health initiatives, including teacher training programs for mental health awareness (Mohney, 2013). It issued the final rule on guidance to implement the regulations regarding the 2008 act. The final rule requires transparency of health plans on how they interpret medical coverage for mental health problems. The final rule should strengthen the impact of the 2008 act. The final rule, which became effective on July 1, 2014, applies to health insurance plans (Moran, 2013).

BACKGROUND OF MENTAL HEALTH SERVICES

Mental Health Professionals

Mental health problems affect not only the individual but family members and friends as well. As a result of the vast impact of mental health disabilities, behavioral services are provided by psychiatrists, psychologists, social workers, nurses, counselors, and therapists (Shi & Singh, 2008). Social workers will receive training in counseling, normally a master's degree, and can provide support for an individual with a mental health disability. Family and vocational counselors as well as recreational therapists also may be involved in the treatment plan. Mental health can be such a complex condition that affects so many aspects of a mentally ill person's life that often many different mental health professionals are needed for support and treatment. Most of these mental health professionals provide outpatient or ambulatory care. Inpatient care may be offered in the psychiatric units of a hospital, mental hospitals, or substance abuse facilities (Pointer, Williams, Isaacs, & Knickman, 2007).

Psychiatrists are specialty physicians who can prescribe medication and admit patients to hospitals. **Psychologists**, who also participate in the treatment of mental health, cannot prescribe drugs but provide different types of therapy. Social workers focus on mental health counseling. Nurses also may specialize in psychiatric care. There may be additional counselors and therapists who participate in the treatment of the mentally disabled.

However, mental health professionals may face liability issues. A recent study (Woody, 2008) noted seven reasons mental health professionals are at high risk for liability and complaints:

- When mental health professionals provide services to both children and their families, they are at risk for more complaints from their patients regarding care. Families may be wary about mental health professional providing services to their children.
- Because of the increased government regulations of the licensing of practitioners, professionals no longer have a say in establishing standards for care.
- The litigious U.S. society has included the mental health profession in their complaints.
- Patients have become more distrustful of their providers and are not always willing to adhere to treatment guidelines. If they are not cured, they blame the provider.
- Managed care has imposed restrictions on the number of sessions that have increased the liability of providers.
- Because of the high cost of health care, more patients are abandoning their healthcare treatment, which has reduced revenues. As a result, practitioners have developed practices to cut costs, which may result in more errors.
- Mental health practitioners are ignoring their professional liability issues and do not hire professionals to resolve their problems. As a result, many practitioners are ill-prepared to defend their actions and are found liable.

Mental Health Commitment Law

Commitment laws are laws that enable family members, law enforcement, or healthcare professionals to commit a person to a facility or a treatment program. **Voluntary commitment** occurs when people commit themselves willingly to receive care. If a person voluntarily commits for treatment, that person can leave of his or her own free will. **Involuntary commitment** occurs when people are forced to receive treatment or are committed to a facility against their wishes. A hearing must be held to prove the person is dangerous to him- or herself or others or is suffering from a mental disorder. If they are committed, they are not free to leave (Pointer et al., 2007). An involuntary commitment may occur as an outpatient mental health treatment plan. This type of involuntary commitment is normally a court-ordered program for mental health services.

Managed Care Behavioral Organizations

Mental health services are provided by distinct components of the healthcare system. There are specialty healthcare providers, as explained previously, such as psychiatrists and psychologists. However, the primary care provider (e.g., family physicians, internists) often is the initial contact for the mentally ill and may serve as the treatment provider. Important providers of mental health care are social service sector employees, such as social service workers and counselors, who provide assistance to both the individual and the family. Finally, there is a growing sector of nonprofit groups and organizations for the mentally ill that provide education and support, including the **National Alliance on Mental Illness (NAMI)** and **Mental Health America**. These components are known as the **de facto mental health service system** (**Figure 11-1**) (U.S. Public Health Service, 1999).

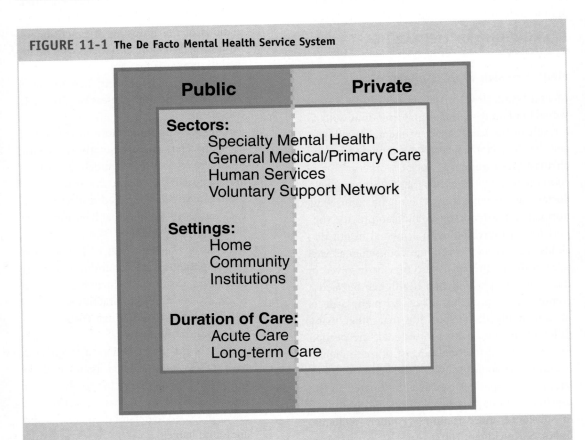

FIGURE 11-1 The De Facto Mental Health Service System

Private insurance coverage for mental health conditions and substance abuse or behavioral care is less generous than the coverage for traditional medical care. Many small companies do not offer mental health coverage. Employers routinely impose higher employee copayments and may limit outpatient visit reimbursement. The **Mental Health Parity Act of 1996**, enacted in 1998, provided the mental health field with more equity for health insurance coverage to ensure mental health services were being reimbursed on an equal level of traditional medical care. The **Mental Health Parity and Addiction Equity Act of 2008** requires group health insurance plans (those with more than 50 insured employees) that offer coverage for mental illness and substance use disorders to provide those benefits in a way that is no more restrictive than any other medical and surgical procedure covered by the plan. It does not require group health plans to cover mental health (MH) and substance use disorder (SUD) benefits, but when plans do cover these benefits, MH and SUD benefits must be covered at levels that are no lower and with treatment limitations that are no more restrictive than would be the case for the other medical and surgical benefits offered by the plan (SAMHSA, 2016b). Many mental health advocates were dismayed by the weakness of this legislation, so in November 2013, a final rule was issued in the 2008 act that includes the following consumer protections:

- "Ensuring that parity applies to intermediate levels of care received in residential treatment or intensive outpatient settings;
- Clarifying the scope of the transparency required by health plans, including the disclosure rights of plan participants, to ensure compliance with the law;
- Clarifying that parity applies to all plan standards, including geographic limits, facility-type limits, and network adequacy; and
- Eliminating the provision that allowed insurance companies to make an exception to parity requirements for certain benefits on the basis of 'clinically appropriate standards of care,' which clinical experts

advised was not necessary and which is confusing and open to potential abuse" (MHPAEA, 2016).

Medicare and Medicaid are a large source of mental health funding, particularly for those individuals with serious mental disabilities who often cannot work. Medicaid is the single largest payer for state-financed mental health care (Shi & Singh, 2008). Medicare imposes a 50% copayment rate for outpatient services other than initial diagnoses and drug management. The normal copayment rate is 20% for traditional medical care (Anderson, Rice, & Kominski, 2007). However, as a result of cost concerns over mental health care, managed care organizations contracted with external vendors that focused on mental health care. These external vendors became known as **managed behavioral healthcare organizations**.

There is still a stigma attached to being mentally disabled. Individuals may be embarrassed to admit they may have a mental health problem and ignore it, or they may not understand what is happening to them. Families can be embarrassed by a member that is mentally disabled. A patient's primary care provider also may be uncomfortable dealing with a patient who may have a mental health disorder.

Who Are the Mentally Ill?

The *Diagnostic and Statistical Manual of Mental Disorders (DSM)* is a guide published by the American Psychiatric Association that explains the signs and symptoms that mark more than 300 types of mental health conditions. Traditionally, mental health providers use the *DSM* to diagnose everything from anorexia to voyeurism and, if necessary, determine appropriate treatment. Health insurance companies also use the *DSM* to determine coverage and benefits and to reimburse mental health providers (Mayo Clinic, 2016). The *DSM* has been in publication since 1952 and periodically publishes an updated manual. The most recent update, DSM-5, was in 2013.

The **National Institute of Mental Health (NIMH)**, the world's largest funding agency of mental health research, has refused to endorse the 2013 *DSM* and will no longer fund mental health research based on the *DSM* mental health categories. The NIMH states that the *DSM* has not categorized mental health disorders based on objective science but more from inconsistent information gathered from clusters of symptoms that are then categorized as a mental health disorder. The NIMH is developing a new classification system of mental health disorders based on science and genetics. There have been petitions requesting an external review of the DSM-5 (American Psychiatric Association, 2016b).

FAMILY AND CAREGIVERS

As with any chronic condition, family members and caregivers are often impacted by caring for those inflicted individuals. Caregivers often do not think of themselves as needing any attention because their focus is on the afflicted family member. It is important to take some personal time out of the "caregiver mode" to take care of reflect on the emotional needs of the caregiver. The following is some advice for caregivers on taking care of themselves:

1. Support groups: Caregivers may feel guilty if they resent their caregiver role. Do not judge your thoughts as bad, thus increasing your stress; recognize that others may have the same feelings. Going to support groups to discuss your feelings provides an opportunity to deal with these issues.

2. Do not ignore personal relationships: Caregivers may unintentionally lose contact with friends. Set up times, even monthly, to see friends if only for a short period of time. These personal times provides an opportunity to step away from the caregiver mode.

3. It is difficult to take care of someone else if the caregiver does not take care of him or herself first. For additional information, please contact 1-800-950-NAMI (6264) or info@nami.org.

Additional resources about mental health illness support include the following (SAMI, 2016):

- **Anxiety and Depression Association of America (ADAA)** provides information on prevention, treatment, and symptoms of anxiety, depression, and related conditions.
- **Children and Adults with Attention-Deficit/Hyperactivity Disorder (CHADD)** provides information and referrals on ADHD, including local support groups.
- **Depression and Bipolar Support Alliance (DBSA)** provides information on bipolar disorder and depression, offers in-person and online support groups and forums.
- **International OCD Foundation** provides information on OCD and treatment referrals.
- **Schizophrenia and Related Disorders Alliance of America (SARDAA)** maintains the Schizophrenia Anonymous programs, which are self-help groups and are now available as toll-free teleconferences.
- **Sidran Institute** helps people understand, manage, and treat trauma and dissociation; maintains a helpline for information and referrals.
- **TARA (Treatment and Research Advancements for Borderline Personality Disorder)** offers a referral center for information, support, education, and treatment options for BPD.
- See more at http://www.nami.org/Find-Support/NAMI-HelpLine/Top-25-HelpLine-Resources#sthash.LZlIFKub.dpuf.

SPECIAL POPULATIONS

Children and Adolescents

According to the NIMH, just over 20 percent (or one in five) children, either currently or at some point during their life, have had a seriously debilitating mental disorder. They can be diagnosed with the following: attention deficit hyperactivity disorders (ADHD), posttraumatic stress disorder, panic disorder, bipolar disorder, autism, depressive disorders, borderline personality disorder, eating disorders, social phobia, and schizophrenia. In some instances, these disorders can follow them throughout their lives. It is particularly difficult to assess teen mental disorders because of their stage in life. Many teens are worried about peer pressure, family issues, schoolwork and activities, and making decisions about going to college or not. It is important that children and teens have open communication either with their parents, counselors, or friends to ensure that, if there is a mental disorder, it will be addressed. Suicide is a major concern among children and adolescents and is the fifth-leading cause of death among ages 5–14 years (Agency for Healthcare Research and Quality, 2002; NIMH, 2016a).

Treatment for Children and Adolescents

According to the APA, it is important that parents recognize problems in their children so that they can be treated appropriately. The most common mental disorders are depression, ADHD, and conduct disorders. Although there is limited research on mental disorders in children, it is estimated that 1 in 10 children may suffer from persistent feelings of sadness, which can lead to depression. In some instances, children may not be able to verbalize their emotions, so it is important to notice any behavioral changes such as poor school performance, loss of interest in hobbies, angry outbursts, anxiety, alcohol or drug abuse, and irrational behavior. Treatment for children can consist of therapy or a combination of therapy and medication (SAMHSA, 2016a).

Elderly and Mental Health

As the U.S. population ages and continues to live longer, mental health disorders in the elderly will become more prevalent. As we age, we will experience loss of family members and friends, which is a major trigger of depression and possibly suicide. Unfortunately, many elderly are not treated for mental illness for several reasons. Often the elderly are being treated for other traditional illnesses, so the focus is on treating those illnesses. Also, as we age, society assumes that we lose our memory and some of our faculties as part of the normal aging process, so primary care providers and family members do not attribute these symptoms to dementia or Alzheimer's disease, both mental disorders. It is also more difficult to see a specialist because of lack of transportation. The elderly are focused on seeing their primary care provider for their main ailments, so both the patient and the provider may ignore the symptoms. Also, the primary care provider may not be comfortable addressing mental health issues. If the primary care provider does refer the elderly patient to a psychologist, a recent APA survey indicated that fewer than 30% of psychologists have had graduate coursework in **geropsychology**, which deals with mental health issues in the elderly. and the survey also found that 70% would be interested in attending programs in geropsychology. The APA has provided geropsychology guidelines for older adults (American Psychological Association, 2016). Finally, the family of an elderly person may not want to acknowledge the problems because they may be afraid of hurting their feelings. Alzheimer's disease and other dementias are difficult for a family member to acknowledge, knowing the end result of these diseases. It is important that the primary care provider, the family, and the patient work together to assess the elderly patient's mental status (Older adults and mental health, 2016).

COMMON TYPES OF MENTAL DISORDERS IN THE ELDERLY

Depression and Dementia

Depression may strike more than 10% of the elderly population. It can imitate dementia because its victims withdraw, cannot focus, and appear confused at times. **Dementias**, which have symptoms of memory loss and confusion, often are considered a part of growing old, but they are not an inevitable part of the aging process. Only 15% of the elderly population suffers from dementia. Of that percentage, more than 60% suffer from Alzheimer's disease, for which there is no cure as of this writing. Approximately 40% of dementias can be caused by conditions such as high blood pressure or a stroke or other diseases such as Parkinson's and Huntington's, which are disorders that, in their advanced stages, can cause dementia (Types of dementia, 2016).

Alzheimer's Disease

Alzheimer's disease causes the death of brain cells that control memory. The longer the person has this disease, the greater the memory loss as more cells die. One million people 65 years or older have severe Alzheimer's disease with approximately 2 million in the moderate stages of the disease (Types of dementia, 2016).

Pseudo (False) Dementias

Pseudo dementias may develop accidentally as a result of medications, drug interactions, poor diet, or heart and gland diseases. Many elderly have multiple prescriptions, so it is important to note any potential interactions that could result in dementia. Also, if the elderly person does not eat well and has poor nutrition, this habit also could cause dementia. It is important that family members or providers monitor the dietary habits of the elderly patient. Fortunately, because of the causes, most of these pseudo dementias are reversible if treated (American Psychiatric Association, 2016).

MENTAL HEALTH AND CULTURE, RACE, ETHNICITY, GENDER, AND HOMELESSNESS

Mental health disorders occur across race and culture; however, according to NIMH, diverse communities often are underserved. These groups include the LGBTQ community, African Americans, Latinos, Asian Americans, American Indians and Alaska Natives, women, and homeless people. All of these groups experience **minority stress**, which stems from various stigmas including social stigma, prejudice, denial of civil rights, victimization, and family rejection.

With any population that experiences mental health distress, it is important for individuals to feel comfortable reaching out for assistance. It also is important that the mental health system recognize and adapt to accommodate the differences in cultural beliefs and other barriers such as language differences. Hiring mental health counselors and providers from the same culture would be a first step in encouraging culturally diverse individuals to use the system. The following is mental health information related to each of these groups.

LGBTQ

The **LGBTQ**—lesbian, gay, bisexual, transgender, and questioning—**population** is almost three times more likely to experience depression or an anxiety disorder. For LGBTQ people ages 10–24, suicide is one of the leading causes of death. An estimated 20–30% of LGBTQ report substance abuse problems compared to 9% of the population.

The fear of coming out or being discriminated against for sexual orientation can lead to mental health disorders. Thoughts of suicide and substance abuse can be issues with this community. Some LGBTQ members also hide their orientation from the mental health system for fear of being ridiculed. These feelings can be emphasized by the movement of **conversion therapy**, which is spiritual or psychological counseling that makes the assumption that being heterosexual is normal, so counselors try to persuade the LGBTQ to convert to that norm. In October 2015, SAMHSA published the first in-depth review of conversion therapy, condemning it as potentially harmful and emphasizing that variations in sexual orientation are normal (HHS, 2016).

The following is a list of resources to locate LGBTQ-specific providers:

- Use the Gay and Lesbian Medical Association's Provider Directory to look through a list of inclusive medical providers.
- Check out the Healthcare Equality Index to find the LGBTQ inclusive policies of organization leaders in health care.
- Review resources on the rights and experiences of LGBTQ people in mental health care, including the Center for American Progress and the National Transgender Discrimination Survey (NAMI, 2016).

African Americans

African Americans are hesitant to access mental health care due to prior misdiagnoses, inadequate treatment, and cultural misunderstandings. Although the percentage is increasing, only a small percentage of psychologists, psychiatrists, and social workers are African American. African Americans rely on religious and social communities for social support, so rather than visit a specialist, they may rely on spiritual guidance. Unfortunately, there is a higher percentage of African Americans in the foster home system, homeless population, and prison. Those environments have a higher level of mental health disorders than other environments.

Latino Community

Approximately 16% of Hispanic adults live with a mental health condition. The Latino population has been identified as a high-risk group for depression, anxiety, and substance abuse. Like the African American population, Latinos may seek treatment from the clergy rather than specialists. Only a small percentage of Latinos are mental health professionals, so the comfort level is lower between the patient and provider. This lower comfort level also is tied to language barriers. Like African Americans, Latinos are overrepresented in the prison and juvenile justice system (NAMI, n.d.).

NAMI has established an educational program "Sharing Hope" for both the African American and Latino communities with the goal of increasing mental health awareness in their communities and the resources available to them.

Asian Americans

Approximately 14% of Asian adults live with a mental health condition. The Asian American population is composed of 50 cultures with different languages and religious traditions. Asian Americans have the highest life expectancy of any ethnic group in the United States. Mental health disorders are lower among Asians than whites. They are much less likely to report mental health disorders to friends or medical professionals because they feel it is shameful and consider it a personal weakness. The suicide rates of elderly and young Asian American women are higher than women of other ethnicities. They will seek help for mental health disorders from alternative medicine providers; however, because they delay treatment for so long due to embarrassment, their problems are more severe. Like the Hispanic population, there also may be issues with language (APA, 2016).

American Indian and Alaskan Natives

More than 28% of American Indian and Alaska native adults live with a mental health condition. Recent statistics indicate that American Indians and Alaskan Native youths use alcohol by 14 years old. They use marijuana and prescription drugs at twice the rate of the national average. Many of these youths believe their parents are permissive with this type of behavior, which encourages them. However, the federal Indian Health Service (IHS) has established a public health marketing campaign targeted to youths to resist drug and alcohol use. The IHS currently funds 11 centers nationwide that address mental health and substance abuse disorders by providing holistic health care, which is accepted by this culture.

The IHS also uses **tele behavioral health**, which is a method of service delivery that broadens the availability to, quality of, and access to care across all behavioral health program areas. Using video-conferencing technology, tele behavioral health services allow "real-time" visits with a behavioral health specialist in another location who can assist in the evaluation, diagnosis, management, and treatment of health problems (IHS, 2016).

Women and Mental Health

Depression affects women nearly twice as often as men. They tend to experience it earlier, longer, and more severely. Women may experience depression as a result of biologic and social reasons. **Premenstrual dysphoric disorder**, a severe disorder that relates depression and anxiety to menstruation, affects between 3–5% of women. Women also may feel depressed as a result of infertility, miscarriage, and menopause. Married women suffer depression more than married men. The more children a woman has, the more likely she may suffer from depression. Women who have been victims of sexual abuse or domestic violence also may suffer from depression.

By the year 2030, 20% of the population will be 65 years or older. Each decade above 65 years of age, the proportion of women increases because their life expectancy is higher than men's.

Older women comprise the large majority of nursing home residents. Unfortunately, women in nursing homes do not often receive mental health care. Throughout their lives, women have been traditional caregivers. Women may provide up to 13 hours of care a day for more than 20 years for both physical and emotional illnesses (Bradley, 2003). As a result of this role, many elderly women experience more depression and anxiety. Unfortunately, research indicates that healthcare providers do not provide appropriate mental health care to a large majority of older females (Qualls, Segal, Norman, Niederehe, & Gallagher-Thomson, 2002).

The Homeless and Mental Health

An estimated 26% of homeless adults staying in shelters live with serious mental illness and an estimated 46% live with severe mental illness and/or substance use disorders. The health status of the homeless is overall poor because of lack of housing. They are exposed to more disease and do not have adequate access to health care, thus their health status deteriorates over time. Mental health and substance abuse problems are common in the homeless population. As a result of their lack of stability, it is difficult to provide adequate mental health care and general health care (National Alliance to End Homelessness, 2016).

MENTAL HEALTH ISSUES AND DISASTERS, TRAUMA, AND LOSS

Disasters can have an impact on communities and their citizens. Disasters can be natural, such as hurricanes, earthquakes, floods, and tornadoes, or manmade events such as the September 11, 2001, terrorist attacks or the wars in Iraq and Afghanistan. Many losses occur after these events, such as the loss of family and loved ones, pets, neighbors, colleagues, and the community infrastructure such as schools, churches, and homes. The disasters may be short or long term. Individuals who experience disasters may be affected emotionally, and they may develop fear and anxiety because of the uncertainty in their lives. According to the **International Society for Traumatic Stress Studies (ISTSS)**, individuals may experience

feelings of shock, disbelief, grief, anger, guilt, helplessness, and emotional numbness. They may have difficulty with cognitive thinking and may experience physical reactions such as fatigue and illness (ISTSS, 2001). They also may have difficulty interacting with others. As with any mental health condition, it is important for these individuals to reach out for assistance before the condition controls their life.

Mental Health Impact of Terrorist Attacks and Natural Disasters

September 11, 2001

Terrorist attacks are different from natural disasters such as hurricanes, earthquakes, avalanches, or tornados because these attacks are deliberately aimed at harming populations. An evaluation of the federal emergency mental health program indicated that more than 1 million New Yorkers received one or more face-to-face counseling or public education services as a result of the September 11 terrorist attacks (Neria et al., 2007). Interestingly, the emotional impact of the terrorist attacks was felt nationwide. The federal emergency preparedness model of the **Federal Emergency Management Agency (FEMA)** and the **Substance Abuse and Mental Health Services Administration (SAMHSA)** is helpful to victims with short-term mental health issues as a result of different types of disasters (Felton, 2004). The **American Psychological Association Task Force on Promoting Resilience in Response to Terrorism** has produced fact sheets that are intended to provide information to psychologists assisting those target populations impacted by terrorist events (APA, 2016). However, those afflicted with long-term mental health issues as a result of these types of events often are not treated. The assumption is that the traditional healthcare system will treat those long-term mentally ill. However, as discussed previously, individuals who have long-term mental health issues feel stigmatized about seeking mental health services. Those individuals who have experienced traumatic events often feel uncomfortable because they feel that they should have recovered from the events without help.

Recent Tragedies

The September 11, 2001, terrorist attack created the need for mental health support and services, and these services provided support for many other horrific events in U.S. history. Mass murders such as the incident at Sandy Hook Elementary School in Newton, Massachusetts; the Boston Marathon bombing; and other horrific events have had a mental impact not only the victims' families but also affected millions of people across the nation. Most recently, the terrorist massacre at the Pulse Nightclub in Orlando, Florida, created a national outcry of support and anguish for those victims, their families, and the entire LGBTQ community. The shooting deaths of five policemen and the injury of many at a peaceful demonstration in Dallas, Texas, by a mentally ill individual has many asking questions about mental health treatment for those who had committed these crimes and for those people who have been affected by these events.

Hurricane Katrina

Hurricane Katrina devastated nearly 90,000 square miles that were declared a natural disaster area. At least 1 million individuals, including 370,000 school-aged children, were displaced. Many were evacuated throughout 46 states (Cook, 2006). Victims were very anxious because their homes were destroyed and so they had to start a new life elsewhere, which was not their choice. The Centers for Disease Control and Prevention (CDC) surveyed Hurricane Katrina survivors in October 2005 and found that 50% needed mental health services and 33% needed an intervention, with only 2% actually receiving mental health assistance (Weisler, Barbee, & Townsend, 2006). Mental health providers reported grief, anxiety, and fear among the victims. This experience was magnified for survivors who had a previous history of trauma and who already suffered from mental health disorders. Long-term mental health care is needed for the survivors of Hurricane Katrina. It is critical that mental health issues be included in the health care of those impacted by events such as terrorist and natural disasters. Mental health issues not only affect the survivors but also the providers of care to those survivors.

MENTAL HEALTH AND VETERANS

With nearly 155 hospitals serving nearly 8 million war veterans and current members of the armed forces, the VA operates the largest healthcare system and is the largest single employer of psychologists in the country. In 1989, the **National Center for Posttraumatic Stress Disorder** was created within the VA to address the needs of the military-related PTSD (National Center for PTSD, 2016). Of the 1.7 million veterans returning from Afghanistan and Iraq, 20% suffer from **posttraumatic stress disorder** or major depression. Mental health issues are the leading cause of hospitalizations for active duty military. According to recent research, military suicides are the result of untreated mental illnesses (American Psychiatric Association, 2016). Many veterans seek help outside the VA healthcare system. Their main reason for not seeking help is the fear of being stigmatized for seeking these types of service. This fear of stigmatization is similar in the general population. There are new military healthcare models to ensure that mental health services are offered confidentially to allay these fears. The Department of Defense follows privacy guidelines established by HIPAA and the Privacy Act.

The **Embedded Behavioral Health (EBH) model** is a model that focuses on early intervention and treatment to promote solider readiness (pre, during, and post deployment). The EBH develops multidisciplinary teams to improve continued access to behavioral care by setting up work areas and working with unit leaders to ensure availability of these resources. The EBH serves as entry into behavioral health care. The EBH is currently working with the Army (EBH, 2016).

MANAGED BEHAVIORAL HEALTH CARE

Managed behavioral healthcare organizations (MBHOs), also known as behavioral healthcare carve outs, are specialized managed care organizations that focus on mental health services.

According to the NCQA, an MBHO can be part of a health plan, an independent organization, or be supported by healthcare providers.

MBHOs dominate private mental health coverage. Research has indicated that MBHOs have reduced mental health treatment costs (Zuvekas, Rupp, & Norquist, 2008). The National Committee for Quality Assurance's **Managed Behavioral Healthcare Organization Accreditation Program** provides consumers, employers and others with information about the quality of the nation's managed behavioral healthcare organizations. National Committee for Quality Assurance (NCQA) accreditation includes a rigorous review against standards for improving behavioral healthcare access and services and the process of credentialing practitioners. Currently, there are 300 MBHOs that serve 120 million U.S. citizens. The NCQA program is designed to:

- Develop accountability measures for quality of care
- Provide employers and consumers with MBHO information
- Develop quality improvement MBHO programs
- Encourage coordination of behavioral care with medical care treatment (NCQA, 2016)

NATIONAL INSTITUTE FOR MENTAL HEALTH STRATEGIC PLAN

As the lead federal government agency on mental health, NIMH developed a long-term or strategic plan for mental health care in the United States. Revised in 2013, the plan identifies four core areas of focus, which include:

Strategic Objective 1: Promote Discovery in the Brain and Behavioral Sciences to Fuel Research on the Causes of Mental Disorders

We will support basic, translational, and clinical research to gain a more complete understanding of the genetic, neurobiological, behavioral, environmental, and experiential factors that contribute to mental disorders.

Strategic Objective 2: Chart Mental Illness Trajectories to Determine When, Where, and How to Intervene

We will chart the course of mental disorders over the lifespan in order to understand ideal times and methods for intervention to preempt or treat mental disorders and hasten recovery.

Strategic Objective 3: Develop New and Better Interventions That Incorporate the Diverse Needs and Circumstances of People with Mental Illnesses

We will improve existing approaches and devise new ones for the prevention, treatment, and cure of mental illness, allowing those who may suffer from these disorders to live full and productive lives.

Strategic Objective 4: Strengthen the Public Health Impact of NIMH-Supported Research

Through research, evaluation, and collaboration, we will further develop the dissemination capacity of the Institute to help close the gap between the development of new, research-tested interventions and their widespread use by those most in need (NIMH, 2013b).

THE VIRGINIA TECH MASSACRE: A CASE STUDY OF THE MENTAL HEALTH SYSTEM

On April 16, 2007, a senior Virginia Tech student, Seung Hui Cho—who had been diagnosed with and treated for severe anxiety disorders in middle school until his junior year of high school, had been accused of stalking two female students at Virginia Tech, had been declared mentally ill by a Virginia special justice, and was asked to seek counseling by at least one Virginia Tech professor—killed 32 people, students, and professors. It was the worst school massacre in U.S. history.

The Virginia Tech Review Panel was charged by Virginia governor Tim Kaine to review the mental health history of Cho. According to the Panel's findings, even as a young boy, Cho was extremely shy and often refused to speak. He was uncomfortable in his school surroundings and was often bullied. As a result of testing, he did receive counseling throughout middle and high school until he was 18 years of age. He had responded well to the counseling but did not want to continue the counseling, so his parents allowed him to stop. When he decided to go to Virginia Tech, the school did not know of his mental health issues because of personal privacy issues. The **Family Educational Rights and Privacy Act of 1974 (FERPA)** and the **Americans with Disabilities Act (ADA)** generally allow for special education records to be transferred to a higher education facility. However, the law prohibits a university from making an inquiry pre-admission about an applicant's disability status. After a student's admission, they may make inquiries on a confidential basis. Cho could have made his disability known to the University but chose not to. Unfortunately, Virginia law allowed Cho to purchase a handgun without detection by the National Instant Criminal Background Check System (NCIS) (Virginia Tech Review Panel, 2007). This tragedy led to the first major federal gun control measure in more than a decade, which strengthened the NCIS, eliminating the legal loophole that allowed Cho to purchase a handgun (Cochran, 2008).

Alternative Approaches to Mental Health Care

Alternative approaches to mental health care emphasize the relationships between the body, mind, and spirituality (SAMHSA, 2009). Established in 1992, the National Center for Complementary and Alternative Medicine at the National Institutes of Health evaluates different types of alternative therapies and treatments and considers whether to integrate them into traditional medicine culture. The following techniques are outlined in a fact sheet from the National Mental Health Information Center. The following is a discussion of the different types of treatment:

- **Self-help organizations**: Many mentally ill individuals often seek comfort in self-help organizations. They find solace with others who have experienced similar conditions. Many of them are nonprofit and are free of charge. They also provide education and support to the caregivers for those individuals who are mentally ill. Often, these organizations are anonymous because of the stigma attached to mental disorders.
- **Nutrition**: Some research has demonstrated that certain types of diets may assist with certain mental disorders. Eliminating wheat and milk products may alleviate the severity of symptoms of children with autism.
- **Pastoral counseling**: Mental health counselors have recognized that incorporating spiritual guidance with traditional medical care may alleviate mental disorder symptoms.
- **Animal-assisted therapies**: Animals often are used to increase socialization skills and encourage communication among the mentally ill. Integrating animals into individuals' lives may alleviate some symptoms of the mental ill.
- **Art therapy**: Art activities such as drawing, painting, and sculpting may help people express their emotions and may help treat disorders such as depression. There are certificates in art therapy for this purpose.
- **Dance therapy**: Moving a body to music may help individuals recovering from physical abuse because the movement may help develop a sense of ease with their bodies.
- **Music therapy**: Research supports that music elevates a person's emotional moods. It has been used to treat depression, stress, and grief.

Culturally Based Healing Arts

Practitioners of Oriental and Native American medicine believe that wellness is a state of balance between the physical, spiritual, and emotional needs of an individual and that illness results from an imbalance (Center for Mental Health Services, 2016). Their remedies focus on natural medicine, nutrition, exercise, and prayers to regain the balance.

Acupuncture is the Chinese practice of inserting needles into specific points of the body to balance the system. Acupuncture has been used to treat stress and anxiety, depression, ADHD in children, and physical ailments. Acupuncture often is used in conjunction with chiropractic medicine.

Ayurvedic medicine practices incorporate diet, meditation, herbal medicine, and nutrition to treat depression and to release stress.

Yoga is an Indian system that uses breathing techniques, stretching, and meditation to balance the body. Yoga is offered at many athletic clubs and gyms and has become a popular mainstream form of exercise. It has been used for depression and anxiety.

Native American practices include ceremonial dances and baptismal rituals as part of Indian health. These dances and rituals are used to treat depression, stress, and substance abuse.

Relaxation and Stress Reduction Techniques

Biofeedback is a technique that focuses on learning to control heart rate and body temperature. This technique may be used in conjunction with medication to treat depression and schizophrenia. Biofeedback may be used to control issues with stress and hyperventilation.

Visualization is when a patient creates a mental image of wellness and recovery. This may be used by traditional healthcare providers to treat substance abuse, panic disorders, and stress.

Massage therapy manipulates the body and its muscles and is used to release tension. It has been used to treat depression and stress.

Technology-Based Applications

Technology-aided development of electronic tools that can be used from home and increase access to isolated geographic areas can increase access to mentally ill individuals with minimal access to health care.

Telemedicine is when providers and patients are connected using the Internet for communication for consultation. Those who are mentally ill living in rural areas, for example, have an opportunity to have access to providers.

Telephone counseling is an important part of mental health care. As stated previously, because of the stigma attached to receiving mental health services, individuals prefer to talk to a counselor on the telephone because they do not have to face anyone and do not have to tell anyone where they are going if they have an appointment in an office. Counselors receive training for telephone counseling. Like telemedicine, telephone counseling provides an opportunity for outreach for individuals who live in isolated locations.

The Internet, including email services (**electronic communication**), has provided an opportunity to increase an individual's exposure to knowledge regarding his or her condition. Consumer groups and medical websites can be accessed anonymously.

Radio psychiatry has been used in the United States for more than 30 years. Radio psychologists and psychiatrists provide advice, information, and referrals to consumers. Both the APA and the American Psychiatric Association have issued guidelines for radio show programs that focus on mental health.

AMERICAN DISABILITIES ACT OF 1990 AND MENTAL HEALTH

The American Disabilities Act of 1990 (ADA) defines a **mental impairment** as "any mental or psychological disorder, such as mental retardation, organic brain syndrome, emotional or mental illness, and specific learning disabilities." The ADA requires an employer to make reasonable accommodations to employees who are disabled. The definition of **disability** as defined in the American Disabilities Act of 1990 includes individuals with mental illness who meet one of these definitions:

1. A physical or mental impairment that substantially limits one or more major life activities of an individual
2. A record of such an impairment
3. Being regarded as having such an impairment

Examples of reasonable accommodations for people with severe mental illnesses are:

- Providing self-paced workloads and flexible hours
- Modifying job responsibilities
- Allowing leave (paid or unpaid) during periods of hospitalization or incapacity
- Assigning a supportive and understanding supervisor
- Modifying work hours to allow people to attend appointments with their psychiatrist
- Providing easy access to supervision and supports in the workplace
- Providing frequent guidance and feedback about job performance (Mental health, 2016).

CONCLUSION

Mental health issues affect millions of U.S. citizens. Mental health disabilities reduce the life expectancy of individuals by many years. Treatment of mental health disorders have been traditionally underfunded because of the attitude of the traditional healthcare system, confusion by health insurance companies, and fear by individuals who are mentally ill that they will be discriminated against because of their conditions. In 1999, Surgeon General David Satcher's report on mental health brought awareness to the issues with the U.S. mental healthcare system. The Mental Health Parity Act of 1996 was an attempt to establish a fair system of treatment between mental health disorders and traditional healthcare conditions by mandating annual and lifetime limits for mental health care to be equal with those in other healthcare areas. President Bush's Freedom Commission on Mental Health focused on an analysis of the mental health system and made recommendations to improve mental health care.

The Mental Health Parity and Addiction Equity Act (2008) and its 2013 final rules further support mental health care by requiring insurance plans to offer similar benefits to traditional medical benefits and to make cost sharing similar to other medical benefits. Over the past 15 years, increased funding has increased the quality of mental health services. The current administration has recognized the importance of funding mental health initiatives, including teacher training programs for mental health awareness (Mohney, 2013).

The Mental Health Association of New York City (MHA-NYC) is a 50-year-old non profit organization that has provided national support over the years for mental and behavioral health challenges. It works with city, state, and federal government programs to administer national networks for crisis call centers. The organization uses web-based technologies to respond to mental health needs. It has established a subsidiary, Link2Health Solutions, which operates national suicide prevention lines, disaster distress lines, Veterans Crisis Lines, and NFL lifelines. Other organizations across the nation provide these services locally. When mass shootings and other major attacks occur, calls and texts double in the Disaster Distress helplines from people who are anxious and depressed as a result of these attacks (MHA-NYC, 2016).

Despite the progress made in mental health care, issues with the U.S. mental health care system persist. Recent tragedies such as the Sandy Hook Elementary School; the Aurora, Colorado, movie theater shooting; and the Navy Yard massacres were executed by mentally ill individuals. Several questions must be answered in order to understand how mental health care can be administered to individuals who need it the most. Was there adequate access to mental health care for these individuals? Were these individuals properly diagnosed? Did their families recognize their problems? Did they refuse care? The U.S. mental healthcare system continues to be analyzed to ensure that these types of tragedies cease. The health navigator can play a vital role in mental health illness. Because it is a stigmatized illness that many do not understand or are embarrassed about, people who have mental illness may refuse help. A health navigator can provide support and understanding regarding mental health treatment as well as navigating any health insurance issues regarding mental health treatment. Because many minority groups may experience discrimination, which can exacerbate mental health issues, a health navigator that feels affiliation with certain groups could be an asset to assist them.

Summary

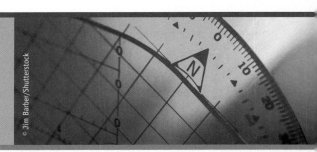

© Jim Barber/Shutterstock

Vocabulary

Acupuncture

Alternative approaches to mental health care

Alzheimer's disease

American Psychiatric Association

American Psychological Association Task Force on Promoting Resilience in Response to Terrorism

Americans with Disabilities Act (ADA)

Animal-assisted therapies

Anxiety and Depression Association of America (ADAA)

Art therapy

Ayurvedic medicine

Biofeedback

Children and Adults with Attention-Deficit/Hyperactivity Disorder (CHADD)

Conversion therapy

Dance therapy

De facto mental health service system

Dementia

Depression and Bipolar Support Alliance (DBSA)

Diagnostic and Statistical Manual of Mental Disorders (DSM)

Disability

Electronic communication

Electrotherapy

Embedded Behavioral Health (EBH) model

Family Educational Rights and Privacy Act of 1974 (FERPA)

Federal Emergency Management Agency (FEMA)

Geropsychology

Hurricane Katrina

Insane asylums

International OCD Foundation

International Society for Traumatic Stress Studies (ISTSS)

Involuntary commitment

LGBTQ population

Managed Behavioral Healthcare Organization Accreditation Program

Managed behavioral healthcare organizations

Massage therapy

Mental disorders

Mental Health America

Mental Health Parity Act of 1996

Mental Health Parity and Addiction Equity Act of 2008

Mental impairment

Minority stress

Moral treatment

Music therapy

National Alliance on Mental Illness (NAMI)

National Center for Posttraumatic Stress Disorder

National Institute of Mental Health

Native American practices

New Freedom Commission on Mental Health

Nutrition

Pastoral counseling

Phobias

Posttraumatic stress disorder

Premenstrual dysphoric disorder

Pseudo dementias

Psychiatrists

Psychologists

Psychotropic medications

Radio psychiatry

Schizophrenia and Related Disorders Alliance of America (SARDAA)

Self-help organizations

Sidran Institute

Substance Abuse and Mental Health Services Administration (SAMHSA)

TARA (Treatment and Research Advancements for Borderline Personality Disorder)

Tele behavioral health

Telemedicine

Telephone counseling

U.S. Commission on Mental Health

Visualization

Voluntary commitment

Yoga

References

Agency for Healthcare Research and Quality (AHRQ). (2002). Specialized training helps ER nurses better manage children at risk for suicide. http://archive.ahrq.gov/research/feb02/0202RA8.htm.

Alzheimer's Association. (2016). Types of dementia. http://www.alz.org/dementia/types-of-dementia.asp.

American Psychological Association (APA). (2003, July). Office of Public Affairs. American Psychological Association applauds final report of President's New Freedom Commission on Mental Health. *American Psychological Association Press Release*. http://www.apa.org/news/press/releases/2003/07/mental-health-rpt.aspx.

APA. (2006). Asian-American mental health. http://www.apa.org/monitor/feb06/health.aspx.

APA. (2016a). Building resilience to manage indirect exposure to terror. http://www.apa.org/helpcenter/terror-exposure.aspx.

APA. (2016b). Guidelines for psychological practice with older adults. http://www.apa.org/practice/guidelines/older-adults.aspx.

Anderson, R., Rice, T., & Kominski, G. (2007). *Changing the U.S. health-care system* (439–479). San Francisco, CA: Jossey-Bass.

Bradley, P. (2003). Family caregiver assessment: Essential for effective home health care. *Journal of Gerontological Nursing, 29*, 29–36.

Center for Psychiatric Rehabilitation, Boston University. (2016). Alternative approaches to mental health care. https://cpr.bu.edu/resources/newsletter/alternative-approaches-mental-health-care.

Cochran, J. (2008, January 12). New gun control law is killer's legacy. http://abcnews.go.com/Politics/story?id=4126152.

Cook, G. (2006). Schooling Katrina's kids. *American School Board Journal, 193*, 18–26.

Embedded Behavioral Health (EBH). (2016). http://armymedicine.mil/Pages/EBH.aspx.

Everett, A., Mahler, J., Biblin, J., Ganguli, R., & Mauer, B. (2008). Improving the health of mental health consumers. *International Journal of Mental Health, 37*(2): 8–48.

Felton, C. (2004). Lessons learned since September 11 2001 concerning the mental health impact of terrorism, appropriate response strategies and future preparedness. *Psychiatry, 67*(2): 147–153.

Grob, G. (1983). *Mental illness and American society: 1875–1940.* Princeton, NJ: Princeton University Press.

Grob, G. (1994). *The mad among us: A history of the care of America's mentally ill.* New York, NY: Free Press.

Health and Human Services (2016). LGBT health & well-being 2015 report. http://www.hhs.gov/programs/topic-sites/lgbt/reports/health-objectives-2015.html.

Indian Health Service (IHS). (2016). Behavioral health. http://www.ihs.gov/communityhealth/behavioralhealth.

International Society for Traumatic Stress Studies (ISTSS). (2001). Mass disasters, trauma, and loss. https://www.istss.org/ISTSS_Main/media/Documents/ISTSSBr-MassDisasters_1.pdf.

Kessler, R. C., Chiu, W. T., Colpe, L., Demler, O., Merikangas, K. R., Walters, E. E., & Wang, P. S. (2006). The prevalence and correlates of serious mental illness (SMI) in the National Comorbidity Survey Replication (NCSR). In Manderscheid, R. W., & Berry, J. T.

(Eds.). *Mental health, United States, 2004* (DHHS Publication No. SMA-06-4195). Rockville, MD: Substance Abuse and Mental Health Services Administration.

Mayo Clinic. (2016). Mental health: What's normal, what's not. http://www.mayoclinic.com/health/mental-health/MH00042.

McFarling, L., D'Angelo, M., Drain, M., Gibbs, D., & Olmstead, K., (2011). Stigma as a barrier to substance abuse and mental health treatment. *Military Psychology, 23*, 1–5.

Mental Health Parity and Addiction Equity Act (MHPAEA). (2016). https://www.cms.gov/CCIIO/Programs-and-Initiatives/Other-Insurance-Protections/mhpaea_factsheet.html.

MHPAEA. (2016). https://www.cms.gov/CCIIO/Programs-and-Initiatives/Other-Insurance-Protections/mhpaea_factsheet.html.

MHA-NYC. Innovations in Mental Health. http://www.mhaofnyc.org/who-we-are/mission/.

National Alliance to End Homelessness. (2016). Snapshot of homelessness. http://www.endhomelessness.org/pages/snapshot_of_homelessness.

National Alliance on Mental Illness (NAMI). (n.d.). Latino community mental health fact sheet. http://www.nami.org/Find-Support/Diverse-Communities/Latino-Mental-Health.

NAMI. (2016). LGBTQ. http://www.nami.org/Find-Support/LGBTQ.

National Center for Posttraumatic Stress Disorder. (2013). About us. http://www.ptsd.va.gov/about/mission/history_of_the_national_center_for_ptsd.asp.

National Committee for Quality Assurance (NCQA). (2016). Accreditation programs. http://www.ncqa.org/Programs/Accreditation.aspx.

National Institute of Mental Health (NIMH). (2016). Older adults and mental health. https://www.nimh.nih.gov/health/topics/older-adults-and-mental-health/index.shtml.

NIMH. (2016a). Child and adolescent mental health. https://www.nimh.nih.gov/health/topics/child-and-adolescent-mental-health/index.shtml.

NIMH. (2016b). The National Institute of Mental Health strategic plan. https://www.nimh.nih.gov/about/strategic-planning-reports/index.shtml

NIMH. (2016c). Introduction. http://www.nimh.nih.gov/about/strategic-planning-reports/introduction.shtml.

Neria, Y., Gross, R., Litz, B., Maguen, S., Insel, B., Seirmarco, G.,... Marshall, R. D. (2007). Prevalence and psychological correlates of complicated grief among bereaved adults 2.5–3.5 years after September 11 attacks. *J Trauma Stress, 20*(3): 251–262.

Office on Women's Health, HHS. Mental health. (2016). http://www.womenshealth.gov/mental-health/your-rights/americans-disability-act.html.

Pointer, D., Williams, S., Isaacs, S., & Knickman, J. (2007). *Introduction to U.S. health care.* Hoboken, NJ: Wiley Publishing.

Qualls, S., Segal, D., Norman, D., Niederehe, G., & Gallagher-Thomson, D. (2002). Psychologists in practice with older adults: Current patterns, sources of training, and need for continuing education. *Professional Psychology: Research and Practice, 33*, 435–442.

Regier, D., Narrow, W., Rae, D., Manderscheid, R., Locke, B., & Goodwin, F. (1993). The de facto US mental and addictive disorders service system. Epidemiologic catchment area prospective 1-year prevalence rates of disorders and services. *Arch Gen Psychiatry*, *50*, 85–94.

Shi, L., & Singh, D. (2008). *Essentials of the U.S. health care delivery system*. Sudbury, MA: Jones and Bartlett Publishers.

Smith, H. (2007). Psychological service needs of older women. *Psychological Services*, *4*, 277–286.

Substance Abuse and Mental Health Services Administration (SAMHSA). (2011). Leading change: A plan for SAMHSA's roles and actions: 2011–2014. http://store.samhsa.gov/shin/content// SMA11-4629/02-ExecutiveSummary.pdf.

SAMHSA. (2013a). Identifying mental health and substance use problems of children and adolescents. http://store.samhsa.gov/shin /content/SMA12-4700/SMA12-4700.pdf.

SAMSHA (2014). SAMSHA 2014 Survey. http://www.samhsa.gov/data /sites/default/files/NSDUH-FRR1-2014/NSDUH-FRR1-2014.pdf.

Sultz, H., & Young, K. (2006). *Health care USA: Understanding its organization and delivery* (5th ed.). Sudbury, MA: Jones and Bartlett Publishers.

U.S. Public Health Service. (1999). Mental health: A report of the Surgeon General. https://profiles.nlm.nih.gov/ps/retrieve/Resource Metadata/NNBBHS.

Virginia Tech Review Panel. (2007). *Mass shootings at Virginia Tech: Report of the review panel presented to Governor Kaine, Commonwealth of Virginia*. http://www.governor.virginia.gov/TempContent /techPanelReport.cfm.

Weisler, R., Barbee, J., & Townsend, M. (2006). Mental health and recovery in the Gulf Coast after Hurricanes Katrina and Rita. *JAMA*, *296*, 585–588.

World Health Organization (WHO). (2010, September). Mental health: Strengthening our response. http://www.who.int/mediacentre /factsheets/fs220/en/index.html.

Woody, R. (2008). Obtaining legal counsel for child and family mental health practice. *The American Journal of Family Therapy*, *36*, 323–331.

Zuvekas, S., Rupp, A., & Norquist, G. (2008). The impacts of mental health parity and managed care in one large employer group: A reexamination. *Health Aff*, *24*, 1668–1671.

Student Activity 11-1

In Your Own Words

Based on this chapter, please provide a definition of the following vocabulary words in your own words. DO NOT RECITE the text definition.

Ayurvedic medicine

Embedded Behavioral Health model

Family Educational Rights and Privacy Act

Involuntary commitment

Mental disorders

Moral treatment

New Freedom Commission on Mental Health

Posttraumatic stress disorder

Psychiatrists

Tele behavioral health

Visualization

Student Activity 11-2

Complete the following case scenarios based on the information provided in the chapter. Your answer must be IN YOUR OWN WORDS.

Real-Life Applications: Case Scenario One

You have been concerned about your grandmother recently. Yesterday, she left the stove on when she went out to the grocery store. Your grandfather has been chronically ill for years and she is his main caregiver. She regularly visits her primary care provider who has told her that it is nothing more than old age. You decide to research mental health issues among the elderly and have found very interesting statistics, particularly for women.

Activity

(1) Provide three statistics about mental health issues in women population; (2) and strategies on how to deal with women's' mental health issues.

Case Scenario Two

You are thinking about going to school to become a mental health professional. However, you have heard that mental health professionals face liability issues and complaints—but you are unsure why.

Activity

Perform research using this text and the Internet to find five reasons why mental health professionals are at high risk for complaints.

Case Scenario Three

The American Psychiatric Association has developed a guide for diagnosing mental health disorders. This guide has been used for years by many mental health professionals. Recently, the APA has been criticized heavily regarding the guide.

Activity

You are curious as to why this guide has been challenged for its quality. Perform research to determine what the issue is with this landmark publication.

Case Scenario Four

You are concerned about your grandmother who recently lost her spouse, your grandfather. You feel she is depressed. You want to take her to her primary care provider for a checkup.

Activity

Prior to taking her to her doctor, you want to familiarize yourself with mental health issues in the elderly. You do some research to find out what mental health issues are common in the elderly population. Discuss how a health navigator can help you with this family situation.

Student Activity 11-3

Internet Exercises

- Visit each of the websites listed here.
- Name the organization.
- Locate its mission statement on the website.
- Provide a brief overview of the activities of the organization.
- How does the organization participate in the U.S. healthcare system?

Websites

http://www.apa.org

Organization Name
Mission Statement
Overview of Activities
Importance of Organization to U.S. Health Care

http://www.samhsa.gov

Organization Name
Mission Statement
Overview of Activities
Importance of Organization to U.S. Health Care

http://www.istss.org

Organization Name
Mission Statement
Overview of Activities
Importance of Organization to U.S. Health Care

http://www.psych.org

Organization Name
Mission Statement
Overview of Activities
Importance of Organization to U.S. Health Care

http://www.nimh.nih.gov

Organization Name
Mission Statement
Overview of Activities
Importance of Organization to U.S. Health Care

http://www.nami.org

Organization Name
Mission Statement
Overview of Activities
Importance of Organization to U.S. Health Care

Student Activity 11-4

Discussion Questions

The following are suggested discussion questions for this chapter.

1. What is the *DSM*? Why is it important to mental health care?
2. Do you believe that mental health care is important to veterans and military?
3. What are some issues regarding the treatment of African American patients who have mental health problems?
4. Do you believe in holistic healing? Support your answer.
5. Do you think the Indian Health Service is important? Discuss its activities.
6. Discuss issues with the LGBTQ population regarding mental health.
7. How can a health navigator assist a patient with mental health care?

Student Activity 11-5

Current Events

Perform an Internet search and find a current events topic that relates to this chapter. Provide a summary of the article and the link to the article and explain how the article relates to the chapter.

CHAPTER 12

Navigating Long-term Care Services

LEARNING OBJECTIVES

The student will be able to:

- Identify three types of long-term care services.
- Discuss the advantages and disadvantages of long-term care insurance.
- List three Activities of Daily Living and three activities of Instrumental Activities of Daily Living.
- Discuss three important historical events that formed the basis of the long-term care industry.
- Identify three ways to pay for long-term care.
- Describe the Medicare and Medicaid payment structures for long-term care.
- Identify and describe three ways a health navigator can assist in long-term care planning.

DID YOU KNOW THAT?

- Many people often pay for long-term care services out of pocket. Some life insurance policies will pay for long-term care.
- Medicaid is the largest source of long-term care financing.
- The Department of Labor has developed a Long-Term Care, Support and Services Competency Model to train workers engaged in long-term care support services.
- According to 2012 estimates, approximately 70% of people 65 years and older will require long-term care services, placing a heavy burden on the U.S. system.

INTRODUCTION

According to the Department of Health and Human Services, long-term care services include a broad range of health, personal care, and supportive services that meet the needs of older people and other adults whose capacity for self-care is limited because of a chronic illness; injury; physical, cognitive, or mental disability; or other health-related condition. People with intellectual and developmental disabilities need long-term care services. Most long-term care is not medical care but rather assistance with the basic personal tasks of everyday life. These tasks are sometimes called **activities of daily living (ADLs)** and include bathing, dressing, eating, and going to the bathroom. Long-term care services also provide assistance for **instrumental activities of daily living (IADLs)** such as housework, money management, taking medications, grocery or clothes shopping, pet care, and using the telephone (HHS, 2013). Individuals may need these services for years. In general, long-term care services usually are provided by unpaid caregivers—family and friends—in home and community-based settings. Over the past 20 years, the shift of institutional long-term care provision has been towards community and home-based settings as a result of the Olmstead decision. The Supreme Court's **Olmstead decision** found that the Americans with Disabilities Act violated the rights of persons with disabilities by keeping them institutionalized, therefore increasing the need for community-based services (Reaves & Musumec, 2015).

HISTORY OF LONG-TERM CARE

From the 1100s through the 1400s, England built about 700 shelters for the elderly. In general, long-term shelters were associated with monasteries. In 1536, King Henry VIII closed all of the monasteries and their elderly shelters. The King appointed a board to oversee long-term care facilities in England. Queen Elizabeth I required communities to care for their elderly as long as possible in their homes and to provide them with facilities as needed. In 1722, England enacted the Poor Law, which created institutions for the elderly. In the 1700s, the American colonies developed nursing home institutions in urban areas, following the English model, and this gradually led to the establishment of nursing homes throughout the United States (LongTermCareEducation.com, 2016).

According to the Kaiser Family Foundation (KFF), long-term care has evolved over the past 100 years to serve the needs of the elderly and those individuals who have physical and mental limitations that preclude both populations from fully engaging in their activities of daily living and instrumental activities of daily living. The following sections represent a timeline of the evolution of long-term care.

Nursing Home Services 1935–1968

1935: The passage of the federal **Social Security Act** provided financial assistance to indigent seniors who were living longer and had no savings to live on. The payments were not given to seniors who were living in public institutions, which at the time provided terrible living conditions. The act became the impetus for the development of private nursing homes. Today these payments are known as the Old Age Survivors Disability and Health Insurance (OASDHI), and deductions to pay for it are taken from an employee's paychecks.

1950: A Social Security Act amendment required residents' payments to be made directly to nursing homes as well as the establishment of state licensing boards for nursing homes.

1965: A Social Security Act amendment established the Medicare and Medicaid programs.

Medicaid programs provided assistance for long-term institutional care, which fostered the start of a nursing home industry.

1967: A Social Security Act amendment was passed to ensure that nursing home administrators were licensed. This amendment was the result of public outcry over abuse of residents in nursing homes.

1968: Social Security Act amendments (Moss amendments) were passed to withhold funding from nursing homes that did not adhere to government standards. A commission appointed by Congress met in 1968 and recommended what today is known as the five Domains of Practice that nursing home administrators must study in order to become licensed. The Domains of Practice include management, personnel, finance, regulations, and resident care.

Development of Community-Based Services

1974: Social Security Amendments provided federal grants for states to support social service programs that included adult day care and health support.

1975: Social Security Amendments created Title XX, which provided assistance for home and community-based services.

1978: Amendments to the Comprehensive Older Americans Act required states to develop a nursing home ombudsman program and to develop community-care alternatives to institutional care.

1980: The Mental Health Systems Act provided support of community mental health programs.

1981: States were allowed to offer non-medical community-based Medicaid programs as an alternative to institutional care.

1982: Authorized under the **Tax Equity and Fiscal Responsibility Act**, state plans were allowed to cover disabled Medicaid-eligible children for community services.

1987: The **Nursing Home Reform Act** imposed quality standards for nursing homes in order to receive reimbursements from Medicare and Medicaid. The Robert Wood Johnson Foundation began to encourage people to purchase long-term care insurance.

1990: **The Americans with Disabilities Act** required state Medicaid programs to cover Medicare premiums for lower income individuals. The Act emphasized the importance of integrating individuals with disabilities into the community and work environment.

2000: The **American Act Caregiver Program** established state grants to fund family and informal caregivers who provide home care.

2005: The Deficit Reduction Act provided federal funding to states to expand community-based long-term care.

2010 Healthcare Reform

2010: The Affordable Care Act provided states with the opportunity under the Medicaid program to improve their long-term care infrastructure.

2013: The **American Taxpayer Relief Act** established a Commission on Long-Term Care.

2014: The Center for Medicare and Medicaid Services provided new standards that community-based services must meet to be considered home and community based.

2015: The Center for Medicare and Medicaid Services improved its Five Star Quality system rating system for nursing homes (KFF, 2015).

TYPES OF LONG-TERM CARE SERVICES

There are home care, community care, and housing programs for long-term care. **Home care** can be provided by family, friends, volunteers, or professionals. Short-term, skilled care is covered by Medicare. Hospice care often is given at home for terminally ill individuals. **Community services** are support services that include adult day care centers, meal programs such as Meals on Wheels, senior centers, and transportation. Adult day care centers offer a break for caregivers who provide ongoing care for loved ones with chronic diseases. The federal government provides housing programs for lower-income individuals who often are seniors. These facilities may provide support

for instrumental activities of daily living (Types of long-term care, 2016).

There are four general categories of long-term care institutional services: independent living, congregate care facilities, assisted-living facilities, and skilled nursing facilities. **Independent living** covers a broad range of settings for individuals who typically do not need regular healthcare services. The target market is 75 years or younger. These facilities typically have age restrictions, have increased security, and offer a range of social activities. The target population in **congregate care facilities** is 55 years or older. There is no assistance with daily activities, and a state license is not required. They fall somewhere between independent living and assisted-living facilities. These facilities will provide assistance for instrumental activities of daily living. **Assisted-living facilities** provide 24-hour supervision and assistance with instrumental activities of daily living. Recreational activities are provided. Depending on state regulations, there may be some medical care assistance. **Skilled nursing facilities** provide care to residents who cannot live independently. Skilled nursing care is provided (Types of long-term care, 2016; Administration on Aging, 2016).

THE ROLE OF THE LONG-TERM CARE NAVIGATOR

The role of the health navigator in long-term care will vary depending on the individual's preference in the type of long-term care services they need, what financial options are available to them, and the state services provided. The long-term care navigator should develop a strategic plan for the individual's long-term care services. The navigator should receive training or have a background in both public and private insurance products. Having experience in long-term care as well as a foundation in basic financial planning would also be an asset. The long-term care navigator should obtain data in the following areas:

1. State options for long-term care
2. Federal options for this individual
3. Insurance options for this individual

4. Personal financial net worth
5. Personal insurance policies

The navigator should collaborate with a personal financial planner to ensure the decision is in the best financial interest of the individual.

HOW TO PAY FOR LONG-TERM CARE SERVICES

In general, long-term care services can be provided at home by home health aides, in the community in adult day care, or in facilities such as assisted-living facilities and nursing homes. Long-term care services can be very expensive. Personal funds, Medicare and Medicaid, and long-term care insurance are ways to pay for long-term care services.

When individuals require long-term care services, they often pay out of pocket for the services until their personal funds are depleted, and then they will access Medicaid to pay for them. Most continuing-care retirement communities and assisted-living facilities are paid for by the individual, although Medicaid may pay for the costs in some states. The Veteran's Administration may help with paying for long-term care costs incurred by disabled veterans. Contrary to many people's beliefs, Medicare does not cover most long-term care costs.

Medicare covers medically necessary short-term or acute care such as doctor visits, prescription drugs, and hospital stays. Physical therapy also is covered by Medicare for conditions that will be improved. Medicare does not pay for the largest part of long-term care services, such as help with activities of daily living. It will pay for a short-term stay in a skilled nursing facility or home health care if the following conditions are met:

1. The patients had a minimum of a three-day hospital stay.
2. The patients are admitted to a Medicare-certified nursing facility within 30 days of a prior hospital stay.
3. Skilled care such as physical therapy is needed.

If these conditions are all met, Medicare will pay for some of the costs up to 100 days.

Medicare also pays for a limited time the following services that are ordered by the patient's physician:

1. Part-time or intermittent skilled nursing care.
2. Physical therapy, occupational therapy, and speech therapy performed by a Medicare-certified home health agency.
3. Medical social services to help cope with an illness.
4. Medical supplies and durable medical equipment.

Medicare covers hospice care for patients with a terminal disease, with a prognosis of six months to live (Administration on Aging, 2016).

Long-term Care Insurance

As life expectancy continues to increase in the United States, more people will require more healthcare services for chronic conditions. Unfortunately, Medicare and traditional health insurance policies do not pay for long-term care. Approximately 70% of people over the age of 65 will require long-term care at some point in their lives. Medicaid will pay for long-term care for patients who qualify. The Department of Veterans Affairs may pay for long-term care for service-related disabilities and other eligible veterans' conditions. *Long-term care insurance* was developed to cover services such as assistance with activities of daily living (personal hygiene, feeding and dressing oneself) as well as care in an organizational setting. The cost of long-term care insurance can vary based on the type and amount of services selected as well as the age at time of purchase and healthcare status. An average monthly cost for a semi-private room in a nursing facility is $6,235, compared with $4,000 for an assisted-living facility (Administration on Aging, 2016).

If an individual is already receiving long-term care or is in ill health, a person may not qualify for long-term care insurance. Most long-term care insurance policies are comprehensive, which means they will cover expenses from home health care, hospice, respite care, assisted living and nursing homes, Alzheimer's special care, and adult day services centers. Long-term care policy costs vary greatly based on age and type of policy. The **National Clearinghouse for Long-Term Care Information** has provided the following information for purchasing long-term care insurance:

- The policyholder can select a daily benefit amount, depending on the healthcare setting. The type of healthcare setting can be identified, such as home health care or skilled nursing facility.
- The policyholder can select a lifetime amount the policy will provide, which can range from $100,000 to $300,000. More expensive policies will allow unlimited coverage with no dollar limit, which is unusual. Premiums are typically $3,000 per year. Most policies will provide long-term coverage from two to five years.
- The policyholder also can select an inflation option, which adjusts the coverage amount as you age.
- Some policies may pay for family/friend long-term care for the policyholder. The policy also may provide reimbursement for equipment or transportation.
- If the patient is are in poor health or already receiving long-term care services, he or she may not qualify for long-term care insurance because most individual policies require medical underwriting. In some cases, the patient may be able to buy a limited amount of coverage, or coverage at a higher "non-standard" rate. Some group policies do not require underwriting (U.S. Department of Health & Human Services).
- This website provides information about long-term care costs in your state: http://longtermcare.gov/costs-how-to-pay/costs-of-care-in-your-state/.

More employers are now offering long-term care insurance as an option to employees. Employers do not contribute to the premium cost but may negotiate a better group rate. Long-term care insurance is becoming more popular because individuals are recognizing that Medicare will not pay for long-term care unless it is a medical necessity. Medicaid will pay for long-term care, but only for those individuals who qualify for the program (DHHS, 2016b).

Older Americans Act Programs

The **Older Americans Act programs** (1965) are federal programs that provide home- and community-based services to older adults. These programs are provided by state and local agencies and include in-home personal care, meals in the community and homebound, local transportation, respite care such as adult day care, and services for older Native Americans. These programs are targeted to low-income, frail or disabled over 60, minority older adults, and older adults living in rural areas (NIH Senior Health, 2016).

Annuities

An **annuity** is a series of payments over a specified period of time. Entering a contract with an insurance company for an annuity may help pay for long-term care services. An immediate long-term care annuity consists of a specified monthly income in return for a single premium payment. **Deferred long-term annuities** consist of a specified monthly income for a specified time period. These annuities are available to individuals up to age 85.

Life Insurance

Life insurance policies are purchased to financially protect a beneficiary in the event of the death of the insured. They typically provide a lump sum to the beneficiary. Some life insurance policies with an accelerated death benefit provide cash advances while the policy holder is still alive. The amount taken from the life insurance policy is subtracted from the amount due to the beneficiaries. **Accelerated death benefits** are available if the policy holder lives permanently in a nursing home, is terminally ill, needs long-term care for an extended period of time, or has a life-threatening diagnosis such as AIDS.

Selling an insurance policy back to the insurance company for its current value is an option to raise cash. This is known as a life settlement and is available to people 70 and older. The proceeds are taxable and can be used for any purpose including long-term care services. As with any of these financial considerations, it is important to consult a financial planner (NIH Senior Health, 2016).

CURRENT TRENDS IN LONG-TERM CARE

CCRCs

Continuing care retirement communities (CCRCs) are a combination of independent living, assisted living, and nursing care all on one campus. This "aging in place" model offers the opportunity to reside in a single-family home on campus, for example, and as individuals age, they can transfer to an assisted-living facility, and eventually to a skilled nursing facility. Seniors must move into a CCRC when they are healthy and can live independently. These housing models often are very expensive; they typically require an entrance free, and residents must pay a monthly maintenance fee depending on their needs. Residents typically sign a continuing care contract. (CCRC, 2015).

There are four different categories of "life care" contracts within a CCRC. **Extensive contracts** include housing, residential services, amenities, and unlimited access to health care at budgeted monthly rates. A **modified contract** includes housing, residential services, and amenities but only limited healthcare access. A fee-for-service contract includes housing, residential services, and amenities but no healthcare services. A **rental agreement** contract on a monthly or annual basis does not give the resident access to healthcare services. There is a Continuing Care Accreditation Commission for these types of housing models. In 2010 (most recent data), there were more than 2,000 CCRCs (Folkeson, 2016).

The Green House Project

In 2001, the Robert Wood Johnson Foundation funded a pilot project developed by Dr. Bill Thomas called the **Green House Project**. This unique type of nursing home focuses on creating a residence that not only provides services but is also a home to the residents, not an institution where they receive care (Fine, 2009).

The home is managed by a team of workers who share the care of the residents, including the cooking and housekeeping. The daily staff members are certified nursing assistants (CNAs). All mandated professional personnel, such as physicians, nurses, social workers, and dieticians, form visiting clinical support teams that assess the residents and supervise their care (Kane, Lum, Cutler, Degenholtz, & Yu, 2007).

Residents are called **elders**, and the word *patient* is not used at all. The Green House is designed for 6–10 elders. Each resident has a private room and private bathroom. The elder rooms have lots of sunlight and are located near the kitchen and dining areas. The residents can eat their meals when they choose. There are patios and gardens for elders and staff to enjoy. Although these new types of nursing homes look like a residential home, they adhere to all long-term housing requirements. They look like other homes in their designated neighborhoods (Fine, 2009).

Residents also can have their own pets, which are not allowed in traditional nursing homes. According to a recent study performed by the University of Minnesota, the residents of the Green Houses are able to perform their activities of daily living longer, are less depressed than residents of traditional nursing homes are, and are able to be self-sufficient longer. Staff members also enjoy working at the Green House, resulting in less turnover (Kane et al., 2007).

The first Green House was constructed in Tupelo, Mississippi. There are now more than a hundred homes in nearly 20 states. Another 130 homes are under development in 10 additional states. Dr. Thomas has partnered with the Robert Wood Johnson Foundation (RWJF) and NCB Capital Impact, which is a not-for-profit organization that provides financial assistance to underserved communities. The NCB Capital Impact has a loan program that provides financial assistance of up to $125,000 to support engineering, architectural, and other expenses for a selected Green House site. The borrower must contribute 25% of the loan amount (NCB Capital Impact, 2016).

Since 2002, the Foundation has awarded $12 million, primarily to NCB Capital Impact, to develop, test, and evaluate the Green House model. In 2011, the Foundation decided to expand its support, with the goal of helping the Green House model achieve greater reach and impact. With NCB Capital Impact, RWJF announced a 10-year, $10 million low-interest credit line to finance the building of Green House homes. Specifically, this investment reduces the cost of financing Green House projects to serve low-income elders. RWJF support is helping to spread the Green House model across the United States. Today, hundreds of Green House homes are open or under development in many states. Research indicates that the Green House operations are comparable in cost to traditional nursing homes (RWJ, 2012).

Village Movement

In 2001, in Boston, Massachusetts, a group calling itself the **Village Movement** formed a nonprofit organization, Beacon Hill Village, which formed a network to provide services to older homeowners that allowed them to remain in their homes longer and maintain their independence. The network typically acts as a liaison to connect homeowners to needed workers. This membership organization's annual dues are approximately $600, and there is a network of contractors and volunteers who offer services that would typically be offered in a retirement community. There now are nearly 200 villages nationwide and more in development (Calmus, 2013).

Long-Term Care Financial Crisis

As the population lives longer, more people will need long-term care services; however, the majority of Americans do not plan for long-term care. Government programs account for 63% of LTC funding, with Medicaid providing for 40% of that amount and Medicare 23%. Nationally, the median annual cost of a private room in a nursing home is more than $90,000 (Calmus, 2013)).

Although Medicaid was originally developed for lower-income individuals, more middle-income individuals will be tapping into Medicaid because they do not have the funds to pay for their long-term care.

The federal government has been examining different alternatives to purchase long-term care insurance options. For example, consumers who have been concerned about the cost of their premiums going to waste if they do not need long-term care can purchase a premium return rider on the policy, although it is expensive. A more grassroots opportunity for the elderly are community networks that the elderly can join so they can access long-term care support services.

LONG-TERM CARE, SUPPORTS, AND SERVICES COMPETENCY MODEL

In 2010, the Employment and Training Administration of the Department of Labor developed a training model for employees to develop competencies to successfully work in the long-term care industry. (See **Figure 12-1**.) This pyramid represents both the general knowledge, skills, and abilities needed for many types of industries as well as specific areas of competencies that apply to the long-term care industry. At the bottom of the pyramid (Tiers 1–3) are personal effectiveness, academic, and workplace competencies that can be applied to many industries. The higher levels of the pyramid, Tiers 4 and 5, represent competencies that relate specifically to the long-term care industry. For examples, Tiers 1–3 training models would include the following competencies: problem solving, effective decision making, organizational ethics, technology, and teamwork. Tiers 4–5 training models would include industry-specific competencies such as knowledge of residential long-term settings, familiarity with the population served, knowledge of long-term care support services, appropriate techniques to assist with activities of daily living and instrumental activities of daily living, and understanding the law and regulations as they pertain to long-term care. A tutorial that provides guidance on how to use the model

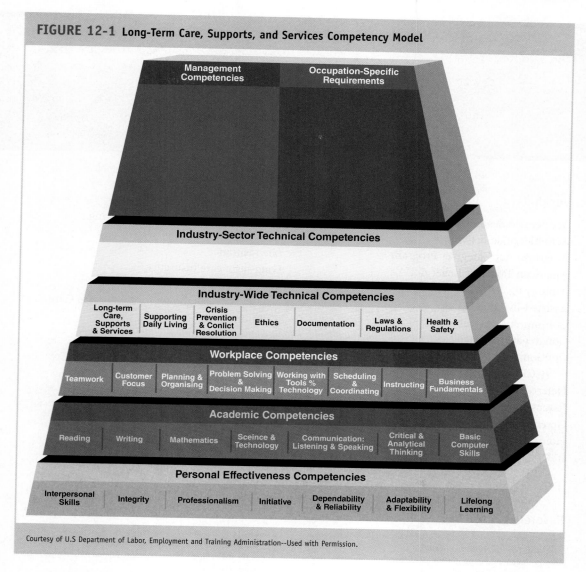

FIGURE 12-1 Long-Term Care, Supports, and Services Competency Model

Courtesy of U.S Department of Labor, Employment and Training Administration--Used with Permission.

can be accessed at http://www.careeronestop.org/CompetencyModel/Tutorials/how-to-use-competency-models-demo.aspx.

CONCLUSION

As life expectancy increases, individuals will require long-term care services, which already comprise a significant percent of national healthcare expenditures paid for by Medicaid. The Commission on Long-Term Care, created by the American Taxpayer Relief Act of 2012, issued a report in 2013 that indicated there needs to be a coordinated program in place that focuses on long-term care services for individuals across the United States, and the Commission recommended funding for a system to be developed. As of this writing, long-term care services vary based on state priorities. In general, healthcare experts recognize the need for creating innovative ways to deliver long-term care services. A component of this type of innovation is the long-term care navigator. This service can assist individuals and their families with researching the different types of long-term care services provided by the state, reviewing their financial support for long-term care services, researching the types of long-term care facilities in their local area, and assisting them with the transition to a long-term care provider.

Summary

Vocabulary

Accelerated death benefits

Activities of daily living

American Act Caregiver Program

American Taxpayer Relief Act

Annuity

Assisted-living facilities

Community services

Congregate care facilities

Continuing care retirement communities (CCRCs)

Deferred long-term annuities

Extensive contracts

Green House Project

Home care

Independent living

Instrumental activities of daily living

Life care contracts

Life insurance

Long-term care insurance

Modified contracts

National Clearinghouse for Long-term Care Information

Nursing Home Reform Act

Older Americans Act programs

Olmstead decision

Rental agreement

Skilled nursing facilities

Social Security Act

Tax Equity and Fiscal Responsibility Act

Village movement

References

Administration on Aging. (2016). Costs of care. http://longtermcare.gov/costs-how-to-pay/costs-of-care/

Administration on Aging. (2016). Medicare. http:/longtermcare.gov/medicare-medicaid—more/medicare.

Administration on Aging. (2016). What is long-term care? http://longterm care.gov/the-basics/what-is-long-term-care/.

A Place for Mom. (2016). Continuing care retirement communities (CCRC). http://www.aplaceformom.com/senior-care-resources/articles/continuing-care-retirement-communities.

Calmus, D. (2013). The long-term care financing crisis. Center for Policy Innovation. http://www.heritage.org/research/reports/2013/02/the-long-term-care-financing-crisis.

Department of Health and Human Services (DHHS). (2016a). Long-term care insurance. http://longtermcare.gov/

Fine, S. (2009, May 31). Where to live as we age. *Parade Magazine*, 8–9.

Folkeson, J. (2016). CCRCs. Military Officers Association of America. http://www.moaa.org/Content/Publications-and-Media/Features-and-Columns/MOAA-Features/Continuing-Care-Retirement-Community.aspx?list=4294967917&cat=4294967326.

LongTermCareEducation.com. History of long term care. (2016). http://www.ltce.com/learn/history.php.

Kane, R., Lum, T., Cutler, L., Degenholtz, H., & Yu, T. (2007). Resident outcomes in small house nursing homes: A longitudinal evaluation of the initial Green House program. *Journal of Geriatrics Society*, 55(6): 832–839.

The Kaiser Family Foundation (KFF). (2015). Long-term care in the United States: A timeline. http://kff.org/medicaid/timeline/long-term-care-in-the-united-states-a-timeline/.

NCB Capital Impact. (2016). http://www.ncbcapitalimpact.org/default.aspx?id=146&terms=Green±House.

NIH SeniorHealth. (2016). http://nihseniorhealth.gov/longtermcare/payingforlongtermcare/01.html.

Reaves, E. & Musmeci, M. (2015, December). Kaiser Commission: Medicaid and long-term services and supports. http://kff.org/medicaid/report/medicaid-and-long-term-services-and-supports-a-primer/.

Robert Wood Johnson Foundation. (2012). The Green House® project. https://www.rwjf.org/en/how-we-work/grants/grantees/the-green-house-project.html.

Types of long term care. (2016). WebMD. http://www.webmd.com/healthy-aging/choosing-long-term-care?page=2.

Student Activity 13-1
In Your Own Words
Based on this chapter, please provide a definition of the following vocabulary words in your own words. DO NOT RECITE the text definition.

Activities of daily living

American Act Caregiver program

Congregate care facilities

Continuing care retirement communities

Instrumental activities of daily living

Life care contracts

National Clearinghouse for Long-term Care Information

Nursing Home Reform Act

Older Americans Act

Village movement

Student Activity 12-2
Complete the following case scenarios based on the information provided in the chapter. Your answer must be IN YOUR OWN WORDS.

Real-Life Applications: Case Scenario One
You have been concerned about your grandmother recently. Yesterday she left the stove on when she went out to the grocery store. Your grandfather has been chronically ill for years, and she is his main caregiver. She regularly visits her primary care provider who has told her that her memory loss is nothing more than old age. You decide to research long-term care options for your grandparents.

Activity
Discuss three long-term care options and the disadvantages and advantages for each option.

Case Scenario Two
Realizing the complexity of long-term care services, you have heard there is a new type of healthcare professional, a long-term care navigator. You would like to know more about this career option.

Activity
Perform research using this text and the Internet to discuss five reasons health navigators can become an essential component to the healthcare system.

Case Scenario Three
You are interested in the concept of continuing care retirement communities as an option for your parents.

Activity

Perform research using the text and Internet. Locate a CCRC in your geographic area and develop a summary report regarding this type of long-term care living option.

Case Scenario Four

You have been assisting your elderly neighbors with grocery shopping and small repairs around the house. However, you are moving to another state and are worried about who will take care of them. You are very interested in the village movement as an option to provide support in the community.

Activity

Doing research using the text and the Internet, locate a village movement and write a summary report. Be sure to include costs and the advantages and disadvantages of this type of long-term care service.

Student Activity 12-3

Internet Exercises

- Visit each of the websites listed here.
- Name the organization.
- Locate its mission statement on the website.
- Provide a brief overview of the activities of the organization.
- How does the organization participate in the U.S. healthcare system?

Websites
http://www.longtermcare.gov

Organization Name
Mission Statement
Overview of Activities
Importance of Organization to U.S. Health Care

http://www.nihseniorhealth.gov

Organization Name
Mission Statement
Overview of Activities
Importance of Organization to U.S. Health Care

https://www.ltcfeds.com

Organization Name
Mission Statement
Overview of Activities
Importance of Organization to U.S. Health Care

http://www.eldercare.gov

Organization Name
Mission Statement
Overview of Activities
Importance of Organization to U.S. Health Care

http://www.webmd.com

Organization Name
Mission Statement
Overview of Activities
Importance of Organization to U.S. Health Care

http://www.thearc.org

Organization Name
Mission Statement
Overview of Activities
Importance of Organization to U.S. Health Care

Student Activity 12-4
Discussion Questions
The following are suggested discussion questions for this chapter.

1. Do you know anyone who uses long term care services? Why do they need them?
2. Do you think the village movement is a good idea? Provide statistics to support your answer.
3. Pick two historical events that you think influenced the development of long-term care in the United States.
4. Discus the Green House project and its impact on the elderly population.
5. Discuss the Supreme Court's Olmstead decision. Do you support this decision? Why or why not?

Student Activity 12-5
Current Events
Perform an Internet search and find a current events topic that relates to this chapter. Provide a summary of the article and the link to the article and explain how the article relates to the chapter.

CHAPTER **13**

Successfully Navigating the U.S. Healthcare System

LEARNING OBJECTIVES

The student will be able to:

- Navigate the Healthcare Marketplace Exchanges.
- Understand federal, state, and local government regulations related to navigating patient care.
- Describe the importance of navigating the public health system as it relates to navigating community health.
- Discuss the importance of navigating inpatient and outpatient services related to hospital care, long-term care and mental health care.
- Describe the importance of health information technology as it relates to navigating patient care.
- Define and discuss the legal and ethical foundations related to navigating patient health care.

DID YOU KNOW THAT?

- A regulated patient navigator program was developed in Canada because most cancer patients there see 32 physicians during their cancer treatment.
- Health literacy is the degree to which individuals have the capacity to understand basic health information and services.
- The Affordable Care Act established insurance navigators to assist consumers with purchasing insurance on the marketplace exchanges.
- The Veterans Administration has a home telehealth service for veterans that allows them to collect symptoms and record vital signs and share the data with the VA.

INTRODUCTION

The U.S. healthcare system has long been recognized for providing state-of-the-art health care. It also has been recognized as a very complex system with many different stakeholders that impact the provider–patient relationship which often is confusing to the patient. Despite the efforts of the Affordable Care Act to increase access to health care, there are still individuals in underserved communities who face barriers to accessing health care. Patient navigators have been in place for more than 20 years. However, the Affordable Care Act has increased recognition of these navigators, resulting in the educational industry's development of curricula for navigator programs.

The role of the patient navigator plays a very important advocate role to ensure that the patient receives the best care possible. However, in order to provide quality patient assistance, a **patient navigator** must develop areas of expertise for each component of the healthcare system. The patient navigator's goal is to increase the health literary of the patient. **Health literacy** is the degree to which individuals have the capacity to obtain, process, and understand basic health information and services. The wide range of skills that comprise health literacy and influence a patient's ability to navigate the healthcare system and make appropriate decisions about his or her health include reading, writing, math, communication, and, increasingly, the use of electronic technology.

This chapter will provide navigation guidelines for each of the areas of the U.S. healthcare system which include navigating the healthcare marketplace exchanges, navigating the roles of all levels of government including public health patient resources, navigating inpatient and outpatient services, understanding information technology as it relates to patient care, navigating legal and ethical ramifications of patient care, and navigating the mental health system. Depending on the professional background of the navigator, a navigator could provide assistance in many of these areas of the healthcare system, but a navigator also could focus on specific areas.

NAVIGATING THE HEALTHCARE MARKETPLACE EXCHANGES

The Affordable Care Act established insurance navigators at the state government level to help with the insurance marketplace websites. According to the healthcare.gov website, a navigator is an individual or organization who is trained and able to help individual consumers, small businesses, and their employees as they look for health coverage options through the Marketplace, including completing eligibility and enrollment forms. These individuals and organizations are required to be unbiased. Their services are free to consumers. The ACA created the Navigator program or In-Person Assister (IPA) as part of its outreach and enrollment assistance to individuals who were purchasing insurance coverage from the Health marketplace. Any marketplace was required to have a navigator program to assist healthcare consumers. Navigators were required to provide education and to assist with enrollment in insurance programs to individuals. The marketplace navigators contracted directly with the Center for Medicare and Medicaid Services which provides a Marketplace Learning Management System (MLMS) for them to complete 30 hours of training.

The 30 hours of training include the following: outreach and public education, expertise in all insurance programs, cultural and linguistic competency, understanding of electronic storage of information and HIPAA requirements of patient information confidentiality, and communication skills development. The following is a summary of the major training components provided by the Centers for Medicare and Medicaid Services:

Outreach and public education

- Targeting the underinsured and uninsured
- Messaging to reach eligible consumers and overcome barriers to reach them
- Identifying community partners to reach consumers
- Utilizing existing media materials
- Creating new materials for outreach
- Developing materials in plain English and non English languages
- Tracking and reporting activities
- Analyzing outreach performance
- Special outreach for vulnerable and underserved populations

Working with underserved and vulnerable populations

- Comprehension of legal requirements for fair treatment
- Reporting violations against other navigators
- Filing complaints
- LGBT issues
- Immigration family issues
- People with disabilities issues
- Working with limited English proficient individuals

Cultural and linguistic competence

- Developing general knowledge of racial, ethnic, and cultural groups including practices and beliefs
- Providing oral and written notice of consumer rights to receive language assistance services
- Accessing and working with interpreters and translated materials
- Health literacy

Access for people with disabilities

- Comprehension of disabilities that need accommodation
- Providing access to materials, websites, and other tools to people with disabilities
- Using TTD/TTY services

Insurance affordability eligibility

- Understanding qualified health plans
- Understanding insurance affordability programs (Medicaid, CHIP)
- Cost-sharing concepts
- Summary of benefits and coverages
- Basic eligibility requirements and application process
- Financial assistance requirements
- Enrollment options (CMS, 2016a)

NAVIGATING THE GOVERNMENT PROGRAMS

The government plays an important role in the quality of the U.S. healthcare system. **Social regulation** focuses on organizations' actions, such as those in the healthcare industry, that affect an individual's safety. Social regulations focus on protecting individuals as employees and consumers (Carroll & Buchholtz, 2015). These types of regulations are common in the U.S. healthcare system and are enforced by government agencies. The federal government provides funding for state and local government programs and sets policy for many aspects of the U.S. healthcare system. The federal government also is responsible for the implementation of Medicare, the entitlement program for the elderly. Federal healthcare regulations are implemented and enforced at the state and local levels. Funding is distributed primarily from the federal government to the state government, which consequently allocates funding to local health departments. Local health departments provide the majority of services for their constituents and collaborate with local organizations such as schools and physicians to increase their ability to provide education and prevention services.

Many federal agencies are involved in the regulation of health care. The U.S. Department of Health and Human Services (HHS) is the most important federal agency. It is a cabinet-level department of the executive branch of the federal government and has 11 operating divisions. The Secretary of the HHS provides advice to the President of the United States regarding health and human services policy (Pozgar, 2014). HHS collaborates with state and local governments because many HHS services are provided at those levels. The Centers for Disease Control oversees public health activities at the state and local levels that directly impact individuals regarding community health services. The Centers for Medicare and Medicaid Services has oversight of both Medicare and Medicaid services that directly impact individuals. The Substance Abuse and Mental Health Services Administration provides policy directives for mental health services and provides resources that affect individuals. The government navigator needs to be familiar with the government activities at all levels but particularly the Centers for Medicare and Medicaid Services. Millions of individuals qualify for Medicare- and Medicaid-covered services, but often they are not familiar with the coverage. The government navigator can provide needed information to the patient to ensure they understand their covered services.

NAVIGATING PUBLIC HEALTH

As a healthcare consumer, it is important to recognize the role that public health plays in our health care. If you are sick, you go to your physician for medical advice, which may mean providing you with a prescription. However, oftentimes you may not go see your physician because you do not have health insurance or you do not feel sick enough. Public health surrounds consumers with educational opportunities to change a health condition or risky health behavior. A public health navigator can assist healthcare consumers with accessing free information provided by the CDC or with visiting their local or regional health department regarding preventive services. All navigators should be familiar with public health initiatives including outreach education that can benefit their patients. Navigators with a masters of public health could be very beneficial to patients.

For example, Memorial Hermann Health System in Houston, Texas, implemented a pilot program in 2008 for patient navigation. The workers were bilingual state-certified community health workers trained in peer-to-peer counseling. Their focus was to educate underserved populations who were uninsured, publicly insured, or U.S. immigrants about the importance of primary care. A health navigator establishes medical home for these populations, schedules appointments, and collaborates with social work services. One of the primary goals of the program was to reduce the number of emergency department visits by these populations who used the ED visits for their primary care. The program places four certified community health workers designated as patient navigators in three Hermann Health Systems emergency departments. Analysis indicates that there was more than a 75% reduction in ED visits as a result of this program. Hermann has received national recognition for this navigator program (Enard & Ganelin, 2013).

NAVIGATING INPATIENT SERVICES

One of the most stressful events in an individual's life is spending time in a medical facility because of a health event or surgery. It can be a fearful time for the patient depending on the circumstances. For example, if a patient experiences a health episode requiring hospitalization or an inpatient stay at a rehabilitation center, the patient may need assistance with the care. If a patient has scheduled a surgery, the person may need assistance from a navigator to understand the care. An inpatient care navigator can be very helpful to both the patient and the facility.

Typically, an inpatient care navigator has a clinical background so the navigator can communicate with the patient's physicians and staff to review medication schedules and care management of the disease to avoid any readmission to a facility for not following orders. The Cleveland Clinic uses care coordinators to provide support to its patients and families, to collaborate with nurses, and to encourage patients to be proactive in their health care (Albert, 2012).

NAVIGATING CHRONIC DISEASE MANAGEMENT SERVICES

Over the years, disease management has become more of an outpatient service. Advanced technology has enabled more ambulatory surgeries and testing, which has resulted in the development of many specialty centers for radiology and imaging, chemotherapy treatment, and kidney dialysis. These services often were performed in a hospital. Patients who receive many outpatient services are individuals who have chronic diseases such as cancer who require case management. A chronic disease management navigator, depending on the patient's condition, must develop a trust and personal connection with patients. Research indicates that outpatient services navigators often identify themselves as both a motivator and supporter of the patient, which often is difficult because the boundaries of a professional relationship must be maintained. When dealing with several outpatient services, the navigator can assist with provider communication, arranging appointments with multiple services, and assisting patients with understanding the different levels of care if needed. Many of these outpatient navigators who worked with chronic disease patients often had both a clinical and social work background in order to deal with the many levels of care provided (Phillips, Nonzee, Tom, Murphy, Hajjar, Bularzik, Dong, & Simon, 2014).

NAVIGATING INFORMATION TECHNOLOGY

Increasingly, health navigators need to increase their familiarity with information technology. Specific electronic applications such as electronic patient records, patient portals, and telemedicine have increased across the country. Healthcare consumers need to embrace an electronic patient record. The patient health record can be integrated into the electronic health records that are being utilized nationwide. This will enable patients to be treated effectively and efficiently nationally. Having the ability to access a patient's health information could assist in reducing medical errors. As a consumer, utilizing a tool like HealthVault could provide an opportunity to consolidate all medical information electronically, so if there are any medical problems, the information will be readily available. Having made this recommendation, not all healthcare consumers have routine access to technology nor do they understand how to utilize health information technology. The role of the HIT navigator can be instrumental in improving patient engagement with their care.

An example of how a home Health navigator can be helpful is with a home telehealth service. Home **telehealth** care is remote (electronic monitoring) between a healthcare provider and a patient outside the facility. The goal of home telehealth care is to maintain a patients' maximum level of care, which ultimately reduces costs of institutional care and promotes the "aging in place" goal. The Veterans Administration has a home telehealth service for veterans. Special devices that collect symptoms and vital signs of the patient are transmitted to a VA facility. These devices are easy to use by the patient. A home telehealth navigator can complement the electronic information available with scheduling appointments and discussing the treatments offered to the patient (VA, 2016).

NAVIGATING HEALTHCARE LAW AND HEALTHCARE ETHICS

To be an effective legal navigator, it is important to understand basic legal and ethical principles that influence both the healthcare provider and the patient. Health navigators must be familiar with the different state laws that impact the health organizations and the healthcare consumers they are trying to assist. Both federal and state laws have been enacted and policy has been implemented to protect both the healthcare provider and the healthcare consumer. New laws have been passed and older laws have been amended to reflect needed changes regarding health care to continue to protect its participants. The legal navigator does not replace legal counsel unless the navigator is an attorney. However, a legal navigator can provide guidance on where to seek legal advice.

HEALTHCARE ETHICS

Ethical standards are considered one level above a legal action because individuals make a choice based on what is the "right thing to do," not what is required by law. There are many interpretations of the concept of ethics. Ethics has been interpreted as the moral foundation for standards of conduct (Taylor, 1975). A major area of medical ethics is the treatment of patients who are dying. Euthanasia, including physician-assisted suicide, illegal in all states but Oregon, Washington, Vermont, and most recently, California, has been a controversial patient issue for years. Supporters of physician-assisted suicide believe it is the individual's right to choose when they want to end their life and they should have assistance from a physician, if needed. Opponents believe it is unethical because it is the responsibility of a physician to save a life, not to take a life. The ethics navigator's priority is to support the patient's right to autonomy when making a medical decision such as end-of-life treatment. According to the American Society for Bioethics and Humanities Task Force, Core Competencies for Healthcare Ethics Consultation, an ethics navigator or consultant seeks to "resolve conflict or uncertainty regarding value laden concerns that emerge in health care and to improve the quality of health care through the identification and resolution of ethical concerns ... in a respectful atmosphere" (ASBH, 2011). This can be difficult if there are opposing views from the family or the clinician. Being trained in medical ethics would be necessary to be successful in this area. It is important to be objective when playing this role. The following are recommendations on how to navigate the ethics navigator role:

1. Do not assume the question you are being asked is an ethical issue. If someone is requesting an ethical consult, they recognize there is a problem. It is important to clarify if this is a legal request which should be referred to legal counsel.
2. Develop a standardized, systematic, and thorough approach to the consultation. Ask standardized questions to assess the

situation in order not to prematurely arrive at a conclusion.

3. Document the process and the decision and place the written information in the patient record. This provides clarification for all parties concerned.

4. Perform assessments of your service to ensure you are providing a satisfactory service.

These recommendations reflect the need for ongoing communication among all parties. In larger healthcare facilities, there may be an ethics committee available for consultation. Collaborating with them can be very helpful as well (Carrese, 2016).

NAVIGATING THE MENTAL HEALTH SYSTEM

Mental health issues affect millions of U.S. citizens. Mental health disabilities limit the life expectancy of individuals by several years. Treatment of mental health disorders has been traditionally underfunded because of the attitude of the traditional healthcare system, confusion by health insurance companies, and fear of discrimination by individuals who are mentally ill. The Mental Health Parity Act of 1996 was an attempt to establish a fair system of treatment between mental health disorders and traditional healthcare conditions by mandating annual and lifetime insurance limits to be equal between mental health care and traditional health care. In 1999, Surgeon General David Satcher's report on mental health brought awareness to the issues with the U.S. mental healthcare system. In 2002, President George W. Bush's Freedom Commission on Mental Health focused on an analysis of the mental health system and made recommendations to improve mental health care.

The **Mental Health Parity and Addiction Equity Act (2008)** further supported mental health care by requiring insurance plans to offer benefits and cost sharing similar to traditional medical benefits. However, mental health experts and legislators felt the Act was overall weak and so in 2013 passed a final rule that strengthened

it, increasing parity of mental health insurance coverage with traditional health insurance coverage. The Obama administration recognized the importance of funding mental health initiatives, including teacher training programs for mental health awareness (Mohney, 2013).

Because individuals with serious mental illnesses are at risk for more diseases and have a higher mortality rate than the general population, a mental health navigator can play a very important role for these types of patients. Because of the fragmentation of mental health care, a mental health navigator can bridge the gap between traditional and mental health services. A mental health navigator can provide a care-linkage approach between the mental health providers and their primary care provider. In Southern California, a "Bridge" intervention pilot program was implemented to assess a healthcare engagement and self-management model that provides tools to patient to be proactive with the help of a mental health navigator. In this instance, a bridge model uses a peer mental health navigator. The navigator keeps a log of all contacts, which average three contacts per month with the patient. The mental health navigator spends a minimum of 10 minutes to four hours, which include lab testing, pharmacy or clinician visits, and monitoring prescription compliance. Results of the program indicated improved health outcomes. The navigator provides guidance to the patients to be compliant with their medical care (Kelly, Fuiginiti, Pahwa, Tallen, Duan, & Brekke, 2014).

Telemedicine

Telemedicine refers to the use of information technology to enable healthcare providers to communicate with rural care providers regarding patient care or to communicate directly with patients regarding treatment. The basic form of telemedicine is a telephone consultation. Telemedicine is most frequently used in pathology and radiology because images can be transmitted to a distant location where a specialist will read the results. Telemedicine is becoming more common because it increases healthcare access to remote locations such as rural areas. It also is a cost-effective mode of treatment. It is also possible that employers and health plans recognize the potential to improve access to medical care while reducing medical costs (Gingrich, Boxer, & Brooks, 2008). Avera eCare established eEmergency in 2009, which provides electronic immediate access of emergency-certified physicians and nurses to rural providers to help them with diagnosis of patients with critical conditions. It is an example of tele-emergency services. Rural clinicians and administrators agree that eEmergency services have demonstrated significant impact on the quality of clinical services provided in rural areas. This type of consumer-centric approach is becoming more popular.

Home Telehealth Patient Navigators

Care managers, or care coordinators, are individuals who combine nursing, social services, and disability assistance primarily to individuals who are eligible for both Medicare and Medicaid, suffer from chronic conditions, and often cannot handle managing their own chronic conditions. The goal of a care coordinator is to avoid the patient's placement into a nursing home. The dual-eligible patients utilize 35% of Medicare and Medicaid spending so this type of assistance with patient life issues may reduce government spending. According to the CMS, eight states have signed agreements with the CMS to develop care coordination plans (Dickson, 2013).

Care coordinators are the fastest-growing occupation in the healthcare industry. Most are registered nurses who have received additional training in coordinated care, collaboration, and communication.

RECOMMENDATIONS ON NAVIGATOR TRAINING CURRICULUM

Depending on the type of navigator, the following are general recommendations for training a patient navigator:

1. Familiarity with the specific disease
2. Primary prevention to improve health outcomes
3. Understanding of the care management process

4. Understanding of the language, culture, and beliefs of patients
5. Communication with the doctors
6. Emotional support of patient and family
7. Understanding the different roles of the navigator
8. Protecting patient confidentiality
9. Managing support groups for family and friends
10. Knowing how to work with terminal patients and their families
11. Understanding of financing resources for patients
12. Familiarity with legal and ethical issues of patients
13. Familiarity with community resources
14. Familiarity with clinical trials (Nguyen, Tran, Kagawa-Singer, & Foo, 2011)

The Harold Freeman Patient Navigation Institute remains the gold standard for patient navigation. This curriculum is broad, which enables nonclinicians to participate. The American College of Cardiology Quality Improvement for Institutions launched a Patient Navigator Program in 2014 to provide support for patient health after discharge. There are 35 hospitals across the United States that participate in this program. It was developed to limit the number of patients who were readmitted to the hospital (Patient Navigator, 2016). Other patient navigation programs advertised on the Internet target students rather than healthcare facilities.

CONCLUSION

The U.S. healthcare system continues to evolve. Technology will continue to have a huge impact on health care. Consumers have more information to make healthcare decisions because of information technology. All of these initiatives are exciting for the healthcare consumer. The implementation of an EHR, which will enable providers to share information about a patient's health history, will provide the consumer with the opportunity to obtain more cost-effective and efficient health care. There are hospitals, physician practices, and other healthcare organizations that utilize EHR systems across the country. Even though implementing the system nationally will be extremely expensive—costs have been estimated in the billions—it will eventually be a cost-saving measure for the United States. The Affordable Care Act has provided many incentives to improve the quality of and access to the U.S. healthcare system. The Centers for Medicaid and Medicare Innovation has more than 40 demonstration projects that focus on different types of financing models based on the performance of healthcare providers.

All of these changes can improve health outcomes. However, the U.S. healthcare system continues to be complex. The role of patient navigators can vary across the healthcare system. The patient navigator's role can take many forms. Depending on training, a navigator can focus on different parts of the healthcare system or just one component. A navigator can focus on inpatient care; marketplace exchanges; outpatient care including chronic disease management for HIV, cancer, and other chronic diseases; telehealth; mental health; and legal and ethical consultations. Although navigators have been used for decades in cancer care, HIV, and diabetes, the role has been revisited with the implementation of the Affordable Care Act marketplace exchanges and designation of navigators for those exchanges. The Centers for Disease Control and Prevention indicate patient navigation is an effective intervention for HIV care. The National Cancer Institute has funded research to assess the effectiveness of these programs (Broeckaert & Challacombe, 2014). The Department of Labor, as of this writing, recognizes the community health worker as a navigator for health care. As these navigators prove their success, there are other opportunities for patient navigators to provide advocacy in many areas that are discussed in this chapter. Canada, which provides health care to all of its citizens, has a highly regulated cancer patient navigator system. The system was developed at the request of patients because of the complexity of the system. For example, a cancer patient in Canada may interact with an average of 32 physicians. Having a navigator can assist the patient with this massive communication process. Although the development of navigation programs vary from state to state and may be private or government funded, Canada has a regulated program for cancer. Cancer navigators must have five years of cancer patient experience. The navigator program is expanding its scope to include cultural sensitive navigators for diverse communities (Patient navigators, 2011). This type of program may be an example that the United States could model particularly as it applies to regulations and standard training. The expansion of the concept of patient navigator will continue to grow as more healthcare facilities hire navigators as a way to improve patient health outcomes. Like Canada, at some juncture, there may need to be regulations to ensure quality training for the patient navigator.

Summary

Vocabulary

Care manager
Health literacy
Mental Health Parity and Addiction Equity Act
(2008)

Patient navigator
Social regulation
Telehealth
Telemedicine

References

Albert, B. (2012). Navigating care management. Healthcare Financial Management Association (December). http://www.hfma.org/Content.aspx?id=14138.

American Society for Bioethics + Humanities (ASBH). (2011). HCEC Pearls and Pitfalls: Suggested Do's and Don't's for Healthcare Ethics Consultants.

Bachrach, D., Frohlich, J., Garcimonde, A., & Nevitt, K. (2015). The value proposition of value clinics. http://www.rwjf.org/en/library/research/2015/04/the-value-proposition-of-retail-clinics.html.

Broeckhart, L. & Challacombe, L. (2014). Health navigation: A review of the evidence. http://www.catie.ca/en/pif/fall-2014/health-navigation-review-evidence.

Carrese, J. (2016). Pearls and pitfalls: Suggested do's and don'ts for healthcare ethics consultants. https://www.ncbi.nlm.nih.gov/pubmed/23256404.

Centers for Medicaid and Medicare Services (CMS). (2016b). Navigator and consumer assistance training curriculum online. https://www.cms.gov/Outreach-and-Education/Learn/Get-Training/Get-training-page.html.

Enard, K. & Ganelin, D. (2013). Reducing preventable emergency department utilization and costs by using community health workers as patient navigators. *Journal of Healthcare Management*, 58(6): 412–427.

Hersh, L., Salzman. B., & Snyderman, D. (2015). Health literacy in primary care. *Am Fam Physician*.

Kelly, E., Fulginiti, A., Pahwa, R, Duan, T., & Brekke, J. (2014). A pilot test of a peer navigator intervention for improving the health of individuals with serious mental illness. *Community Men Health J, 50*, 435–446.

Nguyen, T., Tran, J., Kagawa-Singer, M., Foo, M. (2011). A qualitative assessment of community-based breast health navigation services for southeast Asian women in southern California: Recommendations for developing a navigator training curriculum. *Am J Public Health, 101*(1): 87–93.

Patient navigators becoming the norm in Canada. (October 18, 2011). Canadian Medical Association. http://www.cmaj.ca/content/183/15/E1109.full.

Phillips, S., Nonzee, N., Tom, L., Murphy, K., Hajjar, H., Bularzik, C., Dong, X., & Simon, M. (2012). Patient navigators' reflections on the navigator-patient relationship. *J Cancer Educ, February, 29*, 337–344.

Quality Improvement for Institutions. Patient navigators (2016). http://cvquality.acc.org/Initiatives/Patient-Navigator/Features/Patient-Navigator.aspx.

Taylor, P. (1975). *Principles of ethics: An introduction to ethics* (2nd ed.). Encino, CA: Dickinson.

U.S. Department of Veterans Affairs. (2016). Home telehealth. http://www.telehealth.va.gov/ccht/.

Student Activity 13-1
In Your Own Words
Based on this chapter, please provide a description of the following concepts in your own words. DO NOT RECITE the text description.

Cultural competence

Health literacy

Marketplace navigator

Patient navigator

Telehealth

Student Activity 13-2
Complete the following case scenarios based on the information provided in the chapter. Your answer must be IN YOUR OWN WORDS.

Real-Life Applications: Case Scenario One
You just completed your Master of Public Health degree. You are interested in becoming a public health navigator for your community.

Activity
Using the textbook and Internet, perform a search to locate existing public health navigation programs and report your findings back to the class.

Case Scenario Two
You have a friend that you believe is suffering from some mental health issues. You are concerned about him but do not know what to do.

Activity
Do an Internet search and review the different legislative acts that pertain to mental health. Research mental health statistics in the United States. Write up a report that discusses these acts and the data you found regarding mental health in the United States. Discuss how a patient navigator can specifically help with a patient who suffers from a serious mental illness.

Case Scenario Three
A family member who lives in Canada has been diagnosed with cancer. He is very upset and is refusing care. You know he needs assistance and had heard that Canada has an excellent cancer navigation program. You want to be able to help.

Activity
You perform an Internet search regarding the cancer navigation program and provide a summary for the class.

Case Scenario Four

You had heard that the Department of Labor is recognizing the community health worker as a patient navigator. You are interested in this as a career.

Activity

You go to the Department of Labor website to research this job position. You provide a summary to the class regarding the job responsibilities and salary for this position.

Student Activity 13-3

Internet Exercises

- Visit each of the websites listed here.
- Name the organization.
- Locate its mission statement or statement of purpose on the website.
- Provide a brief overview of the activities of the organization.
- How does the organization participate in the U.S. healthcare system?

Websites

http://www.catie.ca

Organization Name
Mission Statement
Overview of Activities
Importance of Organization to U.S. Health Care

http://www.patientnavigator.com

Organization Name
Mission Statement
Overview of Activities
Importance of Organization to U.S. Health Care

http://www.patientnavigatortraining.org

Organization Name
Mission Statement
Overview of Activities
Importance of Organization to U.S. Health Care

http://www.hpfreemanpni.org

Organization Name
Mission Statement
Overview of Activities
Importance of Organization to U.S. Health Care

http://www.onco-nav.com

Organization Name
Mission Statement
Overview of Activities
Importance of Organization to U.S. Health Care

http://www.cvquality.acc.org

Organization Name
Mission Statement
Overview of Activities
Importance of Organization to U.S. Health Care

Student Activity 13-4

Discussion Questions

The following are suggested discussion questions for this chapter.

1. Develop a code of ethics for a patient navigator. What conduct would you include?
2. What is the Veterans Administration's home telehealth system? How can the navigator work with this system?
3. What is eprescribing? Do you think it will help reduce the number of mistakes that have occurred from handwritten prescriptions? How can a navigator assist with prescription drug compliance?
4. What is telemedicine? Telehealth? How would a health IT navigator assist with a patient?
5. What is the Blue Button Project? Perform an Internet search and discuss one healthcare organization that uses the Blue Button.

Student Activity 13-5

Current Events

Perform an Internet search and find a current events topic that relates to this chapter. Provide a summary of the article and the link to the article and explain how the article relates to the chapter.

GLOSSARY

Academic medical centers: These are hospitals organized around a medical school that offer substantial programs and are considered elite teaching and research institutions affiliated with large medical schools.

Accelerated death benefits: Benefits attached to a life insurance policy that enable the policy holder to receive cash advances against the death benefit in the case of being terminally ill, living permanently in a nursing home, needing long-term care for an extended period of time, or having a life-threatening diagnosis such as AIDS.

Accreditation: It is a private standard developed by accepted organizations as a way to meet certain standards.

Activities of daily living (ADLs): These are job responsibilities of licensed practical nurses that include patient observation, taking vital signs, keeping records, assisting patients with personal hygiene, and feeding and dressing patients.

Acupuncture: A Chinese practice of insertion of needles in specific points of the body to balance the system.

Acuson P10: It is a pocket-sized portable ultrasound machine designed for quick and easy use in emergency medicine, cardiology, ICU, and OB/GYN situations for traditional applications of diagnostic and screening tests.

Acute care hospital: A hospital with specialty-care for patients who stay an average of less than 30 days for short-term treatment.

Adult day care centers: These are day programs that provide a medical model of care, with medical and therapeutic services; a social model, with meals, recreation, and some basic medical health; or a medical–social model, with social interaction and intensive medical-related activities, all depending on the needs of the patients.

Advance directives: Orders that patients give to providers to ensure that, if they are terminally ill and incompetent to make a decision, certain measures will not be taken to prolong that patient's life.

Advanced practice nurse (APN): A healthcare professional possessing a degree required for a licensure who may work independently depending on the state licensure requirements or in collaboration with physicians.

Affirmative action plan: A strategy that encourages employers to increase the diversity of their workforce by hiring individuals based on race, sex, and age.

Affordable Care Act (ACA): An act intended to increase health insurance quality and affordability, lower the uninsured rate by expanding insurance coverage, and reduce the costs of healthcare.

Age Discrimination in Employment Act of 1967: An act that protects employees and job applicants 40 years old and older from discrimination as it applies to hiring, firing, promotion, layoffs, training, assignments, and benefits.

Allied health professionals: A segment of the workforce that delivers services involving the identification, evaluation, and prevention of diseases and disorders; dietary and nutrition services; and rehabilitation and health systems management.

Allopathic approach: An approach that actively intervenes in attacking and eradicating disease and focuses its efforts on the disease.

Almshouses: Also known as poorhouses, they were established to serve the indigent by providing shelter while treating illness.

Alternative approaches to mental health care: Therapies and treatments that emphasize the relationships between the body, mind, and spirituality.

Alternative reproductive methods: A collection of methods for conceiving children through medical technology.

Alzheimer's disease: A progressive mental deterioration that can occur in middle or old age, due to generalized degeneration of the brain.

Ambulatory care: It literally means a person is able to walk to receive a healthcare service, which might not always be true; the term "ambulatory care" is used interchangeably with outpatient services.

Ambulatory surgery centers: A center for surgeries that does not require an overnight stay.

American Act Caregiver Program: An initiative that played a crucial role in the development of community-based services by establishing state grants in the year 2000 to fund family and informal caregivers who provide home care.

American Psychological Association Task Force on Promoting Resilience in Response to Terrorism: An association that produced fact sheets that are intended to provide information to psychologists assisting those target populations impacted by terrorist events.

American Recovery and Reinvestment Act (ARRA): An act signed into law by President Obama in 2009 to protect health coverage for the unemployed by providing a 65% subsidy for COBRA coverage to make the premiums more affordable.

American Taxpayer Relief Act: A bill signed by President Obama in 2013 having numerous provisions that affect the income tax bills of Americans. It averted the tax aspect of the "fiscal cliff" by preventing many tax breaks from expiring as scheduled.

Americans with Disabilities Act: A civil rights law that prohibits discrimination against individuals with disabilities in all areas of public life, including jobs, schools, transportation, and all public and private places that are open to the general public.

Americans with Disabilities Act of 1990: An act that focuses on individuals in the workplace who are considered disabled. This act applies to employers who have 15 employees or more and is enforced by the EEOC.

Anesthesiologist assistant (AA): A healthcare specialty physician assistant who assists with implementing an anesthesia care plan under the direction of an anesthesiologist and as a team member of the anesthesia care component of surgical procedures.

Animal-assisted therapies: A type of treatment where animals are often used to increase socialization skills and encourage communication among the mentally ill.

Annuity: A series of payments over a specified period of time. Entering a contract with an insurance company for an annuity helps pay for long-term care services.

Antitrust law: A law to protect the consumer by ensuring there is a market driven by competition so the consumer has a choice for health care.

Art therapy: A type of treatment where art activities such as drawing, painting, and sculpting may help people express their emotions and may help treat disorders such as depression.

Artificial intelligence: A field of computerized methods and technologies created to imitate human decision making.

Assessment: A regular and systematic investigation which includes surveillance, identifying problems, data collection, and analysis of the health problem to determine possible risks and hazards within the community.

Assisted-living facilities: Facilities alternative to a nursing home providing personalized resident-centered support services and health care according to individual preferences and needs for those who require assistance with everyday activities.

Associate degree in nursing (ADN): A tertiary education nursing degree offered as a two-year program by community colleges and a three-year diploma program offered by hospitals.

Assurance: A process of evaluating policies that meet program goals for provision of services to the public either directly or through regulation of other entities.

Autonomy: Is defined as self-rule, is an important concept to health care because it is applied to informed consent, which requires a provider to obtain the permission of a patient who has been provided adequate information to make a decision regarding intervention.

Ayurvedic medicine: One of the world's oldest medical systems that originated in India. Its practices incorporate diet, meditation, herbal medicine, and nutrition to treat depression and to release stress.

Bachelor of Science in Nursing (BSN): The most rigorous of the nursing programs offered by colleges and universities, it normally takes 4–5 years, where students perform both classroom activity and clinical practice activity.

Beneficence: The basic value that the healthcare provider should focus on the patient's best interests when making a decision.

Benefits Improvement and Protection Act of 2000 (BIPA): An act formally called the Medicare, Medicaid, and CHIP Benefits Improvement and Protection Act, which modifies Medicare payment rates for many services.

Bioethics: The study of the typically controversial ethical issues emerging from new situations and possibilities brought about by advances in biology and medicine.

Biofeedback: A technique that focuses on learning to control heart rate and body temperature.

This technique may be used in conjunction with medication to treat depression and schizophrenia.

Biosurveillance: A new form of surveillance that focuses on early detection of unusual disease patterns that may be due to human intervention.

Bioterrorism: An attack on a population by deliberately releasing viruses, bacteria, or other germs or agents that will contribute to illness or death in people.

Black market: Underground economy, or shadow economy, is a market characterized by some form of noncompliant behavior with an institutional set of rules.

Board certifying or credentialing examination: A certification required for specialists to be certified in their area of specialization, which requires additional years of training and is often associated with the quality of the healthcare provider's services.

Board of trustees: It is legally responsible for hospital operations, approves strategic plans and budgets, and has authority for appointing, evaluating, and terminating the CEO.

Boycotts: It means an expression of protest, a means of coercion or abstaining from using, buying, or dealing with and so on.

Brand name drugs: A name given by the pharmaceutical company that makes a drug to stand out in the marketplace, though the product will have a generic name which is the drug's scientific name displayed somewhere on the product in small print.

Cardiovascular technologist: A healthcare provider who performs diagnostic examinations for cardiovascular issues, basically assisting physicians in treating cardiac (heart) and peripheral vascular (blood vessel) problems.

Care manager: A healthcare professional who provide a combination of nursing, social services, and disability assistance primarily to individuals who are eligible for both Medicare and Medicaid, suffer from chronic conditions, and often cannot handle managing their own chronic conditions.

Carpal tunnel syndrome: A medical condition due to compression of the median nerve as it travels through the wrist at the carpal tunnel. It is a wrist injury that often occurs from repetitive hand motions in jobs such as grocery cashiers and computer users.

Carrier testing: Test used to identify individuals who carry a gene that is linked to a disease.

Certificate of need (CON): Laws that ensure that the state approved any capital expenditures associated with hospital and medical facility construction and expansion.

Certification: A process through which an organization recognizes that accreditation eligibility requirements have been met.

Certified midwives (CMs): Healthcare professionals who do not have a nursing degree but undergo midwifery education program, which is accredited by the same organization. They must also pass the same national certification exam to be given the designation of CM.

Certified nurse–midwives (CNMs): Healthcare professionals who have graduated from a nurse–midwifery education program that has been accredited by the American College of Nurse–Midwives' Division of Accreditation.

Certified nursing assistants (CNAs): Healthcare professionals who work under supervision, assisting patients with eating, bathing, and dressing; taking some vital signs; making beds; noticing any changes in the physical or emotional state of a patient; and notifying a nursing supervisor.

Charitable care or bad debt: It means either the healthcare providers do not expect payment after the person's inability to pay has been determined or the efforts to secure the payment have failed.

Chief executive officer: A highest-ranking executive of a hospital who provides leadership to achieve their mission and vision and who is ultimately responsible for the day-to-day operations of the hospital and is a board-of-trustees member.

Chief information officer (CIO): An executive-level position in a company or other entity who manages the organization's information systems and has knowledge of current information technologies as they apply to the healthcare industry and how new technology can apply to the organization.

Chief of medical staff: An in-charge of the medical staff–physicians that provides clinical services to the hospital.

Chief of service: A person who is responsible for leading the specialty or department in a hospital.

Chief technology officer (CTO): An executive-level position in a company or other entity whose occupation is focused on scientific and technological issues within an organization.

Children's Health Insurance Program (CHIP): The purpose of this program is to provide coverage for low-income children (younger than age 19) whose family income exceeds the income-level requirements of Medicaid.

Chiropractors: Healthcare professionals who have a holistic approach to treating their patients, which means they focus on the entire body, with emphasis on the spine, believing that the body can heal itself with no medication or surgery.

Church-related hospitals: These are community general hospitals developed as a way to perform spiritual work.

Civil law: A private law that focuses on wrongful acts against individuals and organizations based on contractual violations.

Civil Rights Act of 1964, Title VII: An act that prohibits discrimination based on race, sex, color, religion, and national origin and it is the key legal piece to equal opportunity employment. It created a concept of protected classes to protect these groups from employment discrimination in compensation and conditions or privileges of employment.

Civil Rights Act of 1991: An act that enables individuals to receive both punitive damages, which are damages that punish the defendant, and compensatory damages for financial or psychological harm.

Clayton Act of 1914: An act passed to supplement the Sherman Act, as amended by the Robinson-Patman Act, which issues further restrictions on mergers and acquisitions.

Cloning: Any procedure that creates a genetic replica of a cell or organism.

Codes of ethics: Guidelines for industry participants which provide a standard for operation so that all participants understand that if they do not adhere to this code, there may be negative consequences.

Collegial model: A doctor–patient relationship that assumes trust between the patient and doctor and that decision making is an equal effort.

Commission on Accreditation of Allied Health Education Programs (CAAHEP): An agency of accreditation which accredits 2,000 U.S. programs that offer 28 allied health specialties.

Committee on Operating Rules for Information Exchange (CORE): It has set up standards and operating rules for streamlining processes between providers and healthcare plans. This system allows for real-time access to patient information pre- and post-care.

Common law: A law established by the judicial system rather than by statutes enacted by legislatures that interprets previous legal decisions regarding a case when giving decisions in individual cases that have precedential effect on future cases.

Common rule: Elements including a written statement that includes the purpose and duration of the study; the procedures and, if they are experimental, any foreseen risks and potential benefits; and any alternative procedures that may benefit the subject.

Commonwealth Fund: A private foundation that aims to promote a high-performing healthcare system that achieves better access, improved quality, and greater efficiency, particularly for society's most vulnerable, including low-income people, the uninsured, minority Americans, young children, and elderly adults.

Community health workers: The frontline public health workers hired by healthcare agencies who focus on population-based health such as promoting healthy behavior. They are often classified with health educators and serve as a liaison between health/social services and the community.

Community preparedness: Is the community's capability to prepare for, withstand, and recover from both the short- and long-term public health incidents.

Community recovery: The ability to collaborate with community partners (e.g., healthcare organizations, businesses, schools, and emergency management) to plan and advocate for the rebuilding of public health, medical, and mental–behavioral health systems to at least a level of functioning comparable to pre-incident levels, and improved levels when possible.

Community services: Support services that include adult day care centers, meal programs such as Meals on Wheels, senior centers, and transportation.

Compensatory damages: A sum of money awarded in a civil action by a court to indemnify a person for the particular loss, detriment, or injury suffered as a result of the unlawful conduct of another.

Complementary and alternative medicine (CAM): A group of diverse medical care practices that are not considered part of traditional medicine.

Computerized physician order entry: It enables a patient's provider to enter a prescription order or order for a lab or diagnostic test in a computer system, which typically is now part of an electronic health record system.

Conditions of participation: A proposed rule issued by Centers for Medicare and Medicaid

Services (CMS) designed to protect patient health and safety and ensure quality of care.

Congregate care facilities: Facilities typically for residents 55 years of age or older where there is no assistance with daily activities but for instrumental activities of daily living. They do not require a state license and fall somewhere between independent living and assisted-living facilities.

Consolidated Omnibus Budget Reconciliation Act (COBRA): A law passed by the U.S. Congress in 1985 that required most employers with group health insurance plans to continue to offer temporary group health insurance for their employees in special circumstances for a period of up to 18 to 36 months depending on the situation.

Constitutional factors: The factors like genetic, biological, etc., that are highly significant for health which are seen as beyond the reach and influence of public health improvement strategies, policies, and practices.

Consumer Credit Protection Act (Title III) of 1968: An act that prohibits employers from terminating an employee if the individual's earnings are subject to garnishment due to debt issues. This act also limits the weekly garnishment amount from employees' pay and is enforced by the Federal Deposit Insurance Corporation (FDIC).

Continuing care retirement communities (CCRCs): They are a combination of independent living, assisted living, and nursing care all on one campus. It is an "aging in place" model that offers the opportunity to reside in a single-family home on campus.

Contractual model: A doctor–patient relationship that is based on a legal foundation. It assumes there is an agreement between the two parties, assuming mutual goals.

Contractual relationship to care for a designated population: A contract to care for a designated population is indicative of a health maintenance organization (HMO) or managed care contract. A physician is contractually required to care for those member patients of a managed care organization. They may sign contracts to provide care for hospitals, schools, or long-term care facilities that have designated populations.

Contractual right to admission: A relationship between a patient and hospital, a contractual right to admission can be considered a contract if a hospital has contracted to treat certain members of an organization, like a managed care organization.

Conversion therapy: Refers to a practice of spiritual or psychological counseling designed to make the assumption that being heterosexual is normal, so counselors try to persuade the LGBTQ to convert to that norm.

Core public health functions: They are health surveillance, planning, and program development; health promotion of local health activities; development and enforcement of sanitation standards; and health services provisions.

Cost plus reimbursement: A reimbursement given to rural hospitals as per the classification of MRHFP, which makes these hospitals eligible for grants to increase access to consumers.

Cost share: A cost that individuals must pay prior to receiving specific medical services or treatments covered by their health insurance plan.

Credentials committee: A committee that reviews and grants admitting privileges to physicians.

Criminal law: A system of law concerned with actions that are illegal based on court decisions. In order to convict someone of a criminal activity, guilt must be proved beyond a reasonable doubt. The most common types of criminal law infractions in the healthcare field are Medicare and Medicaid fraud.

Critical access hospitals: Hospitals that are classified as having no more than 25 acute care beds, and are at least 35 miles away from another hospital, providing emergency care, and are eligible for grants to increase access to consumers.

Cytotechnologists: A category of clinical laboratory technologists, they are specialists who collaborate with pathologists to evaluate cellular material.

Dance therapy: A type of treatment involving moving one's body to music to help individuals recovering from physical abuse because the movement may help develop a sense of ease with their bodies.

De facto mental health service system: A growing sector of nonprofit groups and organizations for the mentally ill that provide education and support.

Defensive medicine: Results when providers order more tests and provide more services than necessary to protect themselves from malpractice lawsuits.

Deferred long-term annuities: These annuities are of a specified monthly income for a specified time period available to individuals up to age 85.

Dementia: A wide range of symptoms associated with a decline in memory or other thinking skills severe enough to reduce a person's ability to perform everyday activities.

Dental assistants: An aide who works directly with dentists in the preparation and treatment of patients.

Dental hygienists: A healthcare professional who cleans teeth, examines patients for oral diseases, provides other preventive dental care, and educates patients on ways to improve and maintain oral health.

Dentist: A healthcare professional who is required to complete four years of education from an accredited dental school after receiving a bachelor's degree, and prevent, diagnose, and treat tooth, gum, and mouth diseases.

Designated health services: Services that include clinical laboratory services, outpatient prescription drug services, physical and occupational therapy, and imaging services such as magnetic resonance imaging (MRI), and the like.

Determinants of health: The social and community networks and macro environmental conditions that influence the status of an individual's health.

Diagnostic and Statistical Manual of Mental Disorders (DSM): It is a guide published by the American Psychiatric Association that explains the signs and symptoms that mark more than 300 types of mental health conditions.

Diagnostic medical sonographer: A healthcare professional who works under the supervision of a physician, this specialist provides patient services using medical ultrasound, which photographs internal structures.

Diagnostic testing: Test used to identify the disease when a person is exhibiting symptoms.

Dignity: The quality or state of being worthy.

Disability: A physical or mental impairment that substantially limits one or more major life activities of an individual, a record of such an impairment, or being regarded as having such an impairment.

Doctor of Medicine (MD): A medical education from an accredited school that is required to apply for a license to practice medicine as physician to diagnose and treat patient illnesses.

Doctor of Osteopathic Medicine (DO): A medical education from an accredited school that is required to apply for a license to practice medicine as physician to diagnose and treat patient illnesses.

Doctors Without Borders: An international medical organization that provides quality medical care to individuals threatened by violence, catastrophe, lack of health care, natural disasters, epidemics, or wars in 60 countries.

Drug Free Workplace Act of 1988: This act requires any employers that receive federal grants or have a federal contract of $25,000 or greater to certify that they operate a drug-free workplace.

Drug–drug interactions: When one drug affects the activity of another when both are administered together, it is called drug-drug interaction (DDI). DDI software programs alert pharmacists and clinicians about potential drug interactions.

Drugstore clinics: Clinics that are run by nurse practitioners or physician assistants who provide routine care.

Durable power of attorney: Also called an advance directive, it is an order that patients give to providers to ensure that, if they are terminally ill and incompetent to make a decision, certain measures will not be taken to prolong that patient's life.

Duty to treat: A code of medical ethics that provided guidelines for the physician–provider relationship, emphasizing the duty to treat a patient.

Edwin Chadwick: Sir Edwin Chadwick was an English social reformer who worked to reform the Poor Laws and to improve sanitary conditions and public health.

Effectiveness: One of the five justifications essential to demonstrate that the public health efforts were successful and, therefore, it was necessary to limit individual freedom of choice.

E-health: Refers to the use of the Internet by both consumers and healthcare professionals to access education, research, and products and services.

Electronic aspirin: A technology under clinical investigation at Autonomic Technologies, Inc. A patient-powered tool for blocking pain-causing signals at the first sign of a headache.

Electronic clinical decision support systems: Systems that are designed to integrate medical information, patient information, and a decision-making tool to generate information to assist with cases.

Electronic communication: A method of communication which refers to the transfer of writing, signals, data, sounds, images, signs, or intelligence sent via an electronic device using Internet, including email services.

Electronic health record (EHR): An electronic record of patients' medical history that can be used in hospitals, healthcare providers' offices, and other types of healthcare facilities. It enables healthcare organizations to monitor patient safety and care.

Electronic medical record (EMR/EHR): An electronic record of health-related information on an individual that is accumulated from one health system and is utilized by the health organization that is providing patient care. EMR is an EHR that can be integrated with other systems.

Electronic patient record: The patient component of the electronic health record, which is an electronic record of patients' medical history.

Electrotherapy: Treatment that uses electric signals to interfere with the transmission of neural pain signals into the brain. It effectively slows down or distracts the message from the nerve to the brain. It is chiefly used in the treatment of various forms of paralysis.

Embedded Behavioral Health model: A model that focuses on early intervention and treatment to promote soldier readiness (before, during, and after deployment).

Emergency medical technician (EMT): A healthcare professional who works with patients who require immediate medical attention, providing basic life support as they care for and transport the sick or injured to a medical facility for appropriate medical care.

Emergency medical technician-paramedic (EMT-P): A healthcare professional who works with patients who require immediate medical attention, providing advanced life support as they care for and transport the sick or injured to a medical facility for appropriate medical care.

Emergency Medical Treatment and Active Labor Act (EMTALA): An act that required hospitals to screen and stabilize individuals coming into emergency rooms regardless of the consumers' ability to pay.

Emergency Medical Treatment and Active Labor Act (EMTALA): An act that requires Medicare participants to receive emergency care from a hospital or medical entity that provides dedicated emergency services.

Emergency operations coordination: It is the ability to direct and support an event or incident with public health or medical implications by establishing a standardized, scalable system of oversight, organization, and supervision consistent with jurisdictional standards and practices and with the National Incident Management System.

Emergency preparedness: A process of ensuring that an organization has prepared for the first and immediate response for any catastrophic events such as bioterrorism; chemical and radiation emergencies; mass casualties as a result of explosions, natural disasters, and severe weather; and disease outbreaks.

Emergency public information and warning system: It is the ability to develop, coordinate, and disseminate information, alerts, warnings, and notifications to the public and incident management responders.

Employee assistance programs: An occupational health program, dating back to the 1940s, as an intervention for employee drug and alcohol abuse.

Employee Retirement Income Security Act of 1974 (ERISA): An act that regulates pension and benefit plans for employees, including medical and disability benefits.

Employee wellness programs: Programs that include promotion of exercise, health risk appraisals, disease management, and healthcare coaching, which have become a popular employee benefit.

Employer health insurance: A health insurance policy provided by an employer for the employees of a company.

Engineering model: A doctor–patient relationship that focuses on patients and their power to make decisions about their health care.

Enterprise data warehouse: It helps organizations in strategic decision making by integrating many computer systems across an organization.

Environmental health: It is the integral component of public health that focuses on the interrelationships between people and their environment, promotes human health and well-being, and fosters healthy and safe communities.

Epidemics: The occurrence of cases of a disease spreading rapidly in excess of what would normally be expected in a defined community, geographical area, or season.

Epidemiology: It is the study of disease distribution and patterns among populations and is the foundation for public health because its focus is to prevent disease from reoccurring.

Epidemiology triangle: It consists of three major risk factor categories for disease, which consists of the host, which is the population that has the disease; the agent or organism, which is causing the disease; and the environment, or where the disease is occurring.

E-prescribing: A form of computerized physician order entry, it consists of medication history, benefits information, and processing new and existing prescriptions. The user–clinician can review the patient's medication list, prescribe a new drug and designate which pharmacy will fill the prescription.

Equal Pay Act of 1963: An act that mandates that all employers award pay fairly to men and women if it is determined their jobs have equal responsibilities and require the same skills.

Ergonomics: The study of working conditions that affect the physical condition of employees.

Ethical standards: Basic concepts of ethics in the healthcare workplace that are considered above legal standards because individuals make a choice based on what is the "right thing to do," not what is required by law.

Ethics: A system of moral principles that apply values and judgments to the practice of medicine.

Ethics in Patient Referral Act of 1989: An act that prohibits physicians, including dentists and chiropractors, from referring Medicare and Medicaid patients to other providers for designated health services in which they have a financial interest. These laws directly prohibit many referrals that may increase a provider's or family members' financial interest.

Euthanasia: An act where a third party, usually a physician, terminates the life of an individual involving, but not limited to, a diagnosis of living in a situation that the individual considers to be worse than death or existing in a coma or in a persistent vegetative state.

Executive Orders 11246 (1965), 11375 (1967), and 11478 (1969): Orders written by the President of the United States, for federal agency directions that focus on discrimination issues, and require affirmative action based on these factors. These orders affect both federal contractors and employers with 50 or more employees.

Exercise physiologists: Healthcare professionals who assess, design, and manage individual exercise programs for both healthy and unhealthy individuals.

Expert system: A technique of artificial intelligence that was developed to imitate experts' knowledge in decision making.

Exploring Accreditation Project (EAP): The project was funded by the CDC and the Robert Wood Johnson Foundation (RWJF) to assess accreditation of public health agencies to ensure that the health departments deliver the core functions of public health and essential public health services.

Express contract: A type of relationship a physician can establish with a patient to provide healthcare, which is a simple contract—merely a mutual agreement of care between the physician and patient.

Extensive contracts: These are one of the four categories of life care contracts within a continuing care retirement community and include housing, residential services, amenities, and unlimited access to health care at budgeted monthly rates.

False Claims Act: An act also known as the Lincoln law, enacted in 1863, was originally passed to protect the federal government against defense contractors during the Civil War. The False Claims Act has been amended several times throughout the years, and, in the 1990s, was amended with a focus on healthcare fraud, most notably Medicare and Medicaid fraud.

Family Educational Rights and Privacy Act of 1974 (FERPA): A federal law that protects the privacy of student education records. The law applies to all schools that receive funds under an applicable program of the U.S. Department of Education.

Family Medical Leave Act (FMLA): An act that allowed employees up to 12 weeks of unpaid leave because of family illness.

Family Medical Leave Act of 1993: An act of the United States federal law requiring covered employers to provide employees job-protected and unpaid leave for qualified medical and family reasons.

Fatality management: It is the ability to coordinate with other organizations to ensure the proper recovery, handling, identification, transportation, tracking, storage, and disposal of human remains and personal effects; certify cause of death; and facilitate access to mental and behavioral health services for the family members, responders, and survivors of an incident.

Federal Food, Drug, and Cosmetic Act (FDCA): It is a set of laws passed by Congress in 1938 giving authority to the U.S. Food and Drug Administration (FDA) to oversee the safety of food, drugs, and cosmetics.

Federal hospitals: Hospitals that do not serve the general public but operate for federal beneficiaries such as military personnel, veterans, and Native Americans.

Federal Trade Commission: It is one of the oldest federal agencies and is charged with the oversight of commercial acts and practices. Two major activities of the FTC are to maintain free and fair competition in the economy and to protect consumers from misleading practices.

Federal Trade Commission Act: An act that outlaws unfair methods of competition and outlaws unfair acts or practices that affect commerce to protect the healthcare consumer and those who provide healthcare services.

Finance committee: A committee that provides financial oversight for the organization.

Flexner Report: A report that evaluated medical schools in Canada and the United States and was responsible for forcing medical schools to develop curriculums and admission testing.

General duty: Each employer shall furnish to each of his employees employment and a place of employment which are free from recognized hazards that are causing or are likely to cause death or serious physical harm to his employees.

Generalists: Healthcare professionals who can be primary care physicians, family care practitioners, general internal medicine physicians, or general pediatricians, whose focus is preventive services such as immunizations and health examinations.

Generic drugs: A drug that is equivalent to a brand name drug, only it has no patent protection and is sold at discounted prices.

Genetic Information Nondiscrimination Act of 2008: This act prohibits U.S. insurance companies and employers from discriminating based on information derived from genetic tests.

Genetic testing: Testing carried out on populations based on age, gender, or other risk factors to determine if they are at risk for a serious genetic disease or if they have a carrier gene that they may pass on to their children.

Geographic maldistribution: An issue that occurs because physicians prefer to practice in urban and suburban areas where there is a higher probability of increased income.

Geropsychology: A branch of psychology that seeks to address the concerns of older adults.

Graying of the population: The increase in the proportion of older people in the population.

Green House Project: An initiative aimed to provide long-term care for citizens becoming grayer and wanting to live as independently as possible for a long period of time.

Gross domestic product (GDP): The total value of all goods and services produced within a nation's geographic borders over a specified period of time.

Group insurance: An insurance that covers a defined group of people and where the risk is spread among those paying individuals.

Hart-Scott-Rodino Antitrust Improvement Act of 1976: An amendment to the Clayton Act, it ensures those hospitals and other entities that entered mergers, acquisitions, and joint ventures must notify the DOJ and the FTC before any final decisions are made.

Hazard Communication Standard (HCS): It ensures that all hazardous chemicals and toxic substances are properly labeled and requires employers to disclose these substances in workplaces and that companies are informed of the risks.

Health: A state of complete physical, mental, and social well-being of a person.

Health Center: Centers that originated in the 1960s as part of the war on poverty, they are organizations that provide culturally competent primary healthcare services to the uninsured or indigent population such as minorities, infants and children, patients with HIV, substance abusers, homeless persons, and migrant workers.

Health education: It focuses on changing health behavior through educational interventions such as multimedia education and classes.

Health information systems (HIS): Systems that store, transmit, collect, and retrieve health information data.

Health information technology (HIT): Technology used to manage the health data that can be used by patients–consumers, insurance companies, healthcare providers, healthcare administrators, and any stakeholder that has an interest in health care.

Health Information Technology for Economic and Clinical Health Act of 2009: This act amends Health Insurance Portability and Accountability Act of 1996 by requiring stricter notification protocols for breach of any patient information.

Health insurance: A type of insurance coverage that pays for medical and surgical expenses incurred by the insured.

Health Insurance Portability and Accountability Act of 1996 (HIPAA): An act passed to promote patient information and confidentiality in a secure environment.

Health literacy: The degree to which individuals have the capacity to obtain, process, and understand basic health information and services.

Health navigator: Also called a patient advocate, a health navigator assists healthcare consumers with making educated decisions regarding their health care and the health care of their loved ones.

Health promotion: A broader intervention term in public health, encompasses not only educational objectives and activities but also organizational, environmental, and economic interventions to support activities conducive to healthy behavior.

Health services administrators: A segment of the healthcare workforce found at all levels of a healthcare organization managing hospitals, clinics, nursing homes, community health centers, and other types of healthcare facilities.

Health Vault: A website developed by Microsoft that enables patients to develop electronic patient records free of charge and it is up to the individual as to how much medical information the person wants to store online with this website.

Healthcare and Education Affordability Reconciliation Act of 2010: An act signed into law on March 23, 2010, by President Barack Obama to improve the accessibility and quality of the U.S. healthcare system.

Healthcare ethical dilemma: A problem, situation, or opportunity that requires an individual, such as a healthcare provider, to choose an action between two obligations.

Healthy People 2000 report: A report released in 1990, titled the National Health Promotion and Disease Prevention Objectives, was created to implement a new national prevention strategy with three major goals: increase life expectancy, reduce health disparities, and increase access to preventive services.

Healthy People 2010 report: A report, Understanding and Improving Health, was released in 2000 which contained a health promotion and disease prevention focus to identify preventable threats to public health; major goals were to increase quality of life and life expectancy and to reduce health disparities.

Healthy People 2020 report: A report released in 2010, it contains 1,200 objectives that focus on 42 topic areas. A smaller set of Healthy People 2020 objectives, called leading health indicators (LHIs), has been targeted to communicate high-priority health issues.

Healthy People reports (2000, 2010, 2020): The series of reports is a federal public health planning tool produced by the CDC that assesses the most significant health threats and sets objectives to challenge these threats.

Hill-Burton Act of 1946: An act, also known as the Hospital Survey and Construction Act, passed because the federal government recognized the lack of hospitals in the United States during the 1940s. Federal grants were provided to states for hospital construction to ensure there were 4.5 beds per 1,000 people.

HIPAA National Standards of 2002: Standards that ensure that individuals' health information is properly protected while allowing the flow of health information needed to provide and promote high-quality health care for patients and to protect the public's health and well-being.

Holistic approach: An approach that focuses not only on the disease but also on the entire person.

Home care: A long-term care service provided by family, friends, volunteers, or professionals to maintain or restore a patient's health or minimize the effects of a disability or an illness.

Home health agencies: An agency that provides medical services in a patient's home; often provided to elderly or disabled individuals or patients who are too weak to come to the hospital or physician's office or have just been released from the hospital.

Home health and personal care aides: A segment of healthcare professionals who help people who are disabled, chronically ill, or cognitively impaired, as well as older adults who need assistance including in activities such as bathing and dressing.

Home healthcare services: Medical care in the home, provided primarily to elderly, chronically ill, or mentally impaired individuals.

Hospice care: A holistic and philosophical approach to end of-life care to make the individual as comfortable as possible during his or her final days, with an emphasis on pain control, symptom management, natural death, and quality of life to comfort the individual's physical body, while also supporting the family members as needed.

Hospital emergency medical services: An integral part of the American healthcare system that provides care for patients with emergency healthcare needs.

Hospitalists: A physician who provides care to hospitalized patients. He or she is usually a general practitioner and is becoming more popular—because they spend so much time in the hospital setting, they can provide more efficient care.

Human Genome Project: A long-term government-funded project completed in 2003, identified all of the 20,000–25,000 genes found in human DNA.

Hurricane Katrina: A storm that was the costliest natural disaster, as well as one of the five deadliest hurricanes, in the history of the United States.

Imaging informatics: Also known as radiology informatics or medical imaging informatics that aims to improve the efficiency, accuracy, usability and reliability of medical imaging services within health care.

Immigration Reform and Control Act of 1988: An act that requires employers with one or more employees to verify that all job applicants are U.S. citizens or authorized to work in the United States.

Implied contract: A type of relationship a physician can establish with a patient to provide healthcare which can be implied from a physician's actions. If a physician gives advice regarding medical treatment, there is an implied contract.

Incident Command System (ICS): It is a coordinator for an emergency event and it controls situations and makes decisions about how to manage emergencies.

Independent living: A general category of long-term care institutional service that covers a broad range of settings for individuals who typically do not need regular healthcare services. The target market is 75 years or younger.

Infection control committee: A committee that focuses on minimizing infections in the hospital.

Informatics: A science of computer application to data in different industries.

Information sharing: The multijurisdictional, multidisciplinary exchange of health-related information and situational awareness data among federal, state, local, territorial, and tribal levels of government, and the private sector.

Information technology (IT): Forms of technology used to create, store, exchange, and use information in its various forms.

Informed consent: A legal written document that an individual signs to agree to a specific surgical or medical procedures or other course of treatment. The procedure is protected under federal and state medical consent laws.

Inpatient services: Healthcare services that involve an overnight stay of a patient.

Insane asylums: A hospital where the mentally ill were housed to be treated with sensitivity.

Institutional Review Boards (IRBs): A group that has been formally designated to review and monitor biomedical research involving human subjects.

Instrumental activities of daily living (IADLs): Activities that require assistance from long-term care services and include housework, money management, taking medications, grocery or clothes shopping, pet care, and using the telephone.

Intellectual disabilities: A disability characterized by significant limitations in both intellectual functioning and in adaptive behavior, which covers many everyday social and practical skills.

Intentional torts: It is a category of wrongful acts, in civil law, such as assault and battery or invasion of privacy.

Involuntary commitment: It is when people are forced to receive treatment or are committed to a facility against their wishes.

Iron Triangle of Health Care: A concept that focuses on the balance of three factors of a healthcare system: quality, cost, and accessibility to healthcare.

Job lock: The inability of an employee to freely leave a job because doing so will result in the loss of employee benefits.

John Snow: A famed British anesthesiologist, he is more famous for investigating the cholera epidemics in London in the 1800s.

Joint Commission: A private, nonprofit organization that continues to improve the safety and quality of U.S. healthcare. It assesses performance improvement and provides accreditation to healthcare organizations.

Justice: In the healthcare industry it emphasizes that patients should be treated equally and that health care should be accessible to all.

Lateral violence: Defined as "nurse to nurse" aggression and demonstrated by both verbal and nonverbal behavior.

Law: It is a body of rules for the conduct of individuals and organizations. Law is created so there is a minimal standard of action required by individuals and organizations.

Legacy systems: Obsolete computer systems whose integration across an organization is crucial for data warehousing. Although difficult, they are worthwhile to integrate as they support strategic decision making.

Lemuel Shattuck: He is known as the architect of public health infrastructure. He wrote the landmark report, Report of the Sanitary Commission of Massachusetts, which became central to the development of state and local public health activities.

LGBTQ population: The acronym LGBTQ refers to Lesbian, Gay, Bisexual, Transgender, and Queer.

Licensed practical nurses: A healthcare professional who works primarily in hospitals, home health agencies, and nursing homes with job responsibilities that include patient observation, taking vital signs, keeping records, assisting patients with personal hygiene, and feeding and dressing patients.

Licensed vocational nurses: Refer **Licensed practical nurses**.

Life care contracts: An arrangement under which one or more persons are guaranteed care and maintenance for their life in return for transferring a property to the caregiver.

Life expectancy rates: The measurement of mortality rates from each age group in a population in a particular year that gives the summary of average number of years of life remaining for those of a particular age. It implies the number of years of expected life at birth.

Life insurance: Life insurance policies are purchased to financially protect a beneficiary in the event of the death of the insured. They typically provide a lump sum to the beneficiary.

Lifestyle behaviors: It refers to the interests, opinions, attitudes, way of life, values, or world view of an individual, group, or a culture.

Lilly Ledbetter Fair Pay Act of 2009: An amendment to Title VII of the Civil Rights Act of 1964 that provides protection against unlawful employment practices related to compensation discrimination.

Living will: A legal document that outlines the wishes of the individual's medical treatment.

Local health departments: These are governmental organizations that provide most of the direct public health services to the population in their designated areas.

Long-term care hospital: A hospital with specialty-care for patients with serious medical problems that require special and intense treatment for an extended period of time, usually more than 30 days.

Long-term care insurance: A product designed to cover long-term services and supports, including personal and custodial care in a variety of settings such as your home, a community organization, or other facility and the policy reimburses policyholders a daily amount (up to a pre-selected limit) for services.

Macro environmental conditions: These are determinants of health which consist of socioeconomic, cultural, and environmental conditions that impact health, such as education, work environment, living and working conditions, healthcare services, food production, unemployment, water and sanitation, and housing.

Managed Behavioral Healthcare Organization Accreditation Program: A program that provides consumers, employers, and others with information about the quality of the nation's managed behavioral healthcare organizations.

Managed behavioral healthcare organizations: External vendors contracted with managed care organizations that focus on mental health services.

Market division: An illegal action as per The Sherman Act of 1890 which occurs when one or more health organizations decide which type of services will be offered at each organization.

Mass care: It is the ability to coordinate with partner agencies to address the public health, medical, and mental and behavioral health needs D194 of those impacted by an incident at a congregate location.

Massage therapy: A technique that manipulates the body and its muscles to release tension, and treat depression and stress.

Meaningful use: Core measures that healthcare providers must meet to determine the EHR system is being adequately used.

Medicaid: A social protection program rather than a social insurance program where eligibility is determined largely by income. It is the largest source of funding for medical and health-related services for U.S. citizens living in poverty.

Medical assistants: An aide employed by physicians more than any other allied health assistant who performs both administrative and clinical duties under the supervision of the physicians.

Medical countermeasure dispensing: It is the ability to provide medical countermeasures in support of treatment or prophylaxis to the identified population in accordance with public health guidelines, recommendations, or both.

Medical director: Refer **Chief of medical staff**.

Medical ethics: Ethics in health care which focuses on the treatment of the patient.

Medical illustrators: A trained artist who visually portrays scientific information to teach both professionals and the public about medical issues, working digitally or traditionally to create images of human anatomy and surgical procedures as well as three-dimensional models and animations.

Medical informatics: The science of computer application that supports clinical and research data in different areas of health care.

Medical malpractice: Improper or negligent treatment of a patient by a provider which results in injury, damage, or loss.

Medical materiel management and distribution: It is the ability to acquire, maintain, transport, distribute, and track medical material during an incident and to recover and account for unused medical materiel, as necessary, after an incident.

Medical records committee: A committee that oversees patient records.

Medical surge: It is the ability to provide adequate medical evaluation and care during events that exceed the limits of the normal medical infrastructure of an affected community. It encompasses the ability of the healthcare system to survive a hazard impact and maintain or rapidly recover operations that were compromised.

Medical tourism: Travel of people to a place other than where they normally reside for the purpose of obtaining medical treatment in that country.

Medical Waste Tracking Act: An act that requires companies to have medical waste disposal procedures so that there is no risk to employees and to the environment.

Medicare: A health insurance program for people age 65 or older, people under age 65 with certain disabilities, and people of all ages with end-stage renal disease.

Medicare Prescription Drug, Improvement, and Modernization Act: A federal law of the United States, enacted in 2003, which created Medicare Part D, a prescription drug plan that provides different prescription programs to the elderly, based on their prescription needs.

Medicare Rural Hospital Flexibility Program (MRHFP): It is a program created as part of the Balanced Budget Act of 1997, which allows a small hospital to reconfigure its operations and be licensed as a critical access hospital (CAH), which enables the hospital to be reimbursed for services provided to Medicare patients for its reasonable cost of providing service.

Melafind optical scanner: A technology that uses missile navigation technologies originally paid for by the U.S. Department of Defense to optically scan the surface of a suspicious lesion at 10 electromagnetic wavelengths.

Mental disorders: A syndrome characterized by clinically significant disturbance in an individual's cognition, emotion regulation, or behavior that reflects a dysfunction in the psychological, biological, or developmental processes underlying mental functioning.

Mental Health America: A nonprofit group for the mentally ill that provides education and support.

Mental Health Parity Act (MHPA): An act that ensures adequate coverage for mental health illnesses and also ensures that annual lifetime reimbursement limits on mental health services were similar to other medical benefits.

Mental Health Parity Act of 1996: An act that provided the mental health field with more equity for health insurance coverage to ensure mental health services were being reimbursed at the same level as traditional medical care.

Mental Health Parity and Addiction Equity Act of 2008: An act that requires group health insurance plans (those with more than 50 insured employees) that offer coverage for mental illness and substance use disorders to provide those benefits in a no more restrictive way than all other medical and surgical procedures covered by the plan.

Mental impairment: Any mental or psychological disorder, such as mental retardation, organic brain syndrome, emotional or mental illness, and specific learning disabilities.

Mid-level practitioners: A segment of healthcare professionals who have experience and education beyond the requirements of a registered nurse and operate between the RN and MD.

Minimal infringement: The least restrictive intervention that infringes on individual choices.

Minority stress: It stems from the social stigma, prejudice, denial of civil rights, victimization, and family rejection that LGBTQ people face.

Mobilizing for Action through Planning and Partnership (MAPP): A community-driven strategic planning process for improving community health that helps communities apply strategic thinking to prioritize public health issues and identify resources to address them.

Modified contracts: These are one of the four categories of life care contracts within a continuing care retirement community and include housing, residential services, and amenities but only limited healthcare access.

Monopolies: These are healthcare organizations that control a market so that the consumer has no choice in health care.

Moral treatment: An approach used earlier in Europe to treat mental health patients in hospitals while participating in work and educational activities.

Music therapy: A type of treatment used to treat depression, stress, and grief based on research findings that music elevates a person's emotional moods.

National Clearinghouse for Long-Term Care Information: A website developed by the US Department of Health and Human Services to provide information and resources to help a consumer plan for future long-term care (LTC) needs.

National Defense Authorization Act: An act to permit families of military service members to take a leave of absence if the spouse, parent, or child was called to active military service.

National Incident Management System (NIMS): A systematic, proactive approach to guide departments and agencies at all levels of government, nongovernmental organizations, and the private sector to work together seamlessly and manage incidents involving all threats and hazards in order to reduce loss of life, property, and harm to the environment.

National Mental Health Act (NMHA): An act to amend the Public Health Service Act to provide for research relating to psychiatric disorders and to aid in the development of more effective methods of prevention, diagnosis, and treatment of such disorders, and for other purposes.

National Practitioner Data Bank: It is an electronic information repository created by Congress, contains information on medical malpractice payments and certain adverse actions related to healthcare practitioners, entities, providers, and suppliers.

National Response Framework (NRF): Created by the DHS, it presents the guiding principles that enable all response partners to prepare for and provide a unified national response to disasters and emergencies.

Native American practices: Practices that include ceremonial dances and baptismal rituals as part of Indian health. These dances and rituals are used to treat depression, stress, and substance abuse.

Negligence: A situation where a provider does not give appropriate care or withholds care, and injury to the patient results. Also, if a patient did not provide informed consent for a procedure or treatment, it is considered a case of negligence.

New Freedom Commission on Mental Health: A commission charged with implementing an analytical study on the U.S. mental health service system and developing recommendations to improve the public mental health system that could be implemented at the federal, state, and local levels.

Newborns' and Mothers' Health Protection Act (NMHPA): An act that prevents health insurance companies from discharging a mother and child too early from the hospital.

Noneconomic damages: It includes compensation for things like pain and suffering and emotional distress.

Nonmalfeasance: The concept that healthcare providers must not take any actions to harm the patient.

Nonpharmaceutical interventions: The ability to recommend to the applicable agency (if not public health) and implement, if applicable, strategies for disease, injury, and exposure control which include isolation and quarantine of diseased individuals; restrictions on movement and travel advisories; and warnings of high-risk areas that may be hot zones for disease outbreaks.

Nonphysician practitioner: A professional sometimes called physician extender because they often are used as a substitute for physicians. They are not involved in the total care of a patient, so they collaborate closely with physicians.

Nonvoluntary euthanasia: It is an act of ending the life of an incompetent patient usually at the request of a family member.

Nurse practitioner (NP): A healthcare professional who is trained and has clinical competence to provide services that are essential in the promotion, maintenance, and restoration of health and well-being of patients.

Nursing Home Reform Act: An act established to ensure the advancement of nursing home residents' rights by the provision of certain services.

Nutrition: A science that interprets the interaction of nutrients and other substances in food in relation to maintenance, growth, reproduction, health, and disease of an organism.

Occupational Exposure to Blood-borne Pathogen Standard: It applies to all employers who have an employee(s) with occupational exposure to deal with blood products to follow behavioral standards such as wearing gloves and other equipment and disposal of blood collection materials.

Occupational Safety and Health Act of 1970: A federal law enacted in 1970, setting forth workplace rules and regulations to promote safety of workers to ensure that employers have a general duty to provide a safe and healthy work environment for their employees, which is very important for the healthcare industry because of potential exposure to bacteria, viruses, and contaminated fluids.

Older Americans Act programs: Federal programs that provide home- and community-based services to older adults. These programs are targeted to low-income, frail or disabled over 60, minority older adults, and older adults living in rural areas.

Older Workers Benefit Protection Act of 1990: An act to amend the Age Discrimination in Employment Act of 1967 to clarify the protections given to older individuals in regard to employee benefit plans, and for other purposes.

Olmstead decision: A civil rights decision for people with disabilities, it resulted in the shift of institutional long-term care provision toward community and home-based settings.

Operational staff: A parallel line of staff with the medical staff responsible for managing nonmedical staff and performing nonclinical, administrative, and service work.

Optometrists: A group of healthcare professionals known as Doctors of Optometry or ODs, they are the main providers of vision care by examining people's eyes to diagnose vision problems.

Oregon Death with Dignity Act: An act that allows termination of life by an individual where a physician provides with a prescription for medications that the individual may use to end his or her life.

Orthotist: A specialist who develops devices called "othoses" that focus on the limbs and spines of individuals to increase function.

Osteopathic hospitals: Hospitals that focus on a holistic approach to care, with emphasis on diet and environmental factors that influence health as well as the manipulation of the body.

Out-of-pocket payments or expenses: The amount of money that individuals must pay for health services or equipment that is not covered by the health insurance policies.

Outpatient services: Health care for individuals needing services that do not require an overnight stay under clinical supervision or long-term care.

Pastoral counseling: A type of counseling provided by spiritual people like ministers, rabbis, priests, and imams.

Paternalism: It is the concern that individual freedom will be restricted for the sake of public health activities because the government infringes on individual choices for the sake of protecting the community.

Patient: Any individual who is being evaluated by a healthcare professional.

Patient abandonment: Is a form of medical malpractice that occurs when a physician terminates the doctor–patient relationship without reasonable notice or a reasonable excuse, and fails to provide the patient with an opportunity to find a qualified replacement care provider.

Patient Bill of Rights: A law or a non-binding declaration that guarantees patients to get information, fair treatment, and autonomy over medical decisions, among other rights.

Patient navigator: A person who educates and assists citizens in enrolling into health benefit plans stipulated in the Patient Protection and Affordable Care Act (ACA). Their role is to increase the health literacy of the patient and ensure that the patient receives the best care possible.

Patient Point: Formerly known as Healthy Advice Network, it provides education to patients electronically while they are in the waiting room or an exam room.

Patient portal: A secure online website that gives patients convenient 24-hour access to personal health information from anywhere with an Internet connection.

Patient Protection and Affordable Care Act of 2010 (PPACA, or ACA): An act enacted to increase the quality and affordability of health insurance, lower the uninsured rate by expanding public and private insurance coverage, and reduce the costs of healthcare for individuals and the government. It introduced mechanisms like mandates, subsidies, and insurance exchanges.

Patient Self-Determination Act of 1990: An act that requires hospitals, nursing homes, home health providers, hospices, and managed care organizations that provide services to Medicare- and Medicaid-eligible patients to supply information on patient rights to patients upon admission.

Perfusionists: A healthcare professional who operates equipment to support or replace a patient's circulatory or respiratory function, including advanced-life-support techniques.

Personal fitness trainer: A professional familiar with different forms of exercise serving clients in one-on-one or in group activities and may closely work with exercise science professionals or physiologists in corporate, clinical, or commercial fitness centers, country clubs, or wellness centers.

Personal protective equipment (PPE): A standard developed by OSHA which required specialized clothing or equipment to employees who might be exposed to hazardous materials or working conditions.

Pesthouses: A shelter or hospital used to quarantine people who had contagious diseases such as cholera.

Pew Charitable Trusts: An independent nonprofit organization. Its stated mission is to serve the public interest by "improving public policy, informing the public, and stimulating civic life."

Pharmacists: A segment of the healthcare workforce who are responsible for dispensing medication that has been prescribed by physicians and also advise both patients and healthcare providers on potential side effects of medications.

Pharmacogenomic testing: It is a test performed to assess how medicines react to an individual's genetic makeup.

Pharmacy benefit manager: A company that administers drug benefits for employers and health insurance carriers. It uses technology-based tools to assess and evaluate the management of the prescription component so it can be customized to address the needs of the organization.

Pharmacy technician: A healthcare professional who performs all pharmacy-related functions, usually working under the direct supervision of a licensed pharmacist.

Phobias: Excessive, illogical fear of objects or activities.

Physician assistant (PA): A segment of the healthcare workforce in the category of NPPs, who provide a range of diagnostic and therapeutic services to patients, take medical histories, conduct patient examinations, analyze tests, make diagnoses, and perform basic medical procedures.

Physician Compare website: A website that helps to find and choose physicians and other healthcare professionals enrolled in Medicare so that patients can make informed choices about the health care, as required by the Affordable Care Act (ACA) of 2010.

Physician extender: A professional also called as nonphysician practitioner and often used as a substitute for physicians. They are not involved in the total care of a patient and so they collaborate closely with physicians.

Physician Payment Sunshine Act: An act passed in 2010 as part of the Affordable Care Act and requires manufacturers of drugs, medical devices, and other healthcare products with relationships with Medicare and Medicaid providers and CHIP programs to submit annual reports regarding payments and items of value.

Physician Self-Referral Laws: Laws that prohibit physicians, including dentists and chiropractors, from referring Medicare and Medicaid patients to other providers for designated health services in which they have a financial interest.

Physician-assisted suicide: It refers to the physician providing the means for death, most often with a prescription for a drug. The patient, not the physician, will ultimately administer the lethal medication.

Piccolo xpress Chemistry Analyzer: A compact, portable chemistry analyzer that delivers blood test results quickly.

Podiatrists: A healthcare professional who provides medical and surgical care for people suffering from foot, ankle, and lower-leg problems and diagnoses illnesses, treats injuries, and performs surgery.

Poison Prevention Packaging Act of 1970: An act enacted to prevent children from accidentally ingesting substances.

Policy development: The creation of comprehensive public health policies based on scientific evidence in service to the public.

Polysomnographic technologist: A healthcare professional who performs sleep tests and works with physicians to provide diagnoses of sleep disorders.

Poorhouses: Also known as almshouses, they were established to serve the indigent by providing shelter while treating illness.

Posttraumatic stress disorder: A mental disorder that can develop after a person is exposed to a traumatic event, such as sexual assault, warfare, traffic collisions, or other threats on a person's life.

Predictive and asymptomatic testing: Testing to identify any gene changes that may increase the likelihood of a person developing a disease.

Pregnancy Discrimination Act of 1978: This act protects female employees who are discriminated against based on pregnancy-related conditions, which constitutes illegal sex discrimination.

Preimplantation genetic diagnosis (PGD): It is used to test embryos for tissue compatibility with their siblings prior to being transplanted into the mother.

Premenstrual dysphoric disorder: A severe disorder in which depression and anxiety co-occur with menstruation, impacts between 3% and 5% of women.

Prenatal testing: Testing to identify fetuses with potential diseases or conditions.

Presumed consent: It means that if a parent does not actively oppose the transplantation, the procedure automatically occurs.

Price fixing: An illegal action as per The Sherman Act of 1890 which prevents consumers from paying a fair price because competitors establish a certain price (by either increasing or lowering prices) among themselves to stabilize the market.

Price information exchange: An illegal action as per The Sherman Act of 1890 where exchange of price information between healthcare providers can also be illegal.

Priestly model: A model which assumes the doctor will make the best decisions for the patient's health. The patient assumes a very passive role, giving the provider great power in the decision-making process.

Primary care: It is often referred to as essential health care and could include health education, counseling, and other preventive services.

Primary Care Information Project (PCIP): A bureau developed by the New York City Department of Health and Mental Hygiene in 2008 to support the adoption and use of prevention-oriented EHRs primarily among providers who care for the city's underserved and vulnerable populations.

Primary prevention: An intervention or an activity that reduces health risks by protecting healthy individuals from illness or disease before it even occurs.

Privacy rule: Is intended to further protect patient's personal medical records and other personal health information maintained by healthcare providers, hospitals, insurance companies, and health plans.

Private law: A part of the legal system that deals with issues among individuals. An example of private law is the civil law that focuses on the wrongful acts against individuals and organizations based on contractual violations.

Procreation: To produce babies or the process of generating children.

Professional associations: Associations that represent healthcare stakeholders like physicians, nurses, hospitals, long-term care facilities, and that guide them regarding their role in the healthcare industry.

Proportionality: It is one of the five justification criteria that considers public health intervention against freedom of choice. Where the proportionality of public health intervention outweighs freedom of choice, then the intervention must be warranted.

Proprietary hospitals: Also referred to as investor-owned hospitals, these are for-profit institutions and are owned by corporations, individuals, or partnerships.

Prosthetist: A specialist who designs "prostheses" or devices for patients who have limb amputations to replace the limb function.

Pseudo dementias: Also known as false dementias, the conditions develop as a result of medications, drug interactions, poor diet, or heart and gland diseases.

Psychiatric technicians and aides: A segment of healthcare workforce who care for people who have mental illness or developmental disabilities. The two occupations are related, but technicians typically provide therapeutic care, and aides help patients in their daily activities.

Psychiatrists: Specialty physicians who can provide diagnosis and treatment of mental illness, prescribe medication, and admit patients to hospitals.

Psychologists: Healthcare providers who collaborate with physicians, social workers, and others to treat illness and promote overall wellness by a study of the human mind and human behavior.

Psychotropic medications: Any drug capable of affecting the mind, emotions, and behavior. Some legal drugs, such as lithium for bipolar disorder, are psychotropic.

Public education: It is one of the five justification criteria where public health workers must provide public education to explain their interventions and why the infringement on individual choices is warranted.

Public health: It refers to the overall health and safety of the U.S. population achieved by preventing disease, monitoring, regulating, and promoting health through organized efforts, including core functions and essential services by several federal departments and agencies.

Public Health Accreditation Board (PHAB): It was formed as a nonprofit organization dedicated to improving and protecting the health of the public by advancing the quality and performance of tribal, state, local, and territorial public health departments.

Public health emergency preparedness: Planning protocols that are in place to manage a large-scale event such as a natural disaster like a hurricane or massive flooding, chemical or oil spills, or human-caused disasters.

Public health functions: The responsibility of local health departments to protect and promote health, and prevent disease and injury, which includes child immunization programs, health screenings in schools, community health services, substance abuse programs, and sexually transmitted disease control.

Public health laboratory testing: It is the ability to conduct rapid and conventional detection, characterization, confirmatory testing, data reporting, investigative support, and laboratory networking to address actual or potential exposure to all hazards.

Public Health Security and Bioterrorism Preparedness and Response Act of 2002: An act that provides grants to hospitals and public health organizations to prepare for bioterrorism as a result of the September 11, 2001, attacks.

Public health surveillance and epidemiological investigation: It is the ability to create, maintain, support, and strengthen routine surveillance and detection systems and epidemiological investigation processes, as well as to expand these systems and processes in response to incidents of public health significance.

Public health/social educational campaign: An educational strategy to inform the community about positive health behavior, targeting those at risk to change or maintain positive health behavior.

Public hospitals: An oldest type of hospital owned by the federal, state, or local government.

Public law: A part of the legal system that enforces relationships between entities and the government. It is created by federal, state, and local governments. An example of public law is the criminal law concerned with actions that are illegal based on court decisions.

Punitive damages: Damages that are intended to punish the defendant.

Quality committee: A committee that is responsible for overseeing and monitoring the quality of healthcare services, including patient and environmental safety, within the Medical Center.

Quality improvement committee: A committee that is responsible for quality improvement programs.

Quaternary care: It is an extension of tertiary care and refers to highly specialized, cutting-edge tertiary care performed in research facilities and highly specialized facilities.

Qui tam: A concept used in antitrust law is Latin for "he who sues." A qui tam provision enables individuals to sue providers for fraudulent activity against the federal government, recovering a portion of the funds returned to the government.

Radio frequency identification: A technology that uses chips that transmit data to receivers. Each of these chips is uniquely identified by a signal indicating where it is located.

Radio psychiatry: A technology-based application where radio psychologists and psychiatrists provide advice, information, and referrals to consumers.

Recreational therapists: A healthcare professional who provides individualized and group recreational therapy for individuals experiencing limitations in life activities as a result of a disabling condition, illness or disease, aging, or developmental factors.

Registered nurse: A trained nurse who has been licensed by a state board after passing the national nursing examination.

Rehabilitation Act of 1973: This law applies to organizations that receive financial assistance from federal organizations, including the U.S. Department of Health and Human Services, and forbids discriminating against individuals with disabilities in terms of employee benefits and job opportunities.

Remote Area Medical (RAM): An organization founded in 1985 to develop a mobile, efficient workforce to provide free health care in areas of need worldwide.

Rental agreement: A life care contract within a continuing care retirement community that does not give the resident access to healthcare services on a monthly or annual basis.

Reproductive cloning: The deliberate production of genetically identical individuals.

Research cloning: It is a procedure that creates a genetic replica, with a focus on replicating sources for stem cells to replace damaged tissues.

Research genetic testing: Testing that focuses on how genes impact disease development.

Residential care facilities: Facilities that provide around-the-clock social and personal care to the elderly, children, and others who cannot take care of themselves. Examples of residential care facilities are drug rehabilitation centers, group homes, and assisted-living facilities.

Respect for autonomy: It is one of the five basic values that all healthcare providers should observe which states that decision making may be different and healthcare providers must respect their patients' decisions even if they differ from their own.

Respiratory therapist: A healthcare professional who performs basic respiratory care procedures, implements and monitors any respiratory therapy under the supervision of a physician or an advanced-level therapist, and reviews patient data, including tests and previous medical history.

Respite care: A program developed to provide systematic relief to those caregivers of chronically ill patients who need a break.

Responder safety and health: It is the ability to protect public health agency staff responding to an incident and the ability to support the health and safety needs of hospital and medical facility personnel, if requested.

Robert Wood Johnson Foundation: It is the nation's largest philanthropy dedicated solely to health, with a goal to help raise the health of everyone in the United States to the level that a great nation deserves, by placing well-being at the center of every aspect of life.

Robotic checkups: Checkup using a device consisting of a mobile cart with a two-way video screen and medical monitoring equipment, programmed to maneuver through healthcare facilities which can make rounds, checking on patients in different rooms and managing their individual charts and vital signs without direct human intervention. This is an innovative method of telemedicine.

Rules and regulations: These are designated to control or govern conduct and are instituted by administrative agencies by interpreting common law and statutes.

Safety Data Sheets (SDSs): A document that contains information on the potential hazards (health, fire, reactivity, and environmental) and how to work safely with the chemical product.

Sapien heart valve: A life-saving alternative to open-heart surgery for patients who need a new valve but for whom surgery is considered high risk. The valve material is made of bovine tissue attached to a stainless-steel stent, which is expanded by inflating a small balloon in the valve space.

Secondary care: It focuses on short-term interventions that may require a specialist's intervention.

Secondary prevention: An intervention to stop or slow the progress of risk factors by early screening or treatment of the disease or injury.

Security rule: Rules that apply to e-PHI, or electronic patient information, because of the increased use of electronic patient records. They are in place to prevent breach of any patient information.

Self-help organizations: These are usually nonprofit and free of charge organizations which provide education and support to caregivers of mentally ill individuals. Often, these organizations are anonymous because of the stigma attached to mental disorders.

Senior centers: A center that provides a broad array of services for the older population, including meal and nutrition programs, education, recreational programs, health and wellness programs, transportation services, volunteer opportunities, counseling, and other services.

Sexual harassment: Is defined as unwelcome sexual conduct that has a negative impact on the employee.

Sherman Act of 1890: Focuses on eliminating monopolies, price fixing, market division, tying, boycotts, and price information exchange in healthcare organizations to protect the consumers.

Sherman Antitrust Act of 1890: The first piece of legislation that ensured fair competition in the marketplace for patients by prohibiting monopolies.

Silver Sneakers: It is a program created to provide free access to organized exercise at national fitness chains and encouraged the elderly to participate in it.

Skilled nursing facilities: They are a part of a long-term care institutional service that provides care to residents who cannot live independently.

Social and community networks: The external influences on health of an individual characterized by interactions between groups of people and/or organizations and institutions.

Social media: An electronic communication medium dedicated to community-based input, interaction, content-sharing, and collaboration.

Social regulation: It focuses on actions of organizations, such as those in the healthcare industry, that impact an individual's safety.

Social regulations: A set of rules aimed at restricting behaviors that directly threaten public health, safety, welfare, or well-being.

Social Security Act of 1935: An act to provide for the general welfare by establishing a system of federal old-age benefits, and by enabling several states to make more adequate provision for aged persons, blind persons, dependent and crippled children, maternal and child welfare, public health, and the administration of their unemployment compensation laws.

Social/public health marketing: It involves creating, communicating, and delivering health information and interventions using customer-oriented and science-based strategies to protect and promote health in diverse populations.

Sonography: A diagnosis test that uses sound waves to generate images of the body for the assessment and diagnosis of various medical conditions.

Specialists: A physician who is certified in an area of specialization after additional years of training and a board certifying or credentialing examination.

Specialty care: A result of the primary care evaluation where the primary care provider will coordinate the overall care of the patient by referring to a specialist for additional care.

Specialty maldistribution: It refers to an issue in physician supply, with an increasing proportion of specialists to generalists.

Stakeholder: An individual or group that has an active interest in an organization or activity. In the healthcare industry, employers outside are also stakeholders because they provide a large percentage of health insurance coverage to individuals nationwide.

Stakeholder management: It focuses on the relationship between organizations and all of their constituents, including shareholders, and how management recognizes the different expectations of each group.

Standard of care: The level and type of care that a reasonably competent and skilled healthcare professional, with a similar background and in the same medical community, would have provided under the circumstances that led to the alleged malpractice.

State health departments: Departments or agencies of the state governments of the United States focused on public health. They monitor communities to identify, diagnose, and investigate health problems and provide education about health issues.

State licensure: State governments oversee the licensure of healthcare facilities, including hospitals, with a focus on building codes, sanitation, equipment, and personnel before granting license to operate.

Statutes: Laws created by legislative bodies such as the U.S. Congress.

Statutory consent: If a patient cannot clinically give consent to a lifesaving medical treatment, it is presumed a reasonable person would give consent to the lifesaving procedure.

Stem cells: These are "starter" cells for the development of body tissue that has yet to be formed into specialized tissues for certain parts of the body.

Stewardship model: It states that public health officials should achieve the stated health outcomes for the population while minimizing restrictions on people's freedom of choice.

Surgeon General: The chief health educator of the United States, who provides information on how to improve the health of the U.S. population.

Surgeon technologist: A healthcare professional responsible for preparing the operating room by equipping the room with the appropriate sterile supplies and verifying the equipment is working properly.

Surgical assistant: A specialized physician's assistant whose main goal is to ensure the surgeon has a safe and sterile environment in which to perform. They determine the appropriate equipment for the procedure, select radiographs for a surgeon's reference, assist in moving the patient, confirm procedures with the surgeon, and assist with the procedure as directed by the surgeon.

Surveillance: It is the monitoring of patterns of disease and investigating disease outbreaks to develop public health intervention strategies to combat disease.

Tax Equity and Fiscal Responsibility Act (TEFRA): A U.S. federal law created in order to reduce the budget gap by generating revenue through closure of tax loopholes and introduction of tougher enforcement of tax rules, as opposed to changing marginal income tax rates.

Teaching hospitals: A hospital that has one or more graduate resident programs approved by the AMA.

Telebehavioral health: Using video conferencing technology, telebehavioral health services allow "real-time" visits with a behavioral health specialist in another location who can assist in the evaluation, diagnosis, management, and treatment of health problems.

Telehealth: It is the broad term that encompasses the use of IT to deliver education, research, and clinical care.

Telemedicine: Remote diagnosis and treatment of patients by means of telecommunications technology when providers and patients are connected using the Internet.

Telephone counseling: Any type of psychological service performed over the telephone.

Temporary care programs: Refer **Respite care**.

Tertiary care: It is a complex level of medical care, typically done by surgeons—physicians who perform operations to treat disease, physical problems, and injuries.

Tertiary prevention: An intervention to prevent further damage or injury, reduce pain, slow the progression of the disease or injury, prevent the disease or injury from causing further complications, and rehabilitate as much as possible to improve quality of life.

Therapeutic cloning: A procedure that creates a genetic replica of a cell or organism, with a focus on replicating sources for stem cells to replace damaged tissues. It is considered unethical because it involves destroying embryos to obtain healthy stem cells for research.

Tort: A category of wrongful acts, in civil law, which may not have a preexisting contract.

Transfusion medicine specialist: A specialist in blood banking (SBB) technology who provides routine and specialized tests for blood donor centers, transfusion centers, laboratories, and research centers.

Transplantation: It is the general procedure of implanting a functional organ from one person to another.

Triple Aim: An act that focuses on three goals: improving patient satisfaction, reducing health costs, and improving public health.

Tying: An illegal action as per The Sherman Act of 1890 that refers to healthcare providers that will only sell a product to a consumer who will also buy a second product from them.

Uniformed Services Employment and Reemployment Rights Act (USERRA): An act that entitles individuals who leave for military service to return to their job.

United Way: A civic organization that is active in identifying health risks and implementing community public health programs to target these risks.

Universal healthcare program: A type of health care where everyone is provided coverage regardless of their income, race, age, pre-existing conditions, gender, or wealth.

Urgent and emergent care centers: A care center used for consumers who need medical care but whose situation is not life-threatening.

Utilization review committee: A committee that evaluates the necessity, appropriateness, and efficiency of the use of healthcare services, procedures, and facilities and ensures inpatient stays are clinically appropriate.

Village movement: A group that formed a network to provide services to older homeowners that allowed them to remain in their homes longer and maintain their independence. The network acts as a liaison to connect homeowners to needed workers.

Visiting nurse agencies: An agency that provides medical services in a patient's home; often provided to elderly or disabled individuals or patients who are too weak to come to the hospital or physician's office or have just been released from the hospital.

Visualization: A technique where a patient creates a mental image of wellness and recovery. It is used by traditional healthcare providers to treat substance abuse, panic disorders, and stress.

Voluntary commitment: It occurs when people commit themselves willingly to receive care. If a person voluntarily commits for treatment, that person can leave of his or her own free will.

Voluntary euthanasia: Assisting a patient with ending his or her life at the patient's request.

Voluntary health insurance: Consists of schemes that range from employer-based for-profit schemes to small non-profit schemes such as community-based health insurance in which the decision to join and paying premium is voluntary.

Voluntary hospitals: These are hospitals that are privately owned and nonprofit facilities considered voluntary because their financial support is the result of community organizational efforts.

Volunteer management: It is the ability to coordinate the identification, recruitment, registration, credential verification, training, and engagement of volunteers to support the jurisdictional public health agency's response to incidents of public health significance.

Women's Health and Cancer Rights Act (WHCRA): An act that helps protect many women with breast cancer who choose to have their breasts rebuilt (reconstructed) after a mastectomy.

Worker Adjustment and Retraining Notification Act of 1989: An act that states employers with 100 employees or more must give their employees 60 days' notice of layoffs and business closings.

Workplace bullying: An ongoing harassing workplace behavior between employees, which results in negative health outcomes for the targeted employees.

Xenotransplantation: Transfer of organs from one species to another.

Yoga: An Indian system that uses breathing techniques, stretching, and meditation to balance the body.

INDEX